PRACTICAL CBT

Using transdiagnostic case formulations and therapies based on problem-maintaining circles

Gary Bakker

AUSTRALIANACADEMICPRESS

First edition — *Practical CBT: Using Functional Analysis and Standardised Homework in Everyday Therapy* — published in 2008.

Reprinted in 2009, 2011

This edition first published 2021 by:
Australian Academic Press Group Pty. Ltd.
Samford Valley, Australia

www.australianacademicpress.com.au

A catalogue record for this book is available from the National Library of Australia

Practical CBT: Using transdiagnostic case formulations and therapies based on problem-maintaining circles
ISBN 9781925644449 (paperback)
ISBN 9781925644456 (ebook)

Publisher: Stephen May

Copy Editor: Rhonda McPherson

Cover design: Luke Harris, Working Type Studio

Typesetting: Australian Academic Press

Printing: Lightning Source

Contents

Acknowledgments

Sincere thanks and gratitude go to my early clinical inspirations:

To Iain Montgomery, who encouraged me to respect the evidence.

To John Warren, who encouraged me to use my common sense.

And to Michael Griffin, who encouraged me to try to genuinely connect with my clients.

Preface

The original edition of this manual, *Practical CBT: Using Functional Analysis, Problem-Maintaining Circles, and Standardised Homework in Everyday Therapy*, published in 2008, introduced the *problem-maintaining circle* (PMC) model of cognitive–behaviour therapy (CBT) as a way to learn CBT, and to teach CBT, both to beginning therapists and to clients, in a way that is easy to learn, is conceptually consistent, is clinically-focused, and that organises and uses the huge evidence base available in the literature.

This is achieved by emphasising just two of the seven distinguishing characteristics of CBT outlined in this volume on pages 7 to10. They are its basis in learning and conditioning theory for the development of interventions, and its focus on PMCs of causes in formulating case conceptualizations. The reader is assumed to have an adequate knowledge of learning and conditioning theory, and is introduced comprehensively to PMC theory and the practical CBT interventions that ensue.

With these emphases (supported by the research literature), CBT becomes an approach to clinical psychological problems (CPPs) that is consistent, easily understandable, and complementary to the allied fields of medicine, psychiatry, and counselling.

A model of CBT is described that guides therapists in CBT-based assessment, case formulation, and therapy selection, but is also simple enough to immediately teach to clients. Clients in CBT are effectively their own therapists. Little is done to clients in CBT. They mostly change through 'homework', rather than through magical procedures or chemical agents imposed on them in the consultation. Therefore, it is essential that clients understand fully the problem formulations developed, the relevance and need for their homework, exactly how their homework will help, and how not to avoid, sabotage, or cheat in their therapy tasks.

A simple example lies in any exposure therapy. Facing fears requires motivation as it is difficult, and is likely to be the opposite of how the client has been coping naturally so far, because to date his/her reactions or coping attempts have not broken operating PMCs. In fact they may well have kindled or promoted PMC formation and perpetuation by, for example, coping by avoidance. A phobic person needs a convincing rationale that they can understand, and needs to know exactly what counts as exposure, and which behaviours are 'safety' behaviours, because most of the exposure will occur out there in the real world without their therapist at hand.

The model of CBT originally outlined in the first edition is based on identifying currently operating PMCs. A basic taxonomy of common, evidence-based PMCs in the areas of Depression, Anxiety, and Anger problems was presented, along with assessment questions aimed at seeking out these PMCs. And likely ensuing therapy homeworks were described, with verbatim introductory scripts fine-tuned over 28 years of trial-and-error application.

This new edition develops further the theoretical basis of the PMC model of CBT by describing the full PMC-relevant CBT model (a 'grand unified theory') behind the simplified one presented to clients, which then extends the recommended assessment questions, taxonomy of PMCs, and verbatim homework/therapy descriptions beyond depression, anxiety, and anger problems, to CPPs in the areas of health anxiety, eating disorders, relationship problems, chronic pain, obsessive compulsive disorder (OCD), substance abuse/dependence, and sexual problems.

So this new edition of *Practical CBT* uses two strategies to facilitate the practice of effective CBT:

1. It describes the PMC-based approach to CBT assessment, case formulation, and therapy tailoring ('PMC theory') by way of a simple, teachable, consistent, evidence-based CBT model.
2. It provides verbatim scripts to guide therapists in the down-to-earth, real-world practice of applying (PMC-based) CBT in all of the problem areas listed.

Three Critical Abbreviations

CBT cognitive behaviour therapy, or cognitive–behaviour therapy, or cognitive–behavioural therapy.

That body of theory, incorporating learning theory and conditioning theory, and related clinical psychological interventions and techniques, that is distinguished by the 7 features and characteristics outlined in Practical CBT (2008) on pages 5 to 7, which are repeated in this volume on pages 7 to 10.

CPPs clinical psychological problems

Those (especially human) problems that are best described and addressed at the psychological level of analysis, and that warrant intervention (i.e., they are 'clinical') because, due to observed or inferred psychological-level maintenance processes (PMCs), they are not expected to abate naturally or spontaneously. The term is used to distinguish the objects of clinical psychological research and intervention from normal, transient, possibly 'healthy', negative psychological states (mundane psychological problems), and psychiatry's 'mental disorders' (see Table 4.2).

PMCs problem-maintaining circles

Any observed or inferred complete cycle of causes (a 'vicious circle') that includes one or more psychological-level elements (cognitions, emotions, behaviours, or stimuli) that can explain the occurrence and maintenance of a CPP, and hence can suggest points of therapeutic intervention.

About the Author

Gary Bakker is a clinical psychologist with 40 years of experience (over 20,000 consultations!) working with children, adolescents, adults, couples, and families in clinics, hospitals, community centres, and for 30 years in private practice. He trained in CBT when it was newly emerging as the evidence-based therapy of choice, receiving the Fiona Allen Prize during his masters program. Gary has since given innumerable seminars and workshops on themes in CBT, all the while honing its presentation, clarity, and acceptability for his clients, resulting in the verbatim suggested scripts that comprise much of this book. He has bridged the gap between attention to the psychotherapy process and outcome research, and the demands of practical real-world therapy. The result is a whole new non-medicalising conception of clinical psychological problems, called *PMC Theory*.

SECTION I

Introduction and Theoretical Basis

Chapter 1

How To Use This Manual

This manual is intended for therapists who have obtained their basic grounding in the theory, origins, and principles of cognitive–behaviour therapy (CBT), but now need to bridge the gap from academic readiness to real-life, real-time application of the model to a real person with a real problem sitting in front of them. Experienced therapists may also benefit, though, from either:

(a) the acquisition of new strategies and homeworks, as these are presented in the form of verbatim scripts which can be adopted and varied as clinical judgement affords; or

(b) the introduction to a conception of clinical psychological problems (CPPs) based on the notion of psychological-level problem-maintaining circles (PMCs) of causes ("PMC theory") as a simple model of CBT which can aid in the choice of assessment questions and strategies, the development of a case formulation which is highly amenable to CBT intervention, selection of interventions and treatments, and in clients' understanding of the case formulation, and hence their motivation to complete their homework.

It is not enough for the therapist to have a good knowledge of the theory behind CBT interventions plus a lexicon of intervention modules in one's head. As touched upon in the Preface, most CBT, most changes, nearly all of the homework, and all of the generalisation of changes to aspects of real life, occur 'out there' away from the therapist's immediate guidance. So clients' correct understanding, motivation, and completion of homework are vital for success in CBT (Kazantzis, Deane, & Ronan, 2004).

Early in my clinical career it was common for clients to return with homework not completed or completed wrongly (sometimes counter-therapeutically) due to my poor attempts at translating and tailoring the textbook procedures, or at explaining and motivating adequately to induce compliance.

The most frequent plea among the many beginning, and even somewhat experienced, CBT therapists that I have trained and supervised has been: 'But how can I get them to *do* any of these things? So many come back with *none* of their homework done, or it not done properly'. It seems that those most in need of change are least capable of taking the necessary steps. This in itself is a likely PMC!

For me, the past 40 years (about 20,000 consultations) have comprised a huge series of trial-and-error, single-case studies in constructing and communicating explanations and homeworks ('scripts and prescriptions') that most clients can understand quite quickly and that can create movement within the CBT model. The dependent variable has been successful homework completion. I hope that other therapists can short-circuit some of this trial-and-error by beginning with or incorporating the scripts and prescriptions outlined in verbatim detail in this manual.

There are two unusual features of this manual. The first is its presentation of verbatim scripts or spiels. These can, of course, be altered markedly when tailoring to individual clients. Educational level and cultural background are two obvious criteria that a therapist will want to allow for in tailoring explanations or homework instructions. But many of the phrases in the verbatim scripts are ones that experience has fine-tuned for me, and a verbatim starting point from which to vary is for many a better one than a general academic instruction such as 'Address these two likely core beliefs using cognitive restructuring'. Exactly what do you say to a client, and what do you get them to *do*, that will result in the right sort of 'cognitive restructuring'?!

For decades now, whenever a pattern of homework noncompliance, misunderstanding, or miscompliance has occurred, I have amended the relevant instructions or 'spiel' until success can be reliably expected. For example, when clients told me that they hadn't completed their '25 Good Things' list (Homework 6) because it felt too much like boasting (a common sentiment among people experiencing compromised self-esteem), I added the 'It's not boasting because I'm *asking you* for this list' clause. When clients returned with Thoughts Journals that had become rumination logs, I insisted on them using structured Negative Emotion Records (NERs; Homework 1). And when many clients returned with NERs that confused thoughts and feelings, I elaborated on my introductory spiel by including Figure 3.1 in my NER Homework 1 spiel.

The second unusual feature of this manual is its emphasis on PMC theory in implementing assessment, case formulation, and CBT therapy selection. The reason for this emphasis is the same as the reason for the spiels and scripts. PMC theory is very palatable, non-stigmatising, logical, and easy to understand for clients. Hence it increases client understanding and therapy compliance.

Some readers will be used to dealing with 'clients' (psychologists, social workers), others with 'patients' (psychiatrists, GPs); and others with 'customers', or even 'service users'. I will use the term 'clients' simply because, as a psychologist, I rarely 'cure' 'ill' 'patients' of their 'mental illnesses'. Mostly, I provide professional advice and assistance to clients and their parents, guardians, or significant others when they present with clinical psychological problems (CPPs) — as opposed to legal problems, accountancy problems, plumbing problems, and so on. I hope the term 'clients' does not grate too harshly with medical readers.

Four Sections

In the remainder of Section 1 (Introduction and Theoretical Basis), Chapter 2, 'Why CBT?', presents the case for the CBT-nature of most of the homeworks. That is, they are overwhelmingly specific, active, supported by outcome research, based on established learning theory, and address especially problem-maintaining factors. Hence the relevance and utility of PMC theory is simultaneously justified. Other models of CPPs, however, are applicable and absorbable within PMC theory — it is a metatheory — in as much as they target maintainers rather than hypothesised historical etiological events, and therefore can identify elements in active PMCs and offer evidence-based procedures to alter these elements.

Chapter 3, 'A Full CBT Model', describes both the simplified model that can help clients to understand PMC theory and subsequent CBT interventions, and the full CBT model, which, it is argued, is the nearest we have to a 'Grand Unified Theory' (a GUT) in clinical psychology, and that, when its neurochemical physiological substrate is understood, will be clinical psychology's contribution to a 'Theory of Everything' (a TOE) for humans. (With acknowledgement to modern physics for originating both of these terms.)

Chapter 4, 'The PMC Approach to CBT', condenses an outline of PMC theory, and how it can provide a logical method of application of CBT assessment and therapy selection. A nascent taxonomy of psychological-level PMCs is proposed, that can serve the functions of psychiatry's DSM system in a way that is more helpful to clinical psychologists.

In Section 2 (Assessment, PMC Taxonomy, and Treatment Selection), Chapter 5, 'The Initial Assessment', includes suggested general assessment questions applicable to almost every client, but with a CBT/PMC slant, in that there is a focus more on the current situation than on history, and more interest in alterable features that could be part of psychological-level PMCs. For example, there are questions about alcohol consumption and exercise patterns, but not about birth trauma or psychosexual history.

How questions then become more problem-specific and tailored is described, as a case formulation or 'CBT functional analysis' is developed focusing on problem maintenance via the identification of operating PMCs.

Chapter 6 introduces a sample taxonomy of the more prevalent PMCs in 12 CPP areas.

Chapter 7 deals with the decision pathways from assessment and PMC-based case formulation to treatment selection; firstly with regard to universal general problem maintenance issues such as self-efficacy and self-awareness/self-monitoring, and then via tables linking assessment questions to inferred PMCs (from Chapter 6), and thus to particular therapies and homeworks (described in Section 3).

Section 3 (Homeworks) describes in detail 72 potential practical homeworks that can be 'prescribed', including verbatim introductory or instructional scripts.

In Section 4 (Scripts), 13 verbatim scripts that do not introduce or instruct followup homework, but instead aim to be therapeutic in and of themselves by being psychoeducational or motivating are presented. That is, they are intended to break PMCs involving lack of knowledge or faulty beliefs, especially about CBT and PMCs! They likely help by increasing homework compliance and fidelity.

It is expected this manual will initially be read through, and the sections that will then be revisited frequently during therapeutic practice (the 'practical CBT') will be:

- the sample PMC taxonomy of Chapter 6; copies of these pages can be used when giving clients homework to identify for themselves the PMCs that they believe are operating
- the tables in Chapter 7 (7.1 to 7.13) describing general and specific assessment-to-treatment decision pathways
- the specific homeworks and scripts in Sections 3 and 4.

Selected Figures and Handouts in this manual for use with clients are also available as free PDFs from the publisher's website in the 'Downloads' menu. A note is shown on each downloadable Figure and Handout in this manual.

Chapter 2

Why CBT?

What is CBT?

There are at least seven characteristics of CBT that differentiate it from the estimated 500+ other schools of psychotherapy that exist today (Beutler, Bongar, & Shurkin, 1998; Eisner, 2000). These characteristics include:

1. CBT, having grown out of the behaviour therapies, rests on a mass of well-established learning theory and conditioning theory research, dating back to Watson (Watson & Rayner, 1920) and Pavlov (1927) and burgeoning especially in the 1950s, 1960s, and 1970s (Skinner, 1953; Wolpe, 1954). It therefore uses many of the same processes or techniques as does behaviour therapy, such as rehearsal, coaching, reinforcement, modelling, extinction, and so on.
2. The particular targets for change in CBT are measurable — or at least reportable — behaviours, cognitions, emotional states, situations, or skills. Any causal attributions involving inferred subconscious motivations or energies are avoided as unprovable and therefore unscientific. Problem formulations therefore tend to be fairly individualistic, citing interconnected or contributory measurable behaviours, cognitions, emotional states, and stimuli rather than general hypothetical constructs or diagnostic categories.
3. Another legacy of growing out of behaviourism is CBT's emphasis on empirical research. Its proponents and developers have undertaken innumerable outcome studies, components analyses, comparison studies, and so on. A dual consequence of this mindset is that:
    (a) There is a vast body of published research supporting CBT's efficacy with a wide range of problems (e.g., APS, 2010; Antonuccio et al., 1997; Butler

et al., 2006; Dobson & Dobson, 2009; Ellis & Smith, 2002; Fisher & O'Donohue, 2006; Hofmann et al., 2012; Nathan & Gorman, 2015).

(b) Cognitive behavioural therapists tend to measure more and ask for self-monitoring more, at baseline and through therapy, than other types of therapists, and to adjust therapy using hypothesis-testing logic along the way.

4. CBT generally aims to help clients learn new and adaptive ways of functioning. As a process this is usually therefore active, progressive, interventive, time-limited, and goal-oriented. Simple support, maintenance, reassurance, or damage control is rarely settled for.

5. The relationship between therapist and client in CBT is more than just facilitative or reflective (as in client-centred therapy). The therapist is coach, educator, change-process expert, and reinforcer. But the process is a collaborative one in which the client's goals predominate and he/she is accepted as the expert in knowledge of his/her own thoughts, feelings, and behaviours. This dimension of manipulation versus collaboration does traverse a continuum within CBT, however. Toward one end is Albert Ellis's Rational Emotive Behaviour Therapy (REBT), in which clients are frequently told exactly where their thinking is going wrong. Another example would be the imposition of contingency contracting, as in a star chart or token economy. Contrasting these are Aaron Beck's Cognitive Therapy, in which clients are helped to test their own inferences, and the coaching of self-control procedures such as stimulus control to assist with study habits or with sleep onset problems. While all cognitive-behavioural therapists would acknowledge the importance of a good therapist–client relationship, unlike other therapy approaches in which the relationship is viewed as a primary change agent, in CBT the relationship is vital only inasmuch as it enables the processes and techniques to be taught and followed successfully. So it is desirable that the therapist's knowledge and advice be respected, that trust, disclosure, and compliance occur, and that there is a comfortable collaboration. But, while Truax and Carkhuff's (1967) relationship conditions for successful therapy (warmth, genuineness, and so on) are seen as useful, they are not regarded in CBT as central or sufficient. In fact, some doubt has arisen in the literature (Feeley et al., 1999; Krupnick et al., 1994; Tang & DeRubeis, 1999) as to whether the correlation observed between a good therapeutic alliance and good outcome actually describes a causal connection in the other direction. That is, could it be that good early therapeutic success produces or predicts reports of positive attitudes towards the therapist and the therapeutic alliance? For example, Strunk et al. (2010) found in a study of cognitive therapy for depression that early inter-session symptom change depended upon therapist adherence to the cognitive methods, to negotiating content, and to structuring sessions, but not on any measure of therapeutic alliance. And the alliance scores were significantly predicted by prior symptom change! This has been found in

a number of time series studies now (DeRubeis et al., 2005), and implies that therapeutic success benefits the alliance more than vice versa. Effective treatment leads to positive regard of the therapist, and this explains the correlation. Satisfaction with care given has consistently been found to depend on the provision of quality psychosocial interventions. Simpson et al. (2011) looked for predictors of outcome in exposure and response prevention (ERP) treatment of obsessive compulsive disorder (OCD). They found that early patient adherence to ERP homework between sessions significantly predicted outcome, but that the effect of the working alliance was fully mediated by patient adherence (which can, by the way, be maximised by the simplicity and clarity of the PMC model). A good relationship meant that homework got done, which produced more progress. Meantime, patient satisfaction has been found to increase as psychotherapy becomes more CBT-like (Stein et al., 2011). With the consistent finding that therapy adherence and structure are critical in CBT outcome (Shaw et al. 1999), 'the optimal balance of structure and relationship factors is probably the most structure possible that does not damage the therapy alliance' (Kuyken et al., 2009, p. 67).

6. Through CBT, therapists hope to alter directly both (a) ongoing, momentary, situational reactions and coping, instances of behaviour, specific thoughts, emotional states, and particular stimuli; and (b) general skills, habits, beliefs, traits, sensitivities, behavioural potentialities, emotional predispositions, ongoing situations, insights, or life circumstances (see Table 3.1.) Generalised changes are preferred over specific momentary ones, but are often achieved through them.

7. An emphasis has grown over the decades on the identification and modification in CBT of maintaining (versus precipitating) causes of distress. Many of the very early studies in behaviour therapy focused, not surprisingly, on the etiology of emotional problems. The conditioned onset of Little Albert's rat phobia is an example (Watson & Rayner, 1920). However, several factors have pushed toward a heavy recent emphasis on problem maintenance, 'vicious circles', or PMCs (Bakker, 2008a, 2008b, 2019a), including:

   (a) The persistent empirical finding that insight into historical events is not universally necessary in the treatment of the majority of clinical psychological problems. For example, most phobias do not arise from a distinct traumatic conditioning experience (King et al., 1998; Menzies & Clark, 1993, 1994, 1995). Most adult psychological problems cannot be linked to childhood difficulties (Paris, 2000). Understanding one's emotional history is not always necessary or sufficient for relieving psychological distress (Bloom, 1994). For example, Bachrach et al. (1991), in a study of psychoanalytic (Freudian) treatment found that half their 42 patients improved but showed no increase in insight into their 'core conflicts'. It is often unclear where problems arose, but it is clearer what is maintaining them.

(b) The preference for reliably measurable factors favours current over historical ones (Bakker, 2008a).

(c) The consistently disappointing results from therapies that aim to reverse or dissolve the presumed ongoing effects of historical precipitating events. Such approaches have included psychoanalysis, abreaction, rebirthing, psychodrama, catharsis, traumatic incident reduction (TIR), hypnotic regression, and so on. Approaches such as these rarely rate a mention in reviews of evidence-based therapies (Devilly, 2005; Glancy & Saini, 2005; Nathan & Gorman, 2015; Roth & Fonagy, 2005).

(d) The recognition that problems that do not self-perpetuate will tend to ease without therapy. This has been found to be the case in most grief reactions (Parkes, 1993; Windholz, Marmar, & Horowitz, 1985), acute stress disorder (Bryant, 2003), anxiety disorders in general (Clark, 1999), and the spontaneous remission of most psychological disturbances (Tennant, Bebbington, & Hurry, 1981). For example, numerous studies have shown that most victims of child sexual abuse do not retain permanent psychological 'scars' or adult psychopathology (Rind & Tromovitch, 1997; Ulrich, Randolph, & Acheson, 2006), nor do they frequently go on to be sexual abusers themselves (Salter et al., 2003). Terr (1983) followed up a group of schoolchildren who had been subjected to a horrific school bus kidnapping. Two years later almost all were found to be recovered and well adjusted. Therapists can be victims of 'the clinician's illusion' (Chapman & Chapman, 1969; Cohen & Cohen, 1984) due to clinicians seeing only those people for whom problems have persisted (i.e. PMCs have formed; e.g. ASD has turned into PTSD). But population research shows that, for example, 75% to 85% of children whose parents divorce cope quite well in the medium to long term (Hetherington, Cox, & Cox, 1985; Hetherington & Kelly, 2002).

(e) The resolution of the 'symptom substitution' debate between the 'core problem' psychoanalysts and the 'symptom alleviation' behaviourists in favour of the latter group (Kazdin, 1982; Montgomery & Crowder, 1972; Wolpe, 1986). That is, when current emotional or psychological 'symptoms' are addressed via behaviour therapy or CBT, in almost all cases the general problem situation is improved, whereas if it were critical that an historically precipitated ongoing underlying hypothetical core problem be addressed, then other 'surface' symptoms would be expected to flare. We now know, for example, that bedwetters successfully treated by Dry Bed Training or an Enuresis Alarm show better general emotional adjustment afterward rather than worse (Baller, 1975). This applies at least when underlying organic conditions are screened out.

So research in CBT is especially focused on the search for maintainers of problem behaviours, cognitions, and emotions. CBT models of CPPs almost invariably include maintaining causal feedback loops, which are most obvious when they are presented graphically. Clinical assessment questions will seek out problem maintainers, case formulations will emphasise them, and treatments will very selectively target them.

Where Did CBT Come From?

The first major movement in psychotherapy, commonly sourced to Sigmund Freud, was heavily analytic and interpretive. Its theory and practice were developed through introspection and subjective clinical practice, rather than through objective experimentation. This led to both a divergence of theoretical assertions among Freud's contemporaries and followers, and an assumption of therapeutic effectiveness without an interest in objective outcome research.

Radical behaviourism (Watson, 1924) arose partly as a reaction to this unscientific, arbitrary, nonaccountable theory-building and therapy provision. And, while experimental psychology was in its infancy, perhaps focusing only on highly measurable variables such as behaviour and environmental stimuli was justified. But practising therapists soon realised that radical behaviourism, while comprehensive enough to explain most animal behaviour, infant behaviour, and some mass human behaviour, did not predict very well individual adult human behaviour.

As the reports of psychological studies accumulated, the inclusion of some 'black box' factors was deemed justified and necessary, so the processes of vicarious learning, or modelling, and social learning theory were incorporated (Bandura, 1969; Mischel, 1973). Increasing validity and reliability of self-report and other measures of people's internal states allowed the (re)introduction of beliefs, emotional status, expectancies, attributions, and images into theoretical models and therapy sessions; but this time in an empirically justified manner. Cognition and emotion were regarded as legitimate alternative targets and mechanisms for change, using the verified methods that behavioural learning theory had developed (Mahoney, 1974; Meichenbaum, 1977). At the same time largely cognitive methods of therapy were being developed (Beck, 1976; Ellis, 1962).

At the very least this provided an alternative point of intervention. Not only could behaviours and situations (stimuli and consequences) be modified now, but so could intervening or triggering internal states. This was a great boost to the face validity of many models of psychopathology and their related treatments. Clients welcomed the re-inclusion of their mental lives in case formulations after seeing radical behavioural techniques as overly simplistic and manipulative.

What Counts as CBT?

The particular scripts and homework assignments described in this manual borrow from many streams of CBT. These streams vary in their emphases on:

1. situational versus cognitive versus affective versus behavioural change targetting
2. targetting specific momentary, ongoing situations, reactions, and coping versus general skills, traits, life circumstances, or beliefs (see Table 3.1)

3. seeking to increase positive behaviours, skills, or coping versus decreasing negative behaviours, habits, attitudes, or feelings
4. whether the process is more one of therapist influence or modification of the client's responses (e.g., in-session exposure therapy), or client self-change through homework exercises (e.g., an in vivo exposure program)
5. the use of imaginal versus real-life or in vivo procedures.

Among the specific techniques described in the literature and generally regarded as conforming to the characteristics of CBT are:

- cognitive therapy (Beck, 1995)
- rational emotive behaviour therapy (Ellis, 1995)
- problem-solving therapy (Nezu, Nezu & Perri, 1989)
- behaviour therapy (Wolpe, 1973)
- self-instructional training (Meichenbaum, 1977)
- stress inoculation training (Meichenbaum, 1985)
- exposure and response prevention (Marks, 1985)
- anger control therapy (Novaco, 1975)
- anxiety management training (Suinn, 1995)
- assertiveness training (Trower, Bryant, & Argyle, 1978)
- bell and pad conditioning/dry bed training (Azrin, Sneed, & Foxx, 1973)
- biofeedback (Andrasik, Coleman, & Epstein, 1982)
- contingency contracting (Kanfer, 1990)
- controlled drinking (Miller, 1983)
- covert conditioning (Upper & Cautela, 1979)
- cue-controlled relaxation (Grimm, 1980)
- multimodal behaviour therapy (Lazarus, 1981)
- paradoxical intention (Weeks & L'Abate, 1982)
- parent management training (Griffin & Hudson, 1979)
- sex therapy (Masters & Johnson, 1970)
- token economies (Kazdin, 1977)
- mindfulness-based cognitive therapy (Segal, Williams, & Teasdale, 2002)
- metacognitive therapy (Wells, 2011)
- and many others.

Because the core model of CBT (see Chapter 3) is a very general and inclusive one, recognising the involvement of any verifiable cognitions, emotions, behaviours, or stimuli, on an acknowledged physiological substrate, very many therapy techniques are admissible as CBTs, so long as they are consistent with the established body of learning theory, and are shown to be effective beyond placebo. In this sense CBT is largely a collection of empirically supported therapies.

The proponents of Acceptance and Commitment Therapy (ACT; Hayes, Strosahl, & Wilson, 1999) on the one hand claim to be part of the 'third wave' of CBT. But they also assert that some learning theory underlying CBT's techniques is in error, and that Relational Frame Theory is a more true alternative. Hence all thought stopping interventions, for example, are to be avoided (Beevers, Wenzlaff, Hayes, & Scott, 1999; Hannan & Tolin, 2005). As these claims denote not just a qualification or subset within CBT, but rather opposition and claimed supremacy (Bakker, 2009), I cannot include ACT in the above listing of CBTs.

CBT is often classed as one of the 'talk therapies', usually by way of contrast with pharmacotherapy. This is not quite right. CBT is a more often a 'doing therapy' (see Script 5). A percentage of CBT, especially in REBT, involves discussion, argument, instruction, and so on. However, there are nearly always homework tasks. One of the scripts introducing clients to the CBT model states that '10% of the changes might happen while we're together, but 90% need to happen out there in the real world between our sessions'.

Why Use CBT?

CBT is the fastest-growing psychotherapeutic model. There are many reasons for this. Some of them are:

- It works. Individual therapists can vary with regard to the criteria they use in selecting therapeutic models or techniques. Some adhere to the approach they were mainly exposed to as undergraduates. Some choose approaches that 'click' with them or seem to suit their temperament (confrontive vs. conciliatory, intellectual vs. emotive, parental vs. collaborative). Others adopt models or therapies that 'sound right' or 'make sense' to them. But insurance funds, government bodies, and research organisations tend toward other criteria. They usually want therapy to be effective for the greatest number of people, in a short time, without side effects, and with the least chance of relapse. CBT fits the bill here, not only in comparison with placebo or waiting-list, but also when compared to other therapeutic approaches (APS, 2010; Butler et al., 2006; Dobson & Dobson, 2009; DoH, 2001; Fisher & O'Donohue, 2006; Hofmann et al., 2012; Nathan & Gorman, 2015). The trend in psychotherapy, as in medicine recently, is toward being 'evidence-based'. The need for such a theme is somewhat of an embarrassment to many of us. What has psychotherapy or medicine been before? Non-evidence-based? Arbitrary? Intuitive? Unfortunately the answer is largely 'Yes'. Or at least 'traditional'.

- It is an active therapy. Not only is CBT effective, but it is also efficient. Most manuals aim to reach the 'relapse prevention' phase in 12 sessions or less. In practice, therapists will see many clients for less than this number. (My own average across all clients is 6 to 7 sessions.) The provision of homework is a major factor in this efficiency. Hence CBT is more feasible than most approaches for general medical practitioners and other busy health and allied health practitioners (Tiller, 2001).
- Much of CBT is verified common sense. "Primary care workers at behavioural workshops have often remarked that much of what they are learning is applied common sense which they use instinctively in consultations anyway" (France & Robson, 1997, p. 7). This makes the approach palatable and consistent with current practice for many helping professionals, such as GPs, as well as easier to explain and 'sell' to clients. The verbatim scripts provided in this manual are much briefer and simpler than would be required to initiate a client into a psychoanalytic or even a medical model of psychopathology.
- Being fairly inclusive, evidence-based, and compatible with common sense, CBT can mesh well with other models of human service provision such as that employed by GPs with their patients and by courts with offenders. GPs are used to short-term progressive interventions, with tests or measures along the way, in a collaborative but coaching/teaching relationship, on problems that are multifactorial and defined functionally as much as diagnostically or categorically. The courts are often more interested in 'What triggered and will change this offender's behaviour?' than 'What theoretical explanation can you verbalise about this offender's behaviour?'
- CBT happily incorporates or works in parallel with the medical model, both theoretically and in practice. Theoretically, the CBT model (see Chapter 3) acknowledges a physiological substrate to all its factor categories (cognition, stimuli, emotions, behaviours), and incorporates medication as a particular input, especially to the affective component. In practice, it has been found that cognitive therapy for depression, for example, does much the same thing for a person as antidepressant medication does, and can do it sequentially or concurrently by, for example, reducing relapse rates (Ellis & Smith, 2002; Fava, 1999; Fava et al., 1998; Hollon et al., 1991; Jarrett et al., 2001; Oei & Yeoh, 1999; Paykel et al., 1999). Often it can even work better than medication (Antonuccio et al., 1997; Butler & Beck, 2001; Evans et al., 1992; Kovacs et al., 1981; Simons et al., 1986). The same compatibility between CBT and medication, especially where relapse rates are to be minimised, can be found with the treatment of OCD (Cottraux et al., 1990).

Another pointed example of CBT/medication confluence in theory and practice is the recent finding that CBT (exposure and response prevention) has the same effect on regional cerebral function in people with OCD, as revealed by positron emission tomography scans (PET scans), as does medication when it works (Baxter, 1992; Brody et al., 1998; Hansen et al., 2002; Jeffreys, 1993; Schwartz, 1998; Schwartz et al., 1996).

Within the PMC approach to CBT, Type III psychological problems (see Chapter 4) are recognised as likely to have a biological-level underlying mechanism, and to benefit especially from biological-level intervention — all presumably within the medical model.

Chapter 3

A Full CBT Model

The Basic CBT Model

In clinical practice the simple CBT model presented in Figure 3.1 (Bakker, 2008a, 2008b, 2019a) will suffice most of the time. It includes the core triad of 'Thoughts', 'Feelings', and 'Behaviours', with stimuli ('Events, Situations') having their effect through the 'Thoughts' element. This particular causal sequence (Stimuli —> Cognitions —> Feelings and Behaviours) is very common in the case formulations that are presented to clients, which explains the frequency of application of cognitive therapies from within the CBT armamentarium, as they specifically address this sequence.

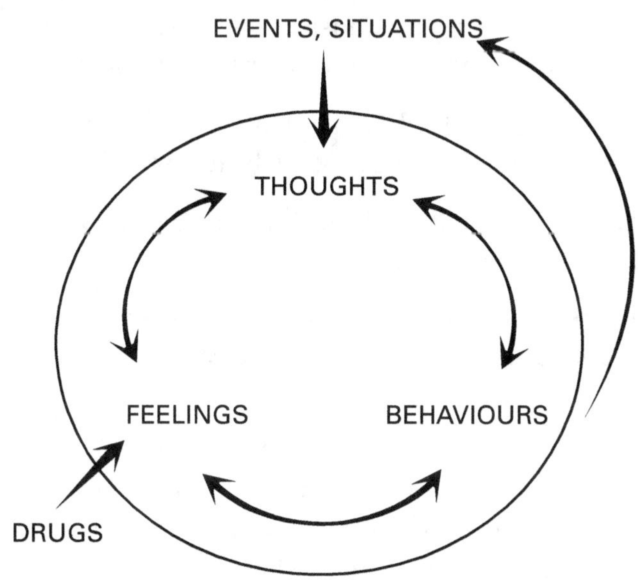

FIGURE 3.1 A CBT model.
(Available as a free download from www.australianacademicpress.com.au)

Because many clients will be either taking or considering concurrent medication, the complication of an input from 'Drugs' has been added. And, although medications can potentially directly affect 'Feelings' or 'Thoughts' or 'Behaviours', their effect on emotional state ('Feelings') is most commonly cited in case formulations (e.g. antidepressants), so only one input from 'Drugs' to 'Feelings' is illustrated in Figure 3.1. This simplified model can then be offered to clients (a) as part of their introduction to CBT, or (b) to explain the likely aetiology of their current CPPs, or (c) to illustrate the problem-maintaining circles (PMCs) that form most of their developing case formulation, or (d) to explain and justify the specific interventions and homeworks that ensue from their PMC-based case formulation (see Script 2).

The enclosed area in Figure 3.1 represents the client. The top downward arrow represents the influence of the client's environment; the majority of psychologically relevant influences on a person ('Events, Situations') initially impinge on that person's brain; that is, the influences are perceived, interpreted, selectively attended to, evaluated, and given meaning. Hence, the proximity of this arrow to 'Thoughts'.

Cognitions/thoughts/beliefs/attributions/schemata — 'Thoughts' — in turn, are modelled as causally influencing either or both (a) feelings/emotions/affective states/autonomic reactions — 'Feelings' — and (b) behaviour/actions/central nervous system responses — 'Behaviours'. The double arrows indicate that these conceptually distinguishable elements can also affect thinking, and can affect each other. A person's behaviour will often logically alter their environment, whether through manipulation or escape/approach. Therefore, there is a feedback loop arrow to the right in Figure 3.1. Finally, medications (prescribed or recreational) can affect the person especially by altering mood. This element is useful to include when so many people with psychological problems are prescribed anxiolytics or antidepressants, or self-medicate with alcohol and other drugs.

Examples abound in the research literature and from common experience of every one of these causal links. But they are most clearly illustrated when a problem or negative experience originates at any of the four identified points:

1. A charging bull (Event), when the danger is perceived, causes a fight-or-flight response and escape behaviour, which means the bull is (hopefully) evaded.
2. Remembering a loved one's death (Thought) causes sadness and crying and a visit to the bathroom to 'freshen up'.
3. Staying home all the time (Behaviour) results in a narrow low-reinforcement environment, boredom, and negative attitudes to the outside world: all depression-cycle risks.
4. A spontaneous panic attack (Feeling) — or the effects of one of Schachter & Singer's (1962) surreptitious epinephrine injections — is attributed to the bus one is travelling in, resulting in a hurried exit, escape, relief, and (perhaps unhelpful) conclusions about future bus avoidance.

These examples begin, respectively, with a stimulus, a thought, some behaviour, and a feeling, but spill into each of the other provinces, often creating a self-perpetuating causal cycle — a PMC.

CBT distinguishes markedly between 'precipitants', which are larger-scale events that can precipitate an episode of disturbance or the decision to seek treatment, and 'activating situations' that are smaller-scale events that result in negative mood or ideation or maladaptive behaviours (Dobson, 2001, p. 95).

Each element in the Figure 3.1 model can be taken to represent either short-term, transient, specific, immediate, situational instances of cause-and-effect, or long-term, general, pervasive causal links (see Table 3.1). An example of the former would be: A bill arrives in the mail —> 'I've already paid this. Another incompetent person I have to deal with' —> Feel angry —> Yell down the phone line. An example of the latter would be: High life stress levels for 6 months —> A negative defensive mindset about the world —> Ongoing anxiety/depression —> Withdrawal from usual social activities. (The potential for both levels of sequence to become cyclic or self-perpetuating is clear in these examples.)

With regard to 'Events, situations', a continuum exists between specific and general causes of psychological reactions or problems. It has been found that the frequency of 'daily hassles' (Kanner et al., 1981) can have an even greater impact on psychological wellbeing than major negative life events (Burks & Martin, 1985; Weinberger et al., 1987). So, for example, Glass and Arnkoff (1997) have recommended that measures of ongoing or momentary internal dialogue be assessed in conjunction with cognitive 'traits' such as anxiety sensitivity or dysfunctional attitudes.

So, where a combination of specific and general factors is included in a case formulation, this can be graphically represented as in Figures 3.2 and 3.3. Figure 3.2 illustrates that the effect of a particular stimulus ('Situation, event') on an ensuing thought/interpretation/self-statement (short term) may be dependent on a person's existing mindset/expectancies/beliefs (long term). Whereas immediate self-talk can be a cognitive mediator, longer-term mindsets are regarded as cognitive moderators (Kwon & Oei, 1992). An example could be a jealous husband who sees his wife put the phone down as

TABLE 3.1 Specific and General Applications of the Model

Elements in model	*Short-term, immediate, specific*	*Long-term, pervasive, general*
Events, situations	Events, stimuli, situations, triggers	The sum of one's experiences, life circumstances, chronic stresses, environment
Thoughts	Self-talk, images, thoughts, self-statements, decisions	Attitudes, beliefs, schemata, knowledge, expectancies, mindset
Feelings	Moods, emotions, feeling states	Sensitivities, conditioned reflexes, temperament
Behaviours	Actions, responses, acts, behaviours	Habits, skills, behavioural tendencies

SITUATIONS, EVENTS + MIND-SET, BELIEFS

↓

THOUGHTS

FIGURE 3.2 Specific and general 'thoughts' in the model.

SITUATIONS, EVENTS + LIFE CIRCUMSTANCES

↓

THOUGHTS

FIGURE 3.3 Specific and general 'situations' in the model.

he enters the room, and thinks 'She's been talking to her lover!' because of an alcohol-problem-induced or past-relationship-problem-induced suspicious mindset.

Figure 3.3 illustrates a combination of specific and general situations affecting a person's thinking. For example, being thrust before an audience (specific) when one has lived as a lighthouse-keeper for 4 years (general) will effectively alter the immediate meaning and impact of that specific situation.

The Full CBT Model

However, Figure 3.1 does not describe the full learning theory-based CBT model of human functioning. Even the processes of classical conditioning, relevant to the etiological formulations, the PMC illustrations, and the treatment explorations of most anxiety disorders, are not included in this basic version of the model. A direct causal link 'Events, Situations' —> 'Feelings' can describe classical conditioning processes, when autonomic responses are triggered and conditioned without conscious thought processes necessarily being involved (though cerebral sensory/perception processes must be). Clients experiencing a Panic Disorder, for example, will often report 'I wasn't thinking anything. It just came on when I went outside. Like a reflex'.

Such phenomena are distinguishable from the operantly conditioned, conscious, cognitive, skeletal, voluntary, central nervous system processes represented by 'Events, Situations —> Thoughts —> Behaviours'. The 'flashbacks' of PTSD would be an example of a classically conditioned problem. And the variant of thought-stopping described in Homework 36 is an example of the use of classical conditioning in therapy.

But stimuli ('Events, situations') can also directly trigger 'Behaviours' without conscious thought processes necessarily being involved. This is exemplified by simple reflexes that rarely involve more than a neural loop to the spinal cord and back, such as pulling one's hand away from the hotplate, though this is of very limited significance in CBT. But the possibility warrants a causal arrow in the CBT model between 'Events, situations' and 'Behaviours' that is bidirectional.

Similarly, the causal links between the environment and both 'Thoughts' and 'Feelings' must be bidirectional when we recognise that one's emotional state *effectively* alters a stimulus by altering its meaning and significance, as do one's thoughts and attitudes.

So, the full CBT model, as illustrated in Figure 3.4 and elaborated and exemplified in Table 3.2, is much more complex and less neat than Figure 3.1, and will rarely be shared with clients. But it deserves to be kept in the mind of the clinician in all etiological analyses, PMC case formulations, and treatment selection processes.

Note in Figure 3.4 the two types of causal influence represented by the two types of arrow heads. Most are what we normally regard as conventional causal links: 'A' materially and sequentially affects or changes or causes 'B' to occur. When an event or stimulus is perceived by a person, and that person has a cognitive reaction to it, we observe the temporal sequence and the material or physical links, and say the thought occurred due to the stimulus.

But some of the arrows in the full CBT model do not represent material and sequential links. They are best described as 'A' 'effectively' causing changes in 'B'. To illustrate, a person in a particularly hypervigilant, worried, or even paranoid mindset (Thoughts) who is exposed to an ambiguous stimulus, perhaps someone calling out his name, is likely to react as though the call is a warning or threat or admonishment. A different mindset could elicit a response of curiosity or even glee. The 'Thoughts' state *effectively* turns a neutral or ambiguous stimulus into a negative one. The calling out is not materially caused, elicited, or altered, – an audio recording will show it is the same sound – but it is effectively changed by the mental state of the responder.

Such 'effective' links are relevant to many PMC formulations. Just one example would be how the effects of drug use are of course materially dependent upon which drugs are ingested, how often, and how ('Behaviour'), but they also depend on the expectations ('Thoughts') and initial emotional state ('Feelings') of the person taking them. Placebo studies show how a person who expects to get drunk, will, and a person in a highly agitated state will hardly be touched by a moderate dose of a sedative. The drug administrations have been effectively altered, even if not materially so.

These 'effective' links are represented in Figure 3.4 by solid arrow heads.

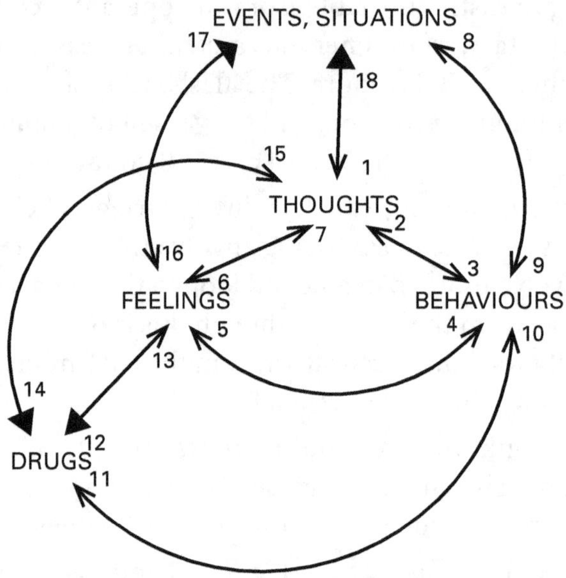

FIGURE 3.4 The full CBT model.
(Available as a free download from www.australianacademicpress.com.au)

The full CBT model applies to both general and specific examples of all the elements represented, and sometimes a combination of these (See Table 3.1 and Figures 3.2 & 3.3). Therefore both general and specific examples of each of the numbered causal links in Figure 3.4 are given in the accompanying Table 3.2.

Uses of the Model

The basic and full CBT models can be guides to assessment, both (1) when exploring a person's history to search for precipitating causes of a problem, and especially (2) when uncovering current maintaining factors:

1. The model is general enough to encompass problem origins in operant conditioning (behavioural or cognitive tendencies reinforced by situational consequences), classical conditioning (autonomic responses linked to new stimuli by temporal association), vicarious learning (cognitive absorption of other's experiences), or didactic learning (absorption at an intellectual, conceptual, or conscious level). It is meant to admit automatic or preverbal thoughts and images that are quick, primed, and therefore difficult to detect (Kahneman, 2011). But not subconscious ones at odds with, or existing in a separate realm from, stimuli, behaviour, and so on, and following separate rules.

2. But with CBT in mind, the model is meant especially to guide exploration and explanation of the ongoing cyclic causal factors that distinguish a passing upset from a distress in need of therapy (a CPP; see Table 4.1). Such a functional analysis has long been part of behaviour therapy. A 'behavioural analysis' (Hersen & Bellack, 1976) involves questioning, observation, and tests to determine the fre-

TABLE 3.2 Specific and General Examples of the 'Material and Sequential' and 'Effective' Causal Links in the Full CBT Model

Specific Example	General Example
1. Upon entering a room full of strangers —> 'Everyone is checking me out.'	1. Lack of interpersonal support and acceptance —> Low self-esteem/self-efficacy.
2. Escape a room full of strangers —> 'I prefer my own company anyway.'[1]	2. An insular lifestyle/avoidant behaviour tendency —> a 'people wouldn't like me anyway' attitude.[1]
3. 'Everyone is checking me out.' —> Escape.	3. Low self-esteem/self-efficacy —> an insular lifestyle/avoidant behaviour tendency.
4. Anxiety state —> Escape.	4. Social anxiety/generalised anxiety —> an insular lifestyle/avoidant behaviour as a coping style.
5. Escape from room full of strangers —> Anxiety state eases.	5. An insular lifestyle —> social anxiety/generalised anxiety (maintained through a lack of opportunity to challenge or decondition anxieties).
6. 'Everyone is checking me out' —> Anxiety state.	6. Low self-esteem/self-efficacy —>Social anxiety/ generalised anxiety disorder.
7. Anxiety state—> 'Everyone is checking me out, and finding fault'.	7. Social anxiety/ generalised anxiety disorder —> Low self-esteem/self-efficacy.
8. Escape —> Social exposure ceases.	8. An insular lifestyle —> Few challenges faced, plus lack of interpersonal support and acceptance.
9. Physical reflexes (e.g., snake recoil).	9. Lack of interpersonal support & acceptance —> An insular lifestyle/avoidant behaviour tendency.
10. Alcohol ingestion —> Walk into room full of strangers.[2,4]	10. Alcohol dependence/abuse pattern —> Mix mostly with other drinkers.
11. Order a drink at the bar —> ingest alcohol.	11. Mix mostly with drinkers —> alcohol dependence/abuse pattern.
12. Anxiety —> Alcohol has less sedating effect.	12. Social anxiety disorder/GAD —> Alcohol's befuddling effects are seen as desirable/relaxing.
13. Alcohol —> Anxiety lessened.[2,4]	13. Alcohol dependence/abuse pattern —> Narrow coping repertoire, Social anxiety/GAD is maintained.[2]
14. 'This drink will help me calm down' —> Alcohol has a confidence boosting effect quickly. (Placebo or expectancy effect.).	14. Low-self-esteem/self-efficacy —> Alcohol's befuddling effects are seen as desirable/relaxing, through lowered self-consciousness.
15. Alcohol —> Thinking becomes less logical and more tangential.[4]	15. Alcohol dependence/abuse pattern —> low self-esteem/self-efficacy.
16. See a room full of strangers —> instant automatic arousal/anxiety (classically conditioned response).[3]	16. Lack of interpersonal support/acceptance —> Social anxiety/GAD, through numerous classically conditioned associations, and few extinction experiences.[3]
17. Anxiety state—> a room full of strangers is an effectively high threat stimulus, not a neutral one.	17. Social anxiety/GAD —> The world effectively looks threatening/unsupportive.
18. 'Everyone is checking me out' —> a room full of strangers is effectively a high threat stimulus.	18. Low self-esteem/self-efficacy —> The world effectively looks threatening/unsupportive.

Note:

1. Cognitive dissonance theory (Festinger, 1957) and self-perception theory (Bem, 1972; Fazio et al., 1977).

2. Note that in the short term (specific example) the effects of a drug, such as alcohol, can be opposite to the long-term effects (general example).

3. Classical conditioning operates predominantly down the left side of the model. Operant conditioning operates predominantly down the right side.

4. The clearest examples of Drugs Affecting Thoughts are the antipsychotics, of Drugs Affecting Behaviour are the stimulants, and of Drugs Affecting Feelings are antidepressants.

(Available as a free download from www.australianacademicpress.com.au)

> quency and duration of problem behaviours, their antecedents, and their maintaining consequences. When self-report began to be accepted as a reliable enough measure of cognitive links in the chain, then the full CBT picture could be assessed (Cautela & Upper, 1975). Ellis's REBT specifies the sequence: (a) activating event, (b) evaluation of the event (beliefs), (c) emotional, behavioural, and cognitive consequences (Ellis, 1994). There is a recognition, but not emphasised in this model, that the appraisal (b) in turn affects the trigger (a) through behaviours and attitudes and emotional state (c). This has been called the self-fulfilling prophecy effect (Dryden & Ellis, 2001, p. 299) and is formally incorporated in our CBT model.

During an assessment interview a client may offer as the presenting problem, a disturbance at any of the four key elements in the model. For example, 'I've had a lot of pressure at work' (Events, situations), 'I'm worrying a lot' (Thoughts), 'I've been feeling really sad and down' (Feelings), or 'I keep washing my hands over and over' (Behaviours). Sometimes the complaint is identifiable with one of the causal arrows *between* the elements. For example, 'Whenever I think of my wife's affair I get nasty to her' (Thoughts —> Behaviours). It is the clinician's task to tease out the usual specific or general antecedents to, and consequences of, these complaints. Exactly what questions to ask (see Chapter 5) should be guided by our research-derived knowledge of common or serious correlates and causes of such complaints. Fortunately, there is a wealth of survey and experimental data informing us of such correlates and causes. For example, we know that depressed people often feel unreasonable guilt (Burns, 1980, p. 181), which in turn worsens mood, self-esteem — and depression! Other commonly encountered PMCs are described in Chapter 6.

When it comes to choosing at which point of a PMC to intervene, the model can also help with clarity of analysis and explanation to the client.

To be effective, a therapy need not directly address the element of the model cited in the presenting complaint. Much evidence suggests that the elements are interdependent enough so that altering one or two will affect all others anyway. The degree of synchrony among cognitive, affective, and behavioural response modes in fear responses, for example, has been thoroughly discussed in the literature (Rachman & Hodgson, 1974; Nelson et al., 1985). However, when CBT targets different elements in the model, comparable results generally emerge.

For example, Rehm (1984; Rehm et al., 1987) found that a self-management program for depression targeting behaviour (activity level) was as effective as one targeting cognitions (self-statements) or one targeting both. Each program was effective regardless of the degree of cognitive or behavioural deficits at pre-test, and each was equally effective in producing changes in cognitive or behavioural targets (Rokke & Rehm, 2001, p. 194). Jacobson et al. (1996) found that a 12-week course of behavioural treatment for depression achieved outcomes comparable to a 12-week cognitive therapy course.

Intervention at the point of 'Feelings' may be more problematic, and this is perhaps why medication is often resorted to.

Targetting 'Events, situations' depends upon just how changeable the client's environment is, and how desirable such change is in the long term. For example, alleviating anxiety by resigning from a stressful job may succeed quite quickly but may not augur well for future coping.

Selection of points in the model at which to intervene will be discussed more fully in Chapters 5 and 7.

Variations on the Model

Underlying the entire Figure 3.1 and Figure 3.4 models is a physiological substrate. 'Thoughts' are at base electrochemical events. 'Feelings' involve hormonal and autonomic nervous system changes. The neurosciences are progressively discovering the neurochemical correlates of what we study and alter at a psychological level. For example, Wykes (2002) found brain activation changes on functional magnetic resonance imaging when schizophrenics were given cognitive remediation therapy.

However, this knowledge is still at a more primitive level with most disorders than is that of the also-young science of psychology. The neurobiology of anxiety (McNally, 1988), of OCD (Hansen et al., 2002), and of posttraumatic stress disorder (Newport & Nemeroff, 2000; Stein et al., 2000) are still at the level of trying to locate relevant neural structures. Meanwhile clinical psychology knows well many of the stimuli, cognitions, feelings, and behaviours that interact to initiate and maintain these problems.

So we are still far from supplanting the Figure 3.4 psychological-level model with a neurological-level one. Even where a treatable biological precipitating cause or trigger is assumed, psychological maintainers are often critical. An example of this is the development of a self-perpetuating panic disorder from one or two drug- or illness-induced panic attacks. Another is the finding that so-called endogenous depressions can be successfully treated with cognitive therapy (Simons & Thase, 1992).

So, even if some clinical psychological problems (CPPs) become somewhat explained or understood at a neurochemical level in the future, many will not. They are not necessarily 'pathological' at this level, and no level of analysis or explanation is intrinsically more real or 'scientific' than any other (Deacon, 2013; Satel & Lilienfeld, 2013). It is no more necessary to explain a depression problem or a jealousy problem neurologically than to compare the poems of Keats and Shelley from a molecular point of view (Dennett, 1995).

However, clinicians who often deal with psychiatric or neurological conditions such as schizophrenia, bipolar disorder, or epilepsy, like psychiatrists, and those who frequently deal with medical complaints as a part of the psychological picture, like GPs, may feel that physiology needs a more direct representation in the model than 'substrate' status. Figure 3.5 displays such an alternative (Radford, 2001).

This model is understandably more useful to people who work directly with a client's/patient's physiology, such as medical practitioners. But to a psychologist someone's nausea, for example, will be regarded as either an Event/Situation they have encountered, or as a Feeling experienced. It is hard to know what is left of 'Feelings' if we take away Situations, Cognitions, Behaviour, and Physiology. Hence, I use a 'three

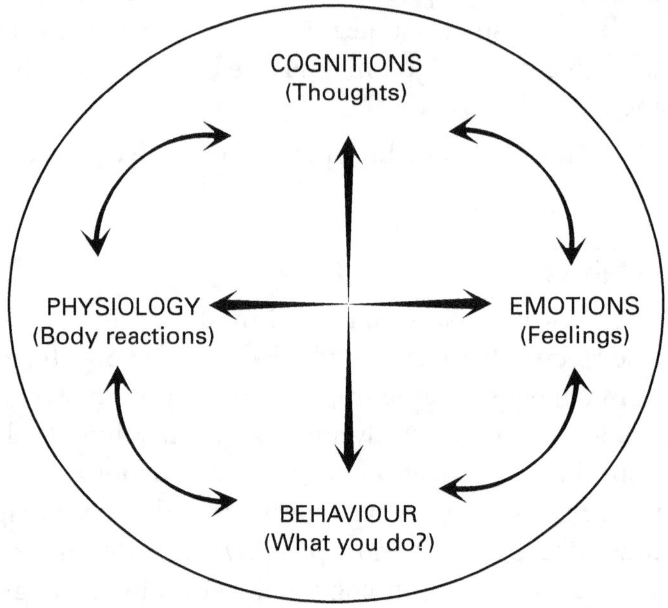

FIGURE 3.5 CBT and a comprehensive model of personal health and personal health care (Radford, 2001).
(Available as a free download from www.australianacademicpress.com.au)

Note:

1. *The circle represents a person. The space outside the circle is their environment.*
2. *The environment impacts on the person, usually via their cognitions.*
3. *Inside the personal circle are 4 areas that work in concert to give overall wellbeing. The areas affect all other areas and are affected by all other areas too (note the direction of the arrows).*
4. *A GP, who is part of a patient's environment, can assist a patient's recovery to positive wellbeing by working, where possible, in all of a patient's internal 4 areas and on their environment.*

factor model' instead of the four that even some psychologists use (e.g., Wilding & Milne, 2010, p.23).

A Grand Unified Theory?

The full CBT model (see Figure 3.4) is a very general model of psychological functioning. This allows it to incorporate and align in one model such historically diverse and theoretically difficult therapeutic concepts as placebo drug effects (Arrow 14), expectancy effects (Arrow 18), classical conditioning (Arrow 16), operant conditioning (Arrow 5), cognitive dissonance theory (Arrow 2), direct instruction/psychoeducation (Arrow 1), multimodal therapies (Lazarus, 1992), PMC theory, and transdiagnostic symptoms and treatments.

In this sense it parallels the 'Grand Unified Theory' (GUT) of physics, which mathematically relates together the electromagnetic, weak, and strong nuclear forces. Physicists are trying to go one step further, and to develop a 'Theory of Everything' (TOE) that will incorporate the fourth basic force, gravity. The equivalent in psychology would be to add to the full CBT model the physiological substrate it sits upon. Then we would have the option and the capacity to intervene with a CPP such as an OCD problem either at the level of behaviour, of cognition, of emotion, of stimuli/environment, or of neurology. But at this point the neurological sciences are much less developed, in relation to clinical psychology, than psychological science is. We have known what can trigger or ease OCD at the cognitive, behavioural, environmental, or emotional level for several decades, but we are still at the stage in neuroscience of pointing vaguely at brain regions, naming them, and claiming that for an undetermined reason they seem to be overactive or underactive. This is still descriptive science, not explanatory or interventive science. For example, it has been claimed that an 'overactive amygdala' is involved in Social Anxiety Disorder (Phan et al., 2006). We cannot yet directly and selectively quieten down a person's amygdala, and even if we could, we may not want to. It is likely to have all sorts of unwanted side effects. Unless we do it via psychological-level intervention!

At this stage knowledge of the neurological substrate to psychological problems provides us only with an alternative level of explanation to offer to our clients. There is no doubt that being able to talk about helping someone's left prefrontal cortex modulate arousal through cognitive therapy of Panic Disorder can help us appear expert and knowledgeable, and hence assist in therapy compliance. But there is also the risk of clients perceiving such an explanation as fatalistic: 'How can I overcome my PTSD if it is hardwired now?!'

Explanations of psychopathology that assist only by making a problem appear known, diagnosed, studied, and labeled can be at any level. For example, explaining the 'freeze' response when a person is highly anxious in terms of norepinephrine and right prefrontal cortex activity, so as to reduce the guilt of someone who did not act in a crisis, could equally be done at the evolutionary level — that we are adapted/programmed to 'play possum' under severe threat as a survival mechanism.

Explanations that also tell us what to do with a psychological problem must be preferred over ones that just help us appear expert. The PMC-based psychological-level CBT model presented is for now only a GUT, without a therapeutically useful neurological substrate to make it a TOE. When the TOE arrives (20–30 years?) it will likely supplant up to 40% of clinical psychological therapies, but it is also likely that disorders triggered and maintained by 'Events, situations' and manifesting in cognitions, behaviours, and feelings will still best be treated at this (psychological) level.

Though we have a useful GUT in clinical psychology we are some way from a useful TOE.

Chapter 4

The PMC Approach to CBT

Problem-Maintaining Circles in the Model

Several features of the introduction to CBT outlined thus far point to the centrality of the concept of problem-maintaining circles (PMCs) of psychological-level causal factors in the development and maintenance of all clinical psychological problems (CPPs). Already, (on pages 9 and 10) five reasons have been presented as to why CBT has grown to focus on and emphasise maintaining (versus precipitating, original, or historic) causes of distress. Hence, both the simplified and full CBT models (see Figures 3.1 and 3.4) are comprised entirely of bidirectional arrows and causal feedback loops.

Almost every time a CBT-related, evidence-based model of a particular CPP is presented graphically in the literature as a causal flow chart, it has included one or more full causal cycles or feedback loops. One of the first highly influential such evidence-based models of a CPP incorporating a full feedback loop, vicious circle, or PMC was Clark's panic cycle (Clark, 1986).

But before this many theoreticians, researchers, and clinicians were noting critical 'vicious circles' maintaining numerous CPPs. For example, Teasdale (1985) noted that, though the onset of clinical depression may occur for a variety of reasons, treatment is most successful when it addresses what is *maintaining* the problem. He suggested that an especially important maintainer is likely to be the 'depression–cognition vicious circle' in which a depressed mindset causes subsequent experiences to be perceived as highly aversive and uncontrollable, which is then a depressant. Hence cognitive therapy is indicated.

Many other evidence-based CBT-related models incorporating clear, graphic PMCs have been developed since, describing a wide range of problems, including general emotional distress (Dobson & Dobson, 2009, p. 44), PTSD (Ehlers & Clark, 2000, p. 321; Zayfert & Becker, 2007, pp. 10–11), panic disorder (McKay et al., 2007, p. 109), worry

(p. 79), general anxiety (Salkovskis, 1996, p. 53; Wells, 1997, p. 9), bulimia (Fairburn, 2008, p. 19), anorexia (p. 21), social phobia (Clark & Wells, 1995, p. 72), depression (Moorey, 2010, p. 178; Persons & Davidson, 2001, p. 98), OCD (Hyman & Pedrick, 2005, p. 127; Rees, 2009, p. 80; Salkovskis, 1985), hypochondriasis (Treatment Protocol Project, 2004, p. 261), and healthy anxiety (Walker & Furer, 2008, p. 370; Warwick & Salkovskis, 1989).

It is a very small step from *explaining* the development of a CPP in terms of a PMC starting to operate, to *defining* a CPP by the operation of such a causal loop. When Clark (1999) explained why problematic levels of anxiety persist (are maintained) in some people, and therefore how to ameliorate it, or when Salkovskis (1996) explained exactly what maintains health anxiety or obsessions such that a 'disorder' arises, they were *defining* the difference between a transient negative state and a CPP.

Case formulations in CBT can be at three levels (Kuyken, Padesky, & Dudley, 2009):

1. They can be purely descriptive. For example, 'Bill experiences severe anxiety in social situations'. This level corresponds to psychiatry's descriptive diagnostic process.
2. They can list precipitating, predisposing, and protective factors. For example, 'Bill had some acutely embarrassing social experiences in the past. He tends to be an anxious person generally. And he has good family support'. Both of these levels can be useful, and they may affect treatment decisions. But they are not critical to these decisions (Kuyken et al., 2009, p. 27). They do not necessarily tell us what needs to be done now to reverse the mechanisms underlying or causing Bill's social anxiety problems. (Few of the interventions/homeworks in this manual intervene at Level 1 or Level 2. Homework 7: Socialisation Messages is an exception. It guides a client toward past experiences that could have precipitated or predisposed toward the development of currently active PMCs. Sometimes a client is only willing to address problem maintainers after background events have been identified and a theory of origin has been proposed.)
3. What will be critical is the third level of formulation: How, based on CBT theory, problems are triggered and maintained; for example, 'Social anxiety + being at a party —> self-criticism + escape —> more social anxiety and escape behaviour'. A number of models have been developed to assist with such maintenance explanations (Kuyken et al., 2009, p. 36), including functional analysis (Hayes & Follette, 1992; Kohlenberg & Tsai, 1991), situation-thought-emotion-behaviour sequences (Padesky & Greenberger, 1995), and several disorder-specific CBT models (e.g., Fairburn, 2008, p. 21). *Practical CBT*'s PMC-based model is one of these options.

Hence, when a CBT practitioner presents a case formulation — whether it be to colleagues, in case notes, or to the client — it will often be in the form of a causal flow chart (Haynes, 1992; Nezu et al., 1997), which — because it will explain and describe problem behaviour-, cognition-, or feelings-maintenance, rather than historical precipitance — will incorporate a feedback loop, vicious circle, or PMC.

Such insights, combined with the profound inadequacy of the medical model of psychiatric disorders and its imposition of DSM diagnoses on clinical psychological practice (Bakker, 2019a; DCP, 2013), has led to the proposition that a conception of CPPs based on PMCs is more in keeping with psychological research and theory, and has inestimably more clinical utility, and case formulation and therapeutic relevance.

The proposition (Bakker, 2008a, 2008b, 2019a) is that CPPs are actually *defined* by whether PMCs have formed and are operating, and that this is what distinguishes a transient upset from a clinical problem warranting clinical psychological intervention. (See Table 4.1.)

Then clinical depression, for example, is not defined by severity of symptoms — a pathological depression can be mild, while a normal grief reaction can be severe. Nor by an alleged 'chemical imbalance in the brain' — this is currently not reliably measurable, and biochemistry is altered in *all* people who are sad. Nor by a distinctive symptom profile, which has not been found to reliably distinguish even claimed endogenous versus reactive depressions (Davidson et al., 1984; Nelson & Quinlan, 1981; Young et al., 1986; Zimmerman et al., 1986).

Instead, a clinical depression is defined or is diagnosable when a low mood, or negative thinking, or behavioural inactivity, or sleep disturbance, or social avoidance have deeply entrenched enough or for long enough to form one or more self-perpetuating causal circles (PMCs). With depression, these circles can involve social withdrawal removing the possibility of pleasant events or of self-esteem recovery; or sleep disturbance, which saps energy and drive; or irritability, which pushes a person's major people-supports away.

So, under this conception of CPPs, the difference between the negative but normal, transient, and even healthy, psychological reactions of Table 4.1 (such as being anxious

TABLE 4.1 Normal, Negative Psychological Situations or Reactions ('Psychological Problems') and Their Corresponding Psychopathological Counterparts, if PMCs Form

Reaction	*Corresponding CPP*
Grief reaction	Depression
Acute stress reactions	Post-traumatic stress disorder
Binge	Bulimic disorder
Anxious state	Anxiety disorder
Episode of substance abuse	Addiction
Misbehaviour	Conduct disorder
Argument	Relationship problem
Diet	Anorexic disorder
Pain	Chronic pain syndrome
Tantrum	Impulse control disorder
Worry over health	Somatoform disorder
Fussiness	OCD

in the presence of a dog), and a CPP involving similar behaviours, emotions, and cognitions (such as a dog phobia) is not whether a certain number of diagnostic criteria have been met. This medical model conception falls down when the presentation — the 'symptoms' — are identical. The difference is in whether the anxiety abates, habituates, or extinguishes naturally (anxiety being an aversive state, rather that self-reinforcing, see footnote under Table 7.2), or is somehow maintained or even grown by a 'vicious circle' (PMC), such as the negative reinforcement that comes from the ease felt when one escapes the presence of the dog (coping by avoidance). Evidence of this way of coping would suggest that a full maintaining perpetuating cycle of causal factors had begun to operate. When currently-operating PMCs are identified, the subsequent case formulation (Bakker, 2008a, 2008b, 2019a) readily suggests relevant therapy approaches. In this example Exposure Therapy is indicated.

If PMCs have not yet formed (see Table 4.1), then supportive counselling or guidance may still be useful, perhaps to speed the (linear) recovery processes of normal coping or spontaneous remission. But clinical psychological intervention is not yet justified. This is a useful, theory-based, and consistent distinction in the use of the terms 'counselling' and 'therapy'. Generally, the negative emotions, behaviours, or cognitions in the left-hand column of Table 4.1 may benefit from supportive counselling, but do not require or justify interventive therapy. No identified PMCs need (yet?) be broken.

Illustrations of a variety of such PMCs are presented in Figure 4.1. Each is research-derived, generalised, explanatory (versus merely descriptive), treatment-relevant, can be detected by a comprehensive psychological assessment and functional analysis, and can be presented in a communicable codified case formulation. The first two operate within an individual and serve to maintain, respectively, a depression problem and a chronic pain CPP. The third functions *between* people. And the fourth is overtly transdiagnostic, describing the onset and mutual perpetuation of a social anxiety problem and an alcohol abuse problem.

Examples abound in the research literature and in common experience of the reciprocity of causal links at a psychological level — of self-fulfilling prophecies, or vicious circles, or deepening spirals. Just one example is Heiby's (1982) finding that depressed people score lower on his self-reinforcement questionnaire, and that low questionnaire scorers are more likely to respond with depression to low levels of external reinforcement (Heiby, 1983). Many other researchers and theorists have written in general terms about 'self-fulfilling prophecies' in this sense (Haynes, 1992; Levenson & Strupp, 1997; Nezu et al., 1997; Wachtel, 1991).

Therapeutic implications also leap from such studies. Kwon and Oei (1992) undertook a careful analysis of the relationship between negative life events and depressive symptoms. They concluded that dysfunctional attitudes (a cognitive moderator) interact with negative life events to produce negative automatic thoughts (a cognitive mediator), which then form a vicious circle with depressive symptoms. Cognitive therapy is clearly indicated in such a situation.

Teasdale (1985) found evidence to support a critical 'depression–cognition vicious circle' involving 'depression about depression', which can explain the effectiveness of

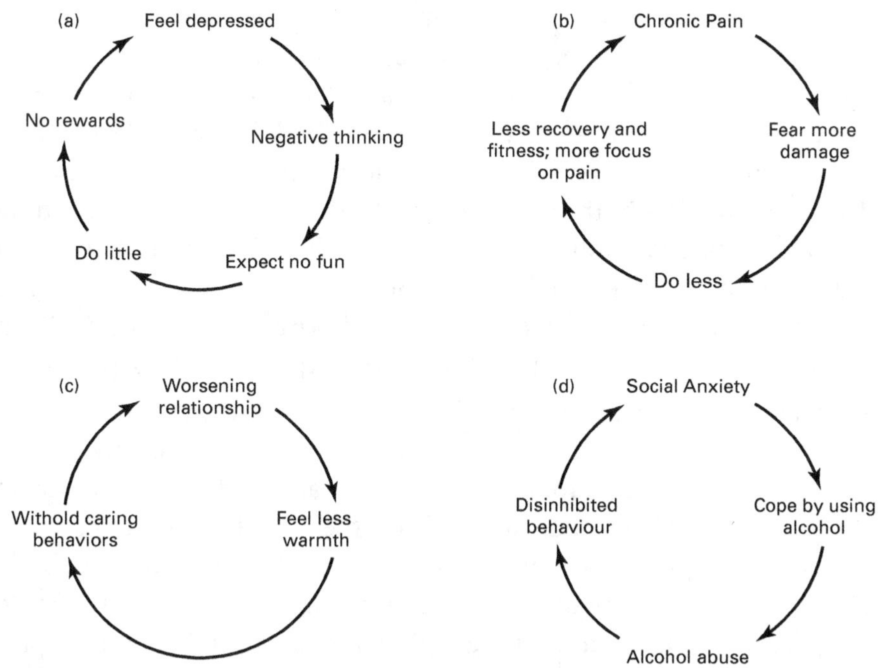

FIGURE 4.1 Examples of PMCs defining CPPs

specific psychological treatments. Hsu and Holder (1986) proposed the 'bulimia cycle' of: dieting —> feeling hungry and deprived —> (with some moderator variables) —> binge-eat —> feel guilty —> vomit or fasting —> feel hungry. Points at which to intervene therapeutically subsequently emerged. Fairburn et al. (2003) have presented a more elaborate and inclusive cyclic model of eating disorders, with subsequent treatment implications. Bilodeau (1992) has proposed a circular explanatory model of anger problems.

The causal spirals that occur in panic attacks have often been described (Hackman, 1998; Pauli et al., 1991), as well as the 'vicious circle in social phobia' (Gruber & Heimberg, 1997), and a mutual relationship between social phobia and alcoholism (Lepine & Pelissolo, 1998).

Scott and Stradling (1992) have proposed a model of the maintenance of PTSD symptoms involving reciprocal causality between intrusive imagery, avoidance behaviours, and disordered arousal.

The paradox that depression can produce sexual dysfunction, which is worsened by the side-effects of selective serotonin re-uptake inhibitors (SSRIs), has been called a 'stress–illness vicious circle' (Wheatley, 1998). And Lindwall, Larsen, and Hagger (2011) have shown that, while depression frequently halts regular physical activity, exercise can prevent depressive symptoms (see Figure 6.4 [u]).

A particularly insidious PMC arises from the fact that the occurrence of a problem can diminish a person's very capacity to cope — their coping repertoire. This has been noted by Wheatley (1997), who argued that depression inhibits a person's ability to cope with stress, worsening the depression. He saw antidepressants as having a role in breaking this cycle. Elsewhere (Wheatley, 2000) he described that stress leads to physical and psychiatric symptoms, which both worsen the stress situation and decrease one's ability to cope. He gave examples in the areas of anxiety, depression, sexual dysfunction, sleep disturbance, and impaired immunity. Meanwhile Seiffge-Krenke (2000) has pointed out that withdrawal as a form of avoidant coping produces its own emotional and behavioural problems, which then lead to more withdrawal. This is a justification of the coping-skill deficit model. (SeeFigures 6.4 [v], 6.6 [a] and [b], 6.12 [b], etc.)

PMCs can occur *between* people to maintain or exacerbate a problem, as well as within a person. (See Figures 4.1 [c] and 6.8.) For example, Patterson (1982) and Patterson, Dishion and Chamberlain (1993) have described how parent–child interactions frequently directly reinforce deviant behaviour, and outlined the role of parent–child discipline practices in the development and maintenance of aggressive behaviour in children. These insights led to the development of the most empirically supported treatment for conduct disorder — parent management training — in which the aim is to interrupt or alter the dysfunctional negative spirals of emotions and behaviours between people.

PMCs can also occur between elements that represent what DSM would regard as different, separate mental disorders. (See Figure 4.1[d]) (This can explain DSM's profound problems with the very high comorbidity rates between its putatively distinct disorders. Why do a majority of people who contract GAD also suffer a MDD around the same time?!) Cosci et al. (2010) have found that cigarette smoking and panic each have the capacity to serve as a causal factor or facilitator in the development of the other. Liedl et al. (2010) found evidence of mutual maintenance between pain and PTSD, mediated by arousal symptoms at 3 months after a traumatic event. Schindel-Allon et al. (2010) took a time series of measures that found that depressive symptoms and PTSD are time synchronous and that, in particular, depression may be critical in the development of PTSD symptoms. Robinson et al. (2011) found evidence that anxiety disorders, mood disorders, and substance use disorders are likely to be causally reciprocal, with anxiety often pre-dating depression and substance use, and substance use pre-dating depression in males, while depression pre-dates substance use more often in females. Most of the evidence for a direct causal relationship between major depression and anxiety disorders is in support of anxiety disorders leading to the development of depression problems (Mathew et al., 2011). Such findings have been cited in support of transdiagnostic approaches to treatment.

PMCs are not an exclusively psychological phenomenon. They can occur at any level of analysis. A sociological example could be: National or class poverty —> poor educational opportunities —> generational poverty continues. A medical-level example could be: Bacterial infection —> physiological stress —> immune system suppression —> worse infection. The term 'CPP' is justified when a *psychological-level* link is identified. For example: Bacterial infection —> unable to go to work —> fear losing job —> anxiety —> immune system suppression —> worse infection. Therapy, then, based on the CBT model of Figure 3.1, can target this PMC's behavioural links (go to work anyway), cognitive links (better self-talk about job loss prospects due to sick leave), affective links (reduce anxiety by relaxation strategies), or situational links (get a guarantee from the boss).

A psychologist who was highly experienced in working with unemployed people once provided me with a taxonomy of eleven PMCs that serve to maintain one's unemployment (a situational problem) involving subsequent and exacerbating : poverty, lack of transport, homelessness, diminished self-confidence, reduced energy/motivation, mood problems, etc. (Sarkes, 2014).

Type I, II, and III Psychological Problems

So PMC theory can give us a definition — a threshold criterion — for the detection of CPPs which is much clearer and more treatment-relevant than that provided by psychiatry's medical model concept of mental disorders (Bakker, 2019a).

But can all clinical, treatment-worthy problems that affect us at a psychological level be adequately treated by psychological-level PMC-breaking? Surely some are best explained and treated by addressing neurological- or neurophysiological-level underlying mechanisms, rather than purely psychological-level ones? Schizophrenia is a candidate for such a problem, especially as best practice treatment guidelines generally commence with pharmacological treatments (Bradford, Stroup, & Lieberman, 2002). The same can be argued with regard to bipolar disorder (Llorca et al., 2013; Swartz & Swanson, 2014).

Therefore, three types of psychological problem must be distinguished. They are described in Table 4.2. Type I psychological problems are negative or undesired emotional, behavioural, or cognitive reactions that are normal, expected, transitional, probably adaptive, 'linear' in cause-and-effect over time, and may benefit or transition more quickly if supportive counselling is provided. So a conception of CPPs based on the detection of operating PMCs is treatment-relevant, categorical (versus dimensional), essentialist (versus arbitrary or merely a convenient social construction), parsimonious (only 1 or 2 criteria), theory-based (both CBT and PMC theory), empirically-derived, and nonstigmatising.

Type II psychological problems are '*clinical* psychological problems' that deserve therapeutic intervention because they are not likely to abate, spontaneously remit, or transition easily, due to the operation of PMCs at a psychological (cognitive or emotional or behavioural) level. Most depression problems presenting to psychologists are such. Perhaps 10% or fewer involve non-psychological-level pathologies, such as Bipolar Affective Disorder, post-viral depressions, or seasonal affective disorder.

Type III psychological problems are those presenting in association with an underlying 'psychiatric condition' which is likely to be best understood at a pathophysiological level, and which are therefore unlikely to be explained entirely by psychological-level PMCs, or 'cured' purely by their interruption. These three overlapping but distinguishable problem types are often referred, respectively, to counsellors, clinical psychologists, and psychiatrists.

TABLE 4.2 All Psychological Problems

TYPE I	TYPE II	TYPE III
Normal 'linear' psychological reactions	Clinical psychological problems (CPPs)	Psychiatric problems (mental disorders)
No PMCs identified (yet?)	PMCs have formed.	Breaking psychological PMCs may not be enough. Biological PMCs may also be operating
Refer for counselling?	Refer for clinical psychological therapy.	Refer for psychiatric (and psychological?) therapy
Grief reactions Acute stress disorder Anxiety states Life event stress Life transitions Adjustment disorders Upsets Arguments Burnout	Anxiety disorders (OCD, PTSD, GAD, ...) Depression Eating disorders Sexual problems Relationship problems Substance abuse/dependence Sleep problems Personality disorders Gambling problems	Schizophrenia Schizoaffective disorder Bipolar affective disorder 'Third day blues' Dementia Delusional disorder Autism disorder Seasonal affective disorder Post-viral depression

(Available as a free download from www.australianacademicpress.com.au)

In this light, one way to distinguish 'psychiatric' and 'psychological' problems is the presence of an ongoing, underlying, presumably-biochemical/neurologically-based disorder that daily 'feeds into' possible psychological PMCs, but makes them of secondary importance, relevant to relapse and some maintenance, but not to 'cure'. Breaking some depression or relationship PMCs can leave a person no longer depressed, or a relationship mended. But breaking a family stress PMC for someone with a schizophrenia diagnosis can only reduce this or future episodes of psychosis; it won't dissolve the disorder itself. (See Figure 5.2)

The Transdiagnostic Approach

The PMC-based approach to case formulation and to subsequent CBT, is part of the recent trend toward transdiagnostic theory, assessment, and treatment of psychological problems (Taylor & Clark, 2009).

The debate over whether it is of any use at all to target the symptoms of a psychopathology, rather than its (theory-dependent) historical causes, was long ago resolved in favour of symptom alleviation and against the notion of 'symptom substitution'. (See page 10.)

Supported by the markedly more robust therapeutic effects of the 'symptomatic' treatments such as behaviour therapy, cognitive therapy, CBT, and drug therapies, a deliberate emphasis on studying 'psychological phenomena rather than psychiatric diagnoses' (Persons, 1986) has been developing for over 30 years now. Persons (1986) listed several advantages of a symptom-focused approach, and went on to develop and promote case formulation approaches over categorical diagnostic approaches for many CPPs (Persons, 1989; Persons & Tompkins, 1997).

A recent incarnation of this evidence-based and therapy-relevant movement can be found in the growth of transdiagnostic assessment and therapy approaches sparked by Barlow and his colleagues (Barlow, Allen, & Choate, 2004). Noting the plethora of complex treatment manuals being produced, they pointed out that the commonalities in etiology and underlying structure among the emotional disorders are greater than their differences (Barlow et al., 2011b). They subsequently identified three fundamental therapeutic components in the successful treatment of the emotional disorders: (a) Altering antecedent cognitive appraisals; (b) Preventing emotional avoidance; And (c) facilitating action tendencies not associated with the emotion that is dysregulated (Barlow, Allen, & Choate, 2004). Note that each of these strategies will disrupt a current (cyclic, maintaining) causal sequence — not reverse some historical event.

These three components represent perhaps the most therapeutically useful and theoretically neat categorisation of CBT techniques proposed to date, because they refer to attacks on different points of the CBT/PMC generic model (Figure 3.1). These components can be rephrased as variants on: (a) Cognitive restructuring; (b) Exposure therapy; and (c) Coping skills training. Almost all the homeworks in Section 3 are categorisable under these three headings, and are hence transdiagnostic. For example, thought-stopping (Homework 36), being a coping skills technique, can be useful in depression, anxiety management, anger control, sexual problems, and so on. It is known that aberrant attentional processes are etiologically significant in the development and maintenance of many emotional disorders (Taylor & Amir, 2010). So transdiagnostic applications of attention modification interventions have been developed for the treatment of psychopathology in general (Taylor & Amir, 2010).

Homework 27 ('Graze Foods') may be helpful irrespective of whether the client has an aberrant eating pattern due to depression, anxiety, an eating disorder, a neurological condition, or bacteriologically-caused nausea. So long as a disturbed eating pattern is identified as a likely problem-maintainer in a PMC, then Graze Foods can be part of the treatment because it will target and attempt to disrupt a low-food-intake PMC that can be critical in all of these problems.

Transdiagnostic cognitive-behavioural approaches attempt to develop broad theories of clinical conditions and corresponding treatment protocols that can be applied to a range of conditions (Taylor & Amir, 2010). This describes the PMC-based model and its ensuing treatments. The 'Full CBT Model' (see Figure 3.4) is the ultimate in broad theories of clinical conditions. Such transdiagnostic models and corresponding treatments also lead to a case-conceptualised and flexible use of CBT, rather than a simplistic manualised one (Dobson & Dobson, 2009). This is, again, the essence of the PMC model. PMC-rich case formulations guide one toward highly individualised treatment programs, which contrast greatly with the 'pill for an ill' standardised, manualised treatments that RCTs of 'CBT for diagnosed mental disorder A' have encouraged.

Among the commonalities identified across the emotional disorders — considered often to outweigh the differences — are numerous cognitive and behavioural maintaining factors (McEvoy, Nathan, & Norton, 2009). Hence transdiagnostic or unified treatment protocols invariably target 'common maintaining factors'. Barlow et al. (2011b) describe that when clients "attempt maladaptive emotion regulation strategies ... this pattern may erupt in a vicious cycle of increased physiological and emotion arousal" (p.15), thus linking further the transdiagnostic approach and the PMC-based model of psychopathology. Their 'Unified Protocol for transdiagnostic treatment of emotional disorders' also uses the same, ubiquitous '3-component model of emotions' as the PMC-based one, of Thoughts, Feelings, and Behaviours (Barlow et al., 2011a, p. 63; 2011b, p. 18), and a similar visual PMC case formulation summary (Barlow et al., 2011a, p.86).

McEvoy et al. (2009) have summarised evidence that such unified treatments are effective, can produce benefits in comorbid conditions, compare well with diagnosis-specific treatments, and result in high client satisfaction, good therapeutic alliance, group cohesion, and positive treatment expectations. Barlow et al. (2011b) include in evidence for the commonalities among the anxiety and other emotional disorders the many studies showing that treatments for an anxiety disorder produce improvements in other anxiety or mood disorders (p. 13). This weighs against the 'separate silos' view of traditional psychiatric diagnosis.

Sometimes such transdiagnostic approaches span a limited range of disorder, such as the eating disorders (Fairburn, Cooper, & Shafran, 2003). Sometimes they span multiple processes that are universally applied (Harvey, Watkins, Mansell, & Shafran, 2004). Or they may promote the relevance of a universal single process, such as experiential or behavioural avoidance (Mansell, Harvey, Watkins, & Shafran, 2009).

Currently, the most prominent transdiagnostic model is an incorporation of Gross's (1998) process model of emotion regulation (Gross, 1998, 2002; Gross & Thompson, 2007) with Barlow et al.'s (2011a) unified protocol for the treatment of emotional disorders (Fairtholme et al., 2010). Emotion regulation is implicated in both psychopathology and in its successful treatment (Kring & Sloan, 2010). Emotion regulation difficulties and mechanisms such as experiential avoidance, suppression, cognitive processing, and sleep disturbances cut across diagnostic boundaries. So controlling experiential avoidance, for example, is part of a 'transdiagnostic functional dimensional approach' to psychopathology (Boulanger, Hayes, & Pistorello, 2010), that focuses on function and dimensions more than diagnostic category (Lawrence, Rosellini, & Brown, 2009).

Transdiagnostic theory and treatment have been promoted and used across the range of anxiety disorders (Clark & Beck, 2010), incorporating depressive disorders with anxiety disorders (Chu et al., 2009; de Jong-Meyer, Beck, & Riede, 2009; Titov et al., 2009), and across the eating disorders (Ghaderi, 2010), sexual problems (de Jong et al., 2010), and sleep problems (Harvey, 2010).

However, the transdiagnostic models of CPPs are still models of the development, maintenance, and treatment of the 'mental disorders'. The transdiagnostic viewpoint has not yet replaced DSM diagnosis with clinical psychology's own taxonomy of CPPs.

In Chapter 6 we will see that various CPPs (represented by distinct PMCs) can be operating in anorexia nervosa (AN). Others can be in operation when bulimia nervosa (BN) is the diagnosis. And some PMCs are common in both. Each PMC can represent a distinct CPP, implicating a different required treatment. Fairburn et al. (2008) have identified many of these PMCs, including those in the 'overlap' between AN and BN, which involve an 'overevaluation of shape and weight and their control'. This explains why about 80% of eating disorder patients change diagnosis within two years.

So the next required step for the transdiagnostic treatment movement will be to move on from offering therapies that can each treat several different mental disorders, to developing and offering therapies that treat particular CPPs (i.e. PMCs) irrespective of the diagnosis presented on referral. This is what most practising clinical psychologists do already, and, with its own nascent taxonomy of CPPs, this is what the PMC model of *Practical CBT* aims to do.

One of the many arguments for transdiagnostic approaches (McHugh, Murray, & Barlow, 2009) is that it has been very difficult to spread and adapt specific evidence-based psychological treatments to real world therapists, agencies, and settings, while maintaining a measure of fidelity to, or rigour in, the validated procedures. Transdiagnostic interventions allow much flexibility in the pacing and content of treatment, while still providing structure to enable testing and replication (McHugh, Murray, & Barlow, 2009).

This sums up the strengths of the PMC-based assessment, case formulation, and treatment model. It is simple, clear, and evidence-based, and yet flexible and adaptable to individual cases. A clinician may not choose any symptom, sign, or correlate of a psychological problem to address. There must be evidence that the target is a problem *maintainer*, and hence its modification is intended to be curative, not just alleviative.

Transdiagnostic PMCs versus Psychiatric DSM

Unfortunately, the conceptual, political, and administrative dominance of the psychiatric profession (Brown & Barlow, 2009; Clark, Watson, & Reynolds, 1995; Hyman, 2010; Waterman, 2007), especially since the publication of DSM-III in 1980 (Anand & Mahli, 2011; APA, 1980; Kim & Ahn, 2002), has meant that the level of analysis and intervention which is most appropriate for Type III psychological problems ('psychiatric' conditions, see Table 4.2) has come to dominate research and practice when an adjacent discipline, clinical psychology, addresses Type II CPPs. Even clinical psychologists often blindly adopt the assumption that they are studying and treating 'mental disorders' as defined and diagnosed by the DSM system.

This conceptual 'hegemony' (Anand & Malhi, 2011; Waterman, 2007) is hard to escape. But when the non-equivalence of mental disorders and CPPs is appreciated many benefits ensue. Seven of the advantages of the PMC model of CBT over the medical model's dominance of CBT are described below.

(i) The DSM system is a 'nosology of diseases' (Hyman, 2010). Psychiatry, as a branch of medicine, quite understandably sees a person who has been persistently sad for some time (a CPP) as suffering from a mental disorder, which is reducible to a neurobiological condition. This assumption will prevail despite the fact that no consistent biological mechanism, marker, or substrate for depression has ever been found (Kingdon & Young, 2007; Kupfer, First, & Regier, 2002; Sussman, 2009), treatment at a psychological level is more often effective and for longer than pharmacological treatments (Dobson, Hollon, et al., 2008; Kirsch, 2009), and even stigma — a prime justification for the medicalisation of CPPs — has not been reduced by such labelling. (See vii. below)

Clinical psychologists as a group are not so biologically focused or trained, do not prescribe medications or administer ECT, and in fact in practice rarely and reluctantly diagnose (Bieling & Kuyken, 2003; Carey & Pilgrim, 2010; Hofmann, 2014). Instead, they construct case formulations at a psychological level (Persons, 2008). They look for underlying psychological mechanisms to explain problems and their solutions.

The idea that CPPs can and should be reducible to presumed underlying neurobiological conditions which are somehow more basic, real, or 'scientific' than psychological-level CPPs is not helpful (Deacon, 2013), not logical (Miller, 2010), and, for almost all CPPs, is theoretically premature (Satel & Lilienfeld, 2013). The psychological and the biological are different levels of analysis, assessment, and intervention (Gold, 2009), and any alignment of phenomena at these two levels is, by definition, correlational, not causal (Miller, 2010). It is no more likely that all CPPs will be reduced in the future to neurobiological conditions than that the geological study of earthquakes will be reduced to molecular theory (Gold, 2009, p. 508). 'Mental disorders may be studied at different levels of analysis (e.g., molecular genetics, neurochemistry, cognitive neuroscience, personality, environment), and no level is inherently superior or fundamental to any other' (Deacon, 2013, p.856).

A taxonomy of diseases emphasising form or structure and defined by topographical syndromes (Gresham & Gansle, 1992) is not helpful to explain function (Bissett & Hayes, 1999, p.380), and function is exactly what the overwhelming majority of psychologists focus on in order to develop a (behavioural) functional analysis or a (CBT) case formulation, which in turn implicates psychological-level intervention points and methods.

(ii) Many CPPs are not mental disorders as defined by DSM. For example, clinical psychologists research and address relationship, marital, or family problems in the same way, using the same (often CBT) models and techniques, as they use with anxiety or depression problems within an individual. But, quite rightly, DSM does not try to claim that marital discord represents a mental disorder. It relegates 'relational pathology' to a few 'V-codes' in its 'other issues' section.

But perhaps the largest class of CPPs effectively addressed by clinicians, but barely researched because they are not mental disorders, lies in the third to half of all people who seek clinical psychological help but cannot be given a clear diagnosis because their problems do not fit criteria and categories neatly (Messer et al., 2001). They may be 'subthreshold' (Howard et al., 1996), or 'subclinical' (Westen et al., 2004), or situation-specific (such as being evidenced only at work). High levels of distress commonly occur in the absence of a diagnosable condition (Roth & Fonagy, 2005), as when one or two 'symptoms' occur very strongly, but three or more are required for a diagnosis (Dobson & Dobson, 2009). Should clinical psychologists turn away people presenting with such CPPs because they do not have a diagnosed mental disorder?

(iii) The mental disorders of DSM represent a 'weak medical model' of CPPs (Follette & Houts, 1996) because, although it uses medical concepts such as 'syndromes' and 'symptoms' to 'diagnose' a 'mental disorder' (APA, 1987; Gresham & Gansle, 1992, p.81), its authors admit there is no assumption that these disorders are discrete biologically-defined entities. DSM's syndromal system is purely descriptive, atheoretical, topographical (Bissett & Hayes, 1999), or phenomenological (Hyman, 2010). "The diagnostic categories of mental disorders are not formed around an identified physical aberration of the individual. They are social, and often political, constructions ... diagnostic labels in no way indicate a cause or an explanation for a person's current psychological distress" (Carey & Pilgrim, 2010, p. 453). Even DSM-IV-TR admitted that "there is no assumption that each category of mental disorder is a completely discrete entity with absolute boundaries dividing it from other mental disorders or from no mental disorder" (p. xxxi).

Despite this, "many have come to believe that we are dealing with clear and discrete disorders rather than arbitrary symptom clusters" (Tucker, 1998, p. 159). This results in worthless, tautological, circular definitions, such as explaining a person's agitation when in public by asserting that 'he has a social phobia'. If asked how we know that he has this condition, the diagnoser's reply is to point to the person's agitation when in public (Carey & Pilgrim, 2010)!

The PMC model of CPPs is theoretically rich, and hence is categorical. A person either is or is not currently ensnared in an undesired full operating PMC. This describes a real, discernible entity existing in the world, a 'natural kind' of thing (Zachar, 2008) with an 'essence' (Borsboom, Epskamp, et al., 2011), rather than merely "dimensional variants, social constructions, or pragmatic ways of carving up the psychiatric domain" (Haslam, 2002, p.204) such as 'mental disorders' where an essence remains indefinable (Cramer et al., 2010, p.145).

PMCs are real, measurable entities. They have existed throughout human history. Hippocrates described the phobia of flute music of a man called Nicanor. The Roman, Celsus, described a treatment for hydrophobia in which the patient is 'thrown unawares' into a water tank until "his thirst and dread of water are removed at the same time". This process appears to be a classic enforced PMC breakage.

Animals can be caught up in PMCs. Dogs can demonstrate a 'learned helplessness' state of depression for as long as they are allowed to maintain a negative expectancy of control and consequences (Seligman, 1972).

(iv) Not only does the PMC model of CPPs have the advantage over DSM's medical model of mental disorders of defining CPPs categorically (versus dimensionally) and from a theory base, but it also does so using only two clear criteria: Is a full PMC operating, and is this undesirable?

DSM, on the other hand, invokes, almost at random, at least seven different criteria to determine the presence of a 'mental disorder'. At different times DSM specifies: (i) A certain symptom cluster. Three or more symptoms from a field of seven are required to diagnose an Antisocial Personality Disorder. (ii) A certain level of distress. In OCD 'the obsessions or compulsions cause marked distress'. (ii) A level of dysfunction. This is required for a diagnosis of Specific Phobia. (iv) A certain type of etiology. This marks a PTSD or a Substance-Induced Sexual Dysfunction. (v) A statistical deviation. To diagnose a Female Orgasmic Disorder relies upon a 'clinician's judgment' on what 'would be reasonable'. (vi) The chemistry involved. This determines an Alcohol Dependence. And (vii) duration is a criterion determining the presence of an Acute Stress Disorder or a Dysthymic Disorder.

This theoretical swamp has meant that no 'essence' to a mental disorder has been determined, two people can be given the same diagnosis when they share only one or two symptoms/criteria but differ on innumerable other features (Kim & Ahn, 2002), and enormous, unexplained rates of comorbidity have resulted (Kessler et al., 2005), leading many to query the underlying structure and assumptions of the classification system (Kendall & Jablensky, 2003).

(v) Though it is generally accepted that "the goals of classification of mental disorders should be optimised for clinical utility" (Hyman, 2010, p.160), DSM diagnoses are a minimal guide to treatment selection even for psychiatrists (Hyman, 2007; Johnstone, 2014; Kingdon & Young, 2007), let alone for clinical psychologists (Callahan, Panichelli-Mindel, & Kendall, 1996; Carey & Pilgrim, 2010; Follette, 1996; Kratochwill & McGivern, 1996). Psychiatrists will commonly prescribe antidepressants whether the diagnosis is social phobia, panic disorder, borderline personality disorder, anorexia nervosa, OCD, or major depression. Antipsychotics may be prescribed whether for anxiety problems, depression, bipolar disorder, personality disorder, ADHD, schizophrenia, or even sleep problems (Johnstone, 2014).

The other clear cause of DSM's (psychological-)treatment-irrelevance relates to its topographical, phenomenological, symptom-focused nature. A nosology emphasising form is not helpful to explain function (Bissett & Hayes, 1999, p.380). The problem here is that "several distinct functional processes may explain a particular topography, and distinct topographies may result from the same underlying process" (Bissett & Hayes, 1999, p.380). Bissett & Hayes (1999) give the examples that overdrinking can have multiple functions, such as social compliance or avoiding painful emotions. And the same function, such as avoiding painful emotions, can control multiple behaviours, such as overdrinking, overworking, bingeing, or sexual promiscuity. (Differing PMCs are being listed here.) These problems for DSM are referred to in the literature as the problems of multifinality and divergent trajectories (Nolen-Hoeksma & Watkins, 2011).

Hence a case formulation approach is much more conducive to tailoring of treatments to an individual than is a diagnostic approach (Persons, 2008), especially when considering psychological treatments.

(vi) Despite the emphasis within behavioural and cognitive behavioural approaches to CPPs on individualised, tailored case conceptualisation, hypothesis testing, and treatment planning, these models have long been criticised for using a 'cookbook', manualised approach. Ironically this (mis)understanding arose due to the development of treatment packages and manuals through outcome studies using (allegedly) homogeneous diagnosed groups of 'patients'. Some benefit has accrued from the development of these disorder-specific manuals and packages (Nolen-Hoeksma & Watkins, 2011), but this advancement has plateaued, as evidenced by the recent lack of progress in success rates for most of these putative disorders (Nathan & Gorman, 2015).

This is hardly surprising when we consider that these diagnostically homogeneous groups are very likely to be heterogeneous with respect to the underlying CPPs involved. According to the DSM model, a 90-year-old woman who is sad because her spouse of 70 years has died is suffering exactly the same mental disorder (a major depression) as a 17-year-old girl who is sad due to a 10-year history of deprivation and sexual abuse. It is not useful to regard these as identical CPPs, or to randomly allocate both women into the same RCT to assess the effectiveness of Therapy 'A' for Major Depression.

Although in practice clinical psychologists formulate much more than they diagnose, almost all research in the discipline ignores this fact (Bakker, in submission). To be considered methodologically sound, and hence to qualify for funding, almost all psychotherapy research must be undertaken with formally diagnosed subjects with the intention of 'curing' them of their mental disorders by removing their symptoms. However, in real-world clinical practice, case formulation guides treatment which targets psychological processes, not symptom profiles. Treatment outcome measured by 'escape from diagnosis' is in this light arbitrary, misleading, and inadequate.

Research trials have typically treated highly selected groups with a single diagnosis, while in clinical practice patients have many comorbidities and atypical symptom profiles (Persons, 2008). As described earlier, a third to a half of all people seeking clinical psychological help cannot be given a clear diagnosis because their problems do not fit criteria and categories neatly (Messer et al., 2001).

Furthermore, clinicians are more likely to apply several interventions, and will base this on the individual case formulation they have developed, on the assumption that each technique is targeting something different in the formulation. When experimental subjects are diagnosed and then randomly allocated to comparative treatment groups, they will have an undetermined distribution of relevant underlying mechanisms.

Important comparative studies on various CBTs for depression, such as cognitive therapy (CT) versus behavioral activation (e.g., Cuipers et al., 2008; Dobson et al., 2008), or for anxiety problems, such as exposure therapy (ET) versus CT (e.g., Ougrin, 2011; Powers et al., 2008), have not been able to find consistent differences between comparative treatments. This is unsurprising, though, when subjects are DSM-diagnosed and then randomly allocated to groups, as though they all have the same CPP. It assumes a diagnosis-to-treatment-selection link. This is an example of theory governing the nature of research. However, the medical model of DSM is so entrenched that many researchers would not even see this difference (Hyman, 2010, p. 157).

It is of much greater benefit to assemble research results into clinical guidelines not on 'the treatment of Depression' or 'of Bulimia Nervosa', but on psychological interventions with CPPs A and B, defined by mechanisms, which may cross diagnoses or differ within a diagnosis. For example, we know that targeting specific mediating cognitive processes in social phobia is more effective than standardised generic cognitive-behavioral treatment (Rapee et al., 2009), because the mental disorder 'Social Anxiety Disorder' can encompass a number of (mechanism-defined) CPPs.

We have known for many years now that individual functional analysis and treatment tailoring can be more effective than generic/manualised/battery treatment (Nelson-Gray, 2003). For example Repp, Felce, and Barton (1988) found that the treatment of stereotypic and self-injurious behaviour was more successful if it was based on an assessment of which of three functions it served: (a) self-stimulation, (b) positive reinforcement, or (c) negative reinforcement. These alternatives represent different remediable PMCs.

So *Practical CBT* is not so much a manualised therapy package, but rather an evidence-based flow chart guide through a smorgasbord of choices.

(vii) The medical model of CPPs has often been promoted in an attempt to reduce blame and stigma, and so to encourage admission of problems and help-seeking behaviour (Johnstone, 2014). Advancement of the disease model of alcoholism is an early and clear example of this strategy in action (Tracy, 2007). However, the consequences of medicalisation have been found to include, along with less blaming, more fear and avoidance (Kvaale, Gottdiener, & Haslam, 2013), as psychiatric patients are seen as more dangerous and less predictable (Angermeyer et al., 2011), and having a worse prognosis (Haslam & Kvaale, 2015). The people themselves, upon diagnosis, tend to feel disempowered and socially excluded (Pitt et al., 2009).

Such deleterious consequences are exacerbated by DSM's assertion that all of the following are examples of the one kind of thing. They are all equally 'mental disorders': Mild Tobacco Use Disorder, Schizophrenia, Female Orgasmic Disorder, Delirium, Restless Legs Syndrome, Alzheimer's Disease, a Spider Phobia, and Opioid Intoxication. Admitting to sadness two weeks after one's spouse has died can put one in the same class, conceptually, as a paranoid schizophrenic, a smoker, a person suffering a panic disorder, or a violent psychopath.

These consequences of problem assessment and problem formulation are not inevitable. It has been claimed that a psychological case formulation or functional analysis approach both avoids the problem of stigmatisation (Carey & Pilgrim, 2010) and the abdication of responsibility (Brooke, 2004) of psychiatric diagnosis. It also allows a much greater, and a less stigmatising, distinction to be made between Type I, II, and III psychological problems (See Table 4.2).

Experience to date in the use of a PMC approach to CBT has shown that it is eminently understandable as well as palatable by almost all types of clients (Bakker, 2008a, 2019a). Offering a formulation of a CPP to a client in terms of recognisable PMCs is intuitive, and appeals to 'common sense', as well as reducing the stigma of being diagnosed as 'mentally ill'.

As a PMC approach is so understandable by so many clients, and naturally and logically implies and justifies specific therapies ("Let's break this cycle *here*, by not coping-by-avoiding this weekend"), client adherence to treatment can benefit. And much research has shown a strong effect on outcomes of good adherence to CBT treatment. Simpson et al. (2011), for example, found that any effect of the working alliance in exposure and response prevention therapy with OCD was mediated by better adherence to the treatment protocol. Better understanding of one's case formulation and its justification of the therapy process can be expected to improve therapeutic motivation and compliance. Use of the spiels in *Practical CBT* (2008a) over 40 years has supported this proposition.

In fact more and more evidence is accumulating that client satisfaction is more affected by the "receipt of CBT-oriented, quality psychosocial (but not pharmacologic) care" than by the therapist merely being liked (e.g. Stein et al., 2011). One is more likely to be liked or respected if clear, effective, evidence-based, respectful advice and interventions are offered. The PMC approach to case formulation and CBT intervention can offer this.

So a conception of CPPs based on the detection of operating PMCs is treatment-relevant, categorical (versus dimensional), essentialist (versus arbitrary or merely a convenient social construction), parsimonious (only 1 or 2 criteria), theory-based (both CBT and PMC theory), empirically-derived, and nonstigmatising.

An Embryonic PMC Taxonomy

In practice and in their training programs most clinical psychologists have for some time now almost ignored traditional psychiatric diagnostic systems (Carey & Pilgrim, 2010), in favour initially of the functional analysis of behaviour problems (Butler, 1999; Haynes & O'Brien, 1990; Yoman, 2008), and more recently of CBT case formulations (Bieling & Kuyken, 2003; Persons, 1989. See *Practical CBT*, 2008a, pp. 24–25)

It has been described that formulation is fundamental to clinical psychology in the same way that diagnosis is fundamental to psychiatry (Bieling & Kuyken, 2003). Johnstone (2006) has argued that diagnosis represents the medical model, as it attributes psychological problems to biological causes, whereas formulation attributes them to responses to life circumstances. Alternatively, whereas diagnosis is a system of classification, formulation is a process of explanation and understanding that links theory with practice (Brooke, 2004).

However, a reliable — if also theoretically bereft, arbitrary, and low validity — system of listing and classification can still perform some functions. For psychologists, the DSM has somewhat aided research by enabling some superficial homogeneity in subject groups, and has assisted in communication by providing some standardisation of terms (Hyman, 2010, p.156), as when a diagnosis is required in a legal or insurance report (Follette, Houts, & Hayes, 1992).

But, in the comparison of formulation and diagnosis approaches, the main drawback of the psychological-level, PMC-based functional analysis or case formulation system is "that functional analysis has failed to progress as a system of case formulation and treatment guidance primarily due to the lack of replicability of functional analysis" (Hayes & Follette, 1992). Functional analysis has not been ready to take on a nomothetic role, to be an alternative in this to DSM, because it has been neither specific nor replicable (Bissett & Hayes, 1999). There has not been a set, shared taxonomy of CPPs to allow standardised classification and to ease communication. What is needed are 'functional diagnostic categories' (Hayes & Follette, 1992). The development of such a taxonomy of CPPs/PMCs would systematise functional analysis and give it a listing of labels, if not diagnoses, to aid communication, research, and administrative (legal, insurance, etc.) functions. "The development of functional diagnostic categories... [can] naturally emerge from the repetition of individual functional analyses" (Bissett & Hayes, 1999). "A large set of functional analyses may reveal common functional processes. This could lead to a nomothetic level of analysis that is also functionally derived — a classification system based on functional categories." (Bissett & Hayes, 1999, p. 381).

Since these observations were made, functional analysis, and especially CBT-based case formulation, has been repeated many times, and the resultant evidence-based CBT models of psychopathology have emerged. The taxonomy of PMCs presented in this volume and in *Practical CBT* (2008a, Figure 7) are extracted directly from these many models.

Therefore, for a PMC taxonomy to adequately supplant the DSM — at least for clinical psychologists — it must be codified. The various iterations of the DSM have each drawn contributions from numerous panels of experts over many years. It would be reasonable to expect that a comparable PMC taxonomy — perhaps compiled in a manual entitled 'Standardised Case Formulation in Clinical Psychology: A PMC Taxonomy' — would require a similar ongoing contribution from the profession.

In the meantime though a nascent PMC taxonomy can be proposed:

A taxonomy is foremost a listing. But, like chemistry's periodic table of the chemical elements, astronomy's star charts and classifications, or zoology's domains, kingdoms, phyla, and so on, to be usable the listing should be structured by some classification. The current proposal lists PMCs in categories, such as 'Depression' or 'Substance Abuse or Dependence'. These are not diagnoses. 'Some nomothetic conceptual overlay is necessary as an initial guide to the more in-depth process of individual functional analysis because it defines the domain of interest' (Bissett & Hayes, 1999, p.380). So the categories comprise 'problem areas' or 'presenting problems', not diagnoses. Denman (1995) has argued that case formulations should have diagnostic elements, but they need not be psychiatric. For example, "The problem is 'marital in nature'" is a form of diagnosis, and a useful label when formulating a person's problems to determine treatment (p.168). This is a good example because, as has been noted, marital problems cannot be conceived as mental disorders, but they are a category of CPP, and there are many PMCs that can explain them and that require therapeutic disruption. (See Chapter 6.)

The categories that follow are largely guided by usual, 'practical', clinical practice. Flanagan and Blashfield (2006, 2007a, 2007b, 2010) have studied the usual, natural intuitive problem categories that experienced clinicians adopt irrespective of their theoretical orientation. They found that these spontaneous conceptual taxonomies do not match the structure of the DSM (Flanagan, Keeley, & Blashfield, 2008), that clinical utility is the primary guide (First et al., 2004), and that anorexia nervosa and bulimia nervosa are bracketed under 'eating disorders', substance dependence and abuse are brought together, and so on (Flanagan & Blashfield, 2006). And that 'presenting problem' is the key guiding theme.

The 2008 edition of *Practical CBT* presented a taxonomy of depression-related, anxiety-related, and anger-related common evidence-based PMCs. This follow-up volume has added PMCs to look for in addressing health anxiety, eating disorders, relationship problems, OCD, chronic pain problems, sexual difficulties, and substance abuse/dependence.

Numerous potential criteria for a disorder in the DSM system (seven or more) are replaced by one primary criterion: Has a PMC formed?[1] The nearest to this criterion currently in the DSM system is that of duration. It makes sense that it takes time for a PMC to form, and a disorder that is very short-lived rarely qualifies as a 'problem-deserving-therapy'. But duration is not sufficient in itself. There is great variability in how long it takes for PMCs to form. A grief reaction can last more than six months, during which time one would be unlikely to want to impose a psychiatric diagnosis and insist upon interventive therapy. However, an Acute Stress Disorder is specified as diagnosable between two days and one month after a trauma.[2] If symptoms persist beyond a month, a diagnosis of PTSD is claimed to be justified. Furthermore, it can be argued that the line between some bad nights' sleep and a Sleep Disorder may be 48 hours. If one or two bad nights cause a person to fret about getting a good night tonight, and this keeps them awake half the night, a PMC has developed, and some (paradoxical?) psychological therapy may correct this. There are fast and there are slow PMCs.

Therefore, what follows is a small naïve Proposal for the structure of a full Standardised Case Formulation manual:

It is proposed:

- That clinical psychological problem codes be prefixed with 'PMC' standing for Problem-Maintaining Circle
- That three levels of numerical coding be used, in the format 'PMC x.y.z'. More would be unmanageable. Less would excessively limit the amount of case formulation/functional analytic/treatment implication information conveyed
- That the numerical 'x' codes represent generally recognised, intuitively acceptable presenting problem categories. An example of a start to such a listing is given in Table 4.3.
- The 'y' codes represent the major classes of problematic underlying mechanism (PMC element) that have been identified in CBT models of psychopathology

1 The secondary criterion is: Is the result of the operation of this PMC negative? Is it a vicious or a virtuous circle?.

2 The PMC Model does not regard ASD as a diagnosable disorder. Most ASDs resolve without therapy. In fact, Critical Incident Stress Debriefing has been found to often be counter-productive (Devilly & Cotton, 2003; Devilly, Gist, & Cotton, 2006; Herman, 2005; Wei, Szumilas, & Kutcher, 2010). Counselling may help, but interventive therapy is not justified. In the DSM, ASD should have the same status as a Bereavement or a Panic Attack.

TABLE 4.3 Some Proposed 'x' Codes in a 'PMC x.y.z' Taxonomy

1.y.z	Anxiety and low assertiveness (e.g., Health Anxiety)
2.y.z	Depression
3.y.z	Relationship problems (e.g., jealousy problems)
4.y.z	Eating problems
5.y.z	Anger problems
6.y.z	Chronic pain
7.y.z	OCD
8.y.z	Substance abuse/dependence
9.y.z	Sexual problems
10.y.z	Any psychological problem
11.y.z	Type III psychological problems
12.y.z	Interactive clinical psychological problems
13.y.z	....

TABLE 4.4 Some Proposed 'y' Codes in a 'PMC x.y.z' Taxonomy

x.1.z	Avoidance (implying exposure therapy)
x.2.z	Erroneous cognitions (implying psychoeducation, cognitive restructuring, thought stopping, self-talk coaching, etc.)
x.3.z	Selective attention/hypervigilance/preoccupation (implying attentional control training, thought stopping, mindfulness,etc.)
x.4.z	Sleep disturbance, physical effects, medical problems
x.5.z	Problematic reinforcement
x.6.z	Narrowed coping repertoire
x.7.z	Worry about worry effects, Depression about depression effects, etc.

and in transdiagnostic research, and that commonly occur in one or (often) more types of presenting problem. A preliminary listing is provided in Table 4.4. The list of potential problem-maintenance mechanisms is enormous. Table 4.4 lists only some of the most researched, frequently recognised, or treatment-triggering ones. This abundance is the reason that 'underlying mechanism' or 'treatment implication' is not coded at 'x'.

- To describe a problem as being maintained 'by avoidance', or 'due to reinforcement' is too broad to implicate specific treatment approaches. Therefore, it is proposed that 'z' codes represent more specific evidence-based mechanisms under each mechanism type. An example listing is provided in Table 4.5.

- Type III psychological problems ('psychiatric' problems) are those problems that are not fully explained by psychological-level PMCs, and are rarely fully 'cured' by interventions that disrupt them. However, PMCs are frequently involved, and psychological therapies can often help management, reduce symptomatology, or avoid episodes of relapse. For some such problems, this

TABLE 4.5 Some Proposed 'z' Codes in a 'PMC x.y.z' Taxonomy

x.1.1	Cognitive avoidance
x.1.2	Emotional avoidance
x.1.3	Behavioural avoidance
x.2.1	Lack of information
x.2.2	'Irrational beliefs'
x.2.3	Negative self-talk/rumination
x.3.1	Seeing threat everywhere
x.3.2	Seeing failure everywhere
x.3.3	Seeing dislike/disrespect everywhere
x.4.1	Low energy levels
x.4.2	Poor concentration/decision-making
x.4.3	Effects of nightmares
x.4.4	Mood effects
x.5.1	Attention-seeking reinforcement
x.5.2	Tangible, concrete reinforcement
x.5.3	Escape conditioning
x.5.4	A low reinforcement environment
x.6.1	Resorting to alcohol/drugs
x.6.2	Resorting to escape/denial
x.6.3	Resorting to aggression
x.6.4	Resorting to self-harm
x.6.5	Reduced social support
x.6.6	Reduced exercise/activity
x.6.7	....

TABLE 4.6 Some Proposed 'PMC 11.y.z' Codes in a 'PMC x.y.z' Taxonomy

11.1.z	Schizophrenia
11.2.z	Bipolar disorder
11.3.z	Autism
11.4.z	ADHD
11.5.z	Delusional disorder
11.6.z	Chronic fatigue syndrome
11.7.z	Premenstrual dysphoric disorder
11.8.z	Dementia
11.9.z	Seasonal affective disorder
11.10.z	Post-viral depression
11.11.z	Menopausal symptoms
11.12.z	....

is currently the best form of therapy available. Table 4.6 lists some of the conditions currently considered to be Type III (psychiatric) problems.

TABLE 4.7 Some proposed 'PMC 13.y.z' codes in a 'PMC x.y.z' taxonomy

13.1.z	Anxiety & Depression (Mathew et al., 2011; Robinson et al., 2011; Schindel-Allon et al., 2010; Wheatley, 1997)
13.2.z	Anxiety & Substance Abuse (Cosci et al., 2010; Lepine & Pelissolo, 1998; Robinson et al., 2011)
13.3.z	Depression & Substance Abuse (Robinson et al., 2011)
13.4.z	Chronic pain & Anxiety (Liedl et al., 2010)
13.5.z	Chronic pain & Depression (Hilderink et al., 2012; Linton et al., 2011)
13.6.z	Depression & Sexual Dysfunction (Atlantis & Sullivan, 2012)
13.7.z	Depression & Sleep Problems (Baglioni et al., 2011)

- The 'z' codes in PMC 11.y.z problems (see Table 4.6) would specify various evidence-based PMCs known to occur in some cases of the disorder, which exacerbate symptomatology, and suggest psychological-level therapies that have been shown to ameliorate, if not resolve, the condition, such as family therapy with schizophrenia or Social Rhythm Therapy (Frank, 2007) for Bipolar Disorder.
- 'PMC 13.y.z' codes represent PMCs which have been found to occur *between* traditionally-distinguished CPPs, suggesting that, if detected, treatment targeting PMCs within either or both problems may be indicated. Table 4.7 lists examples of these, along with supportive research evidence for their existence. Comorbidity is then not a diagnostic problem. It is a naturally occurring, informative, and explainable risk, that broadens treatment options.

The interactive problems listed in Table 4.7 do not represent separately diagnosed mental disorders in the DSM sense. They represent clusters or fields within the symptom matrix of the network model (Cramer et al., 2010). Hence the labels are chosen for their clinical utility only. For example, 'Anxiety' includes PTSD, Social Phobia, and so on; and 'Sleep Disorder' could be elevated to the status of a separate comorbid presenting problem, or remain a part of the network field incorporated in 'Depression', 'Anxiety', and so on.

As PMC theory is a meta-theory, any field of therapeutic endeavour can assemble its own taxonomy of relevant PMCs. Note that 'Situation, events' frequently contributes critical, and changeable, elements to these PMCs, so a team approach (including social work) is desirable.

SECTION 2

Assessment, PMC Taxonomy, and Treatment Selection

Chapter 5

The Initial Assessment

Based on the simplified CBT model of Figure 3.1, a client can describe a presenting problem in terms of situational stresses, negative cognitions, uncomfortable feelings, or maladaptive behaviours. It is then the clinician's task to fill out the picture, which, if the CBT model is being used, involves lots of questions (and perhaps observations) about the causal links between each of these elements, around the presenting problem. Generally this will mean assessment questions targeting:

(a) the presenting problem's frequency, duration, intensity, triggers, current attempts to cope, and so on ('How often have the memory flashbacks happened to you in the past week?'). This can be termed a 'narrow' functional analysis

(b) the cognitive, behavioural, affective, and situational correlates, causes, and consequences of the presenting problem ('When you're in a crowded shop, what are you saying in your head that makes you so nervous?'). This can be viewed as a broader or CBT functional analysis, case formulation, or case conceptualisation

(c) some universally important factors in psychological coping, such as support network, medications, employment, and so on.

This directive form of assessment can be justified in a CBT framework because (1) it can be assumed that the client's narrow formulation of the problem has not been adequate to lead to change, or they would not be now seeking help, and (2) the direction of questioning can already be introducing the client to the CBT model/viewpoint. The client is already absorbing, from the direction of questioning, what may be important issues in the problem.

Universal Assessment Questions

Which factors are universally important enough to routinely include questions about in every initial assessment is open to debate. This will depend upon the clinician's orientation or training. Psychiatrists, for example, routinely ask about family history of psychological/psychiatric problems. The questions also depend upon the client's age, cultural background, and so on.

Some agencies will include a full life history assessment in their intake interview, as well as some formal personality or intellectual testing, especially for a first inpatient admission to a psychiatric unit. But few solo or privately practising clinicians could justify this time and expense for their clients.

Table 5.1 lists some suggestions for questions that are important enough to ask of all clientele early in an assessment. It is a much more condensed assessment than a full life-history questionnaire. For example, it does not address schooling, or sexual history, or even a family history of problems.

The primary criterion for selection of questions in Table 5.1 is treatment relevance. Some questions are necessary in treatment planning for practical reasons; for example,

TABLE 5.1 General Psychological Assessment Questions

Age?
Who is living at home?
What is your spouse's name? How old is he/she? How long have you been together? How are things between you generally?
Children's names? Ages? How are they going? Any worries about them?
Who are your main supports these days? Is this list good enough or big enough for you? How many people know what you're going through?
What are the main worries or stresses on you generally?
How has your health been generally? Spouse's? Children's?
Any money worries recently?
Where do you work? Doing what? How long have you been there? How is it going?
Where do you live? How long have you been there?
Are you taking any (other) medications?
How much alcohol do you drink in an average week?
Do you smoke dope?
How much tea or coffee do you have each day?
Apart from work and home, what are you into these days?
Do you get any regular exercise?
Do you have any goals or plans you're working toward? At home? Holidays? At work? …
What sort of a person would you describe yourself as? How would others describe you?
Has the problem left you feeling suicidal at times?
What therapies or counselling or medications have you had for this problem in the past? Did they help?

(Available as a free download from www.australianacademicpress.com.au)

'Who is living at home?' Some suggest treatment directions in a wide range of problems; for example, 'Do you get any regular exercise?' And some are part of the search for stressors that may have etiological relevance, and may be reversible; for example, 'How is it going at work?'

The question of a family history of problems — being an irreversible possible etiological factor — is not very treatment relevant unless a client seems to need a tidy etiological model before being able to move on to treatment; in which case, a few questions about family history, childhood experiences, later traumas and recent stressors can usually produce such a model. The most vital task usually is to detect current reversible stressors or PMCs.

"In considering the potential significance of a risk factor, it is important to consider the extent to which a variable is open to modification and could be targeted in preventive interventions (e.g. cognitive style) versus those that are fixed but can be used to identify those at increased risk (e.g. … death of a parent)" (Shortt & Spence, 2006, p.2). In CBT — being so PMC-focused — immediate, proximal, *changeable* factors are especially sought in assessment. So, in assessing a depression problem, for example, we need to "focus on proximal factors that are closer to the individual and/or closer in time to the onset of depression (e.g., family functioning and cognitive style) because they are more easily accessed and therefore amenable to change" (Shortt & Spence, 2006, p.19).

A 'Narrow' Functional Analysis

A narrow functional analysis is illustrated in Table 5.2. This is similar to a 'behavioural analysis', but can operate whether the client is complaining of excesses or deficits in behaviour, feelings, cognitions, or stresses (situation).

However, the scope of such an analysis is usually limited to a 'stimulus-response', or at best a 'stimulus-response-consequence' focus. Therefore all elements of the Figure 3.4 (full) CBT model are not necessarily considered, and so many PMCs can remain undetected through this type of assessment.

Such analyses are common among behaviour therapists, (pure) cognitive therapists, situational change experts such as financial counsellors or domestic violence professionals, and pharmacotherapists.

Table 5.2 A 'Narrow' Functional Analysis

Open-ended questions to obtain a general description of the problem(s) or reason for attendance.
Problem frequency, intensity, duration, fluctuations.
Triggers or circumstances it occurs in, or does not occur in.
Consequences, negative or positive.
Change hopes, aims, or goals.
Significant others relevant to the problem.

A CBT Case Formulation or Functional Analysis

A broader CBT functional analysis or case formulation is essentially the application of the whole of the Figure 3.4 model to the presenting complaint. It can commence with open-ended questions guided by the model ('And how do you feel when you drive since the accident?'). But, with a knowledge of common or serious cyclic antecedents and consequences of various problems, it is possible to become quite specific with hypothesis testing ('Have you still been playing golf since you felt depressed?').

Enquiries will seek out which, if any, of the specific, situational or general, underlying long-term PMCs listed and illustrated in Chapter 6 are likely to be currently operating. Then Tables 7.2 to 7.13 provide examples of the questions a CBT functional analysis may include, and possible ensuing therapies or homework.

An Etiological Analysis

A CBT assessment tends to focus more on current maintaining causal factors than on historical precipitating causes of a problem. However, most clients come with a desire to understand where their problem came from. Even if precipitating causes are no longer relevant, an etiological theory can suggest future prevention strategies, and can help make a problem seem more confined or remediable. (Alternatively, some etiological theories can result in people feeling more trapped or fatalistic.)

Therefore, some time early in the assessment may be devoted to a Figure 3.1 model analysis of the client's background, early learning, family of origin experiences, and development of attitudes, sensitivities, or habits. Figure 5.1. displays some examples. A similar analysis can be undertaken of the onset events and conditions for the current problem episode. Often the volume and nature of major life events and their meaning or import to the client will emerge here.

However, it will also often become clear that such precipitating factors have long passed away, or have become irrelevant or are unalterable facts of life.

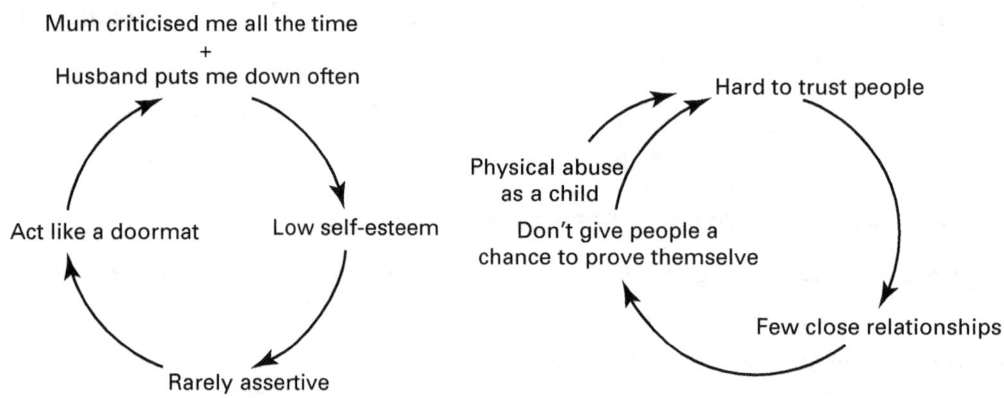

FIGURE 5.1 Examples of etiological analyses.

When a precipitant is judged to be still current or has ongoing relevance, it can be represented simply by an element in the PMC diagram that only feeds in. Figure 5.2 illustrates some examples. Such a precipitating factor could be (a) an ongoing stressor (such as an unhappy marriage), (b) an organically based mental illness (such as bipolar affective disorder or schizophrenia), or (c) an entrenched habit, tendency, sensitivity, or belief.

Individualising Problem Maintenance Hypotheses

"Treatment starts by developing with patients an idiosyncratic version of the cognitive model of their particular anxiety disorder" (Clark, 1999, p.S16). Bringing the client from this comforting or satisfying analysis and learning-theory-based hypothesis about the problem's origins back to 'So what do we do about all this now?' and an analysis of maintaining factors can be difficult if the client has come along with the expectation that precipitating causes, sometimes in early life, sometimes unconsciously absorbed, (even occurring in a 'past life'!) are what is addressed in psychotherapy.

This is where an individualised PMC diagram can be drawn for and with the client. A small handheld whiteboard is useful for this. Any combination of the cycles illustrated in Chapter 6, or others, may result, but perhaps with a more tailored flavour (see Script No. 3).

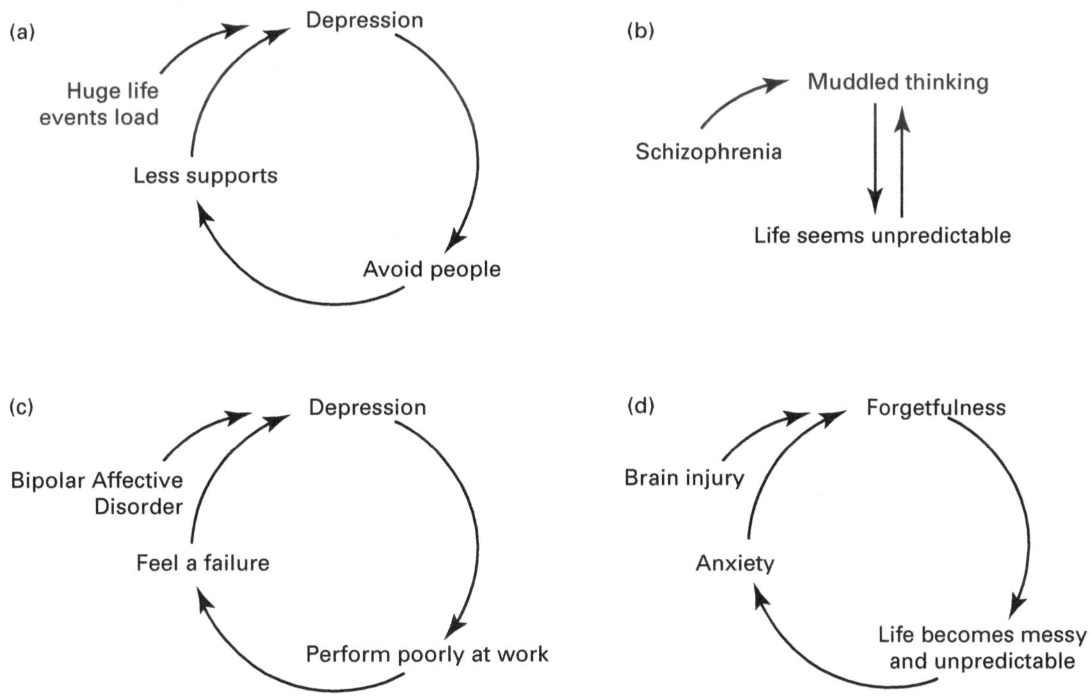

FIGURE 5.2 Problem maintenance diagrams that include currently relevant precipitants.

An example is given in Figure 5.3. This example incorporates the generic Depression PMCs (g) and (h) of Figure 6.4.

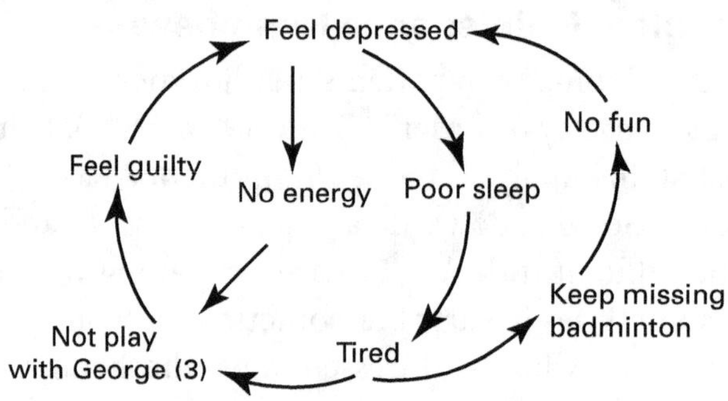

Figure 5.3 Example of an individualised problem maintenance hypothesis.

Chapter 6

A Sample PMC Taxonomy

The proposed PMC taxonomy listing of Chapter 4 is in a compact and academically efficient format. But in terms of clinical utility, if PMCs are illustrated graphically, specifying each causal element that can indicate a point of potential intervention — as in Figure 4.1 — then this becomes infinitely more understandable and intuitive, for our clients as well as ourselves.

Therefore, the following figures, Figures 6.1 to 6.12, illustrate common potential PMCs in 12 different CPP areas. They are presented in such a way that selected pages can be copied and given to a client with the homework of identifying and ticking those that they believe they are currently 'caught up in' (see Homework 72). This can serve as a check on how well the client has grasped the PMC model of CBT and their problems. You may be surprised, as I constantly am, at the level of insight the PMC model engenders, such that clients are often able to develop or confirm the assessment and case formulation much more quickly and in more detail than otherwise.

Figures 6.1 to 6.12 also correspond to the proposed PMC taxonomic categories tabled in Chapter 4. For example, the first five Anxiety PMCs in Figure 6.1 (a) to (e) represent graphically the PMC codes (a) 1.3.1, (b) 1.1.3, (c) 1.2.3, (d) 1.7.2, and (e) 1.4.2 respectively.

Anxiety and Low Assertiveness Problems

A sampling of commonly-occurring or frequently-remediable PMCs that can maintain CPPs that involve anxiety or low behavioural assertiveness is presented in Figure 6.1.

Each CPP area or PMC category (anxiety, depression, relationship problems, etc.) may in the future include subcategories as deemed clinically useful. For example, Anxiety Problems are often distinguished according to *what* the client fears. Health Anxiety and Panic Disorder are useful examples. Therefore, Figure 6.2 illustrates detailed PMCs that may be sought when someone presents with an uncontrolled Health Anxiety CPP.

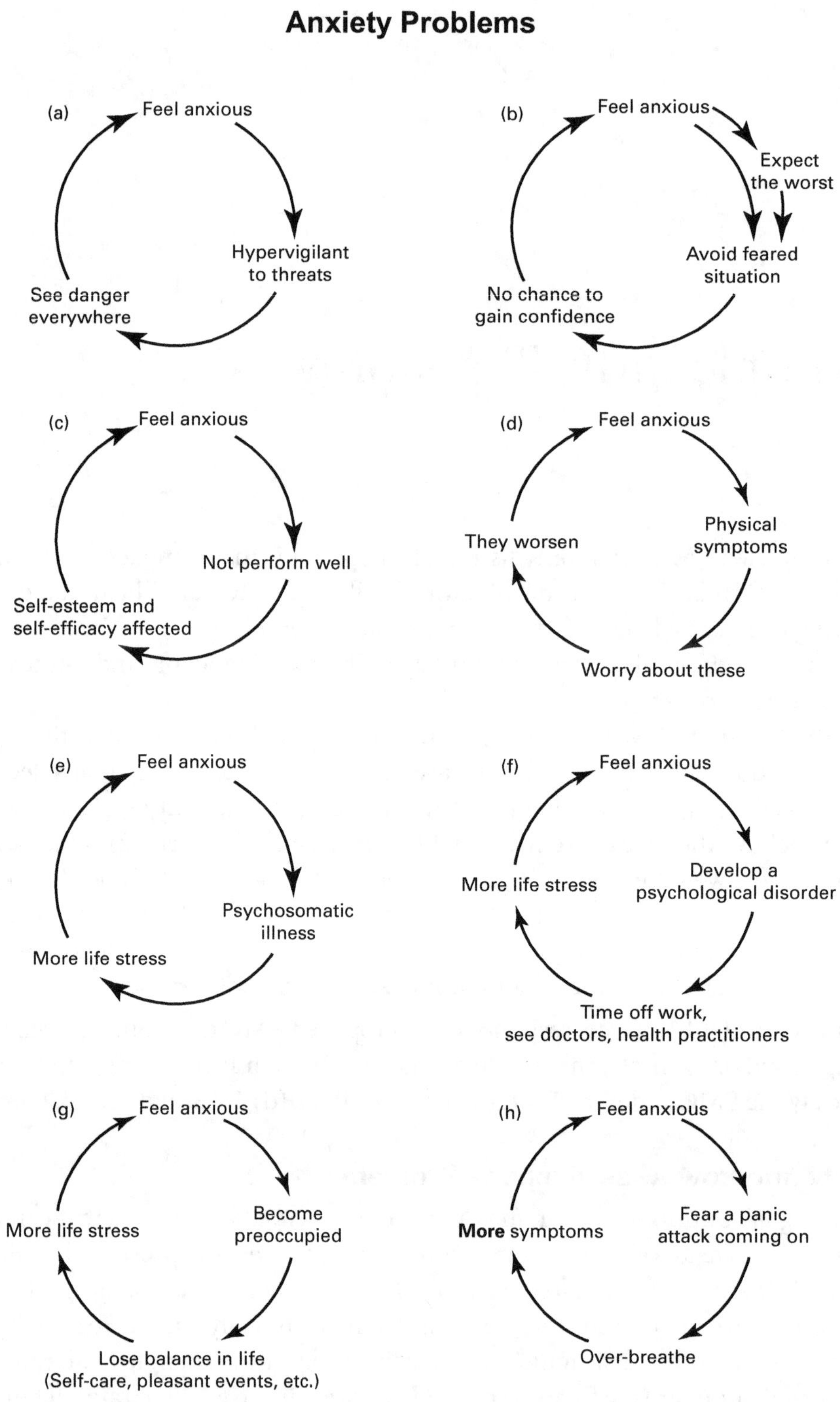

FIGURE 6.1 Some anxiety and low assertiveness problem-maintaining circles (PMCs). *(Available as a free download from www.australianacademicpress.com.au)*

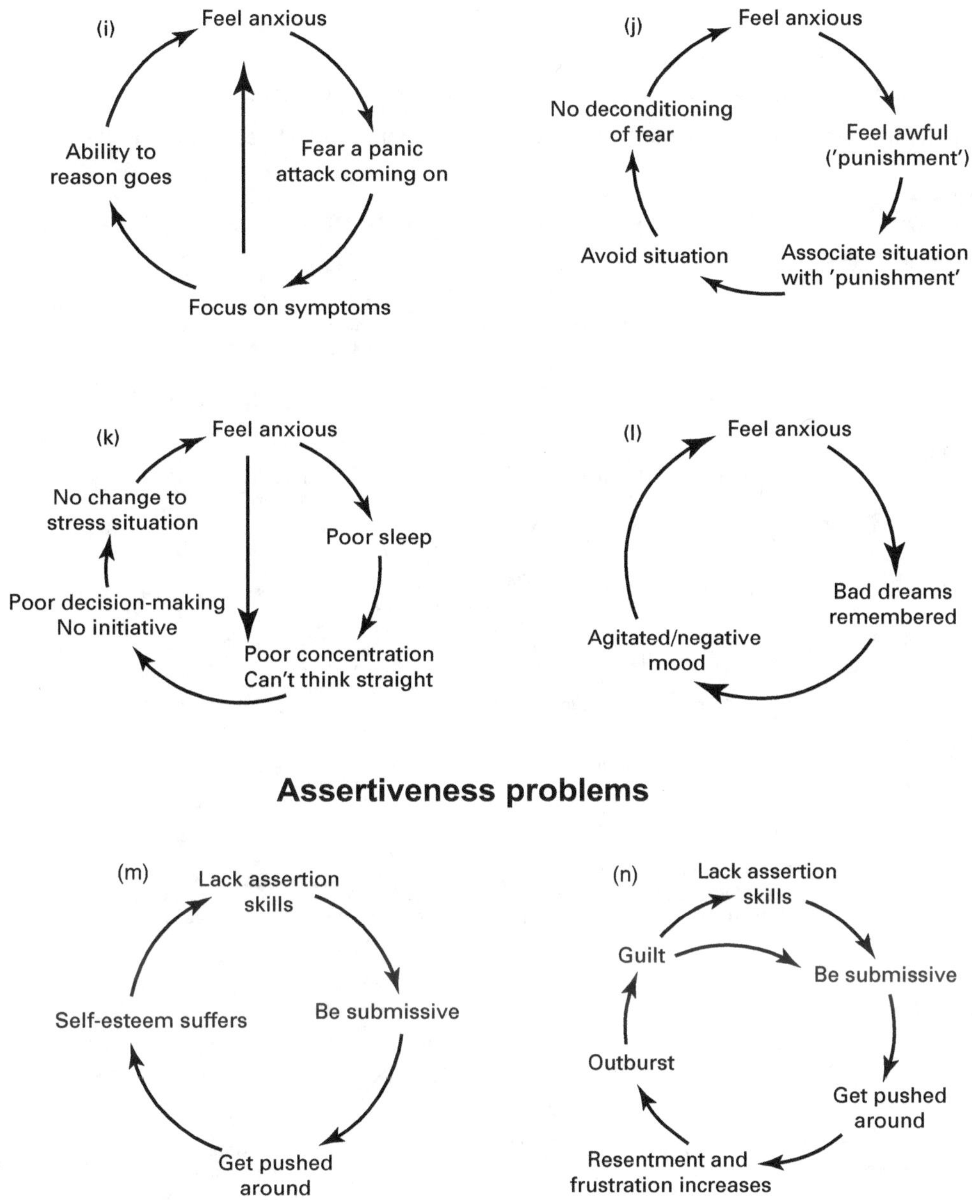

FIGURE 6.1 continued… Some anxiety and low assertiveness problem-maintaining circles (PMCs).

Figure 6.2 is particularly informative because (a) it includes the healthy, 'normal', desired, *linear* causal sequences we hope all people who experience a medical symptom can progress through, so as to distinguish ***problematic causal cycles*** (PMCs). And (b) it makes the point that PMCs within any CPP area can involve *opposite* processes or mechanisms! PMCs can form if we do something *too much or not enough.*

Linear Processes:

Pain/symptom/trigger → Anxious → Curious. Wait and see → Goes away.

Pain/symptom/trigger → Anxious → Book GP → (Counselling?+) Tests → Reassured → Goes away.

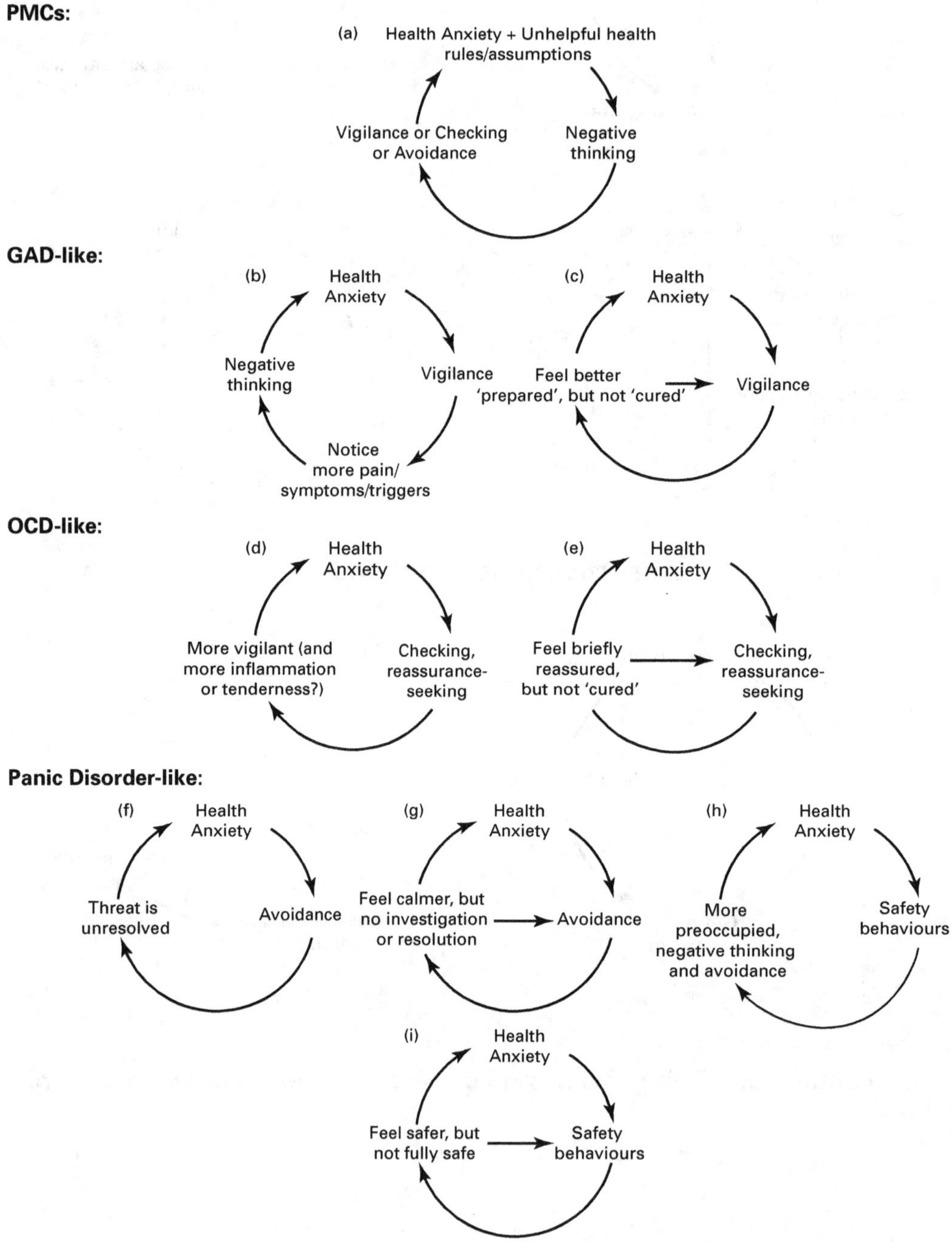

FIGURE 6.2 Some Health Anxiety problem-maintaining circles (PMCs).
(Available as a free download from www.australianacademicpress.com.au)

In the case of Health Anxiety, some clients are hypervigilant (e.g. frequent body checking or excessive doctors visits) and some are too avoidant (e.g. refuse a colonoscopy or never see the doctor). Interventions, then, need to be *opposite*. This emphasises the uselessness of the old derogatory labels and categories of DSM-IV and earlier, like 'hypochondriac'.

DSM's treatment of problems involving health anxiety, illness phobia, psychosomatic symptoms, body image disturbances, etc., has left us with a mess in no small way due to the early input of non-evidence-based psychodynamic theories about 'conversion reactions'. Psychiatrists, especially, have become preoccupied, and confused, by the idea of a physical symptom being 'all in your head'. If this occurs, it is extremely rare (Walker & Furer, 2008) in comparison to the ubiquitous involvement of Health Anxiety or physical symptoms in the PMCs of people who are anxious or depressed (Furer, Walker, & Stein, 2007), or ill or in pain (Tyrer, Cooper, Crawford, et al., 2011), or have OCD, or are young (Campo & Fritsch, 1994; Silverman et al., 1995), or are psychologically naïve or alexithymic.

When a grouping criterion is the 'presence of physical symptoms that suggest a general medical condition… and are not fully explained by a general medical condition' (APA, 2000, p. 445), then this is a clear example of a topographical, descriptive, surface characteristic, or phenomenological grouping, not based on underlying function or process. Clinical psychologists are much more interested in explanatory underlying functional processes (e.g. PMCs) than surface characteristics or 'symptoms'.

Hence a clinical psychologist will identify and treat a person who is caught up in a Body Dysmorphic Disorder PMC similarly to someone with OCD because the PMCs are similar (preoccupation, overvalued ideas, checking behaviour, etc.). It matters little in case formulation whether an OCD involves contamination thoughts, safety fears, harm thoughts, or body dysmorphia. The PMCs and treatment (cognitive therapy, plus exposure and response prevention) will be similar. Inasmuch as a 'Hypochondriasis' anxiety PMC is just one kind of anxiety PMC, similar to a Panic Disorder PMC, or a PTSD PMC, the formulation and treatment will follow the same principles. It will be *transdiagnostic*.

Figure 6.2, therefore, is evidence-based, self-explanatory, nonjudgmental, transdiagnostic, covers multiple problems, and is suggestive of points of treatment or intervention. It includes GAD-like PMCs, OCD-like PMCs, Panic Disorder-like PMCs, and normal linear processes. It is nonstigmatising. It makes it easy to quell a client's 'The doctor says it's all in my head' resentments about being sent to the psychologist with a label like 'Hypochondriac'. It is no surprise that the most successful interventions with health anxiety and 'hypochondriasis' are the cognitive and behavioural procedures commonly used with anxiety disorders (Barsky & Ahern, 2004). Nor is it surprising that attempts to compare behavioural (exposure) and cognitive components of these interventions have been inconclusive (Taylor & Asmundson, 2004; Visser & Baurman, 2001). The PMCs involved, (a) to (i), can involve either or both types of element. Physical symptoms, cognitions about them, and health anxiety also occur as elements in depression-related PMCs (see Figure 6.4), pain-related PMCs (see Figure 6.10), OCD-type PMCs (see Figure 6.11), sexual problem PMCs (see Figure 6.13), and others.

Figure 6.2 is drawn from the evidence-based CBT models of Health Anxiety which appear in many texts and manuals (Anderson, Saulsman, & Nathan, 2011; Walker & Furer, 2008, p. 370). Each causal arrow is supported by experimental, or at least correlational, findings in the literature. For example, Deacon and Maack (2008) found that experimentally manipulating the amount of safety behaviours engaged in directly affected threat overestimation (negative or catastrophic thinking) and avoidance behaviour (see Figure 6.2 [h]). Olatunji et al. (2011) found that when they did the same with health anxiety safety behaviours, it affected levels of health anxiety, hypochondriacal beliefs, and avoidant responses. They further found that this occurred through the mediational influence of an increase in frequency of catastrophic health-related thoughts; see Figure 6.2 [i]. Muse et al. (2010) found that 80% of sufferers of severe health anxiety who reported experiencing recurrent, distressing, intrusive images tended to respond by avoidance, checking, reassurance seeking, distraction, and rumination. They drew treatment implications from this through links with identified 'maintenance cycles'. In developing their approach to treatment of health anxiety, Walker and Furer (2008) drew on recent research on the treatment of Panic Disorder, OCD, and GAD (p. 368). These three subtypes are represented in Figure 6.2.

Depression Problems

There is a vast amount of literature describing maintenance factors in depression problems. For example, Teasdale (1988) suggested that it is the patterns of information-processing that occur once a person is mildly depressed that determine whether an initial depressed state will escalate to the level of major depression. That is, whether a largely cognitive PMC will develop. Similarly, response-style theory (Nolen-Hoeksema, 1987, 1991) posits that cognitive responses to depressive symptoms determine the severity and duration of depressive symptoms. The relevant three main response styles are (1) rumination, which intensifies and prolongs depression (via some obvious PMCs); (2) problem-solving, which eases depression (by preventing the formation of such PMCs); and (3) distraction, which prevents rumination, and so helps in the short term, until problem-solving can kick in (Butler & Nolen-Hoeksema, 1994; Strauss et al., 1997; Trask & Sigmon, 1999). (Hence the positive role that thought-stopping can play as an immediate coping strategy.)

Few researchers and clinicians have, before now, considered that, in investigating depression maintainers, they have been investigating and describing the *essence* of clinical psychological depression problems (depression CPPs) — that is the difference between 'healthy', natural, justified, understandable, transient sadness and distress, and a continuing, perhaps even spiraling or deepening, depression problem warranting and requiring interventive therapy to escape from.

One theorist that has appreciated this perspective, and whose model of depression as a CPP is all about cyclic maintenance processes, is Moorey (2010), who proposed a 'vicious flower' model for depression (see Figure 6.3). This model incorporated two maintaining cognitive cycles (automatic negative thinking and rumination), a mood/emotion cycle, two behavioural cycles (withdrawal/avoidance and 'unhelpful behaviours') and one motivation/physical symptoms cycle. Moorey's model was a mini PMC taxonomy. He saw the purposes of 'maintenance diagrams' as including to aid collaborative conceptualisation of presenting problems, as a way to introduce the CBT model (see Figure 3.1) quickly and simply, and as a rationale for therapy interventions (Moorey, 2010, p.174).

Therefore, his model was deliberately a maintenance model, not a 'developmental model', because maintenance is much more critical in therapy (p. 176). He embedded the model in a network theory, admitting that the six cycles do not operate in isolation from one another. All elements can interact (p. 177). However, this interaction is not represented in his flower, and this makes it more limited than a systematic Depression PMC taxonomy. Despite admitting that 'external events and environmental factors may… play an important role in maintaining depression' (Moorey, 2010, p. 180), causal arrows to and from the environment (Events, situations) are not represented in the flower model. This is another limitation. 'Withdrawal and avoidance' cycles, for example, often maintain problems *through* their effect on the person's environment/stimuli/input/experiences.

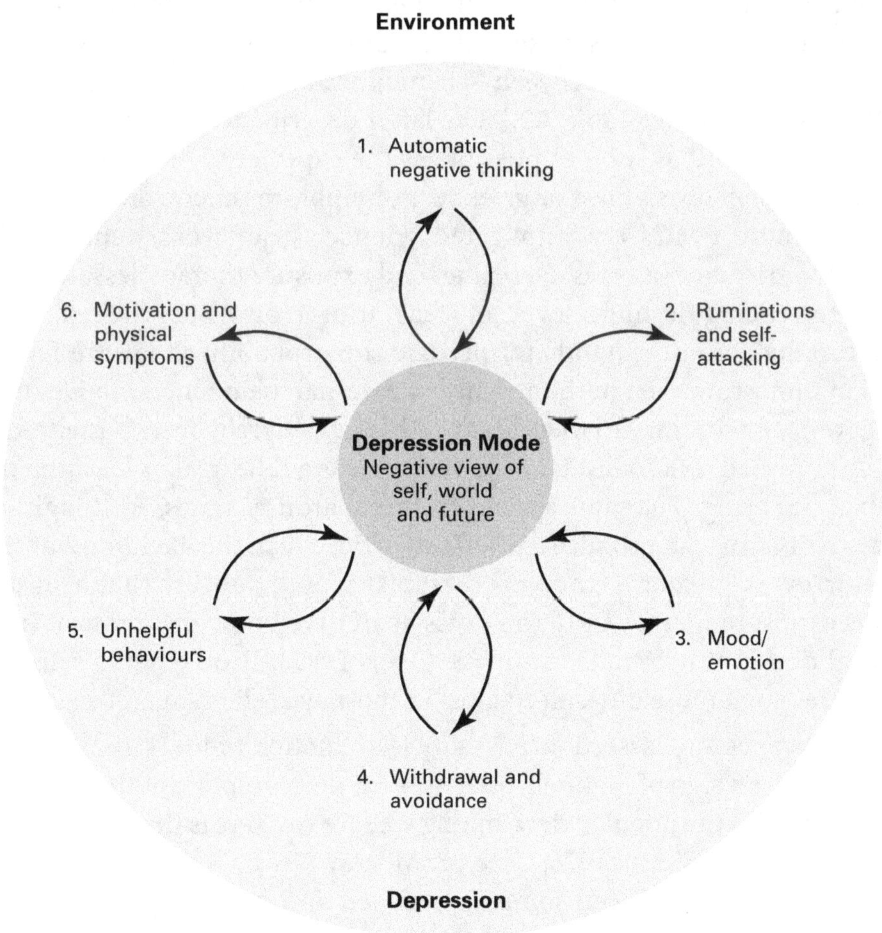

FIGURE 6.3 Moorey's (2010) 'Vicious Flower' model of depression.

In terms of subsequent logically-inferred interventions or therapies, Moorey (2010) supplemented his vicious flower model with a 'virtuous flower' (p. 182) specifying the interventions most likely to be implied by each of his six maintenance cycles, intended to generate positive cycles instead.

Figure 6.4 illustrates a fuller — though still relatively nascent — taxonomy of depression-related PMCs.

PMC theory is a *meta*-theory, in the sense that *any* model of CPPs (that emphasises current maintaining, rather than historical, factors) can be incorporated, and that *any* therapeutic process that has been shown to effectively address those factors is then justified or indicated. For example, interpersonal psychotherapy (IPT) has been shown to be effective with especially recurrent depression problems to a degree comparable with CBT (Cuijpers, Geraedts, et al., 2011). It is no surprise, then, to note that many *interpersonal* PMCs have been identified among depressed clients, and that these have implicated particular CBTs (Dobson, Quigley, & Dozois, 2014) *or IPT* to address those specific PMCs.

Anger Problems

A sampling of commonly-occurring or frequently-remediable PMCs that can maintain CPPs and that involve anger is presented in Figure 6.5.

A distinction can be made between 'self-reinforcing' and 'non-self-reinforcing' emotions. (See footnote under Table 7.2.) The latter describe feeling states that a person is happy to leave behind as soon as possible as the experience of them is itself aversive. These generally include sadness or grief, fear or embarrassment, and pain. If these persist, one or more PMCs are implicated. Hence, 'grief work' tends to lessen the experience of grief and sadness over time; and exposure therapy lessens the probability of experiencing a high level of fear tomorrow. But the experiencing of 'self-reinforcing' emotions tends to *increase* the probability that the feeling will be indulged in tomorrow, even in the absence of external maintainers. This can occur with anger/aggression (contrary to theories of catharsis) whereby its experience, unless significantly 'punished' externally, tends to function as a rehearsal or learning trial, due to the 'rush' it can bring. The same applies to sexual arousal states. Although such states, if leading to orgasm, can produce a brief 'cathartic' effect, the likelihood of similar feelings tomorrow is greater. Hence no therapist would suggest that a paedophile be treated by exposure therapy until the urges abate! We know that fantasy-induced sexual arousal does not habituate (Smith & Over, 1987). Problematic 'self-reinforcing' emotions are much more difficult to alter in therapy (Seligman, 2007).

If submissiveness/nonassertion/passivity is a function of low self-esteem, then logically aggression is a sign of high self-esteem. ('I'm more important than you, so you had better give up'). But the popular view among welfare workers is that aggressive criminals have low self-esteem (Eitzen, 1976; Green & Murray, 1973; Worchel, 1960). The research on this question has produced some very mixed and confusing results (Baumeister,

Depression Problems

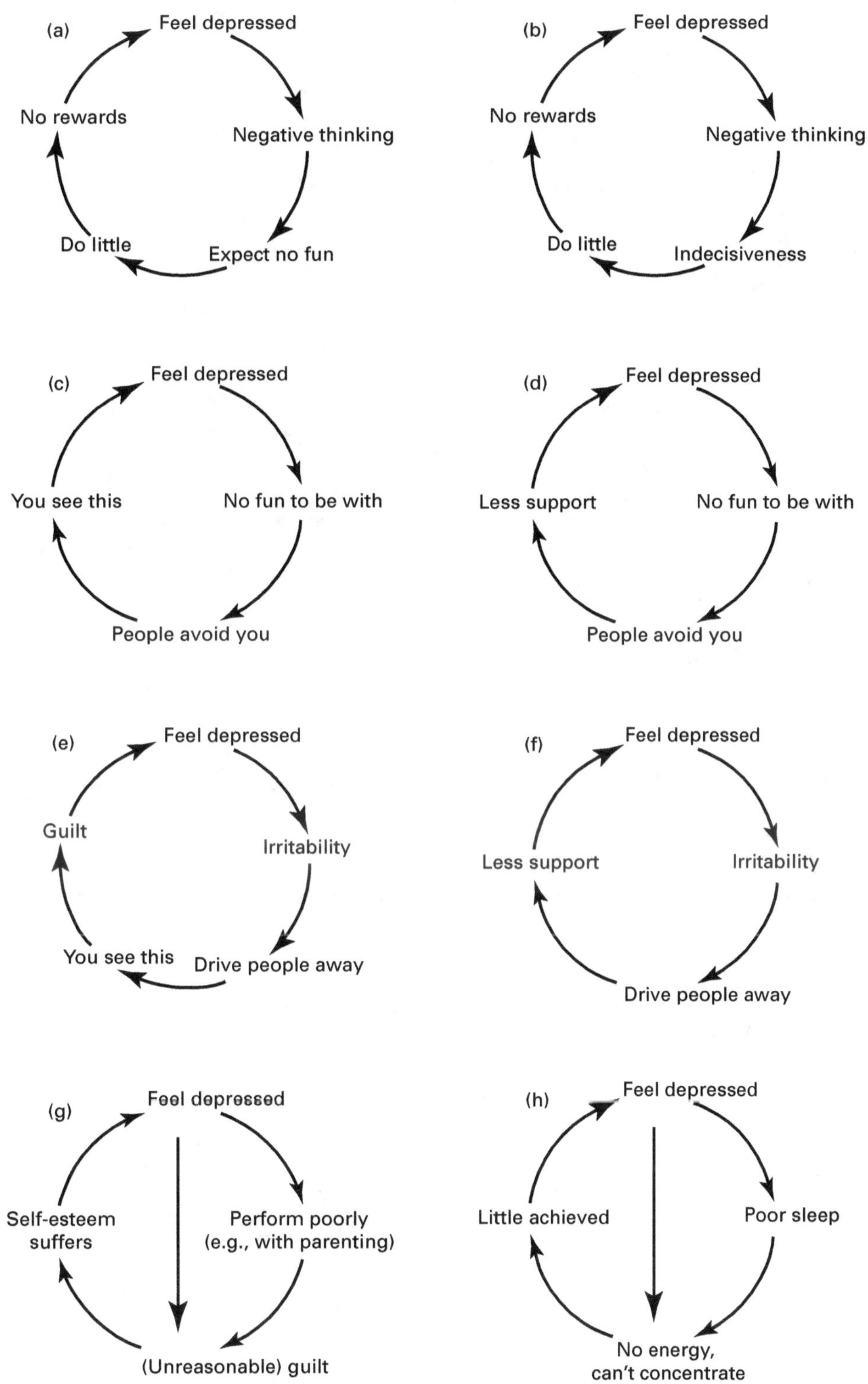

FIGURE 6.4 Some depression problem-maintaining circles (PMCs).
(Available as a free download from www.australianacademicpress.com.au)

Depression Problems (continued)

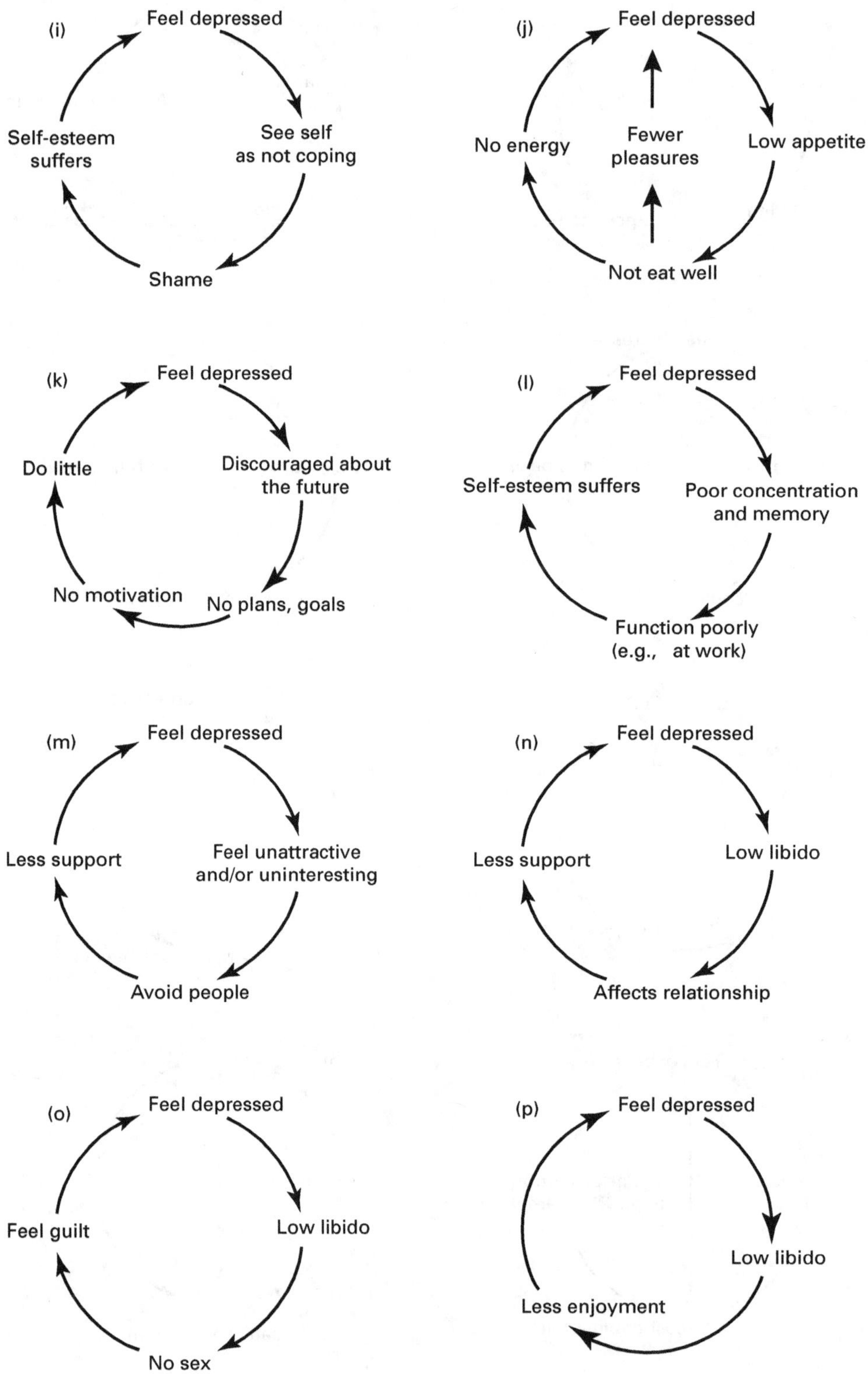

FIGURE 6.4 continued... Some depression problem-maintaining circles (PMCs).

Depression Problems (continued)

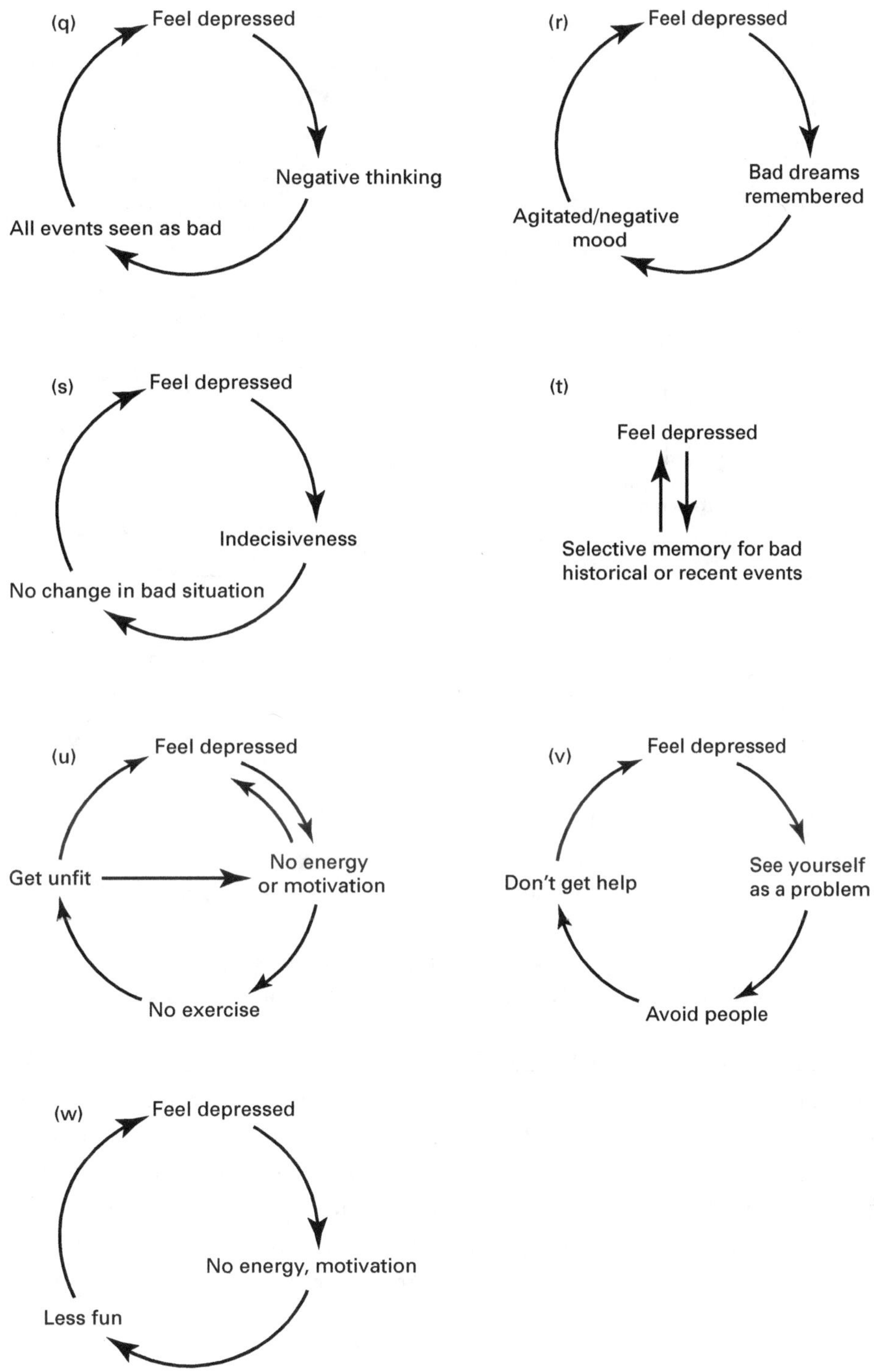

FIGURE 6.4 continued... Some depression problem-maintaining circles (PMCs).

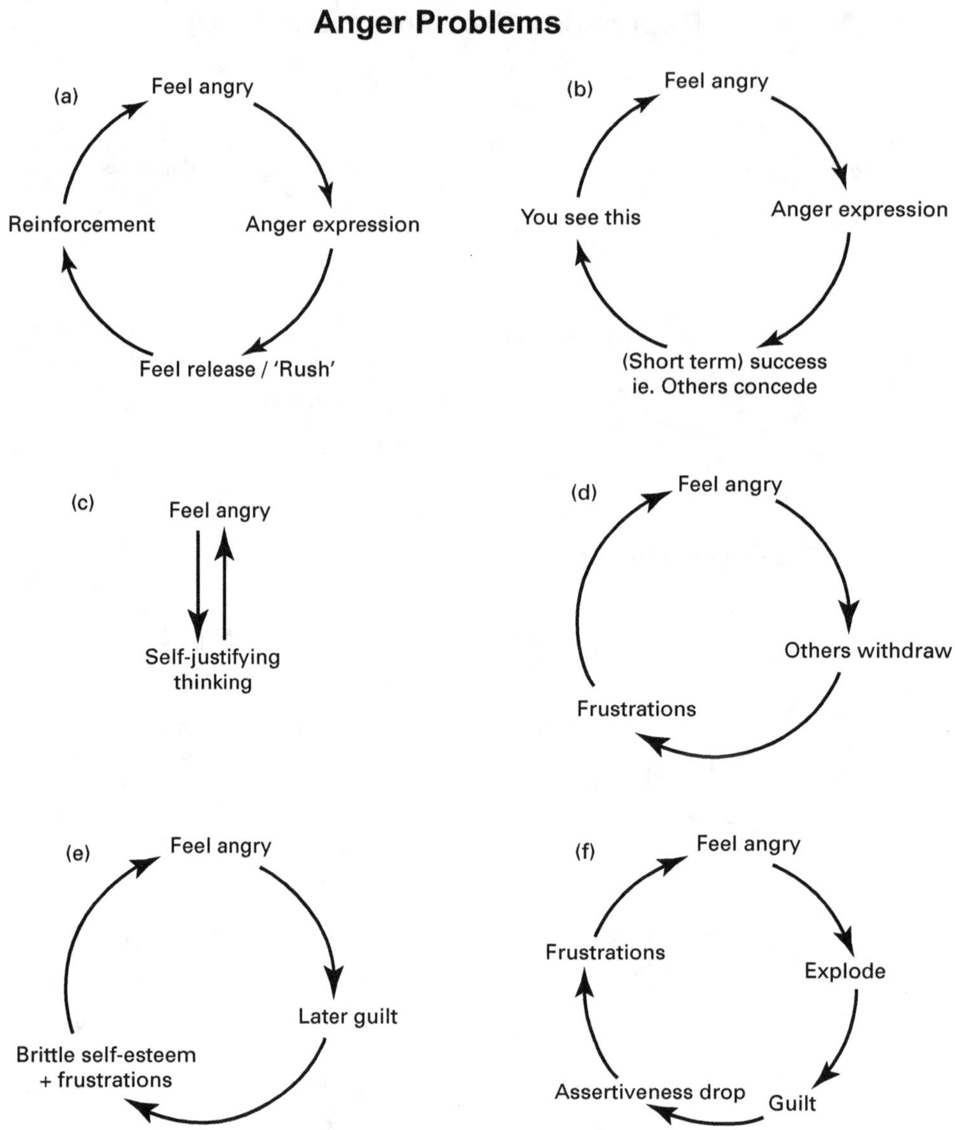

FIGURE 6.5 Some anger problem-maintaining circles (PMCs).
(Available as a free download from www.australianacademicpress.com.au)

Smart, & Boden, 1996; McGuire & Priestley, 1985). A solution lies in the notion of 'delicate' or 'brittle' self-esteem, or 'threatened egotism' (Baumeister, Smart, & Boden, 1996; Bushman & Baumeister, 1998). These studies have shown that violence is most common among people whose self-esteem is inflated but unstable or tentative. Salmivalli (2001) has also noted a certain subset of people who report high self-esteem, but are aggressive. He saw this as showing up empirically as an unstable self-esteem. This can show itself by a tendency to boast or show off, or to react with a 'fight-or-flight response' when challenged.

'Any Psychological Problem'

Some PMCs are near-to-universal among people experiencing a CPP. Experienced clinicians will subsequently find themselves spending a deal of time with almost all clients,

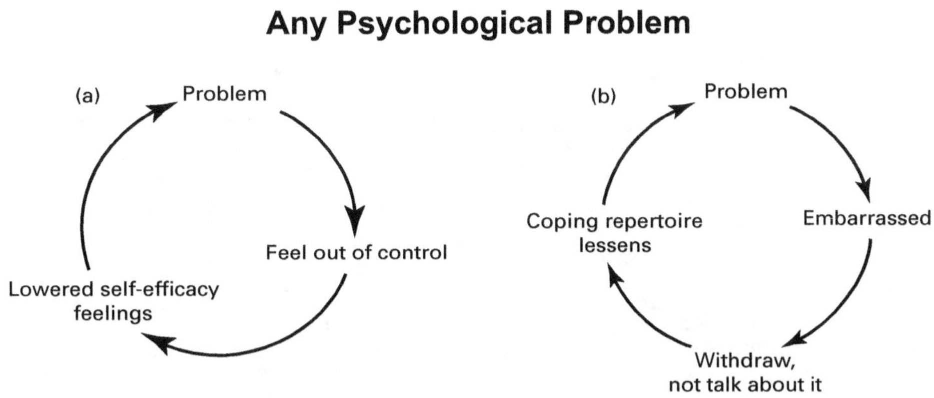

FIGURE 6.6 Some problem-maintaining circles (PMCs) that worsen any psychological problem and can make it 'clinical'.
(Available as a free download from www.australianacademicpress.com.au)

after the initial assessment and early in the intervention process, attempting to restore some feeling of self efficacy or self-esteem, as people become self-deprecating, embarrassed, feel guilty, or feel impotent *as a consequence of developing a CPP*.

Further, when people become stressed or depressed they commonly revert to simple, early-learned, and often problematic coping strategies, such as escape/withdrawal, alcohol or drug use, 'comfort eating', aggression, dissociation, and suchlike. Unfortunately, such a narrowing of one's coping repertoire often only serves to worsen a problem.

Two general 'any psychological problem' PMCs are illustrated in Figure 6.6, and are discussed in Chapter 7.

Eating Problems

The majority of Eating Disorders diagnoses are not for Bulimia Nervosa (about 30%) or for Anorexia Nervosa (about 10%) or for Binge Eating Disorder (about 5%), but for Eating Disorder Not Otherwise Specified (about 60%; Fairburn, 2008). Furthermore, movement between these categories is common, frequent, and multiple. About 80% of patients change diagnosis within 2 years.

The Eating Disorders are a prime example of the utility and validity of the *transdiagnostic* CBT approach (Fairburn, Cooper, Shafran, & Wilson, 2008). Hence some of the PMCs illustrated in Figure 6.7 are centred on 'Binge Eating' and some on 'Dieting, Starving', but they overlap, include common elements, and infer similar treatment Homeworks, irrespective of technical psychiatric diagnosis (see Table 7.6). In fact Fairburn et al. (2008) have suggested that the central problem in the transdiagnostic category of eating disorders that requires intervention — the element that should be at the top of all the PMC diagrams in this category — should be 'abnormal attitudes and beliefs regarding shape and weight'.

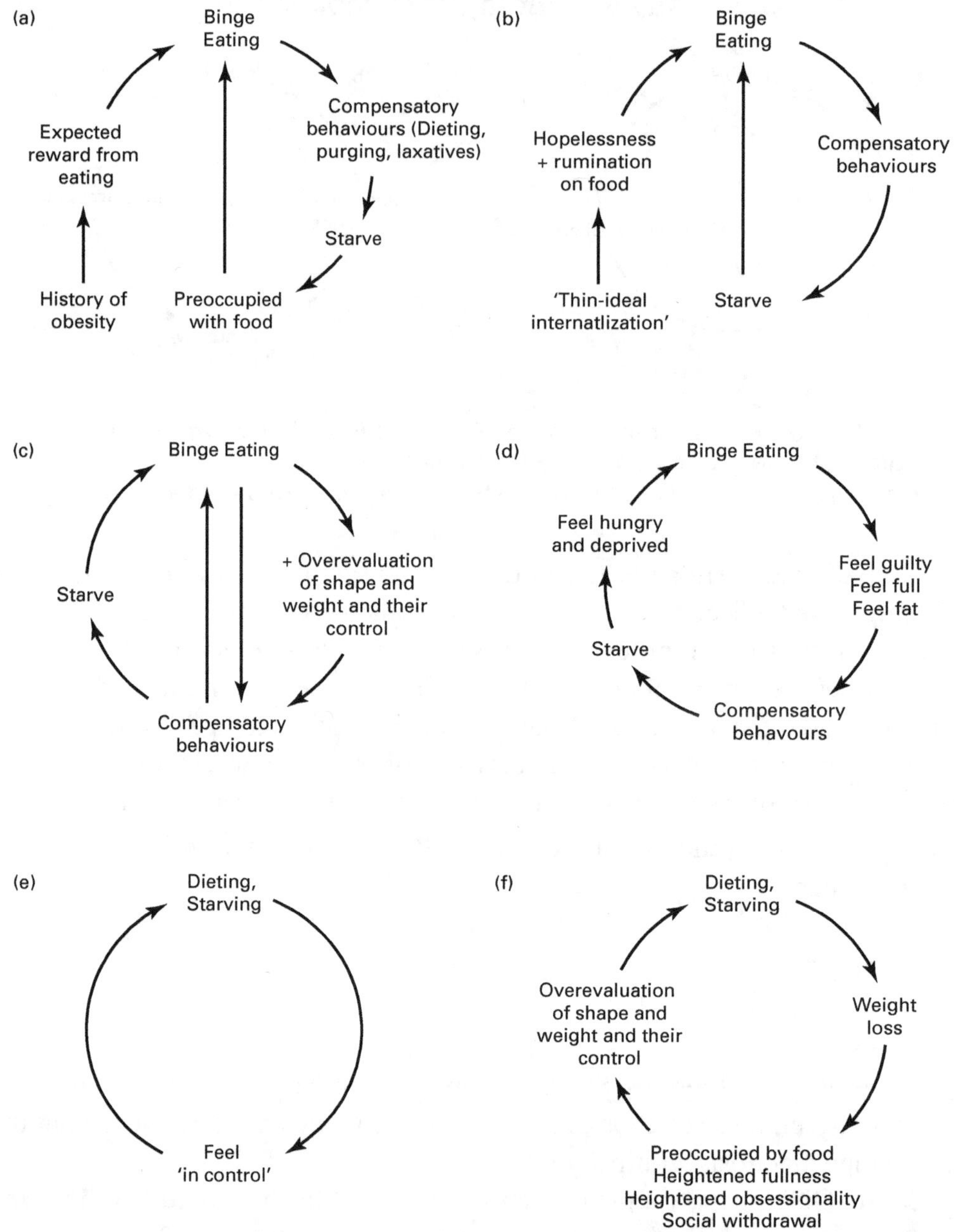

FIGURE 6.7 Some eating problem-maintaining circles (PMCs).
(Available as a free download from www.australianacademicpress.com.au)

Relationship Problems

When PMC-based CBT case formulation in clinical psychology replaces traditional psychiatric medical model-based diagnosis, the CPPs that can be targeted are much better specified and justified. The 7 or more types of diagnostic criteria we find in DSM (see page 42) point us to 'pathologies', 'symptom clusters', or presumed neurobiochemical processes which appear to bear some clinical utility with problems such as schizophrenia or bipolar disorder (clear Type III psychological problems), but are useless at best,

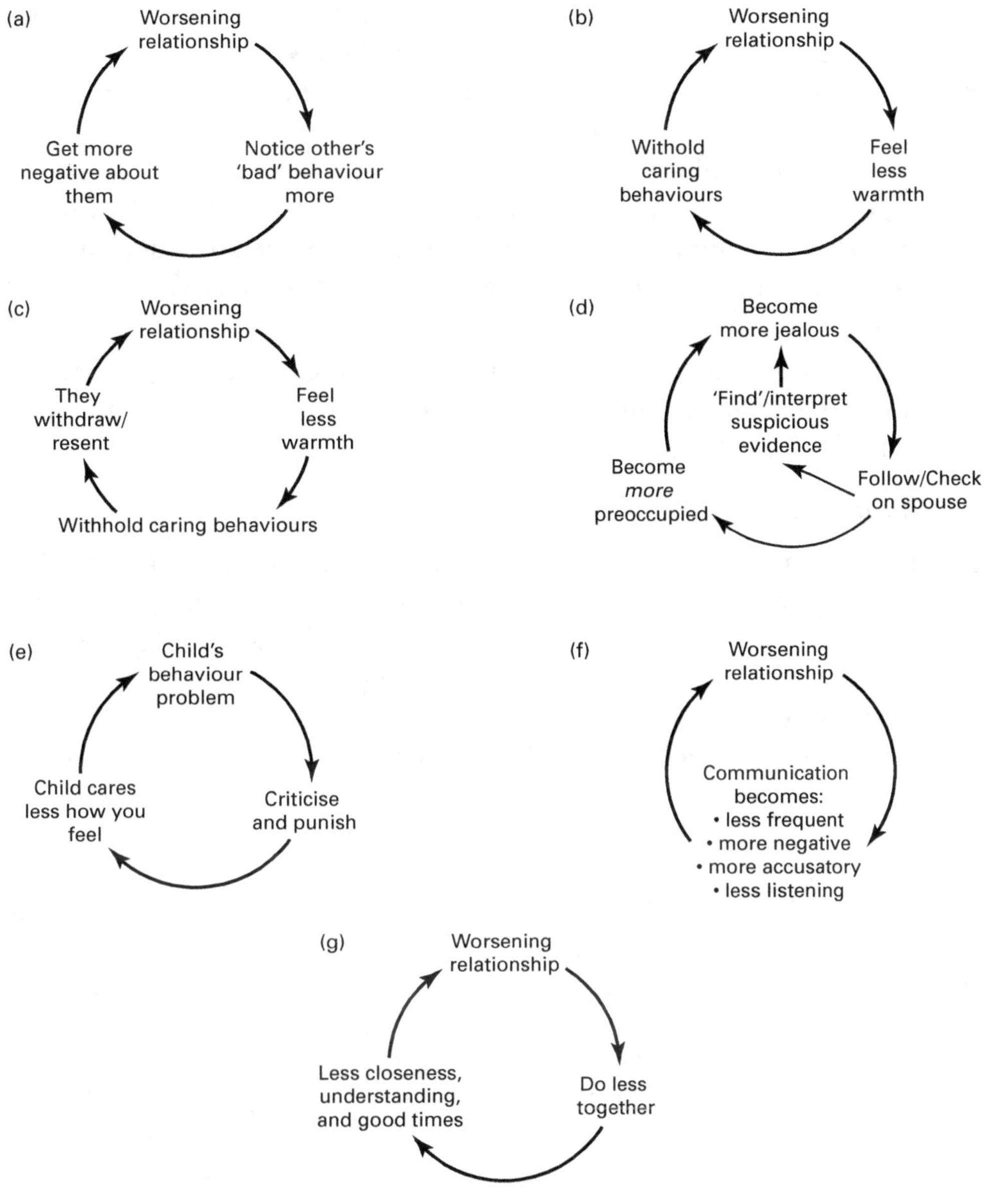

FIGURE 6.8 Some relationship problem-maintaining circles (PMCs).
(Available as a free download from www.australianacademicpress.com.au)

and misleading and stigmatising at worst, with the "high prevalence" CPPs such as anxiety and depression problems.

On the other hand, PMC-based CBT case formulation asks only two main questions: Is this an ongoing negative situation that we want to change? And does it involve PMCs including elements categorisable as 'Thoughts', 'Feelings', 'Situations/Events', or 'Behaviours'? (If the elements in PMCs are predominantly or critically physiological, they are more medical problems than CPPs [see Bakker, 2008a, p. 20]. If the elements in PMCs are predominantly or critically situational, such as poverty, an unsatisfying job, or criminal charges, the other professions will be more useful that a clinical psychologist, such as a financial counsellor, social worker, vocational counsellor, or lawyer.)

But, unlike Type III psychiatric conditions, PMCs at the level of Thoughts, Feelings, Situations/Events, or Behaviours (i.e. CPPs) are not limited to single individuals. They can occur *between* people. This is a major conceptual and practical advantage of the PMC-based CBT model over the psychiatric diagnostic model. Clinical psychologists can be very useful in helping to change relationship problems, as they all involve people's Thoughts, Feelings, Situation/Events, and Behaviours. But DSM-5 deals with this category of 'Other Conditions That May Be a Focus of Clinical Attention' in a few pages of afterthought, assigning 'V' codes to some 'relational problems'. This is clinically useless to a psychologist.

Therefore, a treatment-relevant sampling of some common interpersonal PMCs is illustrated in Figure 6.8. Each implies one or more therapeutic intervention points (as indicated in Table 7.7).

Jealousy Problems

There has been as much solid clinically relevant research on relationship PMCs and their treatment as there has been on other CPP areas. Just one example is research on, and CBT model development of, jealousy problems. Leahy and Tirch (2008) have formulated a 'Conceptual Model of Jealousy' (see Figure 6.9). Note that, as with all comprehensive PMC-based CBT models, it includes (a) inputs to the PMCs, such as 'Childhood history of attachment' or 'Situational triggers', and (b) PMCs involving Thoughts, Feelings, Situation/Events, or Behaviours, such as 'Provoke, punish, devalue' <—> 'Increased relationship conflict', or 'Increased relationship conflict'<—> 'Search for reassurance'.

As with all PMC-based CBT interventions, there will be less focus on the inputs than on the PMCs themselves. A 'childhood history of attachment' may be assessed and acknowledged, but therapy outcome studies have shown that such historical inputs are not necessarily — or even usefully — addressed or reversed in successful therapies (Bachrach et al., 1991; Bloom, 1994; Paris, 2000). Also, the tactic of removing or avoiding or preventing in the future all 'Situational triggers' is unrealistic and unhelpful. (It is the *opposite* of exposure therapy.)

So, Leahy and Tirch's (2008) model can be the source of PMCs for our developing taxonomy, just as other evidence-based models of 'psychopathology' have been. (See pages 29–30 for a listing.) The single quotation marks here are necessary, as problem jealousy is not a distinct psychopathology in the 'mental disorder' sense. It is not listed separately in DSM-5. It *is*, however the basis of many CPPs, especially interpersonal ones. Once again mental disorders and CPPs are shown to be different concepts.

Chronic Pain

Within the PMC model, the essential difference between a person in pain and a person who has a chronic pain problem requiring clinical psychological intervention beyond simple pain relief (a CPP, see Table 4.1) is the formation of perpetuating causal circles. Such PMCs can be at a purely physiological level, such as the central sensitisation that can occur at a neural level producing neuroplastic pain (Woolf, 2011). Or the PMCs can

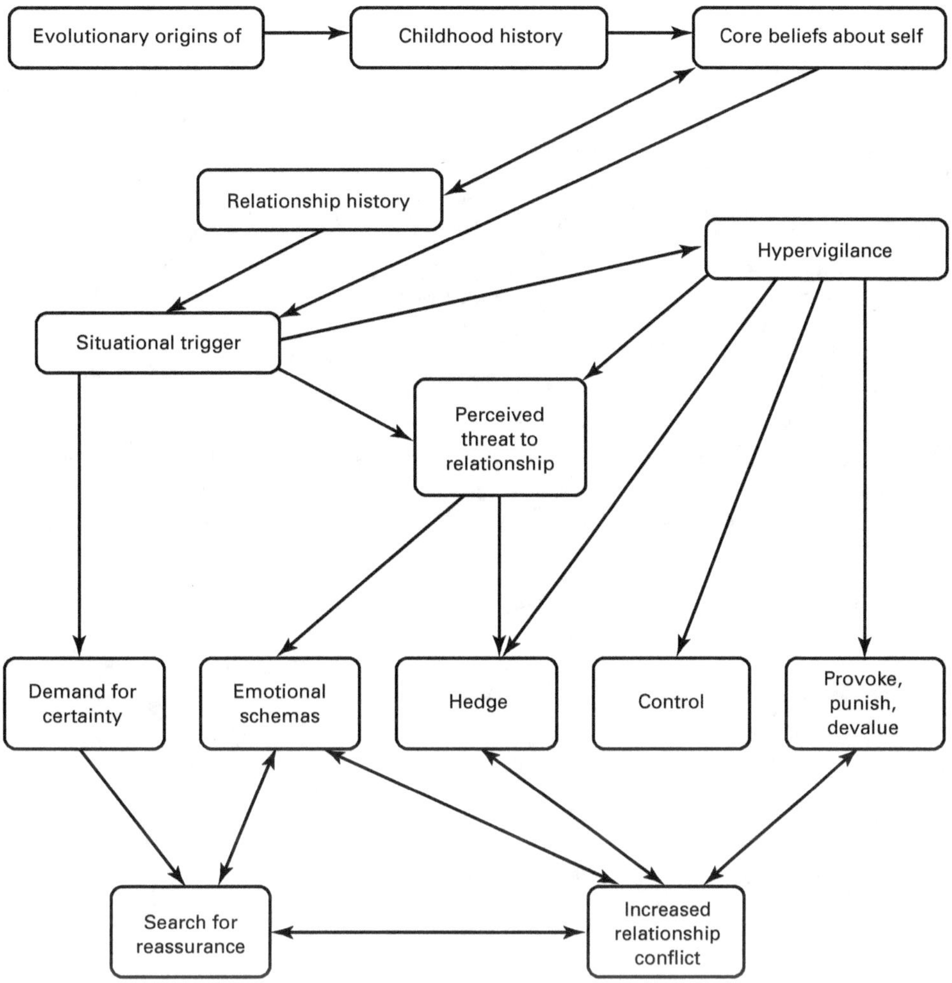

FIGURE 6.9 Conceptual model of jealousy (Leahy & Tirch, 2008).

include psychological-level causal elements, justifying intervention by a psychologist. (See Figure 6.10.)

Most evidence-based psychological-level interventions for chronic pain are CBT therapies (Simon, 2002), and most CBT models of chronic pain — and hence most PMCs to be discovered in this problem area — involve a 'fear of injury or re-injury' model (Vlaeyen & Linton, 2000).

Before the Gate Control Theory of Pain (Melzack & Wall, 1983) emerged in 1965 most formulations of persistent, preoccupying, or excessive pain report were psychodynamically based. Hence the preponderance of diagnoses such as Conversion Disorder in which the pain problem was considered to be 'all in your head'. We unfortunately are still handicapped by this assumption within the community when a pain patient is referred to a psychologist. The diagnosis is still common in the United States, and I have known a psychiatrist to have explained away a Complex Regional Pain Syndrome

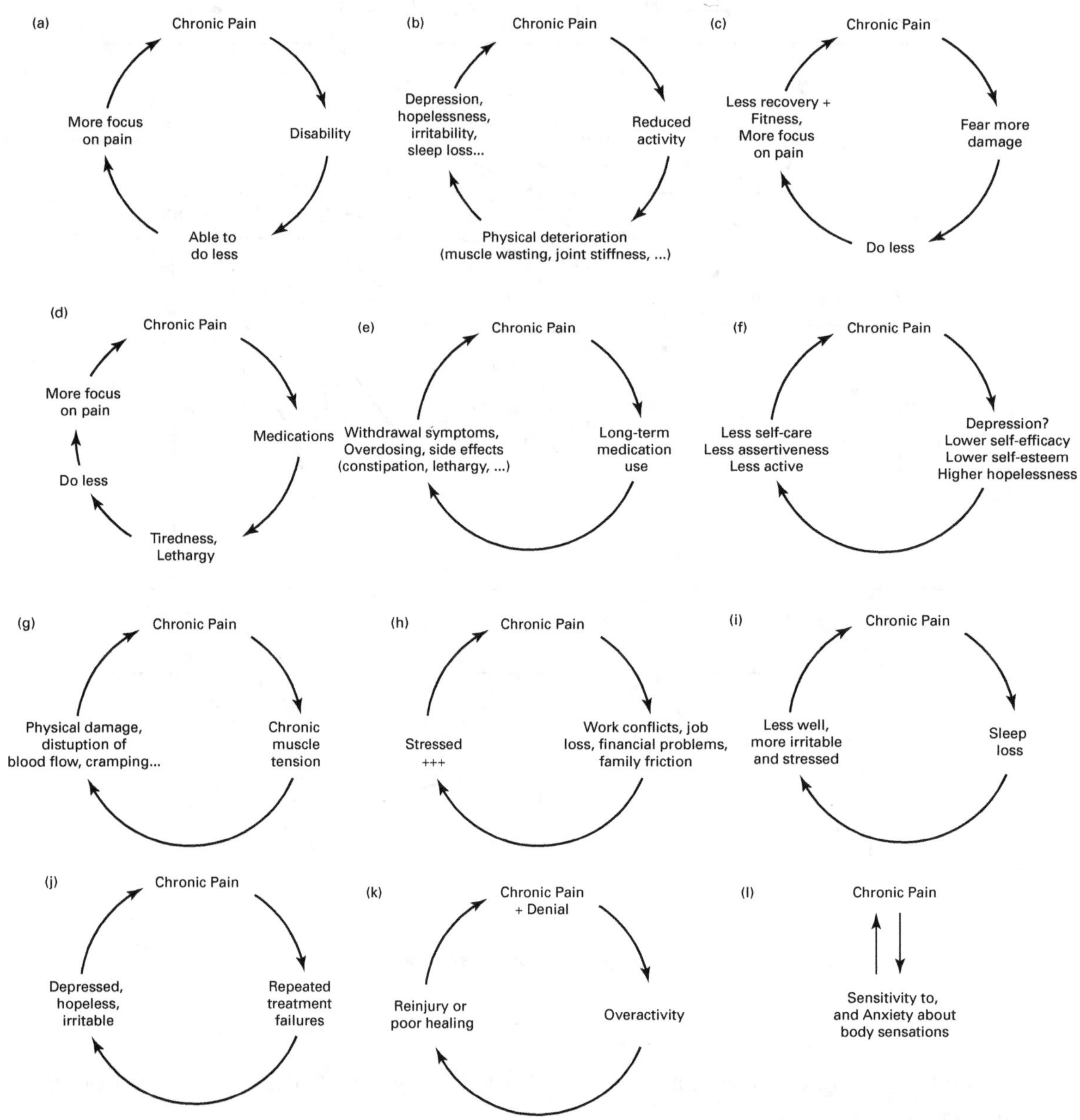

FIGURE 6.10 Chronic pain problem-maintaining circles (PMCs).
(Available as a free download from www.australianacademicpress.com.au)

(Reflex Sympathetic Dystrophy) in these terms.

Now we accept that pain is pain. It is rarely imagined. (See discussion in the Health Anxiety section.) But it is exacerbated by many psychological factors, including by excessive focus, and by inactivity or overactivity, and that the disability due to chronic pain can be lessened, even if the pain levels persist. And that it is greatly worsened or prolonged by depression, stress, and anxiety (Hall et al., 2011). Hence workshops on evidence-based psychological interventions for chronic pain patients are now more likely to be titled 'Psychological Management of Persistent Pain' than 'Psychotherapy for Chronic Pain'.

Almost all the 'yellow flags' that have been found to predict long-term disability and work loss subsequent to injury (Kendall et al., 1997) are identified PMC risks. They include: (a) belief that pain is harmful, and subsequent fear-avoidance behaviour; (b) a passive attitude to rehabilitation; (c) extended rest and withdrawal from activities of daily living; (d) a boom/bust cycle of activity; (e) sleep quality affected; (f) increased alcohol or drug intake; (g) depression; and (h) anxiety over body sensations. All of these are represented in the PMCs of Figure 6.10.

Note that few PMCs in Figure 6.10 describe maintenance or exacerbation of pain per se. Only PMCs (g) and (k), and perhaps (h), do this directly. Most describe the contribution of focus and mood on the *experience* of pain — (a), (b), (d), and so on — or the degree of disability ensuing from the problem — (a), (b), and so on. Hence, most effective interventions do not seek to remove pain per se, but rather address all other elements in the Chronic Pain PMCs. Most are therefore transdiagnostic therapies, and do not comprise a separate section of Homeworks in this manual. (See Table 7.8.)

Whereas mindfulness-based stress reduction has been found to improve pain acceptance, it does not necessarily lessen pain intensity or subsequent disability (Cramer et al., 2012). Other CBT approaches are known to effectively alter both acceptance and disability (Hall et al., 2011). These approaches can include (from the Position Statement of the Australian Pain Society, November, 2002): (a) Cognitive therapy to address unhelpful attitudes and beliefs or self-talk, such as catastrophising; (b) Behavioural approaches to address lowered activity levels, secondary gains, or to restore well behaviours; (c) Relaxation techniques; (d) Anxiety management approaches; (e) Depression management; (f) Sleep management strategies; (g) Management of sexual problems; (h) Assertiveness training; (i) Anger management; (j) Education; (k) Marital or relationship work; (l) PTSD treatment.

Most meta-analyses comparing the CBT treatment of chronic pain problems with treatment as usual reveal only small to moderate effect sizes (e.g., O'Keeffe et al., 2016; Ramond-Roquin et al., 2014). This may well be a result of (a) seeking effects on the pain intensity itself, rather than acceptance or consequent disability, or (b) the fact that all treatment trials reviewed in these meta-analyses have to date involved (DSM) diagnosed groups rather than experimental subjects identified in their CBT formulations as experiencing specific relevant chronic pain PMCs. Diagnosed groups of chronic pain sufferers are most likely to be very heterogeneous with respect to the mechanisms of maintenance they are engaged in, and hence likely to respond differentially to different CBT interventions.

Obsessive Compulsive Disorder

Although OCD has traditionally been classed among the anxiety disorders, there are many reasons to see it as particular and distinct. Firstly, the evidence for a particular neurological base underlying the condition, distinct from other anxiety problems, is growing (Radua et al., 2010), although treatments at the psychological level are still the most effective we have (Foa et al., 2005), and may remain so for some time.

Secondly, many theorists are seeing OCD as quite distinct from other anxiety-related problems in terms of etiology, phenomenology, natural history, and incidence (Phillips et al., 2010), to the extent that even DSM-5 now classes it within a separate group of 'obsessive-compulsive and related disorders' which includes hoarding disorder and body dysmorphic disorder (Hollander, Braun, & Simeon, 2008).

Although compulsive behaviour is "best conceptualised as an escape behaviour (i.e., from obsessional distress) that is similar in nature to avoidance or safety behaviours in other anxiety disorders" (Storch, Abramowitz, & Goodman, 2008, p. 338), the main PMC involved is distinct, namely "a vicious cycle of intrusion —> misinterpretation —> anxiety —> rituals —> intrusion" (p. 339). "The cognitive-behavioural model implicates normal human learning principles (i.e., conditioning) and normal cognitive processes in accounting for the nature and etiology of OCD with greater parsimony than do models that appeal to the presence of chemical imbalances, disease states, or general deficits in attempting to explain the nature and etiology of OCD" (p. 339).

Thirdly, and most importantly, best practice treatment of OCD is, due to the distinctive PMCs involved, also quite particular and distinct from such treatment of the other anxiety-related problems (Bakker, 2009). Whereas similar conditions are best addressed using some form of exposure therapy, plus usually elements of cognitive therapy, best practice with OCD involves cognitive therapy, exposure, and response prevention. This makes several steps in the treatment process all the more critical. To some degree, insight and control of response during exposure treatment of a simple phobia are of marginal significance. We have long known that exposure extinguishes a classically conditioned fear response whether a subject knows this is going on or not, and that relaxation, for example, during systematic desensitisation is not a critical component (Gillian & Rachman, 1974).

However, because OCD treatment involves response prevention, the client must understand the process and must cope in nonavoidant, 'nonrelaxation' ways for treatment to be effective.

This is reflected in the steps necessary in OCD therapy as prescribed by numerous theorists and therapists. For example, Schwartz's (1996) four steps — relabel, reattribute, refocus and revalue — incorporate the two requirements of understanding (the client has to 'get it') and coping in a non-neutralising, nonritualising, nonreassuring way. This second requirement can be technically a challenge to discern, so quite some expertise may be needed to ensure it is detected and averted. For example, even the innocent-looking appeals of the client for reassurance that they were okay not to perform compulsion x can be neutralising behaviours, and sabotage treatment. So referral to an expert clinician is a good idea with most OCD clients.

However, the first of the key requirements listed — a shared understanding — can be attempted by most primary therapists, and appears to be just as crucial as an expert treatment process. In comparing the majority of OCD clients who progress in treatment, with

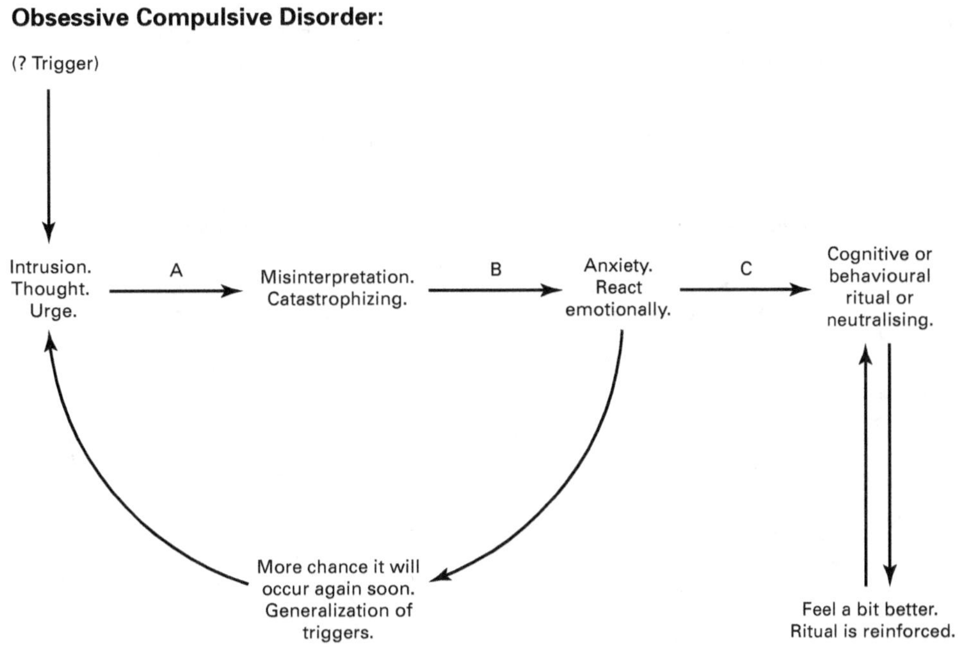

FIGURE 6.11 A general problem-maintaining circle (PMC) model of OCD.
(Available as a free download from www.australianacademicpress.com.au)

those that seem never to have, despite numerous therapists, therapies, and years of suffering, my clinical impression is that this group 'just don't get it' (Bakker, 2011).

Once they grasp the idea that certain of their thoughts/fears/urges are aberrant false alarms, although they feel real, then they can begin treatment in a consistent way. But some clients never truly grasp this. They persist in responding internally, if not externally, as though there is some reality to these thoughts/fears/urges.

Script 11 describes specific attempts to help an OCD-type CPP client to 'get it'. Many anxiety-related PMCs may occur when someone has OCD (see Figure 6.1). Those specific to OCD are illustrated in Figure 6.11, including the points at which Cognitive Therapy (A), Exposure (B), and Response Prevention (C) attempt to break the PMCs. Links between Figure 6.11 and suggested relevant Scripts and Homeworks are presented in Table 7.9.

Substance Abuse or Dependence

Some PMCs to be discovered among people experiencing substance abuse or dependence problems are peculiar to this area, such as those involving withdrawal symptoms or cravings; for example, Figure 6.12 (a). Others have key elements in common with other CPP areas, such as effects on sleep, relationships, or available coping repertoire; for example, Figure 6.12 (b), (c), (d), (e), or (f). Therefore, although the early phases of therapy may benefit from specialist input (e.g. medical support during initial withdrawal), much successful therapy can be provided by a general clinician — especially one offer-

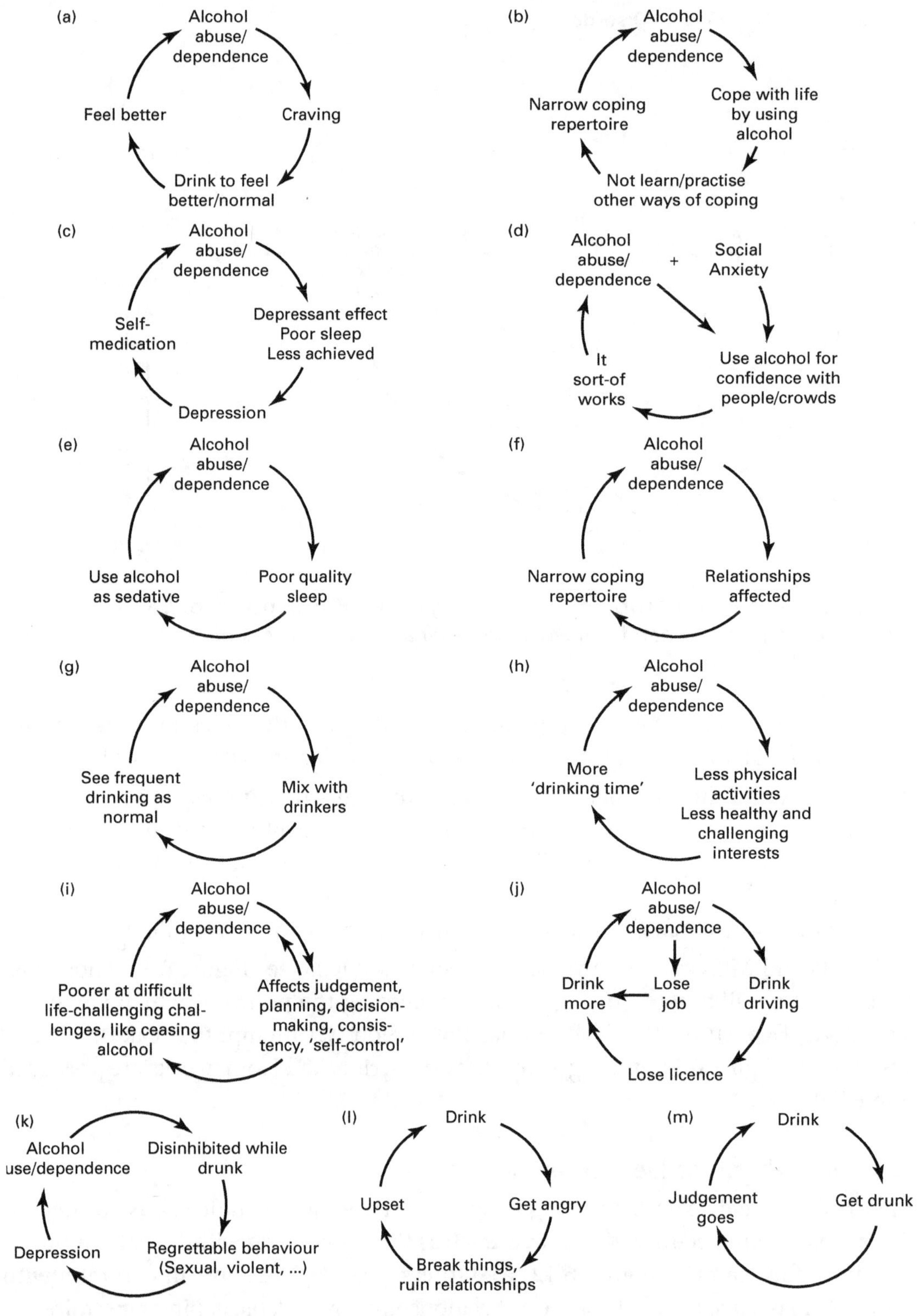

FIGURE 6.12 Substance abuse/dependence problem-maintaining circles (PMCs).
(Available as a free download from www.australianacademicpress.com.au)

ing a transdiagnostic PMC/CBT-based approach within a coping skills model (Dobson, 2001, p. 219).

Figure 6.12, being illustrative rather than exhaustive, focuses only on alcohol abuse/dependence PMCs. Many of these are more physical (e.g., craving), or social (e.g., mix with drinkers), or situational (e.g. lose licence or lose job), than they are psychological (e.g. using alcohol as a coping technique). All identified PMCs in a case formulation should be considered as targets in therapy. So, as well as (from the above examples) medication to reduce craving, advice and assistance in changing one's social network, and help to remain active despite unemployment, therapy may need to re-broaden or restore a client's ability to cope with feelings, people, stressors, etc. without using a drug.

Based on this model, many of the Homeworks recommended in other problem areas will be useful with substance abuse/dependence problems. However, the most specific to the re-development or restoration of a narrowed, immature, undeveloped, or reduced Coping Repertoire are Homeworks 1 and 2. These homeworks are then only the start — the introduction — to an ongoing process of coaching in coping with feelings, stresses, people, frustrations — with life — in non-chemical ways.

This process needs to be explicitly introduced to the client, so that they know the goals, the reasons for their homework, that it will take time, what examples of coping or not coping to write down or tell you about, etc. In this introduction it is always useful (and often likely to be true) to explain a client's 'acopia' in terms of 'missing out on lots of practice in coping with life in healthy ways, by using chemicals all the time instead'. This can explain, for example, a 30 year old with the emotional maturity of a 14 year old, after 15 years of heavy marijuana use.

A similar theme in the psychological therapy of substance abuse/dependence problems is that the drug use occurred for a purpose — it performed a function. If this ceases, it will leave a large gap in the person's life. This gap may be in ability to cope, or it may be a social life gap, or leave them bored and with no interests or commitments.

So other frequently-applicable homeworks may be Homework 21: Pleasant Events Schedule, or Homework 5: Social Challenge Diary.

Therefore, explicitly working on a coping skills gap is only part of working on any gaps left by the removal of substance use. This then is another explicitly explored theme with the client: What did the drug/alcohol used to do for you, specifically? What functions did it perform? Not just with the goal of insight. (Insight-oriented therapies have a poor record with substance abuse/dependence problems.) But with the goal of replacement.

Reviews of outcome studies in the treatment of substance abuse/dependence problems (Nathan & Gorman, 2015; Roth & Fonagy, 2005) — especially alcohol problems — have consistently recommended CBT therapies in the Coping Skills domain. This includes social skills training, self-control training, stress management training, problem-solving training, and cue exposure. Recommendable adjuncts or supplemental approaches have included behavioural marital therapy, motivational interviewing, and behavioural contracts.

Hence few of the homeworks described in Section 3 are specific to substance abuse/dependence problems. Most of the evidence-based treatments in this area are transdiagnostic. This occurs because the elements in the PMCs requiring intervention are mostly generic ones such as depressed mood, a narrowed coping repertoire, or social anxiety. (A rare exception to this is 'craving'. However, after a person has completed a 'detox'/withdrawal phase much physiological craving should have abated, and what remains is more psychological craving which must be coped with or 'deconditioned'.)

No convincing support has been found for confrontational interventions, psychodynamic therapy, or aversive techniques (electric shock, nausea), although there is mixed support for covert sensitisation.

Selection of interventions from the above recommended options (especially working on the coping repertoire) should be guided by the PMC-based case formulation. This is reflected in Table 7.10: Therapies for Substance Abuse/ Dependence, and Table 7.11: Assessment-To-Treatment Links for Substance Abuse/Dependence Problems.

Sexual Problems

Over recent decades, the frequency of presentation of sexual problems to therapists and counsellors in developed countries has declined (McCarthy, 2001). This has occurred in my practice too. Hence I have not in recent years had sufficient numbers of clients in this area to confidently suggest trial-and-error-derived verbatim scripts for Homeworks in this area. Instead, the reader is referred to already published guides to such specific strategies as sensate focus, the squeeze technique, systematic desensitisation, and so on. (See Table 7.12.)

There are many possible explanations for this decline in overall rates of presentation of sexual problems. Information on sexual techniques and behaviour is more readily available. Medical aspects are better understood in the community. Variability in sexual behaviour is more accepted.

But one likely cause for the decline is that the majority of referrals in decades past have been for 'inhibited sexual desire' (Knopf & Seiler, 1990), particularly in women, which has variously been called 'female orgasmic disorder', 'female impaired sexual interest' or 'sexually unresponsive women'.

Partly because no consistent underlying or concurrent psychological pathology has been found in this group of presentations (e.g., Whitehead & Matthews, 1986), society's and therapists' attitudes to this group have changed dramatically, such that 'desire discrepancy between partners' is now more commonly the focus of treatment (Kilmann et al., 1986). This does not necessarily involve PMCs, as it is an attempt to alter a 'natural' state of affairs, and may therefore be addressed with work on the relationship generally, counselling (assistance in progressing through a natural 'linear' developmental process), or information provision, rather than psychotherapeutic intervention to correct a 'pathology' or break an unnatural problematic PMC.

A similar shift is occurring in attitudes to premature ejaculation. It may be useful to assist a man in controlling the pace of his sexual response. But it is hard to see high sexual responsiveness as a pathology, or even a function of a PMC. Premature ejaculation is so common and uncorrelated with any other psychological issues that it is more often now regarded as a natural state of affairs deserving of psychoeducation and counselling rather than corrective therapy.

These changes in attitude are a backlash to the medicalisation of people's discontents, and to the propagation of psychiatric diagnoses, suspected to be initiated by drug companies, who it has been claimed sometimes develop medications and then invent and promote pathologies that their drugs can treat (Carlat, 2010; Whitaker, 2010).

The changes in how we perceive 'inhibited sexual desire' and 'premature ejaculation' are supported by the finding that, although initial success rates in the treatment of these two problems can be good (Kilmann et al., 1986), long-term outcomes are generally 'very poor' or 'disappointing' (Hawton et al., 1986) when compared, for example, to long-term outcome with vaginismus or erectile dysfunction. We seem to be temporarily altering a natural state of affairs?

Despite these qualifications, the general area of the treatment of sexual problems parallels closely the treatment of other problem areas such as anxiety or depression. The similarities include:

- The fact that CBT is far and away the most supported treatment approach (Almas & Landmark, 2010; Hawton et al., 1986; Sarwer & Durlack, 1997). For example, Almas and Landmark (2010) reviewed psychodynamic, hypnosis, behavioural, cognitive, cognitive-behavioural, educational, marital, group therapy, sex therapy, and bibliotherapy approaches. They found that therapy that focuses on the sexual problem is more effective than indirect treatment of underlying problems like anxiety or communication problems.
- The PMC model applies well. It even helps us distinguish those problems we can assist through psychoeducation, support, 'permission', or counselling, and those we need to intervene in to break some identified PMCs (see PLISSIT model, Permission, Limited Information, Specific Strategies, Intensive Therapy).
- Sexual problems can be the result of past traumatic experiences (Becker & Skinner, 1983), but most are not (Schmidt & Arentewicz, 1983), and effective treatment is likely to be similar anyway (Becker & Skinner, 1983). This parallels what we know about, for example, the treatment of phobias (see Bakker, 2008a, p. 6).
- Relevant PMCs can occur within a person or between people. Most effective sex therapy is with couples.

Therefore many Anxiety PMCs, Depression PMCs, and Relationship PMCs can be relevant in the presentation of a sexual problem, and in its case formulation. Figure 6.13 illustrating sexual problem PMCs includes only those with a specific sexual performance element. [It also includes some linear non-PMC causal chains, that can indicate a need only for counselling, if detected; for example, (b) and (g).] Suggested homeworks from Table 7.12 are linked with these PMCs in Table 7.13.

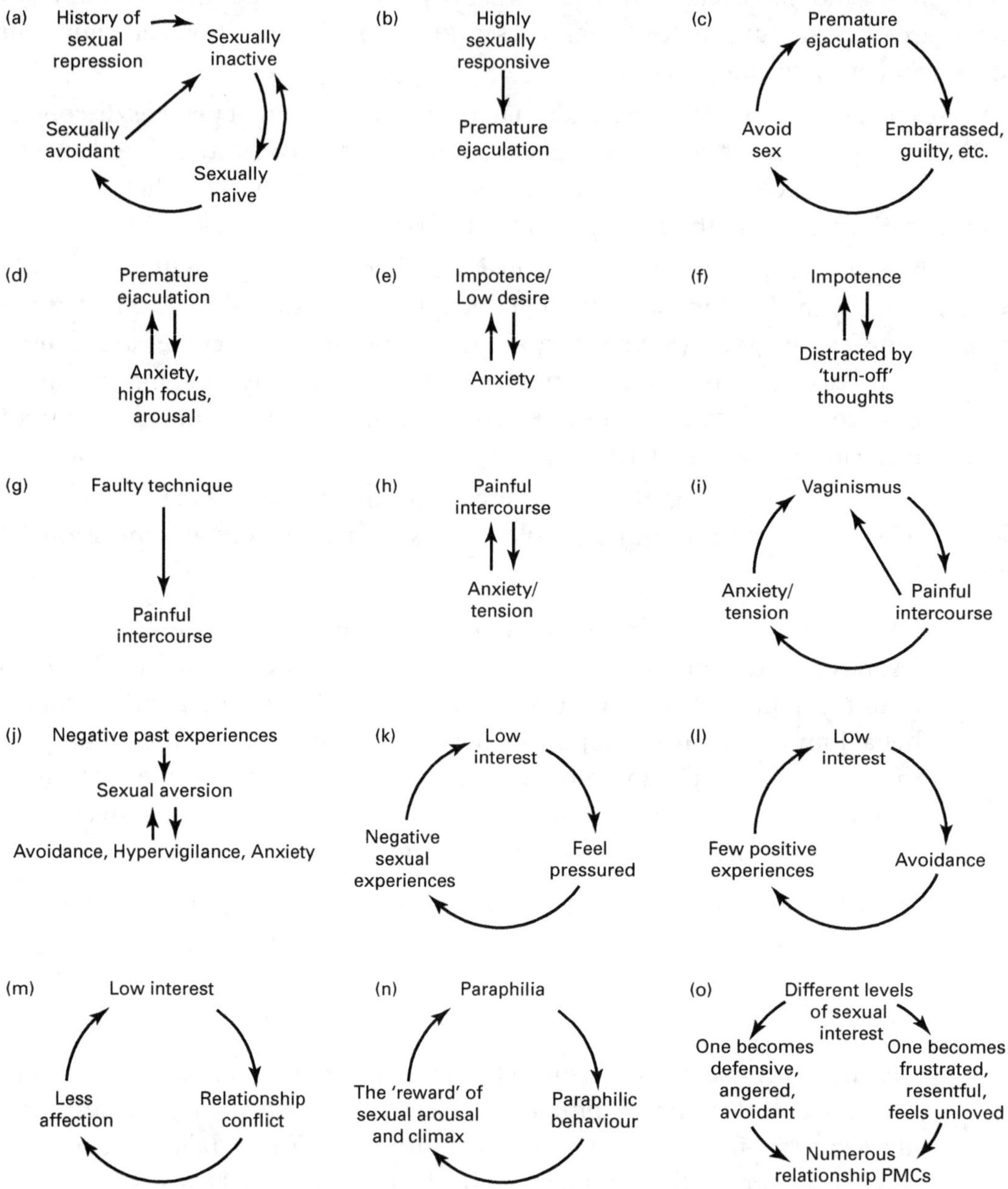

FIGURE 6.13 Some sexual problem-maintaining circles (PMCs) (or linear causal relationships).
(Available as a free download from www.australianacademicpress.com.au)

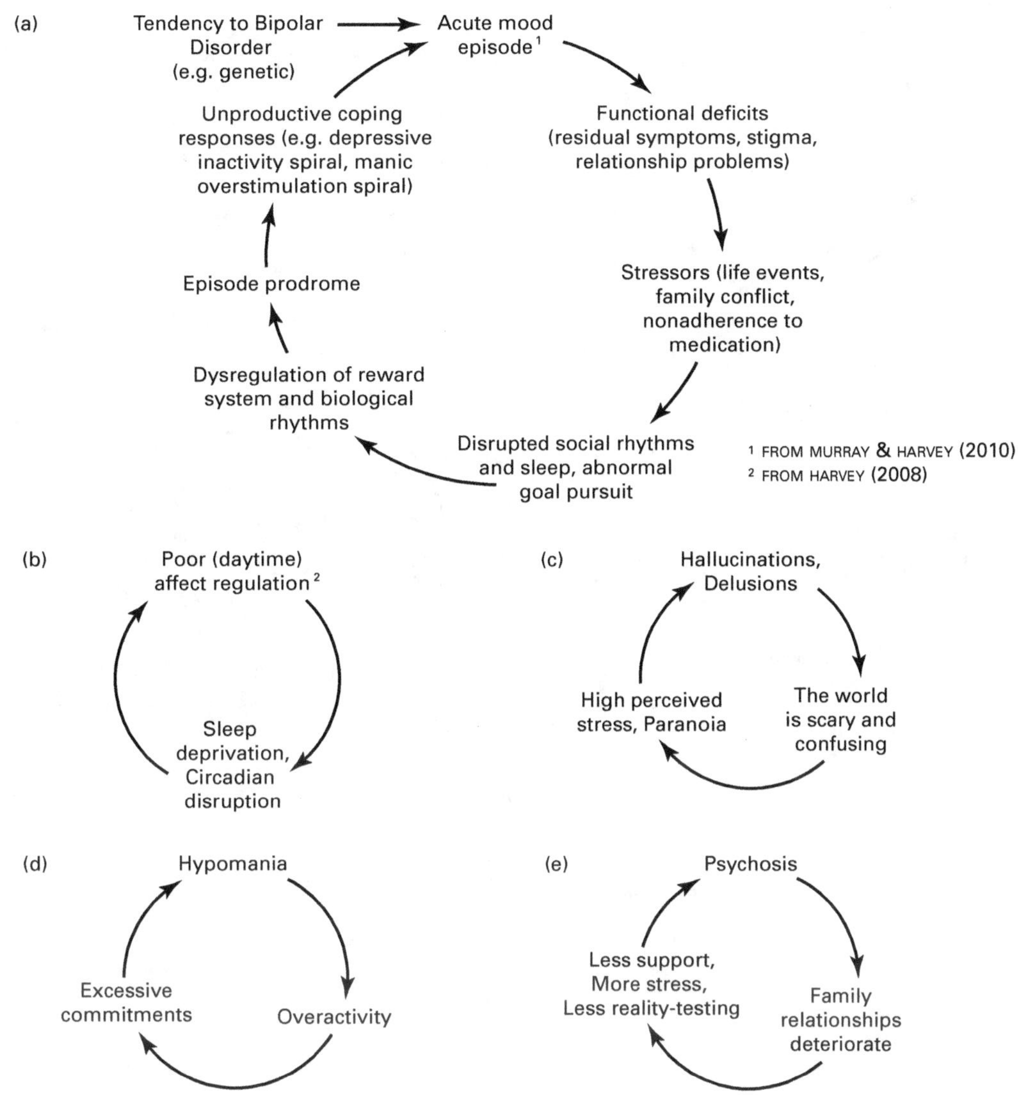

FIGURE 6.14 Some Type III psychological problem-maintaining circles (PMCs).
(Available as a free download from www.australianacademicpress.com.au)

The main distinguishing features of PMC-based CBT treatment of sexual problems are:

1. It can be even more important than in other areas to have medical aspects checked and screened, including the effects of medications, before assuming psychological PMCs are sufficiently explanatory.
2. Most PMCs and most treatments involve more than one person.

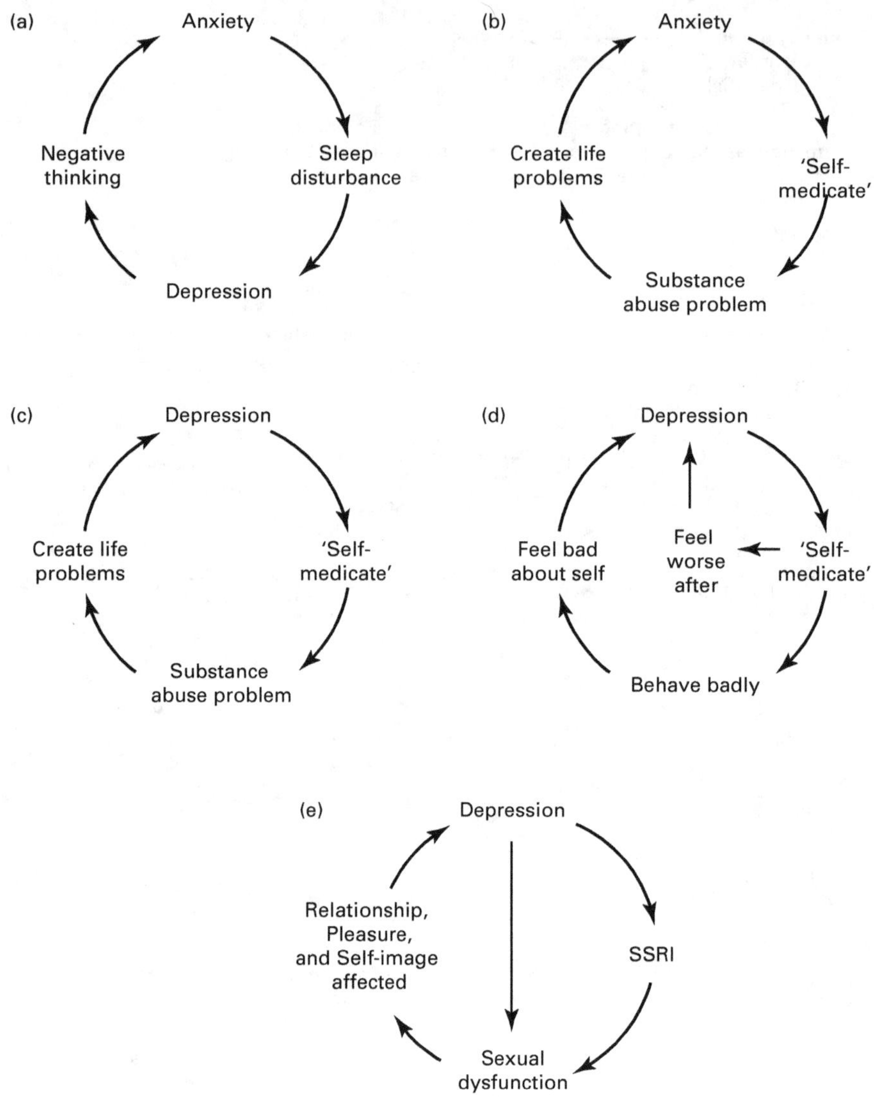

FIGURE 6.15 Some interactive clinical psychological problem-maintaining circles (PMCs).
(Available as a free download from www.australianacademicpress.com.au)

Type III Psychological Problems

Some psychological problems are best considered 'psychiatric' on the basis of two related, but separable, criteria: (a) There is some evidence that the underlying mechanism is predominantly neurological/biochemical/organic, rather than psychological-level; and/or (b) front-line, best practice, or evidence-based treatment guidelines comprise mainly pharmacological or other physico-medical interventions.

In such cases psychological-level PMCs may be operating, but they are not fully explanatory, and their disruption is not expected to 'cure' the condition — only to ameliorate it or to reduce the relapse or hospitalisation rates, or medication dosages.

Therefore, some of the PMCs in Figure 6.14 include organic elements as well as psychological elements, and represent current understanding of underlying neurochemical mechanisms; for example: Figure 6.14(a). And some are purely at a psychological level;

for example, Figure 6.14(c), but do not fully explain a psychiatric condition. Both, however, implicate psychological-level points of intervention.

Many of the Depression PMCs of Figure 6.4 can apply in Bipolar disorder, Chronic fatigue syndrome, Seasonal affective disorder, Post-viral depressions, and so on.

Interactive CPPs

The imposition of the medical model of mental disorders onto the field of CPPs has resulted in the problem of explaining the numerous large comorbidities between diagnoses, such as between GAD and MDD, or between anorexia nervosa and bulimia nervosa. Such profuse correlations are not a theoretical problem, though, when we operate at a purely psychological level. In fact at this level we expect high causal interactions and hence correlations – whether coming at the issue from a common factors, emotion dysregulation, transdiagnostic point of view (Barlow, Allen, & Choate, 2004; Kring & Sloane, 2010) or from a symptom network theory point of view (Borsboom et al., 2011; Cramer et al., 2010).

The Network Model, especially, emphasises the many potential links between, for example, Anxiety CPPs and Depression CPPs. They share — and can be causally linked by — such 'symptoms' as sleep disturbance, negative thinking, reduction in coping repertoire, reduced support system, poor self-care, compromised self-esteem or self-efficacy, and so on.

Hence Figure 6.15 illustrates just a tiny sampling of the multitude of transdiagnostic interactive PMCs that are possible some of which are also listed in Table 4.7.

Chapter 7

Assessment-To-Treatment Decision Pathways

After a general assessment, a CBT functional analysis or case formulation, perhaps an etiological hypothesis has been formulated, and importantly some PMCs have been proposed, it is then the CB therapist's task to select points in the assumed operating PMCs at which to intervene.

Some PMCs can be so apparent that interventions can be initiated even at the end of session 1. The fear of panic attacks in panic disorder may be an example. PMCs in panic disorder — see Figure 6.1 (h) and (i) — may be so clear, and remediation points via psychoeducation and homeworks so well known, that the process from assessment to treatment can begin soon, and along predictable paths.

But, with several options as to what point in a multi-element PMC to address, or which of several PMCs to attack first, and with an array of well-supported procedures available within CBT to address any particular element, the process of treatment/homework selection can be a complicated one.

Several crucial aspects that the outcome studies show need consideration early on, and are quite ubiquitous, include:

- How stuck, impotent, or hopeless does the client feel? Does this need to be addressed before any homework or progress is possible? (self-efficacy) (see Figure 6.6 re 'Any psychological problem'.)
- Do we need to know more about the problem? And can we make this process therapeutic already? (self-monitoring).
- Is this mainly a situational problem? And when the client is no longer unreasonably stressed, could there be no psychological issue to address? (situational changeability).

Self-Efficacy

It has already been commented that even the nature and direction of initial assessment queries can begin to lead the client toward insights about relevant problem linkages. This can be therapeutic already (see Script 2).

It can also be therapeutic to admit a problem to a helper; to feel that someone — an 'expert' — is now on their side, and that the clinician has not become dismissive, horrified, contemptuous, or panic-stricken when told of the problem; to feel that someone seems to understand; and that a course is being plotted.

We now know that many of the benefits accruing from these nonspecific therapeutic factors occur through their effect on the client's self-efficacy expectations (Bandura, 1977, 1997). This refers to the client's estimate about whether they can successfully execute a certain behaviour or control certain cognitions (Kent & Gibbons, 1987). The intention of much of CBT is to increase this sense of self-efficacy. This will determine whether or not a behaviour is initiated, how hard the client will try, and how long they will persist. This applies not only to the alteration of the problem behaviour/thinking/feelings/situation during the course of therapy, but also to the client's initial commitment to therapy. (See self-esteem and self-efficacy references in Figures 6.1, 6.4, and 6.6, including under 'Any psychological problem'.) It is important to restore damaged self-esteem by describing how common the problem is, how it occurs in normal people, and so on, and then to restore some feelings of control by providing a plan and strategies/options/techniques.

Therefore, perhaps one of the first assessment-to-treatment decision pathways is to check how negative, self-blaming, embarrassed, or helpless the client feels, to counter with an aura of determined confidence in the face of some hard work, and to include early on a variation of Script 1.

Self-efficacy improvement can result from (Rokke & Rehm, 2001, p. 176):

- actual accomplishments or successes
- vicarious experiences
- changes in affect
- verbal persuasion.

But regardless of how it improves, it will affect subsequent performance (Bandura, 1982). It is often suggested that a less demanding problem from the client's list (or within a PMC) be addressed first, so that some early success may lead to more hopefulness (self-efficacy) and a better result with greater challenges later. So, caffeine reduction (Homework 39) is a more advisable session one intervention than a full relaxation skills program (Homework 33: Mini-Relaxers).

Self-Monitoring

After the initial assessment, including a CBT functional analysis, decisions must be made about further more specific or ongoing assessment and initial therapy interventions. The distinction between these (ongoing assessment and initial therapy) can be blurred, as it is well known that self-monitoring exercises can be highly reactive (Becker & Heimberg, 1988; Kanfer, 1975). That is, the process of attending to, recording, and reporting ongoing behaviours, circumstances, feelings, or thoughts can alter their occurrence or at least their perception. This is a pure-research nightmare, but a clinical bonus.

Therefore, another early question is: 'Would it be useful for assessment, or perhaps even therapeutically, to ask the client to record aspects of the problem between appointments?'

There are innumerable ways this can be done. The three I use are:

1. on a (system) card (e.g., Homeworks 9, 24, and 34)
2. in a provided diary (e.g., Homeworks 4, 5, 20, 23, and 24)
3. on special 'Negative Emotion Record' sheets (Homeworks 1, 2, and 3).

Or people can, of course, record on their electronic devices. Numerous apps are available to help structure this. Some of the best CBT-based apps are listed in Table 7.1.

Situational Changeability

As discussed in Chapter 3, the point at which an intervention can be attempted in a hypothesised PMC is not necessarily determined by the locus of the presenting complaint. But it can be, as in the case of a clearly changeable problem situation.

If, for example, a client describes an exceptionally distressing work environment, it may emerge that their 'self-talk' in this situation is quite understandable and reasonable, even adaptive and healthy. Their subsequent anxiety or depressive symptoms or anger may also be reasonable or appropriate, and their assertiveness or withdrawal, or even days off with sick leave, may seem the best they can do to cope.

In this circumstance the primary target for change should be the situation, and the CBT clinician should perhaps refer on to a vocational counsellor. CBT work is then a supplemental alternative, targeting such areas as problem-solving training (Homeworks 13 and 14) or assertiveness training (Homeworks 6–11), but only with the goal of assisting the client to change their situation.

TABLE 7.1 CBT-Based Apps That Include a Self-Monitoring Component

App	*Purpose*	*Platforms*
MoodMission	CBT-based tracking and tailored strategies for dealing with low moods and anxiety	iOS and Android
Moodnotes	Mood tracking and thought recording	iOS only
Sanvello	Anxiety and stress management and tracking	iOS and Android
MoodKit	Suite of CBT tools	iOS only
HealthyMinds	Mood tracking, thought recording, and mental health activities	iOS and Android
MoodPrism	Daily mood tracking	iOS and Android

As noted in Chapter 3, such a formulation is a matter of judgment, because it is assumed that this client would cope happily in most work environments and likely will in their new one. Otherwise, their cognitive, affective, and behavioural response patterns are worthwhile targets for change.

Selecting Homework Tasks

When a healthier level of self-efficacy has been achieved, therapeutic self-monitoring has been considered, and the presenting problem is judged to *not* be purely situational, then most ensuing homework will depend upon the formulations developed through the CBT functional analysis. But not on the simple formula:

Complaints about worry or negative thinking → Cognitive Therapy

Behavioural excesses or deficits → Behaviour Therapy

Feelings out of control → Drugs or Relaxation Training

On what criteria, therefore, can we select points of intervention (apart from the overarching criterion of the outcome studies)? Four possible such criteria are:

1. Although not necessary, it may still be desirable to target that aspect of a PMC cited by the client in their presenting complaint — for example, cognitive therapy for a complaint of excessive worry. This strategy saves some need to justify identifying and targeting antecedents and consequences. As it is already the client's focus, the therapy may be more readily acceptable. The specific presenting complaint is likely to be the most bothersome part of the cycle to them, so they may be more motivated to do their homework, or have more insight into this aspect. Though debated, there is some evidence that anxious children, for example, who present primarily with worry may respond better to cognitive therapy, while those that present with somatic complaints are helped more by relaxation training, when both groups are also undergoing exposure therapy (Eisen & Silverman, 1993, 1998).

2. When a formulation includes long-term or general elements (such as beliefs, skills, or habits) then homework or therapies designed to target these are indicated; for example, discussion of irrational beliefs in REBT, or Homeworks 6 or 9. When the formulation includes short-term specific examples of the PMCs, then homework or therapies designed for these can be selected; for example, a desensitisation session with a phobic client in a car while coaching relaxation skills, or Homeworks 1 or 4.

3. The psychotherapy outcome research has shown that we have a far better record in helping with some problems and some maintaining elements of a problem than with others (Seligman, 2007). In general, the technology for intervening at the level of behaviours and cognitions is more research supported than at the level of emotions, except where drugs are used. And some anxiety-provoking situations are easy to alter or avoid (e.g. giving media interviews) and some are difficult (e.g. aches and pains in an illness phobia).

Some interventions are easy to implement, such as beginning to use decaffeinated coffee, and some difficult, such as broadening one's support network. Therefore, homework or therapy selection can be guided by what the research or the client's individual situation indicates is more possible to change.

4. Although difficult to judge, a clinician may elect to target those elements of a PMC that appear to be the most powerful or contributory to a problem's maintenance; for example, 'If I feel a bit sick [this is very hard to control or prevent] then I just know I'm going to vomit, and then I always get really panicky'. The cognitive link or expectation in this sequence is a powerful one. Little will be achieved until it is broken. This criterion — how contributory or crucial a link in the problem formulation appears to be — is at this stage of CBT research a difficult and still largely subjective one. Some problem maintainers that our intuitions have not highlighted have, when researched, been found to be more crucial than was suspected. For example, Morawetz (2001) has consistently found that a sleep improvement program has helped the majority of depressed clients, not only with their sleep, but with their depression as well!

Therefore, while bearing some of the above therapy selection criteria in mind, I recommend giving homework to attack several elements in a PMC at the same time, as long as the client is not quickly overloaded. It is easier to overload a client who:

(a) has a smaller, more peripheral, problem and is not willing to turn their life upside down to overcome it. They may have come along expecting that ten minutes of hypnosis will do, but 6 weeks of hourly thought recording is unreasonable.

(b) is depressed. This by definition means they lack the energy, decision-making efficiency, confidence, etc. to undertake a comprehensive, small-step-at-a-time, ambitious therapy program. Although debated (DeRubeis, Tang & Beck, 2001, pp. 370–372; DeReubis et al., 1999) it has been argued that Cognitive Therapy is less useful when depression is severe. If this is true, it is likely to be because severely depressed people lack the energy/insight/decisiveness/optimism to do their homework.

(c) has low feelings of self-efficacy, low self-esteem, external locus of control (Cloitre et al., 1992; Rotter, 1966), or questionable motivation for change.

While being cautious not to overload a client, the potential advantages of a 'multi-pronged' attack on a problem are numerous. They included:

(a) Invaluable research is being undertaken to determine which clientele are most likely to benefit from which type of therapy (Elkin et al., 1995; Roth & Fonagy, 2005). However, at the individual clinical level a therapist may still opt for an N = 1 experiment to find out which approach(es) are accepted best or are most impactful for a client (Rokke & Rehm, 2001, p.186).

(b) Such 'therapy-oriented assessment' promotes a quick start on therapy, increasing efficiency, and keeping the focus on change, rather than merely diagnosis or explanation (Dryden & Ellis, 2001, pp. 335–336).

(c) Offering a choice of coping strategies can increase perceived control and self-efficacy (Rokke & al'Absi, 1992; Rokke & Lall, 1992).

(d) The CBT model (see Figure 3.1) can be used during explanation to a client as to why the therapist will be giving homework aimed to alter stimuli and/or thinking and/or feelings and/or behaviour. It is logical to assert that the chances of breaking PMCs are greater if all or most elements are attacked than if only one is. This can be offered as an explanation as to why about 50% of people who cease their antidepressant medication within 12 months (without concurrent CBT) will relapse (Evans et al., 1992; Paykel et al., 1999). Only one element is being directly attacked here, but relapse rates after medication plus CBT, or for CBT alone (which addresses several elements in the cycle) are approximately half of this (Antonuccio, Thomas, & Danton, 1997; Butler & Beck, 2001; Ellis & Smith, 2002; Fava et al., 1998; Hollon & Beck, 1994; Jarrett et al., 2001; Kovacs et al., 1981; Simons et al., 1986). This same pattern has been noted with OCD (Cottraux et al., 1990).

(e) On the one hand, we must avoid overloading our clients — especially those battling depression. But on the other, we need to make an impression on them. We need to inject ourselves into their lives. About 35 years ago I was getting nowhere with a young lady with a trichotillomania (hair-pulling) problem. She was not even doing her behaviour-recording homework. My mentor at the time (Iain) questioned whether I was being taken notice of by her. Perhaps I should give her more homework, not less. This turned the corner for us. The prescription of 4 placebo pills a day leads to faster ulcer recovery than 2 a day (de Craen et al., 1999)! This is presumably because the 'treatment' is more intense and intrusive.

(f) Consistent with all of the above, Harvey et al. (2004) found that, while behaviour therapy effects (on chronic insomnia) are more immediate, and cognitive therapy effects are more lasting, CBT (a concurrent and combined approach) offers both benefits.

The bridge from initial assessment to therapy intervention requires clinical judgment. Outcome studies are often not naturalistic, indicate statistical rather than clinical significance rates, and so forth. Therefore, what to offer this client, with these problems, with these strengths, in this situation must entail some tailoring. "Standardised protocols treat disorders; formulation-driven therapies treat patients" (Persons & Davidson, 2001, p. 106).

Unfortunately, especially since the publication of DSM-III in 1980, almost all outcome studies have been undertaken to assess the efficacy of therapy packages on groups of subjects diagnosed with a 'mental disorder'; not on particular behaviour change principles applied to groups of subjects identified through case formulation as experiencing certain PMC-based clinical psychological problems (CPPs). Therefore treatment guidelines are usually vague, sweeping, and clunky rather than precise, specific, and elegant. (See Bakker, 2019, in submission, for a fuller description of this historical problem.)

However, a compromise must be found between tailoring and standardisation. There is a risk that clinicians can develop idiosyncratic formulations based on fad, lore, or unreliable clinical judgment (Wilson, 1998). For example, it has been found that clients with anxiety disorders who were treated with a standardised exposure-based treatment had better outcomes than those who received individualised treatment (Schulte et. al., 1992). This has been explained by the observation that as clinicians stray from standardised treatments of anxiety disorders, they stray from the principle of exposure (Page, 2000).

(I must admit that the specific interventions and homeworks included in this manual have a selective bias arising from my own cognitive style. Imagery techniques, though well supported by outcome research, are underrepresented, because I am more naturally a verbal processor or coper. I unfortunately project this bias onto my clientele. Clients who would benefit more from imagery techniques such as rational emotive imagery (Velten, 1988), covert conditioning (Cautela & Kearney, 1986), or orgasmic reconditioning (Laws & Marshall, 1991), may respond better if they see another CB therapist.)

Why 'Homeworks'?

Homework is a central feature of CBT (Helbig & Fehm, 2004; Kazantzis et al., 2005). Most therapy with most clients within CBT is 'self-therapy', in the sense that it occurs outside the therapy session. Some therapeutic processes, such as psychoeducation, do occur primarily in-session; although even here homework may often include some reading or online research.

Also, some exposure therapy can occur in-session, either in the office (e.g. modelling touching the floor and then licking one's fingers with a cleanliness OCD problem) or in the field (e.g. a drive in traffic with a post-MVA phobic client).

But specific individualized homework that is conscientiously reviewed (Bryant et al., 1999) has been shown to improve CBT outcomes significantly (Cammin-Nowak et al., 2013; Kazantzis et al., 2005).

The Decision Pathways

The functional analysis, including suspected PMCs, and the general psychological assessment should provide early answers to the questions relevant to treatment or homework selection listed in Tables 7.2 to 7.13.

Table 7.2 presents general questions, each suggestive of particular 'scripts' or 'prescriptions' (spiels or homeworks), detailed in Sections 3 and 4, which may apply regardless of the category of CPP identified. Some relevant PMCs are included.

Tables 7.3 to 7.13 present specific assessment questions, implicated PMCs, and suggested therapy directions or Homeworks for Anxiety problems (Table 7.3), Depression-related CPPs (Table 7.4), Anger problems (Table 7.5), problems around Eat-

TABLE 7.2 General Assessment-To-Treatment Links

(a) Does the client feel bad about him/herself because they have the problem? For example, Figure 6.1 (c) and (m); Figure 6.4 (g), (i), (l), (m), (v); Figure 6.5 (e); Figure 6.6 (a).
→ Script 1, Homeworks 6, 7, 8, 42.

(b) Do they grasp/accept the CBT model? If not
→ Script 2.

(c) Do they see how it fits their problem? If not
→ Script 3.

(d) Is the problem best regarded as a situational one (e.g., excessive or prolonged stress) with appropriate, understandable, or even useful, emotional disturbance as a response?
→ Reassure about normality of current responses (Homework 42).

? Educate about anxiety or depressive/grief symptoms (Script 6).

? Educate about prevention of PMCs (Script 3).

? Refer on to situation-change professionals (e.g., social worker, financial counsellor, GP).

? Offer assistance in situation-changing (e.g., problem-solving training — Homeworks 13 and 14, assertiveness training — Homeworks 6–11).

(e) Is it possible that any hypothesised PMC is being ongoingly 'fed' or 'pushed along' by a biochemical, psychiatric, medical, or neurological condition? For example, Figure 5.2 (b), (c), (d).
→ Refer for psychiatric/medical assessment.

(f) Is there an unreasonable fear of having the problem forever? Or of worse relapses? Or an expectation that recovery will be 100% and permanent? For example, Figure 6.6 (a).
→ Script 4.

(g) Does the client expect only 'Talk Therapy' from you?
→ Script 5.

(h) Does (this episode of) the problem seem to have arisen as a result of accumulating life stresses/changes? For example, Figure 5.2 (a).
→ Homework 42.

(i) Is the client preoccupied with, or seeming to suppress/ignore/deny, these stresses? For example, Figure 6.1 (a), (b), (g).
→ Homework 31.

(j) Is the client in a dilemma about a changed or changing life circumstance? For example, Figure 6.4 (b), (k).
→ Homework 13.

(k) Are they being indecisive or feeling stuck with the situation? For example, Figure 6.4 (b), (s).
→ Homework 14.

(l) Is motivation to change suspect or variable over time? (Especially common in eating disorders, aggression problems, paraphilias, substance abuse problems; i.e., problems with 'self-reinforcing'* emotions.)
→ Homework 43.

Note: *A distinction can be made between 'self-reinforcing' and 'non-self-reinforcing' emotions. The latter describe feeling states that a person is happy to leave behind as soon as possible as the experience of them is itself aversive. These generally include sadness or grief, fear or embarrassment, and pain. If these persist, one or more PMCs is implicated. Hence, 'grief work' tends to lessen the experience of grief and sadness over time; and exposure therapy lessens the probability of experiencing a high level of fear tomorrow. But the experiencing of 'self-reinforcing' emotions tends to increase the probability that the feeling will be indulged in tomorrow, even in the absence of external maintainers. This can occur with anger/aggression (contrary to theories of catharsis) whereby its experience, unless significantly 'punished' externally, tends to function as a rehearsal or learning trial, due to the 'rush' it can bring. The same applies to sexual arousal states. Although such states, if leading to orgasm, can produce a brief 'cathartic' effect, the likelihood of similar feelings tomorrow is greater. Hence no therapist would suggest a paedophile be treated by exposure therapy until the urges abate! Problematic 'self-reinforcing' emotions are much more difficult to alter in therapy (Seligman, 1994).

Table 7.3 Assessment-To-Treatment Links for ANXIETY Problems

Assessment question	*PMCs implicated* *Figure 6.1*	*Suggested homeworks*
Generalised anxiety problem?	All or any of (a) – (l)	Script 6 1, 32, 33, 34
With a large cognitive/'worry' element?	a, b, c, d, g, i, k	30, 31, 35, 36
Are 'thinking errors' evident?	a, b, c, d, g, k	3, 30, 35, 37
Narrowed coping repertoire?	b, c, f, g, k, Figure 6.6	2, 30, 31, 33, 36
Specific phobic reactions? (e.g., PTSD)	b, f, j	1, 4, 33, 34
Especially a social phobia?	a, b, c, d, f, g, h i, j, k	5, 6, 7, 8, 33, 34, 37
Panic disorder?	b, d, f, h, i, j	4, 33, 34, 36, 38
Life narrowed due to withdrawal/avoidance?	b, g, j	4, 21, 22, 23
Lost direction? Indecisive? Over-submissive?	g, k, Figure 6.6 a	13, 14, 15, 16, 17
Loss/lack of assertiveness, or assertiveness needed to remove stressors?	b, c, k, m, n	9, 10, 11
Preference for 'burning off' stress over counteracting it with relaxation?	d, h, i	24
Bad dreams worsen daytime mood?	k, l	29
Poor sleep?	k	28
Low self-esteem a cause or consequence of anxiety problem?	b, c, Figure 6.6 a	Script 1 6, 7, 8
Forgetful, disorganised, or priorities muddled?	c, g, k	15, 16, 17, 18
Overwhelmed by workload, responsibilities, or size of the challenges/tasks?	a, b, c, g, j, k	19, 31
Can become frantic, hysterical, out-of-control?	a, d, h, i	25
Language or revealed attitudes show a feeling of loss of control?	c, b, g, i, k Figure 6.6 a	12
High caffeine intake?		39
Little anxiety insight, describes physiological or psychosomatic problems only?		1, 42

Table 7.4 Assessment-To-Treatment Links for DEPRESSION Problems

Assessment question	*PMCs implicated* *Figure 6.4*	*Suggested homeworks*
Almost any depression problem with a cognitive* element in a literate adult or adolescent.	a, b, g, i, k l, m o, q, t, v	1
Has the client's Coping Repertoire narrowed with becoming depressed?	(Almost universally occurs)	2
Are 'thinking errors' evident?	a, b, g, i, k, l, o q, s, t, v	3
Is self-esteem affected – by having a depression problem? – in any way?	i c, e, g, i, l, m,v	Script 1 6, 7, 8
Is lowered assertiveness worsening the depression or the situation?	Figure 6.1 m, n	7, 9, 10, 11
Has the client lost direction, motivation, purpose, decisiveness, or become overwhelmed by multiple problems or demands?	b, k, q, s	13, 14, 15, 16, 17
Become inert, disorganised, or forgetful?	a, b, g, h, k, l, s, w	18, 19, 20
Overall activity level has dropped? Little chance to derive daily pleasures in life?	a, b, c, d h, j, k p, s, w	21, 22, 23
Little or lessened regular exercise?	u	24
Sleep disturbance?	h	28
Upsetting dreams?	h, r	29
Serious dips, when usual coping strategies become impossible?	All or most of a-w at once	25
Noticeable self defeating speech revealing helpless or external locus of control beliefs?	a, b, i, k, q, s, v Figure 6.6 a	12.
Suicidal ideation?	Figure 6.6 a, b	26
Low appetite, eating little or poorly?	j	27
Gets upset, worried, or down about nearly anything that happens?	q	30
Is the reaction, at least partly, a natural reaction to a real or current stressor?		Script 6 31, 42

*Note: * It is conceivable that some, especially organically-based, depressions have little precipitating or maintaining cognitive element. For example, the new mother, three days post partum, with tears streaming down her face, who says 'Look, don't mind me. I'm having a funny turn here. It'll go. The tears just keep welling up.' Some clients in less clear-cut situations also insist that there are no persistent negative thoughts or triggers associated with their down feelings. This could be true, or could reflect a serious lack of insight. A clinical judgment is required over this.*

Table 7.5 Assessment-To-Treatment Links for ANGER Problems

Assessment question	*PMCs implicated* *From Figure 6.5*	*Suggested homeworks*
Need to know triggers? Self-talk? Frequency? Intensity?	a–f	1, 3
Identifiable frequent or key anger-inducing self-talk or beliefs?	c	35, 36, 40
'Delicate' or 'brittle' self-esteem?*	c, e	6, 7, 8
Poor assertiveness ability, or a cycle of outbursts → guilt → submissiveness → outbursts	e, f	9, 10, 11
Outbursts after provocation/buildup?	a–f	24, 41

ing (Table 7.6), Relationship problems (Table 7.7), Chronic Pain (Table 7.8), OCD (Table 7.9), Substance abuse or dependence (Table 7.11), and Sexual problems (Table 7.13).

As the PMC-based CBT model is transdiagnostic in nature, many of the suggested homeworks are shared not only within, but even between, these domains, because the PMCs implicated are almost identical. Hence, in some domains, a listing of relevant homeworks in Section 3 is replaced by a table of generally understood therapeutic techniques. This applies to therapies/homeworks in the domains of Substance abuse/dependence (Table 7.10) and Sexual difficulties (Table 7.12).

TABLE 7.6 Assessment-To-Treatment Links for EATING Problems

Assessment question	*PMCs implicated* *From Figurc 6.7*	*Suggested homeworks*
Chaotic or restricted eating pattern?	a, b, c, d, e, f	44
Binges occurring?	a, b, c, d	45
Purging/voluntary vomiting?	a, b, c, d	46, Script 9
Some foods are identified 'binge foods'?	a, b, c, d	47, 48
Preoccupation with food, weight, calories?	a, f	15, 16, 17, 21, 22, 23, 44, 49
Distorted body image?	b, c, d, f	50, 51

TABLE 7.7 Assessment-To-Treatment Links for RELATIONSHIP Problems

Assessment question	*PMCs implicated* *(From Figure 6.8)*	*Suggested homeworks*
Therapist or clients need more information about issues, and each person's motivation level, and perceptions of the relationship?	a – g	52, Script 7
Communication gone awry?	f	53, 52, 55, 58
Negative perception of partner?	a, e, f	59, 53, 54, 55
Negative behaviour toward partner?	b, c, d, e, f, g	54, 53, 55, 56, 60
Absence of positive behaviour toward partner, or misguided positive behaviours?	a – g	55, 56, 57, 60
Behavioural problems specifiable?	a – g	56
Imbalance or resentment over each other's activities, supports, or independence?	d, g	57, Script 7
Frequent arguments?	a, e, f	58, 53, 55, 59
Little positive time together?	a – g	60, 57

TABLE 7.8 Assessment-To-Treatment Links for CHRONIC PAIN Problems

Assessment question	*PMCs implicated* *(From Figure 6.10)*	*Suggested homeworks*
Disabled and hence less active?	a, b	21, 22, 23
Fears further damage and hence less active?	c	61
Heavily medicated?	d	21, 22, 23, 62, 63
Chronically medicated?	e	21, 22, 23, 62, 63
Associated depression?	f	See Table 7.4
Subsequent muscle tension?	g	64, 62
Pain causing other life changes?	h	Counselling Problem-solving therapy Stress management
Sleep affected?	i	28
Repeated medical treatment failures?	j	61, 63
Denial of limitations?	k	64
High focus on pain? Or high anxiety over it?	l	21, 22, 23, 61

TABLE 7.9 Assessment-To-Treatment Links for OCD

Assessment question	*PMCs implicated*	*Suggested homeworks*
Any OCD problem	Figure 20	65
Limited insight or acceptance?	Figure 20	66, Scripts 11 and 12.
Unsure what is an OC and what is an OK worry?	Figure 20 A	67
Checking rituals?	Figure 20 C	68
Picture complicated by blame or hopelessness in client or family?	Figure 20 B	69
Mainly mental rituals?	Figure 20 B, C	70
General perfectionism?	Figure 20	71

TABLE 7.10 Therapies for Substance Abuse/Dependence

A.	Social skills training (e.g., Homework 5)
B.	Self-control training (e.g., Homework 36, or use of a 'Decision Sheet'; see Homeworks 45 and 46)
C.	Stress management training (e.g., Homework 33)
D.	Problem-solving training (e.g., Homework 14)
E.	Cue exposure/Covert sensitisation or desensitisation
F	Behavioural marital therapy
G.	Motivational interviewing (e.g., Homework 43)
H.	Behavioural contracts

TABLE 7.11 Assessment-To-Treatment Links for SUBSTANCE ABUSE/DEPENDENCE Problems

Assessment question	*PMCs implicated (From Figure 6.12)*	*Suggested homeworks (Especially) from Table 7.10*
Currently physically addicted/craving?	a	Detox
Has used the drug to cope with life? Subsequent narrowed coping repertoire?	b	A, B, C, D
Concurrent depression?	c k	See Table 7.4
Concurrent social anxiety?	d	A, B, See Table 7.3
Concurrent or subsequent poor sleep?	e	Sleep hygienes
Relationship affected?	f	F, See Table 7.7
Mixes mainly with drinkers/users?	g	A, Social changes
Lifestyle dominated by drinking/using?	h	A, B, E, G, H
Judgement, planning affected?	i	B, D, G
Lost job? Licence, etc.?	j	D
Variable motivation to quit?	b, c, g, h, i, j	B, D, G, H

TABLE 7.12 Sexual Therapies (within a PLISSIT model)

1.	Counselling: Give permissions, psychoeducation, sexual information, adjust attitudes
2.	Solo 'sexercises' (Heiman et al., 1976; Montgomery & Morris, 1987)
3.	Sensate focus
4.	Squeeze technique
5.	Increase sexual communication
6.	Relaxation skills
7.	Attention control, distraction, thought-stopping
8.	Vaginismus desensitisation program (with a medical practitioner)
9.	Orgasmic reconditioning via masturbatory fantasies
10.	Body Image exposure/desensitisation
11.	Relationship therapies

TABLE 7.13 Assessment-To-Treatment Links for SEXUAL Problems

Assessment question	*PMCs or linear causal relationships implicated (From Figure 6.13)*	*Suggested homeworks (Table 7.12)*
Is the client sexually inactive and naive and avoidant, perhaps due to a history of sexual repression?	a, j	1, 2, 3, 4, 5, 6
Has this led to faulty technique or to painful intercourse?	g, h	1, 2, 3, 4, 5, 8
Have past negative experiences led to a sexual aversion?	j, a, See Figure 10	2, 3, 5, 6
'Premature ejaculation',* no concurrent problems?	b	1, 2
'Premature ejaculation' and sex is avoided?	c	1, 2, 3, 4, 5
'Premature ejaculation' distorting his focus?	d	1, 2, 3, 4, 7
Performance anxiety with 'impotence'?**	e	1, 2, 3, 5, 6, 10
'Impotence' distorting his focus?	f	1, 2, 3, 5, 7
Painful intercourse plus anxiety about same?	h	1, 2, 5, 6
'Vaginismus' plus anxiety about same?	i	1, 2, 5, 6, 8
Low sexual interest and feel pressured over this?	k	1, 2, 3, 5, 11
Low sexual interest and hence few sexual encounters?	l	1, 2, 3, 5
Low sexual interest and related relationship conflict?	m	1, 2, 3, 5, 11
Paraphilic feelings and behaviour?	n	9
Divergent levels of sexual interest within a couple?	o	1, 3, 5, 11
Are the sexual problems due to another psychological problem?	See other PMC listings	PLISSIT 'Individual Therapy'

Note:

* *Conditions in quotation marks may be no problem at all, or a simple problem requiring permission, information, or counselling, or a clinical problem (a CPP) maintained by a PMC requiring intervention at a psychological level.*

** *Check for medical causes! Check for past traumas, relationship problems, guilt, etc!*

SECTION 3

Homeworks*

Among my primary methods over the past 40 years to engender an understanding of, and achieve compliance with, the homework tasks I have given, is the common sense one that I write all homework instructions on a dated system card which clients take with them. This is to aid memory (essential with so many distressed, distracted, and medicated clients), to keep organised (I generally give multiple homeworks, such as one cognitive, one behavioural, one general, one specific), to make homework instructions official (not just 'words in the air'), to personalise them (I handwrite homework instructions while verbally describing them), and for clients to keep and to refer to if/when relapses occur. On the same cards are written our policies, decisions, mottos, helpful 'self-talk' and so on, as well as personalised PMC diagrams as we identify them. As people leave each session I photocopy for myself their new 'homework card', along with any writings, records, past homework completed, or Negative Emotion Records (see Homeworks 1, 2, and 3) they have brought in. This means I don't have to use valuable session time reading reams. But it also recognises any work done, makes us all more accountable, and gives everyone a copy to keep and use in the future.

* I have yet to discover a better label than 'homeworks', despite its off-putting connotations for many clients. 'Followups', 'action on decisions', 'change strategies' all don't inspire. Other suggestions have been: 'between session activities', 'between session work', and 'between session challenges'. I am open to suggestions!

HOMEWORK 1

Negative Emotion Records (NERs)

Many CBT texts and manuals outline a core paper-based or digital self-monitoring system for clients to record and analyse occasions of problematic distress. Most of these derive from Beck et al.'s (1979) Daily Record of Dysfunctional Thoughts, or Albert Ellis's 'triple-column technique' or REBT Self-Help Form (Burns, 1980; Dryden & Walker, 1996).

The variant I prefer — Negative Emotion Record (NER) sheets — is illustrated in Table H-1.

As a ***clinical*** tool the process described below has been easily adopted by clients, has linked the CBT model (Figure 3.1) to everyday experience, and has allowed expansion to include identification or analysis of 'thinking errors', 'irrational beliefs', or coping style tendencies, and has naturally led on to other homework described in this volume.

Instructions may be altered according to whether anxiety, depression, anger, or other feelings are the likely focus.

Write summary on homework card while saying:

I'd like you to pick a regular time, at least once a day, maybe after dinner or before bed, to sit down with these NER sheets *(provide 3 or 4)* and to jot down any significant bad feelings you have experienced in that day.

You don't have to carry these sheets around with you all the time. This isn't a coping technique to use in the middle of an upset. It's meant to help you learn more about what's going on, and how to cope better, for **tomorrow** or the next time the feeling happens.

But it all does have to be fresh in your mind, so at least once a day would be good.

So when you pull these out of the drawer, I want you to have a think about when you've felt the worst. Hopefully there'll be days when you have a think, and put them back in the drawer! That's great. But there could also be days when two or three separate things have really gotten to you. **You** can decide what's significant enough to bother putting down.

If you think of something, I want you to write on the sheet following the numbers at the top:

After putting in the date, go straight over to '2' *(point)*. Here you write one or two words to describe the bad feeling. *(Give examples.)*

Then, right next to it you score or rate that feeling that happened maybe a couple of hours ago. If you haven't written anything for a while, and you're picking just some little thing that happened so we get something down, give it a '1'. If it completely shattered you, and you went straight home and cried in bed for the rest of the day, give it a '10'. (Vary for different expected target emotions.)

TABLE H-1
Negative Emotion Record

1 *Date*	4 *Situation/event/trigger*	5 *Negative automatic thoughts*	2 *Feeling/emotion*	3 *Emotion rating 1 to 10*	6 *Useful/true/reasonable/thoughts*

(Available as a free download from www.australianacademicpress.com.au)

Then, you go across to '4' and in a few words you describe what you were reacting to. Hopefully you can put your finger on some trigger. But maybe sometimes it's not clear and you'll write just 'Got out of bed'. Some triggers can be external, like someone says something to you. But some may be internal, like 'remembered such-and-such'.

(Present sheet with Figure 3.1)

Then we get to the psychologically interesting bit. We now know that nearly all triggers cause an emotional reaction, **through your brain** *(while pointing to 'Thoughts')*. Often we can't **prevent** upsetting things happening, but we **can** change how we **see** these, so that the feelings aren't so bad *(point to 'Feelings')*.

If it's the first time you've experienced something, this process of perceiving or evaluating a trigger or event can be quite slow, and we can see it happening. 'Is this dangerous? What are my rights here? How likely is this bad thing?' And **then** we react emotionally. But if it's the 10th or the 100th time you've experienced something, the whole thing can happen in a flash *(quickly point from 'events/situation' to 'feelings' on Figure 3.1)*. But the interpretation or perception still happens. It's just very quick. That's why we've got 'Negative **Automatic** Thoughts' in there.

So your job is to put into words, into a sentence, what **about** the situation led to you reacting emotionally.

So far, this is a description of what happened maybe 3 or 4 hours ago. But I don't want you to just sit and write out all of your upsets, so you just feel them all over again. So, the last thing this record asks you to do *(pointing to column 6)* is to add something new. In the last column you write down answers or opposites to the negative automatic thoughts — what you **could** have said to yourself at the time that would have caused a different or better feeling reaction.

(Write in now an example entry perhaps drawn from the client's recent experiences.)

Even if it's hard to come up with something for column 6, maybe because the feeling is still with you, I'd like you to try. Perhaps you could imagine what I'd say or what (spouse/parent/etc.) would say to help you see it differently.

To request NER-writing sessions more than once a day is entirely reasonable, especially with de Craen et al.'s (1999) finding in mind, that 4 placebo pills a day can work better than 2, presumably because this is a more frequent, more intrusive, more active, and therefore a more powerful therapy regime! For people who live alone, the NERs may be helpful as a coping technique, and not just an analysis/educational process. The process can perform the function of 'debriefing' without a support person:

For example, if you get home from a horrible day at work and X says, 'What's wrong with you?' *(point to column 2)*. You'd say, 'I'm angry.' X asks 'How come?' You might say 'Bob at work said I don't do the accounts right' *(point to column 4)*. Then X asks, 'So why did that get to you?' and your answer *(point to column 5)* could be, 'He doesn't appreciate how hard I work. No-one does. The job is a total pain', or other negative 'catastrophising' thinking.

> Then, hopefully, you or X might get to the point of admitting things like *(point to column 6),* 'Do I really care what he thinks?!' 'I know I'm good at the job', 'This was because he was in a bad mood', and so on.
>
> If you don't have someone at the time to go through this with, at least the NERs can help you do it yourself.

The potential benefits of NER homework are numerous:

It can identify and perhaps assist people who have great difficulty in recognising or labelling their emotions. This inability has been referred to as alexithymia (Taylor, 1984). It is reportedly more common in males, (Blanchard et al., 1981), chronic pain patients (Mendelsohn, 1982), substance abuse, PTSD, and depression (Taylor, 1984). It makes psychotherapy difficult (Kennedy & Franklin, 2002) and may suggest the use of behavioural techniques. Biofeedback could be considered as a way to train such people to 'listen to their bodies'. Inasmuch as alexithymia may be a consequence of faulty or inadequate early learning, Script 7 in Section 4 may be used as an introduction to subsequent homework, such as NERs. There is support for the effectiveness of cognitive–behaviourally based therapies for alexithymia, using homework-recording procedures very similar to the NER approach (Kennedy & Franklin, 2002), or in the early stages of therapy for other conditions (Levant, 1998). The process can be regarded as one of 'affective education' (Braswell & Kendall, 2001, p. 259).

NER homework can also help identify whether an emotional problem is more one of anxiety, or depression, or anger, or something else. Often clients will present with a mixture, such as an 'agitated depression'. It may be useful to obtain evidence as to whether they have an anxiety problem (e.g social phobia) that has limited their life to such an extent that they have become depressed; or whether they have become depressed and this has robbed them of confidence in facing life's demands and stresses. Day-to-day sampling can help unravel such dilemmas.

Further, a person may present with an anger problem, because that is what the family or school are upset about, but the person may be experiencing much more (unrecognised) depression. NERs provide information regarding frequency of emotions and their intensity (column 3).

NER homework can tell us what situations or events are resulting in the most frequent emotional responses and the strongest responses. This can be vital in making clinical judgments about whether to target changeable situations, or self-talk about unavoidable situations, or feeling states subsequent to reasonable self-talk, or behaviours subsequent to entrenched thinking and feeling reactions (discussed in Chapter 3).

A key function of NER homework is the identification and addressing of negative thinking patterns — a central source of PMCs. When a sampling of Negative Automatic Thoughts is obtained, it is possible to bracket or classify them in several ways; for example, thinking errors, irrational beliefs, or Seligman's (1990) explanatory styles. This can help simplify the client's ensuing task — that of detecting negative thinking as it occurs in the real world.

The effectiveness of cognitive therapy for depression has been found to correlate with the 'concreteness' of work done early on. That is, the more symptom-focused and active the therapy is, the better the later results (DeRubeis & Feeley, 1990; Feeley et al., 1999). One measure of this concreteness was whether the client was asked early on to record his or her thoughts.

Finally, the NER homework gives clients practice at formulating helpful thoughts. The chances of 'two voices arguing' in one's head are greater after this, as opposed to one negative 'voice'.

The analysis and rehearsal benefits of NER homework can be extended by ensuing homework assignments such as Homeworks 2 and 3.

HOMEWORK 2

NERs + Coping Options

Cognitive–behavioural therapies have been classified into three main types, according to their targets — cognitive restructuring therapies, problem-solving therapies, and coping skills therapies (Mahoney & Arnkoff, 1978). The latter have been supported by a wealth of research into measures of coping style (e.g., Endler & Parker, 1994), treatment/coping style interaction effects (Beutler, Harwood, & Caldwell, 2001, pp. 152–154), and preferred or most effective coping reactions under certain stressors (Miller et al, 1985).

Certain coping options have been shown to be more effective in reducing the problematic results of stress than others. For example, Miller et al. (1985) found getting angry with oneself or others, rumination, drinking alcohol, or smoking, were less useful than talking things over, prayer, relaxation techniques, distraction, or reappraisal. But what is effective depends on many factors, including whether the stressor is, or is seen as, removable or not (Parkes, 1984).

The issue remains, when a certain individual's coping responses are identified in therapy (perhaps via NER recording), as to whether this information is to be used to find their natural coping style to guide therapy selection, or whether their natural reactions can be assumed to be inadequate (or they would not be in therapy), and therefore new, different, better coping responses need to be encouraged or coached.

This dilemma can be avoided if a third approach is taken. It is known that feelings such as anxiety at higher levels interfere with coping (Krohne & Laux, 1982; Schonpflug, 1983; Spielberger, 1972; Van der Ploeg et al., 1984; Wheatley, 2000). So whether the samples of coping response obtained in interview, inventory completion, or daily recording (NERs) are best developed or are best compensated for, any additional coping responses selected and coached can be seen as *broadening the client's coping repertoire.* The research cited indicates a narrowing of coping style under significant stress. Desperate people are more likely to run away, get drunk, take pills, or stew, than to reappraise a situation, problem-solve, or talk it over (Miller et al., 1985). This represents not only a decline in quality of coping responses, but also a narrowing of repertoire. See Figure 6.6(b).

The concept of rebroadening a client's coping repertoire is also an acceptable and easy way to provide a rationale for change. Criticising a client's usual response (e.g. phobic avoidance) is more negative and arguable than suggesting we need a range of coping responses for a range of life situations.

Therefore, a useful adjunct to many instances of NER homework can be:

With recently introduced or completed NER record sheets on the desk:

So far, the NER sheets have given us a chance to find out from real-life examples: What triggers are causing bad reactions, what thinking leads to the bad reactions, what sort of bad reactions, and one way to fight them; that is, talking to yourself differently about the triggers (column 6). But this self-talk is only one better way of coping. There are lots of ways people can cope better with bad situations or feelings. Here are just some (show Table H-2).

The one practised on the NERs in column 6 is No. 3 — 'Have a good calming talk to yourself.' But, depending on the situation, one of the others may work as well or better. For example, if you sit an exam, and the results come out in 3 weeks, what should you do in the meantime? General Coping Option No. 2! Go to the movies. But if your doctor says you have to stop drinking or your liver will explode, is No. 2 a good option? No.

So, to cope well we need a good repertoire of coping options to use.

When a person is under stress, we know that unfortunately their coping repertoire will narrow down usually to the more primitive, early-learned coping options, like running away or getting drunk or collapsing in a heap. People in a falling plane don't think things through deeply (General Coping Option No. 8) or get better organised (General Coping Option No. 15).

TABLE H-2

General Coping Options

1. Solve the problem. Remove the cause of the upset (by being assertive, or changing routine, or reasonable avoidance, or similar constructive action).
2. Distract yourself. Shelve worries until later (do chores, watch TV, hobbies, keep busy, go for a drive …).
3. Have a good calming talk to yourself. Control your thinking.
4. Counteract the feelings. (If tense, use relaxation procedures. If sad, watch a funny film. If flat or bored, listen to music.)
5. Call, talk to, or be with someone. Share it with others. Talk things over. (To clarify, feel understood, or get advice.)
6. Be brave, accept stress as normal, face the fears, and plough on.
7. Become emotional, fall in a heap, cry for help, try to get rescued.
8. Think things through deeply. Get a handle on it by insight or explanation. Read up. Learn lots. Understand.
9. Write it out. (To clarify, put in perspective, get it off your chest, or help with decision-making).
10. See the funny side. Turn it into a (shared?) joke.
11. Time projection. Look back from a year in the future. Get some perspective.
12. Delegate, hand the problem to someone (an expert?). Get professional support.
13. Take on a 'role'. Put on a front. Be professional.
14. Exercise. Burn off stress build-ups.
15. Get organised, plan ahead, make lists, set goals and steps.
16. Pray.
17. Rest, sleep, naps.
18. Be alone. Keep to yourself. Simplify or tone down life.
19. Eat something.
20. Get drunk.
21. Use other drugs.
22. Get a hug.
23. Get angry. Yell. Let off steam.

(Available as a free download from www.australianacademicpress.com.au)

This seems to have happened with you. I think your ways of coping have become more basic since you've been having more problems and stress. That's been a vicious circle, a Catch-22. ***(Illustrate or exemplify from known history or problem formulation.)*** To help rebroaden your coping repertoire, every time you fill in a bad experience on the NER sheets, I'd like you then to go through the General Coping Options sheet (Table H-2), and ask yourself 23 questions: 'Would this have helped if I'd done it? Could this fit with what I went through? What if I do this one next time?' And I'd like you to ***(writing on homework card)*** write in column 6, one or two or three coping option numbers (from Table H-2) of those Coping Options that could have helped the most. ***(Run through a previously written NER entry.)***

We may end up seeing a pattern develop. For example, if Coping Option No. 5 keeps cropping up as something you could have done that would have helped, but you rarely do it, then we know which Coping Option to rehearse for the future.

Where previous NER entries are available:

To start us off, your first homework will be to write in some best coping option numbers next to the entries we already have from last week/fortnight.

The direction of therapy will subsequently be influenced by the client's, and the therapist's, views on which Coping Options are neglected or potentially most useful. For example, general coping option No. 1 may benefit from assertiveness training, No. 2 from thought-stopping, No. 4 from relaxation skills training, No. 15 from coaching in timetabling, and so on.

HOMEWORK 3

NERs + Thinking Errors

Especially when NERs (Homework 1) have been completed and surveyed, but even during interview assessment, it can be suspected that the client has become especially prone to certain *sorts* of negative thinking. If such patterns can be identified then this narrows the range of problem thinking to look out for, and perhaps the 'self-talk' necessary to combat it. This can be a much more manageable task than "fixing my negative thinking".

Among the systems of negative thinking pattern analysis usable with NERs are:

1. Beck et al.'s (1979) 'cognitive errors' (see Table H-3)
2. Ellis's (1962) 'irrational beliefs'
3. Seligman's (1990) 'negative explanatory style'.

Table H-3 lists eleven 'cognitive errors' that NER homework can reveal. This may be a confusing number for many clients. Shorter listings of key or most common thinking mistakes are available in numerous publications (e.g. Burns, 1980, pp. 49–50; Kidman, 1986, pp. 24–27; Kidman, 1999, pp. 17–21).

TABLE H-3
Definitions of 11 Common Cognitive Errors

1. All-or-nothing thinking: Placing experiences in one or two opposite categories – for example, flawless or defective, immaculate or filthy, saint or sinner.
2. Overgeneralising: Drawing sweeping inferences (e.g., 'I can't control my temper') from a single instance.
3. Discounting the positives: Deciding that if a good thing has happened, it couldn't have been very important.
4. Jumping to conclusions: Focusing on one aspect of a situation in deciding how to understand it (e.g., 'The reason I haven't received a phone call from the job I applied to is that they have decided not to offer it to me').
5. Mindreading: Believing one knows what another person is thinking, with very little evidence.
6. Fortunetelling: Believing one knows what the future holds, while ignoring other possibilities.
7. Magnifying/minimising: Evaluating the importance of a negative event, or the lack of importance of a positive event, in a distorted manner.
8. Emotional reasoning: Believe that something must be true, because it feels like it is true.
9. Making 'should' statements: Telling oneself one should do (or should have done) something, when it is more accurate to say that one would like to do (or wishes one had done) the preferred thing.
10. Labelling: Using a label ('bad mother,' 'idiot') to describe a behaviour, and then imputing all the meanings the label carries.
11. Inappropriate blaming: Using hindsight to determine what one should have done even if one could not have known the best thing to do at the time, ignoring mitigating factors, or ignoring the roles played by others in determining a negative outcome.

(Available as a free download from www.australianacademicpress.com.au)

Using Beck's system as an example:

After examining the homework NERs completed:

It looks as though there are certain **sorts** of 'automatic negative thoughts' that have been happening quite a bit. If we can narrow down the sorts we want to look out for and attack, then our job is a bit easier. So, from now on, whenever you write an entry on the NER sheets, I'd like you to write a number next to the 'negative automatic thought' that categorises the thinking according to this list ***(show Table H-3)***. If the same numbers keep cropping up, we know that certain **sorts** of negative thinking are the biggest problem.

In fact, it would be good to look back at the NERs we have already got, and classify them. ***(For example, discuss a past NER, and which cognitive error it illustrates. Write the corresponding number [1–11] in Column 5.)***

HOMEWORK 4

Challenge Diary

The basic principles and procedures of exposure therapy and all its variations are covered in every basic course in CBT. To do justice to the range of approaches encompassing systematic desensitisation, exposure and response prevention, prolonged exposure, graduated exposure, flooding, stress inoculation training, and so on, would require an entire volume; however, elements of these therapies are covered in Homeworks 4, 5, 11, 20, 33, 34, 38, 51, 65, 68, 70, and 71.

Frequently, a therapist will want to initiate more than just a few specific planned exposure experiences. A habit or policy of taking opportunities to face one's fears as they arise can be a better long-term approach, as this can maximise naturalness and generalisation, and many feared situations are hard to construct. Social situations are frequently thus.

So, as well as planning, constructing, and even coaching specific fear exposure exercises, it may be useful to ask a client to record fearful experiences as they arise or are sought out.

In order to imbue this policy with a positive tone, I refer to these fear-facings as 'challenges'.

The aims of record-keeping in this way include: (a) a minimum number of challenges may be stipulated, so movement is encouraged; (b) discussion and planning at subsequent sessions benefits from good information about progress, difficulties, setbacks, and so on; (c) a client can look back over a time period and be reminded of their progress. (Selective negative memory is notorious in anxiety and depression problems.)

What to ask to be recorded is a matter of clinical judgment. Possible inclusions are: Did what? Date? Time? Duration? Where? And any key variables that make a major difference to difficulty, such as: Alone, or in company? With medication or without? and so on.

Almost invariably it is desirable to also ask for a highest Subjective Units of Distress Scale (SUDS) rating for each entry, 0–10 or 0–100 (see Homework 34). This has also been variously labelled the Subjective Units of Disturbance Scale, the Subjective Anxiety Scale (Wolpe, 1973), a fear thermometer, and the Subjective Units of Discomfort Scale (Wolpe & Lazarus, 1966).)

A specifically planned fear exposure program or hierarchy may emerge from these diary records. Its level of ambitiousness can then be a better compromise between being challenged but not overwhelmed (Dryden, 1985).

As well as progressively facing your fears in the way we have worked out, I'd like you to take opportunities as they come up to practise your coping, beat the fears, and prove to yourself that nothing awful will happen. As these 'challenges' come up I want you to record them, to show me next time, on this card/in this diary.

So apart from the date, we're interested in: Where/Who with/How long for … ***(Tailor this section).***

> Also, to see whether you're really pushing it, or going a bit easy, I'd like you to also jot down a SUDS number. SUDS stands for ***(write)*** Subjective Units of Distress Scale. 'Subjective' means it's just how you feel overall inside. 'Units' go from 0 to 10 (or 0–100) and 'Distress' covers any bad feeling like nervousness, panic, worry, upset.
>
> So zero will represent complete calm, total control. I might feel like this on Sunday morning in bed with a cup of tea and the newspaper and nothing to do for the day. Ten means: the worst panic you can remember. So everyone's 10 is different, but it comes from a real memory.
>
> At any one time you will likely be somewhere between 0 and 10. For example, right now, about where is your SUDS level? It looks about a 3 ***(or whatever)***. How far wrong am I?
>
> If possible it would be good to make a rule that you'll do something to face the fear every day. Your diary will show how well you did with this.'

Recording can be on a smartphone. But I prefer hardcopy. Therefore, I buy inexpensive 'student diaries' in bulk (only about $2 each) and hand these out. This increases commitment to, pressure for, immediate start of, convenience of, and seriousness of the prescribed recording homework.

The record will indicate at subsequent consultations whether the client is confronting or avoiding their fears, and whether other details should be recorded. It will provide opportunities for reward/reinforcement/congratulation. It may clarify the nature and focus of the anxiety. And can suggest current, favoured, and neglected coping techniques. Asking about current SUDS level, in interview, can be revealing as well.

HOMEWORK 5

Social Challenge Diary

Homework 4 describes the prescription of a 'Challenge Diary', and the many advantages of such record-keeping.

Social phobia and social anxieties are generally more complex than the other anxiety CPPs, due to the subtleties of social situations, the complexity of perceptions and self-statements in social engagements, and the variability of and difficulty in controlling exposure to them.

I therefore add a key element to the record-keeping of a Social Challenge Diary, beyond the when, where, who with, how long for, and highest SUDS level reached.

I ask clients to also rate and record a How It Went (HIW) score. To avoid confusion with the 0 to 10 or 0 to 100 SUDS score, I recommend an A to E rating system, where A represents 'The purpose of the encounter was achieved totally, and I've made a friend for life,' and E represents 'We got nowhere, and I've made an enemy for life'. This compound rating of Objective Achieved? and Relationship Enhanced? must be clearly distinguished from How Anxious I Got, which is what the SUDS rating represents.

The purpose of this extra rating is to encourage the client to distinguish and appreciate that anxiety is only one criterion, and does not necessarily negate the others. It may also over time help the client to focus more on the function of the encounter and on the quality of the interaction, rather than just their feelings — this being a major strategy and goal in CBT treatment of social phobia.

On follow-up the lack of equivalence, or even of correlation, between the 0 to 10 and the A to E ratings can be emphasised.

HOMEWORK 6

25 Positives

Previous chapters have described the central role that low or 'delicate' self-esteem, self-respect, or self-efficacy feelings can play in both the onset and the maintenance of CPPs. Often the poor self-image is a consequence of having a problem – a clear PMC! – and can benefit from some correction of this distorted view of the self.

Robust arguments against indiscriminate attempts to elevate self-esteem have been advanced by Albert Ellis (Ellis & Harper, 1997) and by Martin Seligman (1995).

Ellis argues that people need to be taught to respect and appreciate themselves because they are people, not because they have some brittle and impermanent desired capacity or quality; or else their self-esteem can just as quickly (and justifiably?) plummet as they encounter failures or rejection. This is a theoretically consistent and admirable position. But it is horrendously difficult to implement without 15 sessions of intensive REBT.

It can equally be argued that depressed people, for example, have not forgotten their 'inherent worth as a person'. Rather they feel they are a disappointment to their spouse, a bad parent, and useless at work, all largely due to their inadequate performance while depressed! Anything that can break the PMC at this point should help. It appears to me more possible to remind a depressed person of their forgotten good qualities, than to assert their philosophical independence from the vagaries of other people's acknowledgement.

Seligman, meantime, has warned us against blanket indiscriminate encouragement. We can dilute our positive interpersonal reinforcement by making it noncontingent. The modern tendency to praise our children's efforts, no matter how nonsensically, in pursuit of high self-esteem, is an example of this. He feels we should aim to help our children learn to cope, not just 'make them happy'. I very much agree with this. See, for example, Bakker (2019), Guideline 7.

But depressed or anxious people have a self-generated bias in the ***other*** direction. They selectively ignore or dismiss the positives. Restoration of some degree of ***balance*** is then justifiable in order to break a negative PMC.

So I readily admit to clientele that their homework may focus sometimes only on the good side, and we know everyone has their not-so-good side. It's a better ***balance*** of appreciation we are after.

Script 1 may be of use, but another basic introduction to addressing a negative self-concept follows:

> When we get together, we inevitably focus a lot on the negatives: What's going wrong? What don't you like about yourself; or how you're coping? and so on.
>
> Because you've been having problems, you've focused for a while on the negatives, but this is only half the picture. The great things about you that you used to see clearly have been forgotten or ignored. If you're going to be strong enough to fight the problems, then you'll need to feel you've got some strengths, **and** you're **deserving** of a better life.

(While writing on the homework card)

So, I'd like you to come back next time with a list written out, on the back of this card, or in a separate book for our homework, of 25 Good Things About You.

I'd like you to include a range of things in the list, like Abilities you have; Achievements you're proud of; things about your Appearance that you like or other people like; Good Deeds that have benefited others; or general qualities of you that others benefit from. (Write these categories on the homework instruction card.)

You're allowed to ask other people for ideas for the list, like ***(insert close person, X, here)***. But if X says you have nice eyes then you don't write 'X thinks I've got nice eyes'. You only write what **you** believe. This is **your** list. So if you agree with them, you just write 'I have nice eyes'.

You'll have to get through this homework one way or another, because if you came back with 25, and it took you 20 minutes to think of them, then I'd have a look, say 'Great', and we'd move on to the next homework. But if you write 15 and it took you 3 weeks to come up with them, that's a bad sign, and part of the remedy is to keep working away at your list!

You'll have to fight the feeling that you're boasting. I'm **asking** you for this list. And I don't want you to show everyone. I just want you to let me in on what you quietly know in your own mind.

This introduction can vary according to the nature of the related presenting problem.

For example, with depression problems, Beck's 'cognitive triad' (Beck et.al., 1979) of a negative view of self, world, and future can be introduced. With anxiety problems, especially social phobia, the notion of confidence is a useful link. With assertiveness deficits concepts of 'self-respect' or 'personal rights' link in. And with anger problems, suspicion of a 'delicate' self-esteem can be raised.

In an attempt to generalise this homework into real-world coping opportunities, a useful follow-up homework once the list is (sufficiently) completed, discussed, and accepted, is:

The process of remembering, and putting into words, and admitting at least to me, all these Good Things About You is a healthy thing to ask you to do, especially given what you've been going through. But I'm more interested in what happens inside you next Tuesday week at 3 o'clock in the afternoon when ***(give example of a possible challenge to the client's self-esteem/self-efficacy drawn from their problem situation)*** you realise you've been too down to get into the housework again, and you start to criticise yourself, as you've being doing a lot lately.

That's the time when you need to remember the Good Things.

But it's not reasonable for me to expect you to stop everything and tell everyone to leave you alone because you're 'trying to remember No. 14'.

So what we want is a shorthand way for the whole idea to come into your thinking. This is to remind you that there are a whole bunch of Good Things About You that are **permanently** true, even in the middle of a big negative mess, and that you **aren't** all bad.

Even this argument is too long to use in your head in real life. So I'd like you to ***(while writing this)*** decide on a Codename or Label for the 25-list, and write this at the top.

A word, or a phrase, or a sentence at the most, something personalised to you would be good, so you could jumble the letters of your name, or you could pick on a nickname you used to be called; a nice one. Or, you could choose a line or the title of a film or book or poem you identify with or feel inspired by.

From now on that name means, to you and me and X, if you tell them about it, that there is a whole big, good side to you that you tend to forget or ignore.

This codename can then be incorporated into other homeworks or coping techniques. For example, it may appear in Column 6 of the NER homeworks (Homeworks 1, 2, 3).

Informed spouses or parents can also have a quick way to prompt healthier thinking at negative or anxious times.

HOMEWORK 7

Socialisation Messages

Although CBT entails an emphasis on current causal pathways (maintainers) rather than historical ones (precipitants), an analysis of past probable factors, beyond the initial interview or functional analysis, is often desired.

Possible reasons for this include:

- the client's insistence on, or preference for, some historical analysis. Clients who present with a clear expectation that developing a theory about where a problem has come from is necessary (or even sufficient!) for improvement to occur, need to be coaxed toward a more useful focus, not dismissed or ignored or overruled immediately.
- sometimes early causal factors are still bearing on the problem, and may be missed in a current functional analysis
- the details surrounding early causes can help guide assessment of current ones.

Self-esteem and assertiveness issues are possible problem areas in which an assessment of early learning influences may be relevant. But the problem areas within which a therapist may wish to help the client explore such history are potentially much broader. Any time the therapist or client wish for more information about earlier learning as a problem precipitant, the following homework gives the client a structure for using the time between consultations to do their own analysis:

We are all given messages as we grow up about ourselves, the world, and how to behave. These messages can come from people directly talking to us, or from what we're praised or punished for, or from watching how other people handle the world. These messages cover everything from what to eat, to how scary the world is, to our feelings about ourselves, and so on. They come especially from our parents, but from other people too.

These messages can be overlearned or underlearned. Your parents didn't decide 'Today we'll tell Mary to share her things, three times. And tomorrow we'll tell her twice'. It just happens. And those people who get undersocialised may end up in gaol. And those who got oversocialised can be stuck with rigid rules that get in the way of leading a full life.

It looks to me like you may have been oversocialised to feel as though … ***(insert here a relevant example. For example … you should put up with problems and not bother other people; and … the world is a dangerous place, so watch out! … if a problem happens, then there isn't much you can do, so hope for someone to help you out …)***

Here are some examples of what we mean by Socialisation Messages. ***(I provide a copy of 'How Socialisation Messages May Negatively Affect Assertion' [Lange & Jakubowski, 1976, pp. 66–68]. Also see Table H-7.)*** But these are only about messages that affect assertiveness. They can affect **any** of our feelings or thinking or behaviour.

Notice they're very, very simple messages. They have to be. You can't have a deep philosophical discussion with a little kid about the rights and responsibilities of living in Western culture. You just say 'Don't eat dirt' or 'Help Bill up, he's fallen over'.

So I'd like you to think about the early influences that probably led you to feel that … ***(insert issue of interest)***. And to write two or three Messages you learned or overlearned. And **who** they came from, because if we are going to change them a bit, then we have to see them as just coming from someone with their own issues going on; not as 'True Rules coming from God'.

Then I'd like you to write out the adult, balanced, complicated, healthy beliefs that should replace the simple ones, now that you can decide for yourself.

Other examples of issues or problems that may usefully be addressed using Socialisation Messages include:

- Anger problems: If father behaved aggressively often, then one can learn 'If you get annoyed the best answer is to lash out, and you're justified to, even if it doesn't fix things'.
- Sexual inhibitions: 'Sex is about men hurting and using women'. Or 'If you can't get an erection you're not a real man'.
- Anxiety disorders: 'If something makes you anxious, you should keep away from it'.
- Depression: 'You can't control life, so just lump it'.
- Relationship problems: 'Don't trust anyone'.

A focus on Socialisation Messages is another angle from which to approach what others have called Core Beliefs, Irrational Beliefs, Schemas, and so on.

TABLE H-7
How Socialisation Messages May Negatively Affect Assertion

Socialisation message	*Effect on rights*	*Effect on assertive behaviour*	*Healthy message*
Think of others first; give to others even if you're hurting. Don't be selfish.	I have no right to place my needs above those of other people's.	When I have a conflict with someone else, I will give in and satisfy the other person's needs and forget about my own.	To be selfish means that a person places his desires before practically everyone else's desires. This is undesirable human behaviour. However, all healthy people have needs and strive to fulfil these as much as possible. Your needs are as important as other people's. When there is conflict over need satisfaction, compromise is often a useful way to handle the conflict.
Be modest and humble. Don't act superior to other people.	I have no right to do anything which would imply that I am better than other people.	I will discontinue my accomplishments and any compliments I receive. When I'm in a meeting, I will encourage other people's contributions and keep silent about my own. When I have an opinion which is different from someone else's I won't express it.	It is undesirable to build yourself up at the expense of another person. However, you have as much right as other people to show your abilities and take pride in yourself. It is healthy to enjoy one's accomplishments.
Be understanding and overlook trivial irritations. Don't be a bitch and complain.	I have no right to feel angry or to express my anger.	When I'm in a line and someone cuts in front of me, I will say nothing. I will not tell my girlfriend that I don't like her constantly interrupting me when I speak.	It is undesirable to deliberately nitpick. However, life is made up of trivial incidents and it is normal to be occasionally irritated by seemingly small events. You have a right to your angry feelings, and if you express them at the time they occur, your feelings won't build up and explode. It is important, however, to express your feelings assertively rather than aggressively.
Help other people. Don't be demanding.	I have no right to make requests of other people.	I will not ask my girlfriend to reciprocate babysitting favours. I will not ask for a pay increase from my employer.	It is undesirable to incessantly make demands on others. You have a right to ask other people to change their behaviour if their behaviour affects your life in a concrete way. A request is not the same as a demand.
Be sensitive to other people's feelings. Don't hurt other people.	I have no right to do anything which might hurt someone else's feelings or deflate someone else's ego.	I will not say what I really think or feel because that might hurt someone else. I will inhibit my spontaneity so that I don't impulsively say something that would accidentally hurt someone else.	It is undesirable to deliberately try to hurt others. However, it is impossible as well as undesirable to try to govern your life so as to never hurt anyone. You have a right to express your thoughts and feelings even if someone else's feelings get occasionally hurt.

(Available as a free download from www.australianacademicpress.com.au)

HOMEWORK 8

Testimonials

This homework can follow on from Homework 6: Twenty-Five Positives; or it can be an alternative when a client has great difficulty with Homework 6.

It simply seeks to obtain honest positive feedback from people whose opinions matter in the person's life.

As discussed under Homework 6, it is ideally preferable that a person's self-esteem would not depend upon the recognition/acceptance/love/praise of others. But a depressed person, especially, is operating at a more basic level than this. *Anything* that can dent the negative spirals (PMCs) such people are trapped in is worth a try. At least 'everyone hates me' is harder to hold on to when positive feedback intrudes.

> I would like you to ask two (or three) people in your life — people who matter to you — to write down an honest opinion of you. Just a page will do. They can either give it to you, or seal it to pass on to me, or send it straight to me. But they'll know we'll be looking at it together. Ask them to be honest. Who might you ask?

The assumption here is that the majority of descriptions will be overwhelmingly positive. Selecting the right client for this homework can maximise the odds of this occurring. But many depressed and most anxious clients are sensitive people who have put a lot of energy into pleasing others or gaining acceptance and approval. This helps our odds.

Recommending the right people to approach can help too. A concerned and supportive spouse is better than one in the throes of a separation.

Hopefully many people will pick up on the intentions of this homework, and flavour their descriptions accordingly.

I have had only one predominantly negative description to help a client to cope with. This involved cognitive therapy techniques of reframing, seeing the one opinion in context, seeing the motives/explanations behind the opinion, seeing the feedback as something to learn from, etc.

But normally the follow-up to this homework is a process, in session, of reinforcing the content returned, contrasting this with the client's self-concept, extrapolating to how **most** other people would see the client, emphasising the permanence of the positives, and so on.

A 'codename' similar to or the same as the Twenty-Five Positives codename (Homework 6) can then be selected as a prompt for future in vivo recognition of one's positive side.

HOMEWORK 9

Personal Rights Listing

In order to behave more assertively, compatible thinking is generally necessary. The concept of 'personal rights' provides an introduction to assertiveness-compatible thinking that is easy to understand and can be readily linked to a client's presenting problems.

Numerous tests and manuals provide lists of general personal rights recognised in Western culture (Alberti & Emmons, 1974; Bloom, Coburn & Pearlman, 1975; Fensterheim & Baer, 1975; Galassi & Galassi, 1977; Lange & Jakubowski, 1976). I provide a handout with some of these listings, which also incorporates Table H-9.

(While drawing attention to the bottom of Table H-7)

In order to **act** more assertively, we first have to get our **thinking** right. In our culture there are certain 'personal rights' that in general we all agree on most of the time.

For example, if you asked to be left alone to lie in the bath quietly for half an hour, but ***(spouse, child, etc.)*** kept interrupting you, then nearly everyone would agree this isn't right. But you couldn't take ***(spouse, child, etc.)*** down to the police station and get them locked up. We're not talking **legal** rights; we call these 'personal rights'.

When you behave as though other people are **more** important than you are ***(point to Table H-9)***, then you're being submissive or nonassertive. When you behave as though your personal rights are more important than other people's we call this aggression. So that's more than just hitting people. When you behave as though **everyone's** rights are equally important, then you'll be assertive.

So one reason you have found it hard to be assertive about your needs is that you haven't recognised your own personal rights at the time enough.

I'd like you to start writing out on a big sheet of paper an ongoing list of some of your personal rights as they crop up day-to-day. It'll be headed 'My Personal Rights' and it'll start with '1. I have the Right to …' ***(write this out)***. Each day, when you get home, or before bed, I'd like you to add any new ones that you think of because of situations you've had that day.

There are millions of them. This ***(show handout of sample Personal Rights listings)*** lists some general ones I got out of books. But the ones you write will probably be more specific. For example … ***(Illustrate a personal right derived from the client's history or presenting problem. For example, 'I have the right to know what's expected of me at work.')***

You can ask people about what you write, because this is a cultural thing, and people's opinions matter on this. I'd like to see what you write, just to check it doesn't go too far. For example, I wouldn't want to see 'I have the right to have ***(spouse)*** bloody well do as he's told.'

The listing process, because it is happening ***between*** consultations, has a greater chance of producing a generalised effect than discussion and coaching purely in session. It also provides for input from significant others. As well as assisting the client, this can be educative for those others too.

Follow up when rights lists return can take numerous directions. Clinical judgement is then necessary.

(**NB:** A parallel process is possible with clients who present with anger problems. But the personal rights of ***others*** is then subjected to regular listing.)

TABLE H-9
Personal Rights: Mine Versus Others'

Nonassertive, Passive, Submissive	*Assertive*	*Aggressive*
Self, OTHERS'	SELF, OTHERS'	SELF, Others'

HOMEWORK 10

'I' Statements

Numerous manuals and guides are available to assist people in increasing their assertiveness capacity or comfort. When a full training program is not necessary or possible, a few key hints may suffice.

They need to be simple, because generalisation from the therapy session to the heat of the real-life moment is difficult. 'I' statements can be a good start.

Whenever you have something a bit difficult or negative or confronting to say to someone, there are at least two different ways you can go about it: You can talk about them, or about yourself.

If you talk about them — that is, start your sentence with 'you' — first, it can sound attacking right from the start. 'You shouldn't do that!' People can get their backs up right away.

But the main problem with 'you' statements is that the topic of the conversation is the other person. And they are the world expert on that topic. So you're almost sure to be wrong!

If you turn what you want to say into an 'I' statement about yourself, then **you're** the world expert — 'I'm upset about ... I don't like ... I get worried when ...' — then the other person can't really say, 'No you're not'. The worst they can say is 'I don't care'.

The other advantage of 'I' statements is that over time you are educating the other person about the effects of their behaviour on you. This is especially useful with kids. Imagine being told 10,000 times from 5-years-old to 17-years-old: 'You're too noisy. You shouldn't do that. You are a pest ...' versus being told ' I can't hear the TV when you talk so loudly. I'm worried about how much homework you do. I'm getting a headache from your interruptions ...'

People who talk about themselves all the time are a pain. So, I'm **only** talking here about delicate or confronting or negative things that need saying.

So the next time you ***(give example here from known history)*** feel that Bill is being too nasty with the kids, try to stop for 5 seconds before saying anything, and then come out with a statement about how **you're** feeling. Like 'I hate it when everyone yells like this', or 'I want us to handle these things in a nicer way.'

HOMEWORK 11

Positive Assertiveness

We often expect clients to move directly from habitual nonassertion, to assertiveness over negative or contentious issues. This is presumably because it is a negative or contentious situation that has sparked the interest in their assertiveness.

But a useful step in the hierarchy of fear-confrontation is to practise some positive assertion. This still requires honest expression and initiation of significant decisions or changes, but toward a hopefully very rewarding goal, not just the elimination of a negative.

For example, to encourage and coach someone in suggesting a family outing to their partner, or suggesting a purchase, or initiating sex, or arranging a party, involves decisiveness, risks, initiative, and forceful communication, but with a potentially highly positive result.

HOMEWORK 12

Locus of Control Speech Correction

An attitude of helplessness (Seligman, 1990), or lowered self-efficacy (Bandura, 1977), or external locus of control (Rotter, 1966) can be exacerbated by recent events, such as a traumatic experience, or the development of a CPP (a very PMC phenomenon); or, it can take the form of a long-term tendency. In the latter case, more protracted or 'deeper' forms of therapy may be considered, such as dialectical behaviour therapy (Linehan, 1993) or schema-focused cognitive therapy (Young, 1990).

When these attitudes are partly a response to having difficulties, they contribute to many PMCs and are, therefore, worthy of intervention.

Many approaches are available to challenge these attitudes. Which approach is chosen may depend upon the terminology, concepts, or specific attitudes and self-talk expressed by a client. For example, a client who frequently or emphatically describes their unhappiness as a direct result of uncontrollable events may lead the therapist to cite Ellis's fifth 'Popular Irrational Belief', that 'Human happiness is caused by factors outside one's control, so little can be done about it.' Another description by a client of a similar attitude may lead the therapist to suggest a series of self-efficacy-restoring tasks, or of 'experiments' to test out the validity of this helpless stance.

If a negative or helpless attitude is revealed by the ***language*** used by a client, their very word use may be challenged, on the understanding that speech, being a 'Behaviour' in Figure 3.1, influences thinking.

Language that may be worthy of challenging includes 'I can't', 'makes me', 'I must', 'he drives me to it', 'Panic comes over me', and so on.

This approach can be seen as a variant of cognitive therapy that begins with quoting back to a client their precise words in describing a problem. So, some verbatim notes need to be kept. Then their expressions are challenged, perhaps using the Figure 3.1 model.

Example A

'I can't go to that supermarket any more.'

But, you did go last month. So 'can't' isn't quite right. And the more you say 'can't', the more you'll believe it and get more stuck. When you went last month it felt really awful. So do you really mean 'it's hard for me to'? Or ' I don't want to enough'? Or 'I refuse to'? Or something else?

Example B

'The guilt makes me feel terrible.'

We know that when people are depressed, they will think negatively about everything, including themselves. We've also talked about how you've been feeling guilty about a lot of things — even about feeling depressed! And how you've done less with the kids because of being depressed. That's one of our PMCs ***(show Figure 6.4 (e) or (g) or (i) or (o)***. We've also looked at how it is people's interpretations of what's going on that are the real cause of bad feelings ***(show Figure 3.1)***. So how about 'I feel guilty about doing less with the kids'? We can do something about this. But we can't go and shoot the big black furry 'guilt' that has been 'making you' feel terrible.

HOMEWORK 13

Options Clarification

Indecisiveness and muddled thinking are common in distressed states, and contribute to CPPs via many PMCs, such as Figures 6.1 (g), (i), and (k), and Figures 6.4 (b), (h), (l), and (s).

At times the simplest levels of problem-solving or decision-making are dysfunctional.

This can also occur when a person has too many options before them.

At these times the simple act of clarifying, verbalising, and writing down the main options can help a client to:

(a) feel they are being heard

(b) feel less trapped

(c) take the first steps in problem-solving

(d) see the clearly preferred option and vacillate less.

When the client appears uncertain of their policy in future consultations, the written list can be referred to.

As the introductory script for such a procedure is too variable, an example of the process will be given:

It commonly occurs that a client working through the Workers Compensation system will feel caught between: (a) the added stress of prescribed assessments by unsympathetic doctors, the stigma of being 'on compo', the required treatments and rehabilitation stages, the forms, the sense of being on trial, and so on; and (b) the financial support the system provides.

In such a circumstance I may write down with the client such options as:

1. Opt out. Go and do your own thing. Muddle through without them.
2. Play the game. See it as your new, involuntary, full-time job.
3. Push for some sort of settlement very soon, even if it's not the best you can get.
4. ....

Room for further options is always clearly marked on any homework cards. Sharing with partners/parents, and friends, is encouraged.

To feel that there *are* options, even if not taken up, can help a person to feel less trapped, and to tolerate a situation more easily; self-efficacy is enhanced.

A similar tactic is used when the client is asked, 'How bad does it need to get before you'll resign/separate/drop that sport/take the Valium?' Once this is roughly determined, a person can more happily tolerate higher levels of distress. They have an 'out' if it worsens.

HOMEWORK 14

Decisions Book

Difficulty with decision-making is very common when people are caught up in mood-perpetuating Depression PMCs. Unfortunately this can, in turn, prevent a person from altering depressing, negative life circumstances. Common resultant PMCs can include Figure 6.4 (b), (h), (l), and (s).

When anxiety is prominent, balanced decision-making can be impaired, or the execution of decisions can be retarded by the 'paralysing' effects of fear, as in Figure 6.1 (g), (i), and (k).

Such PMCs may be overcome in several ways. The advice, reassurance, or intervention of family or of the therapist may help a depressed or anxious person accept or follow through an important decision. Often people in crisis are advised *not* to make life-changing decisions while in an unbalanced state. But some day-to-day decisions are necessary for a person's problems to be overcome. And, unless a legal care or treatment order is in place, the person with the problem needs to ultimately make or accept the relevant decisions.

The following homework is an example of the 'problem-solving therapy' arm of CBT:

I'd like you to buy an exercise book or a pad ***(or supply one at the time)*** and to label it, or regard it from now on, as your 'Decisions Book'.

You've got a lot to think about and some important decisions to make, to get on top of the problems you've told me about. And in the state you're in, it can be really hard to think straight and be decisive. So getting some of that decision-making out of your head and onto paper may help.

(A computer screen is an option for some clients.)

From here several specific process instructions are possible, depending on whether the client has a current two-option dilemma, or general muddled or slowed thinking, or an identifiable problem-solving skills deficit. Where this homework is motivated by a specific, current dilemma, such as leave or stay with a partner, or resign versus stay with a job:

On page one I want you to write out all the options about ***(insert topic)*** you can think of. You may have only been thinking about two so far. But here I want you to come up with more — at least three or four — even if they don't seem practical at first. Some may be compromises. Then, you write Option 1 across the top of pages 2 and 3, Option 2 above pages 4 and 5, and so on. Then on the left-hand page I'd like you to write all the reasons you can think of to do Option 1. We might head this page 'pros'. On the right-hand page, you'll write all the reasons you can think of not to do Option 1. We can head this page 'cons'. You may get some ideas for either side by talking with ***(insert relevant names)***. Then, do the same for Option 2, and 3, and …

> After you've thought of these for a while, maybe a couple of days, then start giving each argument on both sides of each option a score, maybe out of 10, or out of 100, according to how important each pro or con is to you.
>
> Then you can add up the ratings on each side and see what you get. If you don't like what you end up with, **this** might even be a hint about what you'd really prefer.
>
> But if you baulk at the result, this could just be a fear of short-term pain for long-term gain. So maybe it would help to label each argument on both sides short-term ('s-t') or long-term ('l-t') and add up your ratings again separately under these headings.

The above may become complicated, especially for a person in distress, so the latter stages may need to be coached/guided. This is then problem-solving training in therapy. But the early stages of exploring and specifying some of the pros and cons can be useful solo homework. This way the therapist can concentrate on process, rather than be led by their own preference as to the resulting decision.

Where general muddled or slowed thinking is the indicator for a Decisions Book, its content may be less structured, like a journal. This can be useful when the thinking problem seems to arise from depression, anxiety, medication, acquired brain injury, or even psychosis. It can also be useful in ongoing assessment.

In such circumstances, homework instructions may be:

> In this book I'd like you to write down some of your thoughts about your difficult decisions and problems as they crop up. You don't have to carry it around with you, but if you could jot some things most days, that'd be good. The idea is to get some of this out on paper where you or we can look at it more clearly, instead of having it go round and round inside your head. ***(Give examples from known history/problems.)***

This homework is like a very nonspecific NER exercise (Homework 1).

Direction of therapy subsequent to this homework is limitless. It may lead to more specific problem-solving exercises or more specific cognitive therapy. But, in the meantime, it can be therapeutic in itself.

Some clients present with a long-term generalised problem-solving skills deficit. Their current or presenting problem may be just the most recent expression or result of this deficit. The history may be suggestive of such a long-term deficit (many dubious decisions and maladaptive reactions to difficulties), or current responses to difficulties may appear 'systemic' or 'characterological', rather than out of character due to being in crisis. This requires a high level of clinical acumen to judge, or some convincing test results. Or it can be suggested by pervasive 'external locus of control' language. (See Homework 12.) An early history of exposure to poor problem-solving models can also be suggestive.

In such a circumstance, a Decisions Book will be just one part of a general problem-solving skills training program (Nezu, Nezu, & Perri, 1989); perhaps the part that links therapy sessions with homework assignments.

Homeworks 15, 16, and 17 (Values, Goals, and Plans) offer a parallel decision-making, prioritizing, or clarifying process, that could be completed as homework in the Decisions Book.

All the homeworks so far are examples of breaking a difficult or daunting process down into manageable sequenced steps. This is a very behavioural approach to a cognitive problem, and parallels a fear-facing process.

A Decisions Book also provides a concrete opportunity to trigger communication with significant others, much as showing NERs to a spouse can help. It can be good to specifically suggest this as an option. The client will, of course, choose what they are comfortable showing to whom.

HOMEWORK 15

Values Ordering/Priorities Clarification

Many clients in crisis, or after a sustained period of disruption in their lives, lose perspective with regard to what really matters most to them or can most directly lead to happiness, contentment, or a feeling of control, direction, or purpose in life.

Life stresses (see Homework 42) that result in an anxiety-related CPP can lead also to preoccupation with whatever area of life is dysfunctional (e.g. work) to the exclusion of areas which are usually more closely linked to the person's emotional health and happiness (e.g. family). What is 'usual' in this sense has been thoroughly researched in the general population (Argyle, 1987), but individual differences warrant some assessment of this issue with each client.

Depression commonly entails some loss of motivation and direction. The possibility of restoring this through CBT is greater in areas of life crucial to an individual client. ("If I suggest you should go and do a course, so you can get some sense of achievement back, and if Education/Learning is No. 14 on your list of life priorities, then I'd be barking up the wrong tree.")

Multiple problems or stresses can overwhelm because a person doesn't know where to start addressing them. A clinician may choose to begin with a very remediable problem (e.g. panic attacks while shopping) or a very crucial problem (e.g. communication with spouse). Again, we need to know what is crucial for each client.

This homework can serve as a cognitive equivalent of the behavioural Reinforcement Survey Schedule (Cautela & Kastenbaum, 1967).

This Values Ordering homework and the two following (16: Values Into Goals; 17: Goals Into Plans) also have a parallel in the values work encouraged by Acceptance and Commitment Therapy (ACT; Hayes, 2005; Hayes, Strosahl, & Wilson, 1999). The difference lies in the rationale for the homework. Hayes (2005, pp. 153–154) compares the journey of accumulating life experiences to a bus driver picking up desirable and undesirable passengers. He quite rightly urges against stopping the bus to try to change or eject the troublesome passengers. Instead, he encourages acceptance, and keeping on driving. Recognition of one's route and aims (values and purpose) is helpful in this. In mainstream CBT, and in Homeworks 15, 16, and 17, the intention is not to accept the problem passengers (negative past experiences), but deliberately to travel on to collect compensating, reassuring, strong positive passengers, so the disruptive ones have to sit quietly at the back. ('The mind works by addition, not by subtraction.') ACT encourages acceptance, so one can get on with one's life. Homeworks 15 to 17 encourage getting on with one's life, so that problems can be overcome rather than avoided. The very act of examining and reflecting on one's intrinsic values (e.g. a close relationship) has been shown to directly and immediately assist a person's sense of wellbeing (Lekes et al., 2012).

Read out while writing on homework card:

Put the following areas of your life into current order of importance:

(Tailor list to what is known of the client. For example, with eating disorders 'Being slim' may be included. For a conscientious environmentalist 'Self-sufficiency' or 'Protecting the planet' may be included. But for most people the following may suffice.)

I'll write these down in a random order. There's no right or wrong order. We need all sorts of people in the world. The only way you can be wrong is if you don't **live up to** your priorities, maybe because of pressure from people, or because of what's 'in your face' each day, like work. Then you can forget over time what your real priorities are.

Friends / Social Life	Free time / Leisure
Education / Learning[1]	Religion[5]
Health[2]	Job Satisfaction
A Community Role[3]	Financial Security[6]
Travel	Career Advancement
A Close Relationship[4]	Family[7]
	Other[8]

Explanations to give while writing the list on the Homework card:

1. *Getting qualifications, or just learning as a satisfaction in itself.*
2. *You can break this up into Emotional Health and Physical Health if you'd like. This list is just a guide.*
3. *This is broader than Friends/Social Life. It's about involvement in charities or politics or clubs ...*
4. *I haven't written (spouse/partner) down because this isn't about her/him or how that's going. It's about* ***you****, and how central this aspect is to your life.*
5. *Or Spirituality or whatever is a better label.*
6. *This is a better label than 'Money'. It makes people think.*
7. *Or 'Family Time'. Or you can break this up into 'Extended Family' and 'The Kids' or whatever.*
8. *If there's any big area I've missed, then put it in. This is only a guide.*

(Some people return with 'Happiness' or 'Contentment' or 'Satisfaction in Life' included. This begs the questions, though, of what areas can best provide this.)

Now, this can be a hard thing to do, because most of us want most of the things on the list. But even if we just end up with a 'top half' and a 'bottom half' we're getting somewhere.

Sometimes, in order to get **some** answer from ourselves, it might help to ask all-or-none type questions. For example, with 'Health' and 'Travel', would you rather see the world, but be coping with awful health problems, or would you rather be stuck in X all your life but in great health until you drop dead at 99 years of age? This is hypothetical, but at least it can give you an answer.

Discussion of resulting rankings at the next consultation can take many different directions. Greater therapist understanding of the client generally ensues. Comparison between current lifestyle and the rankings is a useful challenge. Note can be taken of whether the presenting problems are in high or low ranking areas of life, and some perspective can be returned. Further homework suggestions ***in identified key areas*** can be selected.

Frequently, Homeworks 16 and 17 are useful follow-ups.

Where depression is the presenting problem, Values Ordering can suggest areas in which motivation, interest, or pleasure may most easily or crucially be restored. It can also assist decision-making, and feed into any therapeutic Problem-Solving Training (D'Zurilla & Nezu, 2001), as it assists prioritising of needs or wants or goals.

In anxiety problems, Values Ordering can help regain some perspective on what is worth feeling stressed over, and what is not. And it can help rank those life changes that may be necessary and possible to reduce stress.

This homework can also be given to couples in counselling. They should be asked to rank their lists independently before comparing. ***Understanding*** of each other's worldview is the goal. But the hope is that small differences may emerge, but not large ones. Small differences can result in the members of the couple being more interesting or 'mind-expanding' to each other, as when the more socially-inclined partner arranges their social life, or the more financial cautious one does the budgeting. But if one has 'Religion' at the top and the other has it at 14th place, then problems can ensue. And if the positions of 'Close Relationship' are at variance then lop-sided dependence, jealousy, or frustrations can occur. It is a matter for the client as to whether they reveal to their partner where Close Relationship has been ranked.

It is common for people to rank Family, Health, Close Relationship, and Job Satisfaction or Financial Security quite highly. If something else is ranked at number one or two, this does not indicate that the person has their priorities 'wrong'! It tells you something important that you need to know (and accept) about them. Religion seems to emerge at or near the top in a small proportion of people, and toward the bottom for the rest.

HOMEWORK 16

Values Into Goals

Especially if Values Ordering is used to restore some motivation, interest, pleasure, or direction in life, then more than ranked phrases on a page are necessary. The first step in applying them is to ask clients what they mean by Job Satisfaction, for example, and what would count or where they would like to be with this area of their lives.

While writing this on the homework card:

With the top four ***(or three? or five?)*** value areas you've ranked, I'd like you to write out about a half a page — more than a sentence, but not an essay — about where you **hope to head** in each area over the next 5 ***(or another number)*** years.

I say 'hope to head' because I'm not really concerned with whether you actually get there. This isn't a contract. All we want is some **direction**.

As they say, 'Life is a journey'. If you get to somewhere, you'll just have to find a new goal or direction anyway. I just want to find out what Job Satisfaction (or other applicable example) means to **you**.

When this homework returns, once again discussion can go in numerous directions. How realistic, modest, or idealistic a person is may be revealed. An opportunity to explain what matters ***most*** to ***them*** can be useful to the client and for the therapeutic relationship. It is important that this discussion be with an outside person, like you, rather than their spouse, family, boss, or workmates, who are too involved in these priorities and direction in life.

While useful cognitively, this homework does not guarantee a generalised or practical impact on the client's life. Homework 17 is an appropriate follow-up.

HOMEWORK 17

Goals Into Plans

When the client has elaborated on some direction or goals, in those areas of life that they report matter the most to them, it is reasonable to ask: So, what are you going to *do* along these lines, then? This is especially relevant with depressed clients, or those paralysed by anxiety.

While writing this on the homework card:

With each of the four (or five or ...) areas of life you've written about, I'd like you to pick out, and write down, two specific things you will do in each area toward those goals within the next 2 ***(or 3 or ...)*** months.

These don't have to be big things. There'll be eight ***(or 10 or ...)*** of them. But they do have to be **specific** things you will **do**. So that in 2 ***(or 3 or ...)*** months if we sit here I'll be able to ask you: 'When did you do this one?' and you'll say 'Last Tuesday week.'

So 'Be nicer to Mary' is too vague. But 'Phone Bill about applying for that job' is fine.

So the first question was the *philosophical* one about what matters in life (Homework 15). The second was the *psychological* one about what you're after in these areas (Homework 16). And this one is the *behavioural* question about what you're going to do about it.

At the next consultation these can be reviewed for specificity and realism. Often some will have already been undertaken. Ensuing commitments, decisions, pleasures, and so on — anything contrary to depression–maintaining PMCs — is to be encouraged.

Even better is a full review of the listed undertakings after the 2 or 3 months.

(Numbers here are fairly arbitrary. For example a person who is currently unemployed may be given a shorter timeline. They have more time to do their homework. A person who is seriously depressed may be given fewer actions to undertake. Successes — even small ones — are more difficult and more critical for these people.)

Homeworks 15, 16 and 17 form a sequential program aimed at breaking the PMCs involved in most depression or anxiety problems, as illustrated in Figures 6.1 and 6.4. They are sequential in the sense that they progress from the almost-philosophical (Values) to the psychological (Goals) to the behavioural (Plans).

HOMEWORK 18

Self-Organisation

The simplest or clearest point at which to break PMCs is often at the *behavioural* level. Anything that can help a person behave in a nonproblematic way, despite problematic situations, thoughts, and feelings, is likely to help at least reduce the problem maintenance.

Many of us manage to do what we are disinclined to by scheduling ourselves. We write timetables for study. We book appointments at the dentist. We put aside Thursday evenings to iron in front of the TV.

Such calendar/timetable/diary systems have other great benefits. They help us remember, which stressed and depressed people find difficult. They enable prioritising of tasks or duties, by requiring proportionate time allocation and set-time deferments. They help us pace ourselves to avoid boredom or overtiredness. They are a check on balances in life such as overall draining tasks (chores, employment, childcare ...) versus overall recharging activities (socialising, recreation, sleep ...). And they enable decision-making.

People who are depressed, anxious, or in pain are known to be deficient in many of these areas. They are prone to forgetfulness, decision-making difficulty, self-doubts, disorganisation, inertia, poor pacing, and absence of pleasurable or 'recharging' activities.

It is therefore likely that, whatever system a client usually lives with or is currently operating, it will be therapeutically helpful to restore or elaborate on their self-organisation.

Begin with an assessment of usual and current self-organisation systems. People in distress often don't maintain their usual system. This forms its own PMC. Ask about calendars, diaries, lists, electronic organisers, notebooks, timetables, apps, etc.

Have available, to illustrate or provide, diaries (I buy cheap student ones in bulk), pocket notepads, specialised daily or weekly personal organisation sheets (as in Kidman, 1986), and weekly timetable sheets.

Specific instructions or elaborations on a person's system will depend upon their current system, and the purposes in mind. For example, diarising to fight lethargy will be quite different from timetabling to moderate one's pacing with a chronic pain problem, or where hypomanic episodes are to be avoided. A common approach may be:

Most of us need to organise ourselves on paper or electronically, so we will remember appointments and chores and grocery lists. I use ... What do you usually use? ... Have you been doing this much recently? ...

Now in difficult times, like you've been having recently, this sort of thing is even more important. Not only to fight forgetfulness, but for lots of other reasons. Our system can help with making decisions, with getting going when we've got no drive, with pacing yourself, and balancing out the good and the bad.

You've already described to me how it's been hard for you to get motivated to do things/ ***(or)*** your concentration and memory have been bad/ ***(or)*** you're having trouble making decisions/ ***(or)*** you're getting behind with homework, study, time visiting mum.../ ***(or)***) you don't fit nice times for yourself in any more/ ***(or)*** ...

I think you're going to have to use more of a system to organise yourself to get on top of this, for a while.

Exactly what system is up to you, but I'll suggest two things. First, I'd like you to start to carry this pocket notepad and pencil around with you all the time. Keep it with your wallet/purse, watch, keys, or phone, and start jotting down lots of things as soon as they come up or you think of them. Not just appointments, but things to do, things to buy, names to remember, decisions you make, at least once a day then go through it and edit it. Some things will then transfer to this diary ***(provide)***. In the diary you'll write appointments, work times, housework times, things to do. As you do them, tick them off. This is a little reward. Anything you don't get done gets crossed off and right away written in for tomorrow or next week. You'll have to decide how urgent it is, and when you've got time to fit it in easily.

There are other ways you could run a system like this. Some people use a spreadsheet weekly timetable like this ***(show)***. Some use elaborate daily and weekly sheets ***(show)***. Some use an electronic personal organiser, or their computer or smartphone. Or a calendar on the fridge, especially when they have to coordinate with the rest of the family.

Next time we meet I'd like to see how you've gone with the notepad and diary system, or show me any of the other ways if you decide to use them instead or as well.

At the next appointment review the effectiveness and efficiency of the system selected. It needs to make remembering, pacing, and so on, easier; not be another opportunity for a depressed person to fail!

The information such a review provides can be surprising and invaluable. Indications will emerge as to how much and how complex the homework is that a person can cope with. The overall activity level currently occurring will be indicated. I am often surprised at the sparsity of some depressed people's lives, or the huge loads some overstressed people cope with day-to-day. A check on the spread of activities through the week is useful, as is a picture of the volume of 'draining' versus 'recharging' activities.

Regularity of activity, sleep, exercise, eating, and so on, can be gauged too. But the main aim is to assist functioning, self-control, and insight.

Other homeworks with similar goals aim to assist decision-making (Homework 13, 14), prioritising (Homework 15), initiative (Homeworks 16, 17), and balance in life (Homeworks 21, 22, 23).

More basic timetabling or diary use strategies are also available for people whose depression is too severe for them to cope with a normal diary-type system (Homeworks 19, 20).

HOMEWORK 19

15-Minute Time Slots

When depression or the paralysis of acute anxiety is too severe for normal systematic daily self-organisation, like following a routine or a diary system, then goals and expectations need to be reduced, to avoid 'another failure experience'.

For example, if a depressed person has tried to plan their day, but reports that they are too negative or lethargic or indecisive to get started; if they feel overwhelmed by the challenge of the day, such that they don't go to the supermarket as planned because it's all too big a series of decisions and stresses; if a severely anxious agoraphobic is daunted at the prospect of driving into the city to walk through the mall; then I recommend that their day be broken up into steps of 15 minutes only, whether on paper or in the mind.

If this strategy is used purely mentally:

> It's clear that these challenges are too big for you the way you've been thinking and feeling recently. The size of the job in front of you and all the steps involved put you off even starting. From now on I want you to think only of the next quarter-hour. If you see the mess in the kitchen, but it's all too much, and you feel like closing the door and going and sitting somewhere else, I want you to say 'It's five past nine. I'll potter with the washing up until twenty past, and then I'll sit down even if it's still a mess'. When you do this, often you'll end up clearing it all up, or maybe not. But at least you got started. The same with getting to the shops. Don't think about the whole big horrible job in front of you. Make a decision only about the next 15 minutes: 'I'll make a list. Then have a cuppa … I'll get in the car and drive to town. Then I'll see how I feel. I might just go home if it's awful'.
>
> So our goals from now on are just to do something useful for the next ¼ hour, and then see how you are.

Many people report much more activity when they cease to be daunted by the perception of a huge challenge in front of them. This can produce a self-perpetuating ***positive*** causal circle — a 'virtuous' circle, rather than a 'vicious' circle.

HOMEWORK 20

Achievement Recording

Many CBT homeworks involve recording of challenges, steps, or achievements. These are often specific to a defined problem (e.g. Homework 4). But when a person is paralysed by depression or anxiety, *any* activity is an achievement.

Prospective diary use (planning) is often too ambitious for such clients. The best they can manage is retrospective diary writing.

Depressed people will naturally remember the disappointments, omissions, frustrations, and wasted times in the day. This tendency forms a PMC — see Figure 6.4 (t).

Therefore, three versions of a very basic homework for severe emotional problems are:

> I'd like you to sit down at 7.30 every night in the lounge room ***(be specific!)*** with this diary/pad, and write down at least three ***(five? seven? use clinical judgment)*** achievements or good things that happened through the day. I know you remember the upsets really well. The good stuff doesn't seem to register as well. That's the reason for this homework. Show me next time what you've written.

Or:

> I'd like you to keep this diary/pad on the kitchen table ***(desk at work, etc.)***, and set your watch alarm to go off every hour.* When it goes off I want you to jot down, I suppose about 15 times a day, one or two achievements or activities you did in the hour. Show me next time.

Or:

> In this diary ***(provide),*** I'd like you to write, every morning during breakfast, two (or one or three...) good things you expect, predict, or anticipate in that day. And then, after dinner (tea/supper/...) write in two successes, enjoyments, achievements, or pleasures you had in the day. Where will you keep the diary so you'll remember?

Note: * Watch alarms, reminder stickers (e.g. Homework 33), prompting by spouse or parent, code words, cue cards, and so on, are vital in bridging the consultation hour and the real world. Technology is helping; for example, computer prompts, vibrating watch alarms, and so on.

HOMEWORK 21

Pleasant Events Schedule (PES)

Assessment in interview of a client's usual daily activity profile will often suggest a paucity of enjoyable, rewarding, or confidence-enhancing activities. This emerges particularly with clients with depression problems, but also sometimes with others, such as anxiety problems, when fearful avoidance narrows a person's life, or chronic pain problems, when disability cuts out some activities.

This consequence of a person's problems (or even sometimes a precipitating cause) is a common source of PMCs. A low level of pleasant events due to low mood, pessimism, low confidence, and fears will likely produce over time a maintenance or worsening of these factors.

If such PMCs are suspected from initial interview assessment, then the Pleasant Events Schedule (Lewinsohn et al., 1986; MacPhillamy & Lewinsohn, 1982) is a useful tool with which to begin work on the problem (see Handout 1).

Begin with a description of the sorts of PMCs that interview assessment has implicated, such as:

I'm worried that because of all you've been through, your life has narrowed down now, and there isn't much left to help lift you out of the bad feelings. I suspect that if I led your life over the past month or two — even without all the upsets and problems before this — that I wouldn't feel much better than you, just because there is nothing much happening that could lift a person up.

We know that getting down is a result of the **balance** between the horrible things we try to handle, and the nice things that keep us strong or positive or confident. If your son/your daughter/a child gets sick, we naturally are nice to them — we may give them a cuddle, or an icecream, or whatever — to try to balance out the increase in 'yuk' they feel with some extra 'yum'.

But, with you, the yuk has increased, and the nice stuff has **decreased**! It's not even stayed the same. For example, since you've gotten down, you have stopped ***(playing golf/going out on Friday nights/other example)***.

So we could work on the bad stuff that's been happening to you forever, but until the nice stuff catches up we're fighting an uphill battle.

But I'm only suspecting all of this. I need some evidence, if I'm going to ask you to fight your feelings and do the opposite of what comes naturally.

So I'd like to start by asking you to fill out this questionnaire, and return it to me before our next appointment.

(Run through the instructions for the PES.)

> When this comes back to me before our next appointment, I'll be able to go through it and compare the overall picture with all the other people who have been given this, and then I'll either say "It doesn't look too bad; I hope you got some good ideas from it; And we'll keep an eye on it" or "This shows that the overall level of nice stuff has gotten so low that it's now a part of the problem, and if your moods and confidence and feelings about life are going to recover, then we'll have to deliberately do something about it".

At the next appointment I ask what sort of a picture the client feels came from their responses, and then compare this with the three scores yielded by the PES and the 'safe' ranges suggested by Lewinsohn et al. (1986) — see Table H-21.

If there is a little concern from this, I go to Homework 22. If there is a serious concern, I go to Homeworks 22 and 23.

The above needs to be modified if ***anxiety*** is the main identified limiter of pleasant activities. Terms such as 'confidence' and 'avoidance' will replace 'mood' and 'withdrawal'.

If a chronic pain problem has narrowed a client's life, then PMCs involving focus on the pain, negativity, a lack of distractions, anger, sadness, or a reduction in physical fitness can be cited.

TABLE H-21

Average Score Ranges on the Pleasant Events Schedule

Age group	*Mean Frequency score*	*Mean Pleasantness score*	*Mean FXP score*
20–39	0.63–1.03	0.86–1.26	0.99–1.19
40–59	0.57–0.97	0.82–1.22	0.92–1.12
60	0.50–0.90	0.78–1.18	0.86–1.06

HANDOUT 1

(Available as a free download from www.australianacademicpress.com.au)

Pleasant Events Schedule Self-Assessment

The objective of this exercise is to enable you to evaluate your current level of pleasant activities. This will assist you to be able to introduce changes in your life so that you can become aware of many potentially enjoyable activities and introduce and/or intensify some of these activities accordingly.

Taking and scoring this test will take approximately 2 hours. The first part assesses how often these events have happened in your life in the past month.

Please answer this question by rating each item in the frequency scale (Column F) as follows:

0 *This has not happened in the past 30 days.*

1 *This has happened a few times (1–6) times in the past 30 days.*

2 *This has happened often (7 times or more) in the past 30 days.*

Place your ratings for each item in Column F. Here is an example:

Item 4 is talking about sports. Suppose you have talked about sport twice in the past 30 days. Then you would mark 1 in Column F next to Item 4.

Some items list more than one event. For these items mark how often you have done *any* of the listed events. For example, Item 12 is Doing art work (painting, sculpture, drawing, moviemaking). You should rate Item 12 on how often you have done any form of artwork in the past month.

It is not expected that anyone will have done all of the 320 items in a single month.

The second part assesses how pleasant or rewarding each event was during the past month.

Please answer this question by rating each event in the pleasantness scale (Column P).

0 *This is not pleasant.* Use this rating for events that are either neutral or unpleasant.

1 *This is somewhat pleasant.* Use this rating for events that are mildly or moderately pleasant.

2 *This is very pleasant.* Use this rating for events that are strongly or extremely pleasant.

If an event has happened to you more than once in the past month, try to rate roughly how pleasant it was on average.

If an event has not happened to you during the past month, then rate it according to how much fun you think it would have been.

PLEASANT EVENTS SCHEDULE

	Frequency	Pleasantness
1. Being in the country		
2. Wearing expensive or formal clothing		
3. Making contributions to religious, charitable or other groups		
4. Talking about sports		
5. Meeting someone new of the same sex		
6. Taking tests when well prepared		
7. Going to a rock concert		
8. Playing cricket or softball		
9. Planning trips or vacations		
10. Buying things for myself		
11. Being at the beach		
12. Doing art work (painting, sculpture, drawing, movie making, etc.)		
13. Rock climbing or mountaineering		
14. Reading the scriptures or other sacred works		
15. Playing golf		
16. Taking part in military activities		
17. Rearranging or redecorating		
18. Going naked		
19. Going to a sports event		
20. Reading a 'how to do it' book or acticle		
21. Going to the races (horse, car, boat, etc.)		
22. Reading stories, novels, poems, or plays		
23. Going to a bar, tavern, or club		
24. Going to lectures or hearing speakers		
25. Driving skilfully		
26. Breathing clean air		
27. Thinking up or arranging songs or music		
28. Getting drunk		
29. Saying something clearly		
30. Boating (canoeing, kayaking, motorboating, or sailing)		

PLEASANT EVENTS SCHEDULE (CONTINUED)

	Frequency	Pleasantness
31. Pleasing my parents		
32. Restoring antiques, or refinishing furniture		
33. Watching TV		
34. Talking to myself		
35. Camping		
36. Working in politics		
37. Working on machines (cars, bikes, motorcycles, or tractors, etc.)		
38. Thinking about something good for the future		
39. Playing cards		
40. Completing a difficult task		
41. Laughing		
42. Solving a problem puzzle, or crossword		
43. Attending weddings, baptisms, or confirmations		
44. Criticising someone		
45. Shaving		
46. Having lunch with friends or associates		
47. Taking powerful drugs		
48. Playing tennis		
49. Taking a shower		
50. Driving long distances		
51. Woodworking — carpentry		
52. Writing stories, novels, plays, or poetry		
53. Being with animals		
54. Riding in an airplane		
55. Exploring (hiking away from known trails)		
56. Having a frank and open conversation		
57. Singing in a group		
58. Thinking about myself or my problems		
59. Working on my job		
60. Going to a party		

PLEASANT EVENTS SCHEDULE (CONTINUED)

	Frequency	Pleasantness
61. Going to church functions (social groups, classes, or bazaars)		
62. Speaking in a foreign language		
63. Going to service, civic or social club meetings		
64. Going to a business meeting or a convention		
65. Being in a sporty or expensive car		
66. Playing a musical instrument		
67. Making snacks		
68. Snow skiing		
69. Being helped		
70. Wearing informal clothes		
71. Combing or brushing my hair		
72. Acting		
73. Taking a nap		
74. Being with friends		
75. Canning, freezing, or making preserves		
76. Driving fast		
77. Solving a personal problem		
78. Being in a city		
79. Taking a bath		
80. Singing to myself		
81. Making food or crafts to sell or giveaway		
82. Playing pool or billiards		
83. Playing chess or checkers		
84. Being with my grandchildren		
85. Doing craftwork (pottery, jewellery, leather, beads, or weaving)		
86. Weighing myself		
87. Scratching myself		
88. Putting on makeup, and fixing my hair		
89. Designing or drafting		
90. Visiting people who are sick, shut in, or in trouble		

PLEASANT EVENTS SCHEDULE (CONTINUED)

	Frequency	Pleasantness
91. Cheering for a team in a sporting competition		
92. Bowling		
93. Being popular		
94. Watching wild animals		
95. Having an original idea		
96. Gardening, landscaping, or doing yard work		
97. Shoplifting		
98. Reading essays or technical, academic, or professional literature		
99. Wearing new clothes		
100. Dancing		
101. Sitting in the sun		
102. Riding a motorcycle		
103. Just sitting and thinking		
104. Social drinking		
105. Seeing good things happen to family and friends		
106. Going to a fair, carnival, circus, zoo, or amusement park		
107. Talking about philosophy or religion		
108. Gambling		
109. Planning or organising something		
110. Smoking marijuana		
111. Having a drink by myself		
112. Listening to the sounds of nature		
113. Dating/courting		
114. Having a lively talk		
115. Racing in a car, motorcycle, boat, and so on		
116. Listening to the radio		
117. Having friends come to visit		
118. Playing in a sporting competition		
119. Introducing people I think would like each other		
120. Giving gifts		

PLEASANT EVENTS SCHEDULE (CONTINUED)

	Frequency	Pleasantness
121. Going to school or government meetings, or court sessions		
122. Getting massages or backrubs		
123. Getting letters, cards, or notes		
124. Watching the sky, clouds, or a storm		
125. Going on outings (to the park, on a picnic or having a barbeque)		
126. Playing basketball		
127. Buying something for my family		
128. Photography		
129. Giving a speech or lecture		
130. Reading maps		
131. Gathering natural objects (wild fruit, rocks, driftwood or shells)		
132. Working on my finances		
133. Wearing clean clothes		
134. Making a major purchase or investment (car, appliances, house, or stocks)		
135. Helping someone		
136. Being in the mountains		
137. Getting a job advancement (being promoted, given a raise, or being offered a better job)		
138. Hearing jokes		
139. Winning a bet		
140. Talking about my children or my grandchildren		
141. Meeting someone new of the opposite sex		
142. Going to a religious revival or crusade		
143. Talking about my health		
144. Admiring beautiful scenery		
145. Eating good meals		
146. Improving my health (having my teeth fixed, getting new glasses, or changing my diet)		
147. Being down town		
148. Wrestling or boxing		
149. Hunting or shooting		

PLEASANT EVENTS SCHEDULE (CONTINUED)

	Frequency	Pleasantness
150. Playing in a musical group		
151. Hiking		
152. Going to a museum or exhibition		
153. Writing papers, essays, articles, reports, or memos		
154. Doing a job well		
155. Having spare time		
156. Fishing		
157. Lending something		
158. Being noticed as sexually attractive		
159. Pleasing employers, teachers (superiors)		
160. Counselling someone		
161. Going to a health club, or sauna bath		
162. Having someone criticise me		
163. Learning to do something new		
164. Going to a fastfood restaurant (Kentucky Fried, McDonald's, etc.)		
165. Complimenting or praising someone		
166. Thinking about people I like		
167. Being at a club (Leagues, RSL, Sporting, or special interest)		
168. Taking revenge on someone		
169. Being with my parents		
170. Horseback riding		
171. Protesting social, political, or environmental conditions		
172. Talking on the telephone		
173. Having daydreams		
174. Kicking leaves, sand, pebbles, and so on		
175. Playing lawn sports (badminton, croquet)		
176. Going to school reunions, alumni meetings		
177. Seeing famous people		
178. Going to the movies		
179. Kissing		

PLEASANT EVENTS SCHEDULE (CONTINUED)

	Frequency	Pleasantness
180. Being alone		
181. Budgeting my time		
182. Cooking meals		
183. Being praised by people I admire		
184. Outwitting a 'superior'		
185. Feeling the presence of the Lord in my life		
186. Doing a project in my own way		
187. Doing odd jobs around the house		
188. Crying		
189. Being told I am needed		
190. Being at a family reunion or get-together		
191. Giving a party		
192. Washing my hair		
193. Coaching someone		
194. Going to a restaurant		
195. Seeing or smelling a flower or plant		
196. Being invited out		
197. Receiving honors (civic or military)		
198. Using cologne, perfume, or aftershave		
199. Having someone agree with me		
200. Talking about old times		
201. Getting up early in the morning		
202. Having peace and quiet		
203. Doing experiments or other scientific work		
204. Visiting friends		
205. Writing in a diary		
206. Playing football		
207. Being counselled		
208. Saying prayers		
209. Giving massages or backrubs		

PLEASANT EVENTS SCHEDULE (CONTINUED)

	Frequency	Pleasantness
210. Hitchhiking		
211. Meditating or doing yoga		
212. Seeing a fight		
213. Doing favours for people		
214. Talking with people on the job or in class		
215. Being relaxed		
216. Being asked for my help or advice		
217. Thinking about other peoples problems		
218. Playing board games (Monopoly, Scrabble, etc.)		
219. Sleeping soundly at night		
220. Doing heavy outdoor work (cutting or chopping wood, clearing land, farm work)		
221. Reading the newspaper		
222. Shocking people (swearing, making obscene gestures)		
223. Dune-buggy riding		
224. Being in a body-awareness, sensitivity, encounter, therapy, or 'rap' group		
225. Dreaming at night		
226. Playing ping-pong		
227. Brushing my teeth		
228. Swimming		
229. Being in a fight		
230. Running, jogging, or doing gymnastics		
231. Walking barefoot		
232. Playing with a frisbee or throwing a ball		
233. Doing housework or laundry — cleaning things		
234. Being with my roommate		
235. Listening to music		
236. Arguing		
237. Knitting, crocheting, embroidery or doing fancy needlework		
238. Petting, or necking		

PLEASANT EVENTS SCHEDULE (CONTINUED)

	Frequency	Pleasantness
239. Amusing people		
240. Talking about sex		
241. Going to a barber or beautician		
242. Having house guests		
243. Being with someone I love		
244. Reading magazines		
245. Sleeping late		
246. Starting a new project		
247. Being stubborn		
248. Having sexual relations		
249. Having other sexual satisfactions		
250. Going to the library		
251. Playing sport (soccer, rugby, hockey, cricket, etc.)		
252. Preparing a new or special food		
253. Birdwatching		
254. Shopping		
255. Watching people		
256. Building or watching a fire		
257. Winning an argument		
258. Selling or trading something		
259. Finishing a project or task		
260. Confessing or apologising		
261. Repairing things		
262. Working with others as a team		
263. Bicycling		
264. Telling people what to do		
265. Being happy with people		
266. Playing party games		
267. Writing letters, cards, or notes		
268. Talking about politics or public affairs		

PLEASANT EVENTS SCHEDULE (CONTINUED)

	Frequency	Pleasantness
269. Asking for help or advice		
270. Going to banquets, luncheons, or potluck		
271. Talking about my hobby or special interest		
272. Watching attractive women or men		
273. Smiling at people		
274. Playing in sand, a stream, or the grass		
275. Talking about other people		
276. Being with my husband or wife		
277. Having people show interest in what I have said		
278. Going on field trips, or nature walks		
279. Expressing my love to someone		
280. Smoking tobacco		
281. Caring for houseplants		
282. Having coffee, tea, a coke with friends		
283. Taking a walk		
284. Collecting things		
285. Playing sport (volleyball, squash, etc.)		
286. Sewing		
287. Suffering for a good cause		
288. Remembering a departed friend or loved one, visiting the cemetery		
289. Doing things with children		
290. Beachcombing		
291. Being complimented or told I have done well		
292. Being told I am loved		
293. Eating snacks		
294. Staying up late		
295. Having family members or friends do something that makes me proud of them		
296. Being with my children		
297. Going to auctions, or garage sales		

PLEASANT EVENTS SCHEDULE (CONTINUED)

	Frequency	Pleasantness
298. Thinking about an interesting question		
299. Doing volunteer work, working on community service projects		
300. Water skiing, surfing, scuba diving, surfboard riding		
301. Receiving money		
302. Defending or protecting someone (stopping fraud or abuse)		
303. Hearing a good sermon		
304. Picking up a hitchhiker		
305. Winning a competition		
306. Making a new friend		
307. Talking about my job or school		
308. Reading cartoons, comic strips or comic books		
309. Borrowing something		
310. Travelling with a group		
311. Seeing old friends		
312. Teaching someone		
313. Using my strength		
314. Travelling		
315. Going to office parties or department get-togethers		
316. Attending a concert, opera, or ballet		
317. Playing with pets		
318. Going to a play		
319. Looking at the stars or moon		
320. Being coached		

Reproduced with permission (Lewinsohn, Munoz, & Zeiss, 1986)

HOMEWORK 22

PES Sublist

If the PES results (Homework 21) are a cause of concern, then perusal of the responses may be useful, to check whether many items received a zero for frequency (F) and at the same time a two for pleasantness (P). These have, by definition, not been occurring, but are at the same time potentially very enjoyable. If a number of these items were specific (e.g. playing pool or billiards) rather than general (e.g. completing a difficult task), then a good source of pleasant activity ideas has been obtained.

You'll see I've marked some of the items. These are the ones that you haven't been doing recently — they got a Frequency score of 0 — but they can be enjoyable for you — they got a Pleasantness score of 2.

I'd like you, for homework, to write out a separate list of all PES items that got a zero for F and a two for P at the same time; especially the specific practical ones ***(give example)***, not so much the woolly impractical ones ***(give example)***.

This can act as a good source of ideas over the next couple of months.

HOMEWORK 23

PES Diary

There are innumerable strategies that may be followed when a client's pleasant activity profile is identified as deficient, and therefore a probable PMC factor.

As noted earlier, such PMCs can be depression-related, anxiety-related, pain syndrome-related, relationship-related, and so on. The difficulty lies in overcoming the naturally maintained pleasant activity deficit in someone who is pessimistic, amotivational, fearful, in pain, or resentful. Therefore a graduated approach, using insight to overcome reluctance, is necessary. An analogy with 'taking your medicine' or 'going to the dentist' because we know it's good for you, may help. Others may benefit from the ***permission*** to be 'selfish', which is inherent in prescribed homework.

A PES Diary, in which a client is asked to record, usually daily, one or more extra pleasant activities or experiences, attempts to increase the volume of positive experiences and the appreciation of them.

Dobson and Joffe (1986) found that the impact of an increase in the volume of pleasant events is enhanced if a strategy is included to maximise the focus or appreciation of them — a concurrent deliberate cognitive strategy. Diary recording may serve this function, but I also add a requirement to rate the activity's pleasantness, which can further add focus, impact, or appreciation.

Provide some form of diary or journal, while writing:

From now on, every day, I want you to do at least one thing extra that counts as a pleasant activity. It doesn't have to be big — lying in the bath for 20 minutes with the radio on, or raiding the cupboard for some chocolate biscuits, would count — but it needs to be something every day, because what we're after is an overall different level if you filled in the PES again in another month or two.

You may not feel like it, but you have to do something every day because we know it's good for you.

Even if it feels a bit selfish to, say, go for a walk and leave John with the kids for half an hour, you can blame me because this is your 'medicine'. And if you don't do it you'll be no good for John or the kids anyway! But I also want you to write down in this diary — in just a few words — what you do extra on purpose.

And when you do, I'd like you to give the pleasant experience a score out of 10, where 10 is great, and 1 is barely okay. There are two reasons for this. First, I want to see whether it's all 1s and 2s you do, and that doesn't help much. Second, when you write the rating down, this means you have to think about the nice experience again, and that might help it sink in a bit better.

Review of the PES Diary at followup consultations puts more pressure on for compliance. It is also a check on the strength/significance of pleasant events. And can be informative about ***what*** the client can enjoy.

It is hoped that, as well as producing a greater volume of pleasant, rewarding, or confidence-boosting experiences in a simple behavioural-level conditioning sense, this homework can also alter the person's mindset and habits about self-care and assertiveness to bring about a broader cognitive change.

HOMEWORK 24

Regular Exercise

There are at least three psychological justifications for assessing a client's current exercise profile and recommending an increase where little exercise is occurring:

1. It is well known that people who are depressed do less, and have less energy, motivation, and expectation of enjoying an activity. Therefore, they tend to get less exercise. And this can worsen their situation by maintaining a feeling of physical flatness or inertia, reducing their fitness, and blocking a source of social contact, pleasure, or achievement — see Figure 6.4 (u). Whatever the mechanism of problem maintenance that a lack of exercise produces, it is now known that a program of moderate progressive exercise can reduce the experience of depression, irrespective of cause, or concurrent medication (Dunn et al., 2005; Lam & Kennedy, 2004; Mather et al., 2002).
2. The 'fight-or-flight' response of anxiety can be either counteracted (by relaxation procedures, positive self-talk, or halting behavioural avoidance), or it can be 'used up' or 'discharged' in ways other than 'belting someone or running away'. It has been found that aerobic exercise training reduces the increase in sympathetic neural activity following mental stress (Blumenthal et al., 1990; Cleophas, 2000).
3. The same 'fight-or-flight' logic applies to anger problems, — see Figure 6.5 (a) and (f). A regular exercise outlet can prevent the tension buildup that results in 'explosions'.

The homework suggestions surrounding exercise are too varied and idiosyncratic to summarise here. Davis, Eshelman and McKay (2008) offer a relevant chapter on exercise homework for anxiety or stress problems.

Simple examples as applied to depression, anxiety, and anger follow:

Depression

They've found just recently that when people who are depressed get some exercise, a lot of them improve. We still don't know how or why. We just know it makes a big difference, even if nothing else is done. But, when people feel down they just don't feel like getting up and getting going. So, they're caught in a trap, in a vicious circle — or one of our PMCs. So, I'm going to ask you to break this circle; to regard the homework I'm going to give you as your 'medicine'. To do it even when you don't feel like it.

Recommend a homework.

Anxiety

When you're nervous, tense, worried, anxious, uptight, you're having what's called a 'fight-or-flight response'. This is the mind and body's preparation for action: to belt someone or to run away. For millions of years most of the threats we faced were physical ones — trees falling down, and wild animals chasing us. These days the threats we face are things like relationship problems, money worries, and health scares. But still we have the same inbuilt fight-or-flight response, even though it doesn't help — in fact it often gets in the way. So, your muscles tense up, and your heart rate goes up, and your sweat glands get going, and … ***(tailor this to reported symptoms).*** But there's nowhere to run, and no-one you need to fight. So a lot of the time you can feel like an engine out of gear — revving up, but not getting anywhere. This can even hurt you physically. There are at least two things we can do for this: one is to counteract the feelings by using relaxation techniques. The other is to **use up** the adrenalin and glucose that is being pumped into your system, so you can get back to a normal state.

This second option is what I'm going to ask you to do regularly. However, this is different from exercising to get fit. For that you might exercise three or four times a week, and for an hour or so. What I'm suggesting needs to be done more often — preferably daily, as it's no good being revved up for 2 or 3 days before you exercise. It doesn't have to be for long — 10 or 15 minutes might be enough, and it doesn't have to be very vigorous — a good walk would count.

Recommend a homework.

Anger

As above, with a few word changes, and the possible addition of:

If we're going to avoid you getting into a state where you can blow up, then we need to control the situations you get yourself in ***(show Figure 3.1)***, and/or the crabby thinking you do in them, and/or the physical state of tension that can build up. You'll need to do some **regular** physical activity to use up this fight-or-flight tension so it doesn't build for long.

Example

On the back of this card ***(while writing)*** I want you to record what type of physical exercise you do every day. Just a few words will do, like: 'Walked 20 minutes with Mary', or 'dug in the garden for half an hour'. ***(On the reverse of the card, write the day and the date — for example, Tuesday 16th — from today for 3 to 4 days, down left side, leaving full width line beside.)***

If a diary is already a part of homework, this can be used to record daily exercise instead of a separate card.

HOMEWORK 25

Overwhelming Sensory Experiences

By definition, a problem that has formed PMCs is hard to fight because it is being ***maintained***. At times this maintenance can occur acutely, as when a stressor produces anxiety symptoms, which are then a cause of panic when they are misunderstood. Or when negative thinking produces profound sadness and inertia, which is viewed negatively!

Such acute states of anxiety/panic, or depression, or anger, are often too self-perpetuating to be easily or quickly corrected by specific healthy, sensible, constructive, psychological techniques addressing one's thinking (thought-stopping, self-talk ...) or one's feelings (relaxation techniques ...) or one's behaviour ('smile anyway'...) or one's situation (go outside ...).

At such times a more drastic intervention is needed, even be it somewhat negative, in order to allow a possibility of interrupting the PMC.

This is when I give Overwhelming Sensory Experiences (OSE) homework.

What you have described happening yesterday ***(cite a specific example of an out-of-control state)*** sounds too strong a feeling to control at the time with one of our particular sensible little techniques ***(pointing to elements on Figure 3.1 model)*** that try to get your **thinking** straight , or reduce a horrible **feeling**, or put you in a better **situation**, or control your **behaviour**. At times like yesterday, the whole circle is snowballing along so strongly that we need something much more drastic, that can interrupt the **whole** picture, and give you a chance of a fresh start. ***(At this point I shake the paper with Figure 3.1 on it in the air, and place it back on the table.)***

But in the middle of such a bad time, you're not in a good state to stop and think up some good way to stop it all.

So your homework today is ***(while writing on homework card)*** to work out today, while you can think straight, two or three Overwhelming Sensory Experiences that might be drastic enough so that if you put yourself through one next time that you're feeling so X, it might stand a chance of shaking you out of the spiral of bad feeling. And then you need to prepare for them, **before** you need to use them, because you may have to buy something or set something up, or line up someone else to help. But you need to do this **before** the next bad time.

So these OSEs are things you can do to yourself at the next out-of-control time that are drastic enough to shake you up physically, mentally, and emotionally,.

The key words are '**drastic**, but **safe**'. (Write this.)

I can give you some examples, but what you can come up with is up to your imagination and what's available to you.

Some people in the past have set up OSEs like:

- going for a run, even in the rain
- having a punching bag set up in the garage; take to it without gloves
- keeping 2 litres of custard in the fridge to gorge on
- putting on the stereo headphones; play AC/DC loud for 20 minutes; maybe dance
- getting in the shower; put only the cold tap on.
- a small one would be to put a really strong lozenge in your mouth
- a big one would be to up and go camping in the bush for 2 days.

Homework follow-up then involves checking the two or three ideas listed: Are they ***drastic*** enough, but ***safe***? Are they ***quickly*** available? (Effort and self-discipline are absent in out-of-control states.) Have they been ***prepared*** for? Are they available at home, at work, elsewhere?

For example, going for a fast drive in the car is drastic, but not safe; ditto getting drunk.

Finally, have they been used? Have there been times when they should have been used? Did they work? Could they work?

HOMEWORK 26

Options When Suicidal

'Learned helplessness' (Seligman, 1990) and 'hopelessness' (Beck, Kovacs, & Weissman, 1975) are key predictors of suidical behaviour. The most crucial point at which a person may translate these cognitive states into suicidal action is when they are considering the immediate options to swallowing the pills, getting into the car, and so on.

Therefore, when suicidal ideation has been reported or is considered possible:

> I'd like you to come back next time with a list written out, to show me, of four things you may be able to do if you feel bad enough to consider killing yourself.
>
> Contacting someone is usually a good idea. So some or all of your list will be the names and phone numbers of who you could contact. Lifelink/Lifeline might be on the list. I might be on the list.
>
> Here are my phone numbers.
>
> Some items on your list might not be contacting someone. Some people include going for a run or having a long bath. Be careful of these. They need to be powerful enough to really shake you out of it. And getting drunk or driving fast can make it **more** dangerous, not less.

When the list returns, grill the client as to whether it has ***likely*** and ***effective*** alternatives on it. This should involve imaginal rehearsal of options on the list.

Alternative strategies include extracting a promise, even written, to hang in there until the next appointment; or a promise to phone you before doing something harmful ('I'd rather be woken at 3 am by someone in distress, than hear about their death the next day!').

It's fine to be blunt in discussing all this. It models to your client that everything needs to be talked about or talked out. Nothing is taboo. And this issue is so serious that people's feelings about bringing it up come second to the risks.

HOMEWORK 27

Graze Foods

A common symptom of depression is poor appetite. This can create a PMC over time in at least two ways. First, a low nutrient or calorie intake can deplete a person's energy levels, which alters mood quite directly. And second, what is for some people a major source of pleasure (satiation, taste, social dining …) is removed.

A similar concern can emerge with anxiety problems too, when nausea is a prominent symptom.

When weight loss or appetite reduction emerge in an assessment as symptoms of concern, especially if other features of a PMC are reported (such as low energy levels, tiredness, or feeling deprived of daily pleasures) then the following may be 'prescribed':

> At your next supermarket visit on … with … ***(specific instructions always promote compliance more than general advice)***, I want you to wander up and down the aisles and pick out lots of what I call 'graze foods'. Get lots. Remember, it'll cost you less than one of our visits. These are foods that keep well outside the fridge, don't need any preparation, and don't need equipment to eat.
>
> So things like nuts, biscuits, or fruit definitely count. But who knows what you'll find if you browse. Even chocolate biscuits are better than nothing. At least they're calories. Then, I want you to spread them around. Put them in your drawer at work, in the car, by the couch, on your bedside table … The idea is that any time you feel you can get some food down, there it is, have a bit. You don't have to be hungry. This is like medicine. You'll graze because it's good for you, even if you're not hungry.
>
> But it won't happen unless the food's **there**, and it won't be there unless you go and buy it on purpose and spread it around.

(One or two sentences from the above written on the 'homework card' should suffice.)

HOMEWORK 28

Sleep Hygiene

The literature on sleep disturbance and its nondrug management is profuse. I will describe introductory approaches to three types of disturbance only: sleep onset difficulties, frequent waking, and disruption by dreams.

The rationale behind direct intervention with sleep problems, even when they appear to be secondary to anxiety or depression problems, relates to their role in such PMCs as: Figure 6.1 (k) and (l), and Figure 6.4 (h) and (r). This rationale is supported by the finding that when people who are depressed are helped simply to sleep better, without drugs, not only does their sleep improve, but "70% of the insomnia sufferers who were depressed before treatment and learned to sleep better were no longer depressed or were significantly less depressed, once their sleep had improved" (Morawetz, 2001).

If the primary complaint is disruption by disturbing dreams, then 'dream antidotes' may be recommended (Homework 29).

If delayed sleep onset is prominent then the following five 'prescriptions', as an introductory set, take about 15 minutes to deliver.

---

1. Set bed hours: ***(Two lines of written 'prescription' should cover the following)***

   We're going to make a reasonable guess at what would be a good number of hours resting or sleeping in bed, and from what time to what time this should be. (Queries about historical pattern and current sleep-or-in-bed pattern can follow, as well as how refreshed, and allowing for decreasing hours needed with age, and so on.)

   From now on I want you to stick with these hours in bed, whether you're asleep or not, and **only** these hours in bed.

   This means no naps! You may be tempted to catch up in the daytime when you're really tired, but that just means you'll sleep worse the following night, and you'll muck up your daily body rhythm or pattern in the medium-to-long-term. So no naps, even if you're really tempted, and no going to bed early to try to catch up. This would either mean you'll lie there awake anyway, or you'll wake up too early.

   And not much sleeping in, for the same reasons. Get up when the alarm goes, and then you'll have a better chance of sleep the next night.

---

2. Rest is nearly as good as sleep:

   We now know that a lot of benefits can come just from lying relaxed in bed with your eyes closed and with nice stuff drifting through your head. A lot of the rest and recuperation parts of sleep can happen then, even if you're not asleep.

The other parts of sleep that we need — like deep sleep ***(explain if appropriate)*** and dream or REM sleep ***(explain)*** — can be caught up on quite quickly if we do nod off. We know this because if you deprive a person of, say, REM sleep for a couple of nights, which they've done in sleep laboratories, then as soon as you stop interfering, people tend to have a big catchup in their REM sleep, almost as soon as they nod off. The same with deep sleep.

So people can survive quite okay with limited sleep for quite a while. **As long as** they're getting rest the rest of the time.

There are a million things that can muck up one or two night's sleep – noise, heat, worry, pain, tablets … But when they've looked for the **biggest** cause of **ongoing** bad sleep, it's people **worrying about not being asleep**!

So this is another reason why it's important, in bed, at night, when you're awake, to say to yourself: 'Rest is nearly as good as sleep. I'll at least make sure I'm relaxed with nice stuff drifting through my head.'

---

3. Positive serial fantasies:

Through most of your life, you've gone to bed, turned the light out, and waited to see what happened. This is okay mostly, because you soon go to sleep.

This isn't happening now, though. So we have to come up with something different.

We know that if you have nice things going on inside your head, that people find it easier to go to sleep. But if you have negative or scary or upsetting things going on in your head, this actually produces chemicals that are inconsistent with going to sleep.

Unfortunately, recently that's what your mind has been doing, so you can't afford to just turn off the light and see what happens. You will need to consciously **do** something with your brain when you go to bed.

So, for homework, today, what I'd like you to do is to ***(while writing on homework card)*** 'decide on one or two Positive Serial Fantasies to turn your mind to when the light goes out.' Now, these need to be 'positive', nice, enjoyable, interesting. They need to be big ***('serial')***, so they can last a while. Counting sheep is different from this. But they can be about **anything *('fantasies')***, because we're not out to solve problems, or rehearse what to do tomorrow, or work out what happened today, or anything like that. All we want to do is occupy your mind nicely so you can go to sleep.

Some PSFs that people can pick on are things like: What would you do if you won $10 million in the lottery tomorrow? Do this in great detail, or go through a long lovely story, and write your novel in your head, or design your ideal house/mansion in your head. Also in great detail. Colour schemes. Everything. I want you to decide today, before bedtime, because I don't want you fretting in bed tonight about what you could have as a PSF!

These ideas can last a while, because you'll probably find your mind will wander off after a bit, but usually onto something nice.

Then, the next night, it'll take you a minute or two to remember where you were at, then you'll follow the PSF for a bit, and then you're mind will wander off again.

If you find your thinking is back onto negative stuff, the idea is just calmly to bring back in the PSF.

When I see you next, I'll ask which one or two PSFs you've chosen.

The hard part might be to think of using it every night at the right time.

---

4. Pen and pad:

Sometimes what bothers you in bed at night can be 'tomorrow-type' stuff. 'I must remember to talk to Bob about that', 'I should go for a walk after breakfast', and so on.

I'd like you tonight to put a pen and pad by the bed. And then, if you notice any 'tomorrow-type' thinking, turn on the light for just a few seconds, write a couple of words as a reminder, and turn the light off. You know you'll see what you've written in the morning, so your mind has permission to leave it alone. Otherwise, a little bit of your mind will be saying 'Don't forget to …', or 'I shouldn't do X tomorrow …'.

---

5. Time limit:

Through your life, about how long has it usually taken you from lights out to getting to sleep? Add about 20 minutes to that. This can now be your time limit for trying.

I don't want you to look at the clock all night. But if you feel it's been a long time awake, then check the time, and if it's past your time limit, then get up for just a couple of minutes and start again.

So you might just have half a glass of milk or go to the loo or read half a page, and then back to bed and light out.

If you lie in bed awake for a long time, eventually bed gets associated with lying there awake ***(stimulus control)***. We need to break up this link.

Also, if you've been awake a long time there's a big risk of a snowball getting going and it'll only get **harder**. We need a fresh start to avoid this.

With wakings through the night, if they are extended, then some of the above may apply. If they are brief but frequent and therefore problematic, then the following may help:

The Rollover Approach

Using one of the many illustrations of a typical EEG/REM night's profile (e.g., Regestein & Rechs, 1980) or while quickly drawing your own:

We know that people go through cycles in their brain activity through the night. About every hour or hour and a half our brains wake up a bit and we have a time of dreaming or REM sleep ***(explain if appropriate)***. Our brains are quite active then, and it's quite possible to wake up then, even without a trigger.

We can learn lots of things **in our sleep**. We learn not to wet the bed, in our sleep. We learn not to fall out of bed, in our sleep. It's even possible (it happened to me) to learn to turn the alarm off in our sleep. (I had to put the alarm further from the bed, so I had to wake up to turn it off.)

Unfortunately we can learn **bad** habits in our sleep too. And sometimes we 'learn' to wake up habitually from dream arousal states. So this can then happen several times through the night ***(refer to EEG chart)***.

(An interpretation of the effectiveness of the 'controlled crying' technique with infants is that it gives them an opportunity to 'learn' to roll over and go back to sleep, until they do it quickly right through the night.)

In order to 'learn' not to wake up at these times, we need to approximate what we're after; to 'shape' the behaviour. So the best approach is to minimise the whole waking up process. To 'rollover and go back to sleep' quite quickly, so that the next time it takes only a minute, then a few seconds, then we hardly remember waking, then we do it in a drowse, then we do it while still asleep. ***(This can be illustrated with shortening curves on the EEG graph.)*** We want to learn to roll over and go back to sleep, **in our sleep**. So the principle is to start doing it while awake. ***(NB: This approach is useful only if waking frequently is the problem, not if staying awake is the problem.)***

HOMEWORK 29

Dream Antidotes

Bad dreams or nightmares are frequently reported during periods of emotional distress, particularly in PTSD. It can be difficult to discern whether their frequency and intensity increases at these times, or more attention is paid to them, or they are remembered more clearly, or it is the emotional distress that produces them, or medication or alcohol use, or the general sleep disturbance that depression and anxiety can cause.

Irrespective of these uncertainties, there is no doubt that they can become elements in PMCs. The distress or unease that bad dreams produce upon awakening is a bad start to an already-difficult day.

Sometimes the distress is exacerbated by attention to the content of the dreams. Despite the fact that no reliable, and therefore useful, system has been developed for extracting meaning from dream content (Empson, 1989; Oswald, 1987), there is a general view in the community that dream content means something, and therefore people add to their disturbance by asking 'Why did I dream *that*?! There must be something bad or sick in me. Or maybe it's a premonition!'

Reversal of the effects of distressing dreams therefore requires 'antidotes' to the direct effects they have on mood or state upon awakening (a PMC component), and to the unnecessary upset that ascribing meaning to the horror can produce. The 'antidote' to the former, outlined below, is based on a technique described by Marks (1978a, 1978b; Linde & Savary, 1974)

There are two ways that the bad dreams you've described are making the whole situation worse for you. First, you can get upset about **what** you're dreaming. After 100 years of studying dreams, we still don't have a good system for working out what they mean. We still don't even know whether we dream stuff that's not us, to get it out of the system, or we dream stuff we really want, but can't get. All we know is that people during a bad time will have bad dreams, but they're generally just a jumbled mix of bad experiences, bad memories, and bad feelings with no useful pattern. ***(Further explanation regarding REM cycles, dreaming universality, effects of physical sensations on dream content, and so on, can be added when appropriate or sought.)***

But what can we do about the horrible feeling they leave you with in the morning, at a time when life is tough enough already without this.

While writing on homework card:

From now on, the moment you realise you've been affected by a bad dream, even before you open your eyes or get up, if that's possible, I want you to return in your **awake imagination** to the dream. Bring back in your mind where it was, who was there, the sights, sounds, smells. Then I want you to imagine the opposite of whatever bad was happening. So, for example, if in the dream you were falling, this time you'll turn it into flying. If you're being chased by something, when you re-run the dream, you'll stop, turn around, and belt the thing or person so they explode or disappear. Then the sun comes out, everyone smiles, and you have a cup of tea.

So when you get out of bed, you've then got **two** memories in your head: a bad dream, and a lovely opposite imagining.

Sometimes you won't think of doing this until later. Over breakfast maybe. Better late than never. Do it then, at least.

We've found that if you do this, first, at least the horrible effect of the dream has been counteracted somewhat. But also, surprisingly, they've found that the actual number of bad dreams remembered can get less over time. This was an unexpected bonus.

PMCs involving bad dreams can occur in anxiety-related CPPs, such as PTSD, or depression episodes, or any mixed stress/distress period.

Clients' distress at such times is burden enough without waking with an overnight trauma to colour the morning. Providing a 'dream antidote' strategy may help alleviate this, while reinforcing a client's coping repertoire and self-efficacy feelings.

HOMEWORK 30

Worry Questions

When a client does not respond well to a detailed, variable, clerical worry processing system, such as NER recording (Homework 1), they may be more open to a simple, specific, generic, nonclerical one. Also, clients cannot be expected to continue NER recording or suchlike forever. As they stop this, a more convenient process can replace it.

Another difficulty with NER–type processes is that they tend to help by stimulating constructive 'debriefing', or reflection, or maximal learning from emotional reactions, but are not convenient in vivo immediate coping techniques.

The Worry Questions homework can instead, or subsequently, help boost a person's in vivo worry processing or coping (see Bakker, 2019b, Guideline 9):

We all have in our heads a system for processing everything new that comes along in our day, and sifting out what we're going to get upset about, or worry about, or take seriously, and what we're not. We start developing this when we're little, and hopefully it gets better as we get older. We're more able to quickly see what's worth reacting to and what isn't.

So you and I use this quick mental system maybe 50 times a day — every time anything new crops up. And hopefully 48 or 49 times a day our brains quickly say 'No, that's not worth worrying about' and we let it go.

But, unfortunately we know that when someone is down, or over-stressed, or over-tired, or even ill, this system doesn't work so well. Any little or silly thing can get to us.

(Give an example from the client's symptom history. For example, if you get home feeling good, and the kids are noisy, you might just leave the room or turn the TV up. But on a bad day you might yell at them and get even more upset.)

Now, this is just an unlucky thing about human nature; that exactly at the times we need to throw out the rubbish because we are already down, we can't, and it all snowballs on.

This mental worry processing system has happened in you lots of times every day for years. So it's pretty automatic now. But recently it's not been happening automatically enough. Maybe only 44 or 45 times a day? So a few bits of rubbish get through each day.

Anything that is supposed to happen automatically, but isn't happening very well recently, can be improved by doing it **consciously** for a while. We can see this in sports. Or if you're driving along and (spouse, friend or therapist) says 'You didn't indicate at the last 3 corners you came to,' then what you'll do for the rest of the day is to **say** to yourself at every corner 'Indicate!' Then, by tomorrow, it's happening automatically again. We need to do the same thing to the worry processing system in your head.

This system in our heads probably looks something like this ***(show Figure H-30A)***.

There is nothing new on this sheet. You do this sort of thing lots of times a day, whether you're aware of it or not. But lately, instead of maybe 45 times a day, it should be happening properly 50 times, and a few useless bits of worry are getting through.

So what I'd like you to do is ***(while writing on homework card)***: Rewrite the Worry Questions ***(Figure H-30A)*** onto a small handy card ***(give sample card)***.

I say 'rewrite', and not 'copy', because if you want to change any of the words or arrows or questions, that's fine. Everyone has a different way of talking to themselves.

Then ***(while writing)*** I want you to keep this card with you 24 hours a day, because we don't know when worries can crop up, for X weeks ***(whatever appeals as a reasonable time to boost a healthy mental habit)***. How long for depends on how often you think of it. So I want this card to be with your other daily stuff, like your keys, your glasses, your wallet, your phone … If you're concerned people might see it, then you could put it in your wallet or purse, but in the **money** section where you'll see it, not at the back of the credit card section.

What we're after is that, instead of fretting on something for an hour before you realise you're wasting energy and making yourself miserable, you might think of the questions after 20 minutes. Then, next week, after 10 minutes. By the time its down to 2 minutes, you're probably doing as well as anyone at throwing out the rubbish.

With Any Worry:

1. Is it **really** important?
   Does it **really** matter? → No → Then STOP!
   (What is the Worst Possible Outcome?)
   ↓
   Yes
   ↓
2. (If about the future)
   Is it **really** likely? → No → Then STOP!
   ↓
   Yes
   ↓
3. Can I do anything about it now? → No → Then STOP!
   (Is it **my** problem?)
   ↓
   Yes
   ↓
   THEN **DO** SOMETHING!

FIGURE H-30A
The Worry Questions.

(Available as a free download from www.australianacademicpress.com.au)

If you can see over time that it's nearly always Question 1 you forget to ask, or 2, or 3, then that helps us, because it simplifies what you need to be consciously asking yourself more often.

So at our next appointment, I'll ask you **what sort of** useless worry you seem most susceptible to.

Some clients cite this as the most life-changing part of their therapy. Many go on to use it in coaching those around them!

As well as, or instead of, carrying a reminder/cue card about, the Worry Questions can become wallpaper on a client's 'phone or computer.

As I invite clients to change the Worry Questions flow-chart in any way that 'clicks' better for their way of thinking, some illuminating and educative variations come back. For example, one client constructed the version depicted in Figure H-30B.

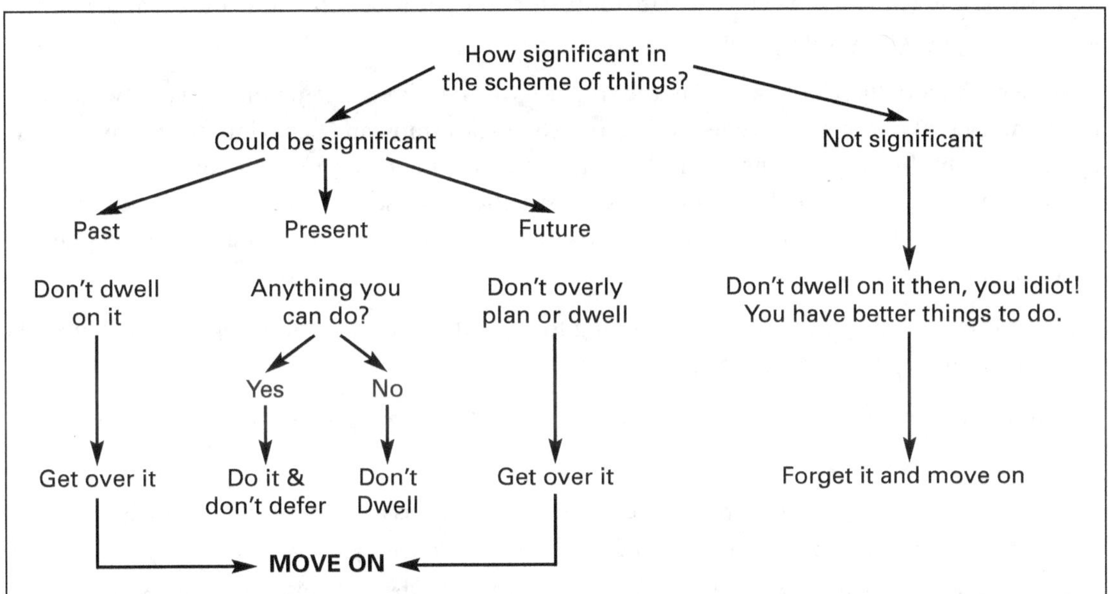

FIGURE H-30B
A Version of the Worry Questions.

HOMEWORK 31

Allocating Worry Time

Some psychological conditions involve negative thinking that serves *no* useful function. OCD is an example. Counting rituals need to be dispensed with completely. Another example would be guilt over past forgiven misdemeanours.

On the other hand, some depressions are still in need of 'grief work' (Parkes, 1993). And many anxiety problems are in situations of significant, real, current stress.

Therefore, it may not be advisable to encourage simple thought-stopping, distraction, or avoidance in these circumstances. The person has two mutually exclusive tasks before them: (a) to confront their fears, or the reality of their loss, or problem-solve, share, grieve, write, plan, or do their homework; and (b) to get on with life, care for their family, be productive at work, eat at mealtimes, keep up with the chores, and so on.

To neglect either of these tasks increases the risk of PMCs developing. Perennial negativity can easily result in inactivity, poor sleep, neglected or strained relationships, and behavioural avoidance. All of these can be problem maintainers. On the other hand, coping by permanent cognitive avoidance, distraction, reassurance, and placation, risks the situations worsening when grief is unconfronted, fears unfaced, and OCD rituals reinforced. Problematic grief reactions can result from 'over-grieving' or from 'under-grieving'.

When it is clear that a client is not responding to this dilemma with some degree of balance, the following homework advice may help:

Introduce the above in a way that is relevant to the client's current problems. For example:

When something terrible happens, like Mary's death, there is a risk of reacting in a way that becomes a problem in itself; of becoming **so** upset it takes you over completely, and your health and the kids and your work suffer badly too. Obviously, Mary wouldn't want this. On the other hand, if you try to forget all about it, you won't be facing reality and it can come back and hurt you later on, and it's not respectful to Mary's memory either.

Or:

Some of what you're going through needs your attention to manage it, and fix what you can. For example, we've agreed that you need to talk with your boss about your hours. And you need to work out what you'll say. But we've seen that if you're bothered by the stresses and problems **all** the time, you feel even worse, and your work suffers, and you hardly sleep.

Or a similar tailored introduction to the following:

So you've got two incompatible things you need to do, that can both spoil each other. You've got problems to face, and you've got life and responsibilities to maintain. If you focus on the worries all the time, your life and health and family will suffer, and the problems will likely get worse! If you ignore the problems altogether, nothing gets fixed.

Replace the word 'worry' with 'grieving' where appropriate.

So from now on I want you to consciously decide when is Worry Time, time for you to think, plan, write stuff, talk to people, see me, your doctor, and so on; and when is 'Get On With Life' time (GOWL time).

During GOWL time don't say to yourself 'That's silly. Stop It', because often it's not silly. Instead, you say 'Not now'. And you can even think 'Tonight after the news; that's Worry Time!' It's easier to say 'Not now' because you know you can come back to it. Often, of course, you won't, but that just means it wasn't important enough.

Some people even write their Worry and GOWL times in their diary!

Next time, I'll ask you for some examples of your Worry times and GOWL times.

Or:

Let's start two lists: Worry times and GOWL times. Under 'Worry times' we can put: 'When with psychologist', 'At the doctor's', and maybe even 'Every night from 7.30 to 8.00'. Under GOWL times we can put: 'When I'm with the kids', 'In bed at night'. Next time, I'd like to see at least three or four more under each heading.

A similar procedure is outlined in White (1999) as a recommended technique with Generalised Anxiety Disorder.

Thought-stopping (Homework 36) may be a useful adjunct.

HOMEWORK 32

Relaxation Sessions

Relaxation sessions of some kind have traditionally been a recommended part of behaviour therapy or CBT for most anxiety disorders (Benson, 1975; Jacobson, 1974).

However, while some research suggests that such sessions can be useful with generalised anxiety disorders (GAD; Borkovec & Mathews, 1988), it seems they are not very effective for more specific anxiety problems such as social phobia (Al-Kubaisy et al., 1992) or panic disorder (Ost, 1988).

For the majority of anxiety problems, relaxation as an in vivo active coping skill, such as in stress inoculation training (Meichenbaum, 1977), or anxiety management training (Suinn, 1977), or cue-controlled relaxation (Russell & Sipich, 1973), or applied relaxation (Ost, 1987), produces better results (Arntz, 2003, Goldfried & Trier, 1974) and has been increasingly favoured (Goldfried, 1979). "Rather than viewing relaxation as an alternative conditioned response ... CB therapists present relaxation as a coping skill to be developed and consciously enacted whenever needed" (Braswell & Kendall, 2001, p. 260).

Therefore, I limit my prescription of relaxation sessions, usually via recorded instructions, to:

- GAD clients
- clients who describe never feeling calm, from waking to bedtime, so that they can at least have an occasional experience of calm
- those clients that request or prefer such sessions
- as an exercise to assist development of a personalised, tailored, brief, in vivo, 'mini-relaxer' procedure (see Homework 33).

If the use of regular intense sessions is decided upon, there are innumerable procedures from which to choose. They include progressive muscle relaxation (PMR), autogenic training, a form of meditation, yoga practices, visualisation techniques, or lying in the bath with the radio on. There is little to choose among these.

Two criteria I use in selecting a procedure are as follows:

1. It has been found that Progressive Relaxation Training is differentially effective with anxiety-related disorders in which there is a prominent physiological component (e.g., a psychosomatic illness; Borkovec & Sides, 1979). It is notably ***ineffective*** with, for example, OCD (Rachman & Hodgson, 1980). As discussed in Chapter 7, Selecting Homework Tasks, a physiological presentation may warrant a more physical relaxation procedure, and a cognitive presentation a more cognitive approach.
2. Some of the relaxation session options are more active and preoccupying (e.g. PMR via a CD) and some require mind-emptying (e.g. meditation). Clients that describe racing/worrying thinking may be better off with an active distracting procedure.

Relaxation sessions, or even skills, are no longer, however, a first line of treatment for many anxiety disorders. It has long been known that relaxation is not a necessary component in systematic desensitisation (Gillian & Rachman, 1974). In fact, in panic disorder it may be a hindrance, in that it can reinforce the client's ability to escape or blunt, rather than face, their primary fear (DeRubeis et al., 2001, p. 368). In acute stress disorder, anxiety management has been found to be a nonessential adjunct to exposure and cogntive therapy (Bryant et al., 1999). And in PTSD, exposure therapy appears to be more effective than relaxation training (Taylor et al., 2003).

Live relaxation sessions during the consultation have been found to be preferable to sessions with take-home tapes (Hoelscher et al., 1987). Given the qualifications surrounding the usefulness of relaxation sessions anyway, I rarely conduct such sessions during a consultation, as they are a very inefficient use of consultation time.

Generally, sessions of 20 minutes to 1 hour are prescribed once or twice a day in the acute phase of an anxiety problem. The rationale assumes a 'carryover' effect to the rest of the day. However, a deliberate process of enhancing generalisation to the rest of the day, especially to anxiety-provoking situations, may be preferred (see Homework 33).

HOMEWORK 33

Mini-Relaxers

Brief, inconspicuous, calming procedures used in vivo, either periodically and habitually, or in response to the occurrence of stressors, are a common component of many CBT interventions such as anxiety management training, applied relaxation, cue-controlled relaxation, and stress inoculation training. This approach falls clearly within the 'coping skills' arm of CBT.

However, to expect a person to usefully employ a half-minute calming procedure from day 1, whenever they experience a crisis, a panic attack, or exposure to a phobic stimulus is unreasonable.

It is also usually advisable to present a variety of different options for achieving relaxation, and to let the client choose and practise those that they prefer (Braswell & Kendall, 2001, p. 261).

I use the three-step process outlined below.

Clients often assume, when the term 'relaxation' is introduced, that they will be introduced to yoga or meditation or PMR sessions. I therefore tend to use a term like 'calming process', and often begin by distinguishing traditional relaxation 'sessions' (see Homework 32) from in vivo relaxation 'skills'.

Step 1: *Development of a mini-relaxer.*

I'd like us to work out a short, maybe half-minute, little calming-down process you can use nearly anywhere, that clicks with **you**. If you lie down for 20 minutes with your eyes closed, then nearly any procedure is going to calm you down a bit, even just lying in the bath with the radio on. But if doing something for half a minute is going to work, it really needs to be tailored to **you**.

So we're talking about just 2 or 3 bits you'll do in your 'mini-relaxer'. They need to be inconspicuous, because you may end up doing your mini-relaxer in the car or at work or walking down the street.

There are hundreds of things a person can put into their mini-relaxer. You may just have to try some and see how it feels. Or you might start by looking at what usually happens to you when you get uptight. Some people are real worriers, but it's hard to see it on them. They need some mental tricks in their mini-relaxer. Some people are leg-jigglers ***(demonstrate)*** or fiddlers or steering-wheel grippers. Some people are frowners, or get tension headaches.

So you can start by looking at how **you** usually react when stressed.

It may by useful to provide literature on stress response profiles here. For example, the 'Cues for Tension and Anxiety Survey Schedule' (Table H-33).

(While writing) Some of the options include: One or two muscle relaxings; a couple of slow deep breaths or sighs; a bit of calming self-talk, like 'What's the worst that can happen?!' or 'I've handled it before'; imagining something, like being on the beach in the sun; or counting down from 10, or remembering a nice time, or imagining feeling warm and heavy ***(autogenic relaxation)***.

If you try out this CD ***(provide)*** it may include bits you especially like.

Any literature on the above can be provided. For example, The Relaxation and Stress Reduction Workbook (Davis et al., 2008).

Step 2: *Selection of cues and start of routine Mini-relaxers.*

Over the next week, I'd like you to look out for regular times in your normal routine when it would be possible to take half a minute to do your Mini-relaxer — whether you need it or not. I want you to choose 3 or 4 or 5 that each might happen 2 or 3 or 4 times a day. They aren't necessarily times when you feel uptight; just times that happen regularly, and are convenient.

So you may choose: Every time you have a cuppa; Or each time you go to the loo; Or just before you get out of the car; Or as you put the phone down at work; Or …

One or two at home, and one or two at work, and one or two elsewhere would be good. ***(Vary this according to need and circumstances.)***

What we're after is a total of around 15 times a day. Less than 10 is probably not worth doing. More than 20 could become a nuisance. So, three cues or reminders that each happen about 5 times a day would be an example.

When you decide on which ones you'll try — tell me next time what they are — put one of these stickers ***(provide about six colourful star or dot stickers)*** at that spot. For example, on your coffee mug, or on the back of the loo door, or on the dash of the car, or … Leave them there for at least a week, until you start to think of the Mini-relaxer without them.

Step 3: *Mini-relaxer use when needed.*

If I asked you to just take two slow breaths and relax whenever you get a panic attack/nervous with people/stressed at work/ … ***(tailor to the client here)***, it would be too hard. The hardest time to calm down is when you're feeling really anxious.

But if you've been doing a particular calm-down procedure 15 times a day regularly for 3 weeks, then you may be good enough at it so it can make a difference even when you're in a bad state.

So, the next step, after a few weeks, is to try to remember to use your Mini-relaxer when you most need it. Then, instead of stickers or cue situations being the trigger, getting anxious itself might remind you.

All of the above must be tailored to an individual client's problem, circumstances, and capacities. And followup coaching and encouragement are crucial.

Accompanied in vivo exposure therapy (in the car, down the street, in the supermarket …) is an ideal time to prompt and coach Mini-relaxer practice, but only after the Step 2 lead-up.

TABLE H-33
Cues for Tension and Anxiety Survey Schedule (CTASS)

Name:..

Date:...

Individuals have different ways that indicate that they are tense or anxious. Check below the ways that apply to you:

Feel tense in:
☐ *a. Forehead*
☐ *b. Back of the neck*
☐ *c. Chest*
☐ *d. Shoulders*
☐ *e. Stomach*
☐ *f. Face*
☐ *g. Other parts*..

☐ Sweat

☐ Heart beats fast

☐ Can feel heart pounding

☐ Can hear heart pounding

☐ Face feels flushed or warm

☐ Skin feels cool and damp

Tremble or shake:
☐ *a. Hands*
☐ *b. Legs*
☐ *c. Other*..

☐ Stomach feels like you are just stopping in an elevator

☐ Stomach feels nauseous

☐ Feel yourself holding onto something tightly (like a steering wheel or arm of a chair)

☐ Scratch a certain part of the body

☐ When legs are crossed, you move the top one up and down

☐ Bite your nails

☐ Grind your teeth

☐ Have trouble with your speech

☐ Feel like you are going to choke

☐ Feel faint

☐ Feel dizzy

☐ Find yourself breathing quickly or heavily

Cues for Tension and Anxiety Survey Schedule (Hersen & Bellack, 1976).

(Available as a free download from www.australianacademicpress.com.au)

HOMEWORK 34

Subjective Units of Distress (SUDS) of 7

When the notion of SUDS (0–10 or 0–100) is introduced (see Homework 4), an opportunity emerges to give guidance in the pacing of exposure therapy. "A moderate level of emotional intensity or distress is motivating and not debilitating; however, a high level of distress can interfere with therapy, and a low level of emotional intensity fails to motivate the patient to change" (Beutler et al., 2001, p. 161).

A target of 70% or 7/10 on the SUDS scale has been proposed as therapeutically optimal during exposure to feared stimuli (Montgomery & Morris, 1992).

After (re)introducing the SUDS concept (see Homework 4): Using the SUDS idea, psychologists have tried to find out how fast people should push themselves to face their fears to get the best increase in confidence over time.

So they've tried different things.

They've asked some people to keep their SUDS as low as possible: to have a 'stress holiday'; to take it easy, stay home, avoid the things that make them anxious.

Second, they've taken people by the hand and pushed them towards their fears, quickly and with no compromises. This is sometimes called 'flooding'.

Or they've asked people to try to push their SUDS up to a number — 3 or 5 or 7 — every day, but not past it.

What they've found is that the people who take a 'stress holiday' feel a bit better at first, but they don't get anywhere. Their fears stay just as strong, or even worsen, and their confidence stays low.

Among the people who were pushed, maybe even into panicky states, some get much better very quickly; but lots pull out of the whole process. It felt awful, they felt out of control, and didn't go on with it.

Among the people who were asked to push it every day up to a certain level of upset or stress, it was the ones who aimed for a SUDS of 7 that improved the most. They really pushed it, but not to the point were they felt out of control.

I'd like you to use 'SUDS of 7' as a guide as to how far and fast to push it when you're ...

(Describe in vivo fear-facing. Compare this with Challenge Diary entries to date.)

When a spouse/parent is involved in exposure episodes:

Tell Bill about what the SUDS mean, and about SUDS of 7. Then he'll know when to give you a little push or encouragement, and when to back off because you're doing a bit much already.

HOMEWORK 35

Reasonable Versus Unreasonable Worries Listing

This homework is useful whenever there is some doubt in the client's mind as to which worries/concerns/anxieties are appropriate, 'normal', useful, or justified and which are over-valued, excessive, pathological, or unjustified. Such doubt is common where a person may have several phobic concerns, as in generalised anxiety disorder (GAD) or obsessive–compulsive disorder (OCD) or agoraphobia, or when there are still significant multiple (precipitating?) life stressors impinging.

Perhaps on the back of the homework card, write headings such as 'Reasonable, Useful Worries' and 'Unreasonable, Useless Worries' at the top of two wide columns, with a separating vertical line. Vary the titles according to the person's vocabulary and the introduction so far as to why their fears/obsessions are a problem.

> Under these headings ***(read them out)*** I'd like you to write examples of upsets or worries that are understandable and probably useful to dwell on because they're real and you need to plan or grieve or psyche up, and examples of the problem worries you've told me about that aren't reasonable and that get you nowhere or hold back your life.

Provide one or two examples of each drawn from the history provided so far; for example, 'My mother has become very ill' versus 'If I use a public toilet I'll get a terrible disease.'

Among the functions of this homework are:

1. It gives the client practice at consciously identifying, distinguishing, and acknowledging target worries.
2. It simultaneously approves 'healthy' worrying, so that phobias, obsessions, and so on are less likely to be total distractors from real, urgent, or fixable life stresses.
3. It assists early identification of worries that need a different response as early as possible; for example, thought-stopping of OCD rituals, rather than reassurance-seeking, or control of breathing during agoraphobic panic.
4. It also provides the therapist with a problem-thoughts listing that may be more comprehensive than that elicited in assessment interview. The client has time to recognise unhelpful thinking or anxious feelings in 'real life' and may be more willing to jot embarrassing fears on a list than admit them verbally with eye contact.
5. The therapist, upon presentation of the dual listing, can then decide whether to focus primarily on therapy/management of the pathological anxieties, or whether to address the client's coping with the 'useful' worries as well (e.g., via grief work, problem-solving training, bibliotherapy, education about psychosomatic conditions, or assertiveness training).

HOMEWORK 36

Thought-Stopping

This group of procedures can be useful whenever an identifiable distressing thought is part of an escalating sequence of responses, or a PMC. Thought-stopping was originally developed with obsessive ruminations in mind (so to speak; Wolpe, 1973). But it has since been successfully applied, usually only as a component of therapy, to many other anxiety, anger, depression, and psychotic problems (Burk, Randolph & Probst, 1985; Peden et al., 2005; Rimm & Masters, 1979).

The original procedure comprises therapeutic sessions in which the client is asked to engage in the troublesome thinking, whereupon the therapist would shout 'stop!' In subsequent trials the therapist would just say 'stop', the client would say 'stop' out loud, and finally would merely think 'stop'.

However, soon variations emerged involving (a) the use of a rubber band flicked on the wrist, pinching of the hand, or even electric shocks, and (b) extension of the procedure to home/self-administered sessions, and to ongoing in vivo problem situations.

With such variability of procedure and application (Rimm & Masters, 1979, p. 400), it is no surprise that the learning theory rationales for thought-stopping's effectiveness are many and varied. In a confusing mixture of cognitive, operant, and classical conditioning hypotheses various authors have implicated thought-stopping training as a form of self-punishment (Mahoney, 1971; Steketee, 1993; Tryon & Palladino, 1979), producing an operant extinction curve (Fensterheim & Baer, 1975, 1977), simply providing a distractor (Cautela, 1979; Cautela & Kearney, 1986; Steketee, 1993), even if it is in the form of an electric shock! (Dengrove, 1985), as reciprocally inhibiting the maladaptive thought (Cautela & Rosensteil, 1979), establishing a habit of thought inhibition by positive reinforcement through anxiety reduction (Wolpe, 1973), developing an assertive response (Davis et al., 2008; Rimm & Masters, 1979), or as a self-control (McGuire & Priestley, 1985; Rimm & Masters, 1979; Wisocki, 1985) or coping skill (Kilpatrick & Amick, 1985).

This mayhem provides much leeway in presenting a rationale to a client and in selecting a thought-stopping procedure to follow. The following 'prescription' is one that has been well understood and well accepted by my clients. It derives from the self-control or coping skills model, which has some support from Marks' (1973) finding that thought-stopping applied to neutral nonobsessive nonphobic thoughts can be as effective as applied to obsessive ones. This suggests a skill is being acquired, rather than a response being modified.

Unfortunately, thought-stopping has received much unwarranted bad press recently. This has not been the result of new solid surprise empirical findings of ineffectiveness or, as claimed, even negative effects. It has come from proponents of the 'third wave' of CBT, namely the Acceptance and Commitment Therapy (ACT) (Beevers et al., 1999; Hayes, Strosahl, & Wilson, 1999) and mindfulness (Hannan & Tolin, 2005) devotees, who have philosophical objections to thought-stopping, due to their assumption that all negative states must always be faced, experienced, and endured rather than modified or avoided.

This opinion ignores 40 years of the successful evidence-based application of thought-stopping techniques in hundreds of studies with thousands of people with dozens of different CPPs (Bakker, 2009).

I therefore recommend direct in vivo rubber-band thought-stopping ('the ouch technique'; Greenberg, 1996) in those situations where the risk of negative thinking is appreciable, which may be 24-hours-a-day (mulling in bed?), or just at work, when out socially, while studying, and so on.

I'm going to ask you to do something a bit weird, so I need to explain properly why. It involves hurting yourself.

Now one way to describe what we've worked out so far, is that when you get into situation X two voices get going in your head. The 'good' voice and the 'bad' voice.

This has nothing to do with schizophrenia or multiple personality. This is just like anyone can have an argument in their head.

The bad voice is saying ***(give examples from assessment, such as 'I'm going to die', 'Germs are all over my hands', 'Jenny is being slow just to annoy me')***, and the good voice, which hasn't been winning very often, is quietly saying 'It's okay, calm down, Stop that rubbish' ***(or a more pertinent example)***.

Now what we want to do is to help the good voice be more powerful, so it wins 90% of the time instead of 10% of the time. ***(Clients often interject here with 'or 0% of the time'.)*** We can make **anything** more powerful for you by simple conditioning. By pairing it — the good voice — with something that is already powerful, enough times so the good voice gets some of that power.

They call this classical conditioning. ***(Give an example, perhaps from Pavlov, perhaps from experience.)***

So we want to pair the good voice saying 'That's rubbish, Stop it!' with a **natural** thought-stopper, for a while.

I'm going to ask you to wear this rubber band ***(provide),*** or a similar one ***(24-hours-a-day/16-hours-a-day/every day at work/other specifier) for (one week/a few days/until our next appointment)***, on your left wrist. It needs to be tight enough so it won't fall off, but not so it cuts in.

Whenever you notice a battle between the good voice and the bad voice, ***(give example)*** which you should notice more easily and more quickly now that we've been talking about it so much, I want you to pull the rubber band out as far as you've got the courage to, and at the very moment you let it go, I want you to say to yourself, with the good voice, 'That's rubbish, Stop it!' ***(or a similar agreed sharp command)***. It's meant to hurt because it's meant to interrupt the bad voice. It's a natural thought-stopper. ***(Demonstrate and request a rehearsal.)***

Then, you'll still have to do something else to distract yourself, or else the bad voice will just kick back in, in a few seconds. But, at least the thought-stopping will give you a couple of seconds to get onto a new track.

What we're after is that in a while the good voice saying 'That's rubbish, Stop it!' will develop some of the power of the rubber-band pain, and you'll get better at stopping, and, therefore, better at throwing out the negative thinking.

So, I don't want you to use a rubber band for the rest of your life. What you'll find is that after a day or a week or a month, one day you'll notice in the car/at work/etc. that the bad voice is getting going. You'll think to yourself 'I'm doing it again. I'd better stop it'. You'll reach for the rubber band, and you'll notice that you don't have to flick, because the thought has gone. That's because you just said to yourself 'I'd better stop it' and the associations in your head with that thought kicked in like a reflex.

When that happens, you might want to keep the rubber band on for a little while, but you can soon throw it away, because the power has been 'conditioned' into you.

Other advantages of doing it this way include that the rubber band is there all the time to remind you of what you're supposed to do. The pain from it can be sharp, but it does no permanent damage. Sometimes you may just need to give yourself a tiny reminder flick, and sometimes a really big shock.

If you find the battle is going on but you haven't got your rubber band, then some people pinch the skin between their fingers with their fingernails. This can work too.

Don't worry if you don't think of using the thought-stopping until you've been ***(worrying/ getting angry/thinking negatively)*** for half an hour. Do the thought-stopping then, because the next time it might be 20 minutes when you think of it, and then 10 minutes. If we can get it down to half a minute, then you're going as well as most of us, because we all have rubbish go on in our heads. It's just a matter of how far it goes before we control it.

So, I'll find out from you next time how much you have used the rubber band, and how good you're getting at thought-stopping without it.

HOMEWORK 37

Social Phobia Self-Statements

Erroneous and catastrophising self-talk is critical in the PMCs of social phobia. As an introduction to the identification and challenging of this self-talk, I ask my clients to tell me which of four levels of negative thinking they most frequently engage in. The intent is to trigger greater self-observation and self-awareness. But the commencement of self-challenging often ensues, even before subsequent homework is set.

I'd like you to start to 'watch' your own thinking ***(list relevant settings: e.g. in town, work meetings, parties)*** to see which of the following thinking mistakes you fall into most often.

(Write these, tailored to the client's own particular fears.)

1. 'Everyone is paying attention to me.'

We know that mostly people are busy with their **own** issues, or their own presentation. You're just another body in their world.

2. 'My anxiety and embarrassment show.'

We've already used the mirror to show that you don't go as red as you feel you do. It all feels big inside. But mostly it doesn't stand out to others.

3. 'When I shake/go red/sweat, everyone can tell why.'

There are hundreds of reasons why people might shake or be red ***(give examples)*** Sometimes people are cold, or have a permanent tremor, or a hangover, or people can be naturally red, or be hot or ill or have a medication side effect, or we just can't tell what causes what, if we see any of this.

4. 'If people pay attention specifically to me, and my feelings show out, and they guess what I'm thinking/feeling, that's **awful** and I should dig myself a hole and go and jump into it.'

(The tone here is deliberately a little flippant.)

You are ***not*** an awful person because nervousness or embarrassment shows. When you can fully accept that, the problem fully goes away.

The following anecdote has helped get the above points across. Hopefully you can remember a similar one to genuinely share with clients:

When I was working at a hospital years ago, we had staff meetings every morning to introduce new patients. One day they were talking about something to do with sex. I suddenly had the thought: 'What if I went red when the topic of sex came up. People would see it. I'm supposed to be able to calmly talk about anything as a psychologist, so that'd be awful.'

After that, every time the topic came up, or I thought about it, I'd feel myself going red. I was caught in a self-fulfilling prophecy (a PMC.)

As a psychologist I knew things that should help, so I tried distracting myself whenever the thoughts or feelings came up. I'd look at the roses outside the window. This helped a bit, but it didn't **fix** the problem.

I started taking slow breaths and relaxing whenever I got a reaction. This also helped a bit, but didn't **fix** the problem.

Then, one day, in the meeting, I was going through my 'I think I'm going red' bit, when I looked around and realised: 'I've been going through all this stress and bother, and no-one knows or cares, or is paying attention! Even if I am going red, they're not noticing, and even if they did, so what! I don't care any more'. From that day, my reactions changed, and stopped keeping the cycle going.

Since then I hardly ever go red, or care if I do!

An anecdote with a parallel message — again you may have a similar one to relate — follows:

I was giving a seminar to a big group of important people once, and I was very nervous, and my papers were shaking in my hands. The seminar happened to be about 'Anxiety and Panic Attacks'. So, when I stood up, I said: 'Instead of just talking today about anxiety and panic attacks, I've decided to demonstate the problem as well'. Then it was out in the open. I had nothing to hide. And within 2 minutes I was feeling fine. I had broken a PMC.

Following such an introduction, it is more possible to extract, challenge, and block socially phobic catastrophic thinking. Each client's reaction and needs will vary, and will require individual coaching.

HOMEWORK 38

Over-Breathing Experiment

The feature that distinguishes panic disorder and agoraphobia from the other anxiety disorders is that what is feared or avoided is panic attacks themselves and certain situations are then avoided only because they are associated with the risk of having a panic attack.

The principle of exposure is then more difficult to apply, because situational exposure only indirectly confronts the client with their primary fear. Over-Breathing Experiment sessions are one way clients can deliberately confront much of what they fear (panic symptoms). There are other ways to create panic-like physical symptoms (e.g. spinning to produce dizziness), but hyperventilating is easy, quick, safe, and re-enacts what actually occurs in most panic states.

Panic disorder clients also usually require convincing that their breathing is a significant PMC factor in panic attacks; see Figure 6.1 (h). An 'experiment' to test the effects of over-breathing or hyperventilation is often useful.

Both these functions are served by an over-breathing experiment — exposure and experiment.

This homework, including the HV Questionnaire (Handout 2), derive from John Franklin's excellent *Self-Mastery Training: A Complete 28 Day Home Treatment Program For Agoraphobia* (1999).

So we've worked out that what you're most afraid of is these panic attacks, because when you have one you feel as though ***(you could have a heart attack/you might faint)***. We now know you won't. It's just a panic attack that feels awful.

Now if you told me you only have a panic when you're near a dog, we'd be off to the RSPCA kennels. Facing what you fear is really important. But how do we arrange to face the feelings in a panic attack?

Also, I've been saying that among the things that make a panic much worse is your breathing. When you get anxious, a part of the 'flight or fight response' ***(explain)*** is that a person will breathe a bit quicker, and their blood pressure goes up, and their heart rate goes up, and so on. All this is to prepare you for action — to hit someone or run away! But, if you don't hit someone or run away, because that's no answer to a panic attack, then you'll get all this extra oxygen and chemicals in your system that aren't used up. We now know that **this** will cause a whole bunch of symptoms that are nearly the same as a Panic Attack!

This ***(show HV Questionaire — Over-Breathing)*** is a list of some of the things that having too much oxygen and not enough carbon dioxide in your system can produce. ***(Pause.)*** Notice how similar the symptoms are to what happens in a panic attack. But you and I can produce a lot of this right now, just by over-breathing.

(While writing.)

So, for two big reasons, I'm going to ask you to do the following: Several times, at home, when you're feeling okay, maybe with ***(spouse/parent/other)*** there — I know what I'm asking you to do is perfectly safe, but you may be wary, so I don't want to contaminate this with anxiety symptoms, I want to find out what the over-breathing does — to sit down and on purpose over-breathe ***(demonstrate)*** until you get some symptoms. Then you'll stop over-breathing, and some symptoms will go away immediately, and some will hang on for a while.

I want you to do this several times because at first you may go pretty easy on yourself. But as you find out it's okay, you can push it a bit harder each time.

When you have a *good* go, then, as you stop over-breathing, I want you to fill in the questionnaire, by putting numbers from this scale into these boxes. Then when you bring it back, I'll be able to see which of these symptoms happened a lot.

It won't be exactly the same as a panic attack, because in those there are other things going on, like the anxiety of being out of control, whereas in this you'll know exactly what is causing what. That's why I want you to over-breathe in a really exaggerated way. So that in one minute you'll get the symptoms that several minutes of 'nervous breathing' might produce.

So this is partly to experiment to find out the effects on *you* of panic-breathing. But it's also to help you face some of the feelings in a controlled way, to face your fears.

Many clients are fearful and reluctant with this homework; if they do not fulfill it as homework, an option at the next appointment is to undertake the exercise with them in session. This has the advantage of providing modelling as well.

 (Available as a free download from www.australianacademicpress.com.au)

HV Questionnaire (Over-Breathing)

Name:... Date: ..../............/............

Listed below are a number of symptoms that people sometimes experience when they over-breathe. We would like you to tell us how much disturbance or distress each of these symptoms caused you when you over-breathed today. Do this by choosing a number from the scale below and placing it in the box that corresponds to each symptom. Be sure to place a number in every box.

0	1	2	3	4	5	6	7	8
Not at all disturbing		Mildly or slightly disturbing		Moderately or definitely disturbing		Severely or markedly disturbing		Very severely disturbed

1. Dizziness, faintness or lightheadedness .... ☐
2. Feeling short of breath or trouble getting your breath .... ☐
3. Numb or tingling sensation in hands or feet.......... ☐
4. Dry mouth .... ☐
5. Feeling unsteady on your feet.......... ☐
6. Feeling nausea.......... ☐
7. Having little stamina and tiring easily .... ☐
8. Trouble thinking clearly .... ☐
9. Trembling hands or legs .... ☐
10. Feelings of tightness or pain in your chest.......... ☐
11. Seeing double .... ☐
12. Fear of having a heart attack.......... ☐
13. Feeling that you or your surroundings are strange or unreal .... ☐
14. Headache.......... ☐
15. Hands tight and hard to open.......... ☐
16. Sensations of numbness or tingling in the face .... ☐
17. Feeling of breathing 'too much' .... ☐
18. Cold pale hands .... ☐
19. Difficulty in talking.......... ☐
20. Feeling 'far away'.......... ☐
21. Crying for no good reason .... ☐
22. Feeling a lump in your throat .... ☐
23. Fear of passing out or collapsing .... ☐
24. Blurred vision .... ☐
25. Feeling of panic.......... ☐
26. Heart pounding or racing .... ☐
27. Nervous stomach .... ☐
28. Sensations of burning, tingling or crawling .... ☐
29. Feeling of rising agitation .... ☐
30. Feeling that you want to run.......... ☐
31. Muscular tension in jaw, neck, back, legs, and so on .... ☐
32. Fear that you may wet your pants.......... ☐
33. Diahorrhea .... ☐
34. Feeling hot or flushed.......... ☐
35. Fear that you may die.......... ☐
36. Feeling trapped and helpless .... ☐
37. Feeling as if the ground was moving and rising up .... ☐
38. Feeling exhausted or completely drained .... ☐
39. Fear that you are going mad .... ☐
40. Losing control, for example, becoming hysterical .... ☐
41. Causing a scene or public disturbance .... ☐

HV Questionnaire reproduced with permission (Franklin, 1999).

HOMEWORK 39

Caffeine Reduction

Among the general psychological assessment questions (Table 5.1) was included *'How much tea or coffee do you have each day?'* This question is useful to ask of almost any client, as caffeine intake or withdrawal can be an aggravating, if not causal, factor in anxiety, pain, mood, eating, psychotic, or sleep problems (American Psychiatric Association, 1994, p. 214; Carter, 1997, pp. 178, 203, 213).

Caffeine is a recognised pseudostressor or sympathomimetic, and as such can increase metabolism, alertness, stress hormone release, blood pressure, heart rate, and CNS reactivity (Greenberg, 1996). Withdrawal commonly produces headache, and perhaps irritability, lethargy, or anxiety (Padus, 1992, p. 229).

The most common source of significant amounts of caffeine is brewed coffee (170 mg–200 mg per cup), instant coffee (90 mg–140 mg), tea (60 mg–100 mg), colas (40 mg–60 mg), and a little in chocolate, especially dark chocolate. The American Medical Association recommends a daily limit of 200 mg (Davis et al., 2008, p.246).

Therefore, a high level of intake or sudden changes in pattern are worthy of intervention. Just because someone says they have drunk a lot of coffee all their life and it doesn't affect them does not remove all concern, as caffeine may not in some cases interfere with sleep until the middle years of life (Evans et al., 1983, p.102).

Where level of intake is a concern — for example, more than 4 cups of instant coffee per day, especially if into the evening — then homework actually written on a card may be warranted. This should be specific and behavioural rather than vague policy. The questions of home versus workplace pattern, and morning versus evening ingestion should be considered.

Explain caffeine as a nervous system stimulant, and a typical homework then might be:

> This afternoon or at the next supermarket visit, I'd like you to have decaf coffee/decaf tea on your grocery list. These days it's quite drinkable, so give the taste a try. Then, make sure it's sitting out where you'll see it at home or at work.
>
> At first I want you to alternate between the decaf and your regular drink; except in the evening when you **only** have decaf.

With a client who has high regular ingestion:

> Keep an eye out for any withdrawal feelings, like a headache.
>
> If you prefer a chocolate drink, or juice, or water, that's fine. But I guess you're used to the tea/coffee as a habit, or associated with a break. So the decaf means you don't have to change completely.

After a while you may go totally to the decaf.

This applies only now, while you're having some troubles. In a while you can go back to drinking what you like.

This won't fix everything, but why have a bit of nervous system stimulant in you making everything 10% worse, when you're already ***tense/jumpy/worried/in pain/finding it hard to sleep/confused/racy in your thoughts/other problem descriptor***.

HOMEWORK 40

Angry Self-Talk

Whether identifying and analysing anger-inducing self-talk in terms of 'irrational beliefs', or 'thinking errors', or 'hot thoughts', a useful homework is to start to list relevant ones as they are identified, either through discussion and introspection, or through self-observation over time, as with NER recording (Homework 1).

Often the expression of these thoughts on paper in words is enough to make a client cringe with how silly the self-talk can look; however, writing reasonable alternatives or answers to them is a logical next step.

Even though the anger seems to flash out of nowhere, nearly always there will be two quick steps before the rush of feeling.

First, there will be a situation or trigger. You've told me about some, for example, when ...

But we can't avoid those situations forever. So what's the next step? ***(perhaps pointing to Figure 3.1)***. The situation or trigger can only get to you if it has some **meaning**. So, something must be going on in your head **about** the trigger that is the **real cause** for getting angry. This **real cause** is the enemy. We need to know the enemy, and this is fixable, even when the situation isn't.

I'm going to have a guess at one or two of the common angry thoughts that can happen to you from ***what you've told me/from your NER records/from the questionnaire***. Maybe one that happens when your son does something annoying: 'He's doing this **just** to get at me'. While driving, maybe it flashes in your head 'People should be as competent as me!' I've written these down. I'd like you as homework to keep the list going, until you have five or six. Then I want you to write a reasonable, or true, or more positive alternative thought for each one.

The list of common or general angry thoughts is huge, some other possibilities include:

- when someone hurts me they deserve to be hurt back.
- when things go wrong, that *makes* me angry
- everything I do has to work out perfectly
- no-one should ever make a mistake
- if people make a mistake, it's laziness
- someone has to pay if there's been a mistake
- things should go perfectly.

These are ***general*** attitudes behind specific instances of angry 'self-talk'. A specific instance, perhaps revealed by NER analysis, may be 'That idiot is driving too slowly'. The general attitude behind this may be 'People should be as competent and thoughtful as me'. It is more ***generally*** useful to be aware of these generic attitudes than the millions of specific thoughts that mediate anger.

Most anger-inducing self-talk involves 'shoulds' (Butler, 1991).

HOMEWORK 41

Time-Outs

To break the anger PMCs of Figure 6.5 using cognitive therapy alone (as in Homework 40) is especially ambitious, as cognitive self-control in the heat of argument, or with such a 'self-reinforcing' emotion (see Table 7.2, footnote) is attempting a sophisticated form of control over a primitive state.

It may be more practical initially to use a behavioural or situational strategy, such as time-out.

This is different from the imposed 'time-out' often used in child management, as it is ***self-administered*** *before* a situation escalates.

A useful preamble is to explore the history of positive and negative outcomes once anger has really set in. 'Did you change her mind after the argument got heated?', 'Did you fix or damage the wobbly chair when you got mad at it?', 'Does snapping at your son when he says something silly make him smarter?', and so on. The point here is to get agreement that nothing good comes of allowing crabbiness to grow to rage, and everyone is better off if things are stopped at the crabbiness level.

Recommended homework:

> So from now on I'd like you and Mary and Bobby to know that when you start to get hot under the collar you are going to — or they will remind you to — excuse yourself for a while, to give some space and time to cool down, or at least to avoid a worsening and a blow-up and things you'll all regret.
>
> From now on everyone will know this is the policy.

If they are not present:

> Your homework is to tell them all about this. So they can remind, or at least understand if you stomp out suddenly. Or **they** might go and do something else, if that's convenient for them.
>
> Anyone can use the codeword 'time-out' or the symbol they use in basketball. You need to break the situation up. It's got nothing to do with who's right and who's wrong or what's fair. It's just about avoiding a worsening while it's still possible. And the person who leaves the situation and breaks the spiral is the one who is doing the right thing. This isn't running away. Any topic can come up again tomorrow.
>
> The break usually needs to be for at least a half an hour. You can judge what time you need. It's good to do something physical or something very distracting during your time-out. But driving fast or damaging things to 'get your anger out' is **not** recommended. ***(Distraction or counteraction versus catharsis can be discussed here.)***

I also provide some pages on time-out strategies and rules by Sonkin and Durphy (1985, pp. 27–31).

HOMEWORK 42

Life Change Units

During an initial general assessment (Table 5.1) hypotheses will emerge as to possible precipitating and maintaining causal factors. It is very common to find an increase in significant life events, changes, or stressors in the period preceding problem onset or referral (Brown & Harris, 1989).

Uncovering a possible problem cause has not only explanatory relevance, but often therapeutic relevance in a number of ways:

1. While some stressors are historic and irreversible (e.g. a death in the family), some will be ongoing and changeable (e.g. arguments with the boss).
2. An overload of life events can include one or two crucial ones, perhaps revealing themselves as such by the nature of the presenting symptoms. For example, generalised anxiety peaking in the car after a life-event excess which includes a motor vehicle accident.
3. In order to minimise PMCs involving self-deprecation for having a problem and functioning so poorly — as in Figures 6.1 (c), 6.4 (g) and (i), and 6.6 (a) and (b) — it can help to have a reasonable causal theory, so that a client may get to a point where they can say, 'Well it's no wonder I'm struggling. I've done a good job just to get through all this. I'll be getting better from here, but I'll need to work on it'.

For any of the above reasons, but especially the third, I prescribe the 'life change units' homework to anyone whose recent history includes a number of possibly cumulative life stressor precipitants.

The original list of 43 life events and corresponding average life change units, the Social Readjustment Rating Scale (Holmes & Rahe, 1967), has been extended and updated to a 74-item list called the Recent Life Changes Questionnaire (Miller & Rahe, 1997). This is reproduced as Handout 3. It is designed to cover a 2-year period, and 6-month totals over 300 life-change units (LCUs) or 1-year totals over 500 LCUs are considered indicative of high recent life stress.

You've had a lot going on to try to cope with — more than the average person can reasonably be expected to handle without something giving. And it's all been happening one after another, without time to get over one thing before the next stress or upset dumps on you as well.

Show Recent Life Changes Questionnaire (Miller & Rahe, 1997) — Handout 3.

This is one way of looking at what you've had to handle: Have you ever seen this before? I'll tell you where it came from:

The researchers started off with a list of significant changes and stresses in a person's life. They decided to give getting married a score of 50, which represented the average impact that has on the average person. Then they got hundreds of people to rate the other events on the list in comparison to getting married, for how much impact they have, and they subsequently averaged everyone's opinion and came up with the scores on the list.

Now, everyone is different, and every event is different, but at least with this list they could do research, because that used group averages anyway.

So they then gave a list like this to thousands of people and asked them to add up a 'total life event score' for themselves for, usually, the last 1 or 2 years.[1]

Then they followed up all those people to see how they went over the next 12 months.

Among the people who had worked out a score of over 300 — a big score due to lots of stressful events — 80% of them, 4 out of 5, developed in the next 12 months a major physical or emotional problem. Physical things included migraines, and ulcers, and heart problems. Emotional things included anxiety problems, or depression, or obsessive–compulsive problems, or irritability to the point of affecting relationships.

Among those who scored between 200 and 300, about 50%, have a problem in the next 12 months; under 200, and it was up to 30%.

Now, exactly what problems cropped up — where the cracks showed — was a bit of a lottery. The exact types of stresses didn't predict it very well. It seems that depends on how you're built, your genes, your background, and so on.

Now, even without doing the calculations, I can tell from the bit of history you've given me so far, that your score for the last ***(year or 2 years — insert appropriate timeframe)*** would be pretty awful.

And we now know that everyone has a limit to what they can take. Your limit might be quite high. But you've got one. We can see that when you've had too much to cope with, it shows up by ***(insert here appropriate lay diagnostic terms, e.g. 'getting depressed', 'becoming panicky', 'obsessive-compulsive habits', 'getting headaches', 'your irritable bowel syndrome getting worse')***.

So, I'm going to ask you to jot down all the significant changes and stresses you've had to cope with over the last 2 years and then give them all a score based on this list ***(Handout 3)***. If anything happened twice, it gets that score twice. Then add them up.

There are at least two reasons I'm asking you to do this. First, you've had very little time for all these stresses to sink in. While you were coping with one, the next one took over. This exercise will at least give you a little chance to see it all and let it sink in a bit better. You may want to do the homework with ***(spouse/parent/etc.)*** so you can talk about it all a bit.

But the second reason is that this exercise will prove that your reaction has been understandable. **You're** okay. It's **life** that's been unreasonable. There is no point or sense in kicking yourself about the problems you've been having. There is a cause for them, and our job is to get on top of them. If you put yourself down because you've got problems, it's not fair, and it'll just make our job harder. You're going to have to be strong and sensible to fight these problems.

These messages can be reinforced when the homework comes back. Often unrevealed stressors may emerge in the list; stressors that bear a direct relationship to the presenting symptoms may also emerge (e.g. a break-in before obsessive–compulsive checking of doors and windows), and stressors that are ongoing and deserve current practical intervention can be discerned (e.g. financial strain).

In addition, clients will have opinions about the rating each listed event warrants. This can be revealing about the special or personal meaning of the stressors to them.

But the opportunity to break self-derogatory PMCs over having an embarrassing, 'weak', frightening, or indistinct problem is critical. Therefore, this does not rely on proof of the etiological life-stress hypthesis, only on its believability.

In some circumstances, identification and subsequent reversal of some of the precipitating life changes can be central to therapy. This may be the case with postnatal depression, for example.

Endnote

1 The literature is confusing as to whether the statistics apply to a sample period of 1 year (Davis et al., 2008; Peterson & Bossio, 1991) or 2 years (Bourne, 1995; Wolfe, 1974), and whether illness over the next 1 (Greenberg, 1996) or 2 years (Norfolk, 1986) is predicted. Some just refer to 'the near future' (Davis, et al., 2008; Padus, 1992).

Recent Life Changes Questionnaire

Life change event	LCU
Health	
An injury or illness which:	
kept you in bed a week or more or sent you to the hospital,	74
was less serious than above	44
Major dental work	26
Major change in eating habits	27
Major change in sleeping habits	26
Major change in your usual type and/or amount of recreation	28
Work	
Change to a new type of work	51
Change in your work hours or conditions	35
Change in your responsibilities at work:	
more responsibilities	29
fewer responsibilities	21
promotion	31
demotion	42
transfer	32
Troubles at work:	
with your boss	29
with coworkers	35
with persons under your supervision	35
other work troubles	28
Major business adjustment	60
Retirement	52
Loss of job:	
laid off from work	68
fired from work	79
Correspondence course to help you in your work	18
Home and family	
Major change in living conditions	42
Change in residence:	
move within the same town or city	25
move to a different town, city or state	47
Change in family get-togethers	25
Major change in health or behaviour of family member	55
Marriage	50
Pregnancy	67
Miscarriage or abortion	65
Gain of a new family member:	
birth of a child	66
adoption of a child	65
a relative moving in with you	59
Spouse beginning or ending work	46

Life change event	LCU
Child leaving home:	
to attend college	41
due to marriage	41
for other reasons	45
Change in arguments with spouse	50
In-law problems	38
Change in the marital status of your parents:	
divorce	59
remarriage	50
Separation from spouse:	
due to work	53
due to marital problems	76
Divorce	96
Birth of grandchild	43
Death of spouse	119
Death of other family member:	
child	123
brother or sister	102
parent	100
Personal and social	
Change in personal habits	26
Beginning or ending school or college	38
Change of school or college	35
Change in political beliefs	24
Change in religious beliefs	29
Change in social activities	27
Vacation	24
New, close, personal relationship	37
Engagement to marry	45
Girlfriend or boyfriend problems	39
Sexual difficulties	44
'Falling out' of a close personal relationship	47
An accident	48
Minor violation of the law	20
Being held in jail	75
Death of a close friend	70
Major decision regarding your immediate future	51
Major personal achievement	36
Financial	
Major change in finances:	
increased income	38
decreased income	60
investment and/or credit difficulties	56
Loss or damage of personal property	43
Moderate purchase	20
Major purchase	37
Foreclosure on a mortgage or loan	58

Recent Life Changes Questionnaire (Miller & Rahe, 1997).

HOMEWORK 43

Reasons To Change

CBT can be hard work. It is no magic bullet, quick fix, mystical cure-all, or fatalistic cop-out. In fact, as discussed in Script 5, one may be suspicious if a client is relieved and placated at the end of a session. This is a good sign only if education and reassurance are the primary interventions. Otherwise, they leave with the knowledge of the challenging homework ahead of them, and the expectation of improvement over time — not with the glow of a 'cured' client.

This challenging nature of CBT has some attractions for a therapist. Malingerers, exaggerators, ambivalent clients, and trivial issues are less likely to clog the lists of CBT therapists than of some other less demanding therapists.

But it also means that consistent motivation over time is required. We know that bad habits, conditioned responses, negative self-talk, and destructive situations can wreak their havoc merely through intermittent reinforcement. This is especially true of 'self-reinforcing emotions' (see Table 7.2, footnote) or of appetitive behaviours such as drug use, or gambling.

Where a client's motivation is suspect from the start — as in compulsory treatment orders, referrals from the courts, pressure from spouse to attend, being delivered by parents to 'get fixed', and so on, or where motivation is variable over time, as revealed perhaps by poor homework compliance — specific work on motivation increase or consistency may be indicated. What follows is a very abbreviated version of Motivational Interviewing (Britt, Blampied, & Hudson, 2003).

While writing on homework card:

Between now and our next appointment, I'd like you to write down, to show me ***(10 or 8 or 5, insert appropriate number here)*** reasons you want to get on top of this problem. For example, from what you've told me so far, I would guess one of them would be ...

Write on card.

It is good to start the list, based on your assessment to date, even if the guesses are not good, to illustrate what sort of reasons we seek. Clients can misunderstand this homework in surprising ways.

So, examples could include:

For OCD:	To live a normal life
For depression:	To care better for my children
For social phobia:	To actually enjoy a meal out
For anger problems:	To keep my marriage
For alcohol abuse:	To save my body/liver/brain

When the list comes back, a review can enlarge upon what *the client* sees as important. (We can have misguided assumptions/projections on this). It can also elaborate upon or enlarge the list.

The 'codeword' strategy is an appropriate next step (as also in Homework 6):

> This list is great. But I'm less interested in what we can intellectually see and agree on now, than in what happens next Tuesday week at 4.00 in the afternoon when you feel it's all too much, and you give in and let the problem take over again, which makes it hard to claw your control back all over again.
>
> But I can't expect you to stop everything and tell everyone to be quiet, because you're trying to remember what reason number 7 was!
>
> So I'd like you to decide on a codename or label or reminder for this list — a word or a phrase or a sentence at the most — and to write this at the top. From then on to you and to me and to ***(spouse? parent? insert appropriate person here)*** this reminder means: 'There are a bunch of good reasons I'm fighting this problem. I'm not going to give in on it now!'

HOMEWORK 44

Recording 3 Meals and 3 Snacks

There are many reasons we may want to re-establish an acceptable eating pattern. This is especially the case when someone has been restricting/dieting. But other CPP areas can involve an inadequate or a chaotic eating routine. This can occur in depression. (See Homework 27: Graze Foods.) But I have also worked with someone whose OCD has crippled their toileting routine (3–4 hours) to the extent that he almost stopped eating so as to avoid the need to excrete!

The central question, irrespective of problem area, is: 'Is absence of a meal pattern, or presence of a chaotic meal pattern, a critical, changeable element in one of the client's PMCs?'

At the same time, the functional analysis and case formulation will often involve a degree of preoccupation, obsession, or hypervigilance around foods and calories. So we likely won't want to reinforce this by, for example, instructing the client to record all they eat, let alone their calorie totals. The case formulation and identified PMCs will mean our goal is regular, habitual, unemotional meals and snacks.

On such occasions we can 'prescribe' 3 meals and 2 to 3 snacks daily, without too much fuss about exactly what comprises them. It is the unemotional routine we are after (food as fuel), rather than a calorie goal. Any improved routine will be better than the low intake or chaotic pattern to date.

A general discussion about what qualifies as a 'meal' or a 'snack' is useful, but ongoing bickering about volumes and calories defeats the purpose.

(After introducing the need for more food and a better routine, usually via PMC analysis ...)

I would like you to record on this card/in this diary from now on, every day, the 3 meals and 3 snacks that you make sure you fit in.The dates go here.And each Meal is marked by an 'M', and each Snack by an 'S'. I suppose the snacks will be usually around mid-morning, mid-afternoon, and in the evening.We are aiming for 3 Ms and 3 Ss by the end of each day.

This is intended to make the client accountable, as well as to record progress. It is meant to be 'reactive' self-monitoring; that is, we want it to be therapeutic, rather than representative, naturalistic, or necessarily accurate.

If Ms or Ss are missed, this is to be discussed on followup. A quick check on what has usually compromised an M or an S is also allowable. But it should not feed any unhealthy preoccupation.

HOMEWORK 45

Binge Decision Sheets

A critical moment in any binge-eating or bulimic problem occurs at the decision point when the person decides whether to stop at the shop on the way home, or open the fridge, or stand at the food table at a party, and so on. At that moment there will be two 'voices' in the person's head: the 'good voice' and the 'bad voice'. (The bad voice may even have a name by now?)

We want the good voice to win more often. We may even use a variant of Homework 36: Thought Stopping to boost the power of the good voice.

All our good intentions and accurate insights and cognitive restructurings in-session are futile if there is not a solid bridge, a mechanism for generalisation to the real world, a self-talk coaching Homework, in place. Binge Decision Sheets (BDSs; see Figure H-45) can provide this.

They are intended to provide accurate, useful, ongoing information on the client's problem behaviour occurrences, triggers, and so on. But especially to help the client to pause, use the 'good voice', make a more rational decision at that moment, and hopefully break their usual behavioural sequence with a healthier alternative behaviour or means of coping.

I'm going to give you a pile of these sheets. They are 'Binge Decision Sheets'. I'd like you to put them, with a biro, in some spots where they will be handy at the right times. So I suggest you put some on top of the fridge at home, in your car, in your drawer at work ... [Your functional analysis will have uncovered the trigger or risk situations. Allow for privacy/confidentiality in the suggestions. For example, where at home will depend on who at home knows of the problems, the ages of children, etc.] As soon as you have the idea or urge to overeat or binge, such as when you are buying your food, I want you to promise me you'll delay what you do about it for the couple of minutes it'll take to write on the sheet.

As you can see at the bottom, you'll later be circling either 'Binge' or 'No Binge' depending on whether you went ahead and overate. But this time it'll be after thinking about the decision much more and much better than you have in the past.

(Then, take the client through one believable example of a BDS entry, using a recent binge experience.)

As with most homeworks, the direction taken after the first batch of BDSs comes back depends largely on the information gathered through them. This batch can tell us about frequency of serious binge urges, and of binges, situational and feelings triggers for those urges, what the client sees as benefits and bad effects, and, especially usefully, alternatives to binge eating. These alternative behaviours or coping methods are not then derived from a textbook, or from the therapist's wisdom or biases, or even from the client's abstract guesses in interview; but are derived at the time, in the situation, with those feelings being experienced. Feasible and effective alternative coping behaviours are more likely to be found in vivo.

Similar decision sheets can be useful with a number of other problem behaviours (e.g. excessive drinking), either as an assessment tool, or to help coach the 'good voice' into action. Homework 46 provides further examples.

TABLE H-45
Binge Decision Sheet (BDS)

Date:.. Time...

Feelings I am experiencing:

Situation or problem behind those feelings:

Benefits of bingeing now:

Bad effects of bingeing now:

(Tick whichever are bigger)

Alternatives to bingeing now:

BINGE NO BINGE

(Available as a free download from www.australianacademicpress.com.au)

HOMEWORK 46

Other Decision Sheets

Compensatory behaviours such as vomiting, laxative use, or dieting can be just as critical, harmful, and alterable in eating disorders as bingeing. If voluntary vomiting is an identified PMC critical element, then 'Throwing-up Decision Sheets' (TDSs; see Figure H-46) can be provided using a similar introduction to that for Binge Decision Sheets.

Script 10: 'Calories and Vomiting' on page 267 may be relevant too.

Any problematic behaviour identified in a PMC can in theory be addressed using decision sheets (e.g. substance abuse or dependence.) This will depend upon factors such as convenience, timing, predictability, and confidentiality of the behaviours. And on whether the 'good voice'/'bad voice' model can apply.

A further CPP example in which I have used decision sheets is with a problem of frequent looking at pornography on the internet. The same decision sheet structure was used as with Table H-45, but with 'bingeing', replaced by 'lapping', (being an abbreviation of 'looking at porn'). Any such verb can in theory be supplanted on the sheets at 5 points to change their target behaviour. A further example I have used is 'Buying Decision Sheets' for compulsive purchasing, or where shopping has become a maladaptive coping technique.

TABLE H-46

Throwing-up Decision Sheet (TDS)

Date:.. Time..

Feelings I am experiencing:

Situation or problem behind those feelings:

Benefits of throwing up now:

Bad effects of throwing up now:

(Tick whichever are bigger)

Alternatives to throwing up now:

THREW UP DIDN'T THROW UP

(Available as a free download from www.australianacademicpress.com.au)

HOMEWORK 47

Sacred Chocolate Block I

Many clients with a binge-eating or bulimic problem will not have successfully resisted the urge to binge on certain foods in a long time. To succeed once in this will be an achievement — perhaps a breakthrough. At least it will be an experiment, a first step, and good practice.

> On the way home today, I want you to stop at a shop and buy one family block of milk chocolate [or another highly binge-risk food, as determined by specific questioning]. When you get it home, I want you to write with a texta a large 'S' on the wrapping, and put it in the fridge. The 'S' stands for 'sacred' or 'special' or 'separate', because I then want you to leave it alone until our next appointment, when I want you to bring it in and show it to me — undisturbed. How long is it since you've had a block of chocolate at home unopened for that long? How hard will this be? How will you do it?
>
> If you feel like bingeing you'll have to buy and eat ***something else*** because this sacred block will be 'off limits'.

The vast majority of clients I have given this task to have succeeded. We then must make a fuss, and ask lots of question about how it was done.

Even with the few who fail, much can be learned about why, at what point, in what way, and so on.

HOMEWORK 48

Sacred Chocolate Block 2

Those who succeed with Sacred Chocolate Block 1, can be asked to take the next challenge, which involves practice and breakthroughs at not just saying 'No', but at saying 'I'll stop now'. Many people with a binge eating problem have not stopped eating a 'binge food' voluntarily, when alone, after a small serving, for many years. To do so can be a breakthrough, or at least an experiment, a second step, and good practice.

Your functional analysis or CBT case formulation should have identified common or powerful binge-trigger foods. Chocolate is a common one.

> I'd like you to take your 'sacred' chocolate block home, and tonight at 7 pm [choose a convenient time] open it and break off 2 squares. Put the rest back in the fridge. Eat the 2 squares, and record on this card [supply], next to the date, that you ate 2 squares, with a tick. Do this every evening at 7 pm. If you miss or forget, you can catch up; but don't forget to put your ticks down. There are x squares of chocolate, so this will last y days. When I see you next, there will be z squares left. Bring them in.

Again, most succeed. A fuss is then appropriate, along with lots of questions about how it was done.

HOMEWORK 49

Remove The Scales

A preoccupation with food and/or calories and/or body weight is almost universal in all CPPs involving eating. We know from learning theory and numerous clinical studies in CBT that acting on a preoccupation, while it may provide short-term emotional relief, (especially in OCD), will usually strengthen the preoccupation and behaviour patterns in the medium- and longer-term (Figure 3.4, Arrow 2). It cements one or more PMCs.

Breaking a PMC is often easiest at a behavioural element because we can see clearly whether behaviours occur. For example, with a jealousy problem, I will usually start with banning all checking/following/interrogating behaviours, because we see more immediately whether this maintaining link is broken than when cognitive or emotional ones are.

In most eating problems frequent weighing is such a behavioural maintainer. Daily weighing will feed the preoccupation [so to speak], while providing unreliable information that will fluctuate greatly and produce unjustified feelings of panic, depression, or relief. The simplest strategy to avert this is to 'put away the scales' (Kausman, 2004, p. 15).

(After explaining the above, and the PMC we wish to break)

We want you to be weighed no more than once a week, preferably once a fortnight or once a month, always on the same scales. Where would be a good place? At your doctor's? At the pharmacy? Meantime, how many scales have you got at home? The easiest way to get around this is to give your scales to a friend or relative for 3 months/6 months. Who could this be? Can you do this today? Will anyone else at home miss them? You may need to tell them why, and that it is important.

(Write the homework, officially, on a homework card.)

Tell me who you gave the scales to, next time.

HOMEWORK 50

Body Image Evaluation

A distorted body image or 'overevaluation of shape and weight' (Fairburn et al., 2008) is central to many PMCs in CPPs involving eating. This is important therefore to assess — especially in a way that enables cognitive therapy, confrontation of inconsistencies, and ongoing tracking of the degree of distortion.

Therefore, much better than 'Do you feel fat?' or 'So how fat do you feel?' or 'Do you feel any less fat now?' — all vague and only verbal — is to use a graphical representation. A computer screen can provide this, or simply presentation of Figure H-50.

> Have a look at these silhouettes. Which of them would you say looks closest to you right now? Which of them is closest to how you looked three years ago? (Choose a pre-eating-disorder time span.) Which would you like to be like? Which do you think I would say is closest to you? Which would (partner, parent, significant other) say is closest to you right now?
>
> If you're really calm and objective about it, which would you say actually is closest to you?
>
> Can you take this sheet home with you, and ask (partner, parent, significant other) to write at the bottom the number of the silhouette that is closest to how you look right now?

The variety of uses of Figure H-50 depends upon the circumstances. But it can be used not only as a one-point assessment. It can also be used to confront the person with their misperception (which can be of a hallucinatory quality!), to reassure, or to challenge, and to bring other trusted parties into the evaluation and challenge:

> Now, you pointed to Numbers 2 and 7. I said, honestly, Number 6. Bruce also said Numbers 5 and 6. We have no reason to lie or exaggerate. We know that many people can get a distorted view if they get over-focused on their weight and body size. It produces Eating Disorders. You've been sent along by Dr Smith because he feels you have an Eating Disorder. So the odds are that you genuinely see or feel that you're like Number 2 or 7, but that it's actually wrong, and you're going too far with this preoccupation with what you eat, and with getting skinnier.

Such blunt language is justified if there is objective evidence of distortion, such as that provided by Figure H-50 evaluations.

FIGURE H-50
Body image evaluation sheet (for females).

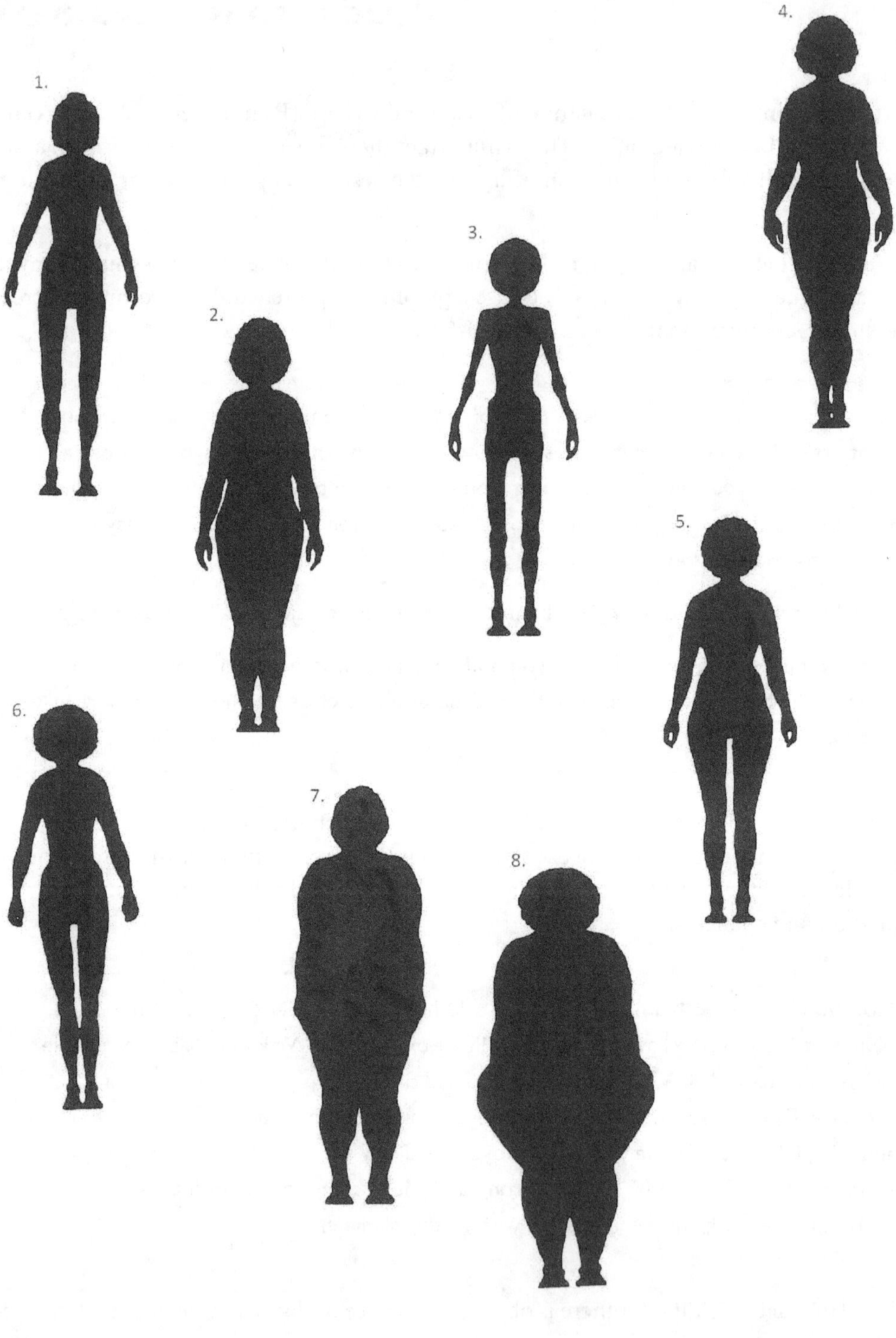

(Available as a free download from www.australianacademicpress.com.au)

HOMEWORK 51

Mirror Exposure

Sometimes your case formulation will pick up that an eating-related or a "body dysmorphic" CPP appears to be maintained by the classical and operant conditioning that occurs in many phobic reactions — a brief distressing exposure to a stimulus, followed by escape, reinforcing an anxiety, or even disgust, reaction.

For example, many people with an eating CPPs will describe catching a glimpse of themselves in a shop window and averting their eyes due to the upset.

The picture can be complicated, because some people with Body Dysmorphic Disorder spend a lot of time examining or checking their 'defect'.

But, if the former (avoidant) profile is described, then a course of prolonged exposure may be useful to break the avoidant/maintaining PMC.

> I'd like you to go home today, and get some time alone. Where are your big mirrors in the house? Go there today, and, wearing what you have on now, stand in front of that mirror, looking at your body, for 10 minutes front on, 10 minutes facing left, and 10 minutes facing right. It's a long time, so you may want the radio on. But you can't read or watch TV, because you have to be ***looking***. Record your 'mirror session' on this card/in this diary. Write in how long, how many clothes, and highest SUDS reached. (Explain SUDS.)
>
> Then, tomorrow I want you to do the same again, but this time wearing … (bra and pants?) Then, on Day 3, I want you to do the same, for the same time, with no clothes on. Do this for two days. It sounds a lot — half hour a day for four days — but if it's boring after a while, ***good***. We want you to 'be over it'/not care/ not get upset/ not react, because so far the reaction's been big and upsetting and wrong and unhelpful.

Explanations of learning theory and PMCs will be necessary to justify this effort, as it will otherwise be seen as either pointlessly upsetting or pointlessly tedious.

The SUDS records will be important to review.

HOMEWORK 52

Relationship Questionnaires

The assessment phase with most problems can be the beginning of the therapeutic phase. Self-awareness and psychoeducation may begin even in Session 1. The nature of the questions asked are already an indication to clients as to what is important or relevant and what is not (Bakker, 2008a, p. 35). If a person is experiencing panic attacks, and the therapist does not ask about their toilet training, but instead asks many careful questions about when the attacks occur, and whether they fear the attacks, psychoeducation has commenced.

Much early self-monitoring or problem-recording also blends seamlessly into therapeutic changes. Homework 1: Negative Emotions Record is a prime example of this.

But sometimes an assessment activity is prescribed *predominantly* for therapeutic reasons. This can especially occur when providing relationship-focused questionnaires to couples.

A reason this can be classed as predominantly a therapeutic activity — a homework — is that, even more than the therapist learning important information about the couple, it is hoped that the couple can learn important information about each other, the current status of the relationship, differences in their perceptions, and specific issues or behaviours that are critical.

Questionnaires, completed separately and without interruption, can help couples be honest and to the point with their information. This is the start of communication therapy.

Another reason for questionnaire assessment with couples, when a similar approach may be less frequent with individuals, is that working with two people feels more than twice as complex as working with one. (I am sure there is a mathematical formula or law in there somewhere.)

Many relationship-focused questionnaires are available that can serve this purpose. Because a primary goal is the facilitation of honesty, communication, and detection of differences, rather than a precise, valid, and reliable score representing degree of current relationship pathology, the instrument chosen needn't be psychometrically powerful, but should have face validity and be clinically comprehensive.

I use the Dyadic Adjustment Scale (Carey et al., 1993; Sabourin, Valois, & Lussier, 2005; South, Kruger, & Iacono, 2009; Spanier, 1976). There are others that are specifically consistent with cognitive–behavioural marital therapy (Dattilio, 1989; Epstein & Baucom, 1989).

HOMEWORK 53

Talk Times

Problems in communication are ubiquitous among couples that present for work on their relationship. The reasons for this include that communication flaws can be a cause or a consequence of relationship problems, or both.

Any issue in a relationship is more likely to arise, or will feel more serious, or will grow, or will fester and prolong, when communication is inadequate.

Hence, some variant of the Talk Times homework is very commonly relevant and useful when working with a couple.

(While writing key instructions on a homework card)

I'm going to ask you to practise, at home, some 'perfect' communication, to see how different it is from how the two of you usually get on, and to see if we can improve the usual communicating that goes on.

What I'm going to ask you to do is a bit artificial. There will be rules, and you'll be doing it because I've asked you to. But there's no way around that. Improving anything is done by artificial practice with effort at first.

So, the first thing I'm asking you to do, is to work out together three (one? two? seven?) half-hour times each week you're going to do this. Maybe you'll need to sit with your diaries on a Sunday night and work it out, like you may do for other things, like childcare rosters. Doing this shows each of you that the relationship is a priority. If you spend 40 hours a week at work or 4 hours a week at tennis or 15 hours a week in front of the TV, then you should spend at least 1½ hours a week on communication and your relationship.

You probably won't need a half hour each time, but I want you to allow for it, because the worst thing in the world is if you're saying something important and your partner stops you because the TV news has started.

When the time comes, first you make sure you're alone and can talk freely, in confidence, and uninterrupted. Then you decide who talks first. It doesn't matter who, or how you decide. Someone might be bursting to start, or you can toss a coin.

Then (a) Talker tells of a negative feeling. It's a *feeling* you describe.

When they've videotaped happy couples and couples with problems while talking about something (maybe which school to send the kids to?) they've found that the couples who like how they get on talk a lot about feelings.

This doesn't seem to come as naturally to the blokes, who on average prefer problem-solving, 'useful', objective talk. But the point of this communication is not to make decisions, or find the truth, or fix something; it's to share each other's worlds, to connect, to *communicate*. So you'll be doing more 'female style' communicating about *feelings*.

It doesn't matter whether you pick on the Iraq War, or your finances, or your partner's recent rotten behaviour, as long as you talk about *feelings*. I hope, actually, you do pick on personal, sensitive, important feelings, because the Talk Times will be the safest time to bring these up; because there will be rules controlling how it goes.

But while describing this feeling, the Talker must use 'I' language. That is, most sentences need to start with the word 'I'. You have to talk about yourself. There are at least 3 ways you can say things: You can talk about yourself: 'I'm feeling very alone;' You can talk about the other person: 'You ignore me all the time'; or you can talk about the world: 'People don't listen'. With the third type — 'It' or 'They' sentences — whoever you're talking to can disagree, you spin off into an argument about people or things, and get nowhere. With the second type — 'You' sentences — it sounds attacking right away. But also you are talking to the world expert on that topic. They have lived their whole lives with themselves, and there's nothing you'll be able to say they don't already know or will disagree with. When you use the first type of language — 'I' sentences — you are the world expert. If you tell someone you're upset, they might try to say you shouldn't be, but they can't just say 'No you're not'. 'I' statements are much less attacking, and they are educational. They tell people what causes what with your feelings.

(Optional Extra: If you tell a kid from age 5 to age 15, 10,000 times 'You're a nuisance' 'You're lazy' 'You shouldn't do that', they feel put down, and they care less what you say because you're negative at them all the time. If you 10,000 times tell them the effect their behaviour is having — I get a headache when you're noisy (notice 'you's can slip in after 'I's sometimes), I'm disappointed in what you did, I need to know you're OK, so phone me next time — then they get educated about you and life and people and feelings. So 'I' statements have really good long-term effects too.)

The next rule is: There are to be no interruptions. We're not Truth-seeking here. We want communication, sharing, understanding each others' worlds. So even if you hear the biggest load of rubbish you've ever heard, you aren't allowed to correct it. At least not at that time. You may store it up to correct it later on, if it's important enough. So I'll write: 'No followup on content until the next day.' If it's that important, and you remember it, then bring it up at breakfast.

In fact, the next rule goes further. Because, after the feeling has been described, using 'I' statements, with no interruptions, the listener then has to summarise back what was said. You don't have to agree with it, but you do have to say something like 'So I think you're saying that the worst thing for you about our social life is ...' There is no better feeling than the confirmation that you've been heard; whether others agree with you or not. So, this may involve a bit of correction if the summary is way off.

Now, Step (b) in these Talk Times is all the same as Step (a), except this time the Talker tells of a *positive* feeling, using 'I' statements, with no interruptions, with a summary back, etcetera. These are to be balanced communication times, not just moan sessions.

The final two Steps (c) and (d) are all the same as (a) and (b), but with talker and listener roles reversed.

Now when you come back in x weeks, I'll ask lots about the Talk Times:

- Did you schedule your 3 each week?
- Did you focus on feelings?
- Did you stick with 'I' statements? Was this hard?
- Were you able to not interrupt?
- Were any topics taken up the next day?
- Were the summaries you got back reasonably accurate?
- Did you pick on 'safe' topics, or did you share things that matter?

The homework card, written as the Talk Times are described, may be as simple as this:

26/04/2017

1. Each Sunday night, schedule 3 half-hour Talk Times for the week in your diaries.
2. Decide who talks first.
   (a) Talker tells of a negative feeling.
   Use 'I' sentences. No interruptions.* Summarise back.
   (b) Talker tells of positive feeling.
   Same rules.
   (c) As for (a) with roles reversed.
   (d) As for (b) with roles reversed.

*A topic may be brought back up the next day.

Of course, much of the relationship/communication therapy can occur at subsequent appointments, when problems in undertaking the Talk Times, and issues raised within the Talk Times are addressed.

People are not expected to have official Talk Times for the rest of their lives. Many effectively do, as they either continue to deliberately schedule 'communication time' or 'couple time' in their lives, or as they continue to deliberately use or prompt the prescribed 'rules' in other natural communications.

But it is hoped that communication practice in official Talk Times can occur for long enough (4–10 weeks?) that 'I' sentences, not interrupting, summarisings, balancing positives and negatives, and *feelings* talk will happen more often and more spontaneously for a long time after.

As well as attacking Relationship PMC (f) – see Figure 6.8 – Talk Times can have a nonspecific positive effect by weakening PMCs (b) or (c). Talk Times can be a medium or venue for showing that you are making an effort, the relationship matters, and you do love your partner, irrespective of what is talked about.

HOMEWORK 54

Three Secret Positives

Several relationship PMCs involve perpetuation of withheld caring behaviours, or of negative perceptions of each other. A simple homework task can start to break these spirals. It uses your influence as a third party to re-initiate some positive relationship behaviours and perceptions or appreciations that would otherwise continue to fade.

The simple instructions are:

I would like you each over the next week to think of three nice things you can do for your partner that are 'extras', that they'd notice. That is, things you don't do already.

But you may not tell your partner about them. Then, I want you to do them. Even then, you may not 'confirm or deny' whether any particular thing you've done is it.

So you each have to think what your partner would like, and do it, and see if you can spot what they've done for you.

When we meet next time, first I'll ask whether you spotted what was done for you, and then I'll get you to tell us what you actually did.

The purposes of this homework are:

(a) To make them guess or remember or recognise what matters/is appreciated by their partner.

(b) To have them do some noticeable positive extras for their partner, perhaps for the first time in ages. Initially they are doing this only because it's homework, but the effect can be the same anyway.

(c) To trigger some attentiveness to their partner's caring behaviours. Many return with wrong guesses, showing they now notice other positives that they have been ignoring.

Follow-up on all this can be very informative. For example, it can reveal misdirected caring behaviours ('But I'd rather cook myself anyway' or 'But when we cuddle I always feel you expect sex every time'). And it can reveal lack of motivation ('I did one, but I couldn't think of any others').

HOMEWORK 55

How You Feel Loved or Show Love

Relationship PMCs often involve withheld caring behaviours — Figure 6.8 (b) reduced closeness, Figure 6.8 (c) or similar. At such times it is critical that attempts to break these cycles, by deliberately behaving positively or by appreciating one's partner's positive behaviours, be usefully targeted. That is, the attempts to change need to be in areas of behaviour that matter to the other person. Helping more with the housework when your partner would rather do it solo so it's done well, and really needs a daily cuddle, is a mistargetted attempt.

Several other homeworks can help clarify specific behaviours and areas of contention most critical to relationship improvement. Especially Homeworks 52, 53, and 56. But this homework also aims to help people recognise and appreciate when their partner is making efforts, even if they may be misguided.

It can be introduced either by genuine personal examples of differences between you and your partner in affection expression or appreciation, or by reference to the general recent popular literature on gender differences (e.g. *Men Are From Mars, Women Are From Venus*). The following script has a personal example, which may not apply to you, and anecdotal examples need to be real for you to be genuine.

Now something I've been picking up is that I've got two nice, sincere, caring [use whatever positive descriptors can honestly apply here] people here. Neither of you is 'the baddie'. But a vicious circle has gotten going. And even when you're trying to stop it by being nicer for a while, it doesn't work. I think there's a good chance you're making your efforts in areas that aren't the best ones. Or that when your partner makes an effort it doesn't work because it's with something that isn't the important stuff for you. [People may respond to this second point (Your partner is misguided) better than to the first (You are misguided).] For example, the thing that makes the biggest impression on my wife is when I help out at home. If I get home and see the clouds and get the washing in, then when she gets home, my wife thinks 'He's so thoughtful. He knows what matters to me'. Now, if it was up to me, I'd leave the washing out there until I needed it. It'd get a good rinse then!

On the other hand, what really matters to me is if I get home and my wife puts her book down, comes over, and gives me a hug. But that's not how she operates. To show love, she cooks for me. Now I suspect there are some differences like this for you two. So, what I'm asking you to each do, separately, as homework, is to write down 3 things which matter to you, which if your partner did them, would make you feel good, and make you feel they care; 3 things you'd like to see more of.

> Then, also, I want you to write 3 things that you naturally do when you're feeling loving; three things you may only do with someone you love, or that just happen when you like someone. Does this make sense?

The major phase of this intervention is the followup, discussion, implications, and learning that occur at the next session when the lists are compared. The aims at this point are to achieve either:

(a) some adjustments in behaviour, either by agreement, effort, and prompting, or by an overt contract, such that one or (ideally) both partners make efforts in the relationship that stand more chance of being effective and appreciated and breaking a PMC, or

(b) one or (ideally) both partners appreciate their partners feelings and efforts more, even if expressed in ways that somewhat 'miss the point'.

It is hoped that both of these are generalization-of-behaviour goals. That is, increased insight and adjusted effort can occur indefinitely — not just this week.

HOMEWORK 56

A Behavioural Marital Contract

The most common specific negative behaviours maintaining a relationship PMC that are reported on presentation are around display of affection and respect, or the absence of these — Figure 6.8(b) and (c). Hence Homeworks 54, 55, 59, and 60 are frequently useful.

However, during assessment of a relationship problem other specific negative PMC behaviours can emerge. Especially as the CBT approach requires that every general statement, such as 'He is angry all the time' or 'She doesn't care what I think', must be followed by queries for examples or illustrations. This is the essence of behavioural or cognitive-behavioural marital therapy (Dattilio, 1989; Epstein & Baucom, 1989).

If the specific complaints can be distilled at least to the level of: 'He does nothing to help at home. It's like having three children at home instead of two', or 'She shows no interest in me or my work. I might as well not come home', then specific PMCs are identifiable that can be attacked initially through a behavioural marital contract.

As with similar programs — such as a Star Chart with a 7-year-old or chores-and-behaviour- contract with a 15-year-old — often the most critical and useful phase of any contract is the preliminary one of clarifying exactly which behaviours are a problem, exactly what each party expects or hopes for, which behaviours are a small irritation and which are game-breakers, the communication and listening required at this step, and the fact that the whole process is bilateral, fair, and blame-avoiding. This arises naturally when the process is seen as a PMC-breaking one. People can see how they both contribute to the maintenance of a relationship PMC, the breaking of which depends upon who has some control of what, not who is to blame and so must give in and change.

The steps involved in a behavioural marital contract are:

(a) Assessment to elicit specific problem behaviours from all parties

(b) Engender understanding and motivation through the PMC model

(c) Homework to specify (3–5?) behaviours that each would like to see more in their partner, and a similar number that each would like to see less

(d) The creative and common sense construction of a trade-off, mutual-effort agreement specified on paper, signed and witnessed

(e) Implementation for a specified trial period

(f) Review and adjustment, and the addressing of emergent critical issues (communication? interference from outside the relationship? lifestyle adjustments? etc.).

HOMEWORK 57

Overlapping Lives

Issues identified in an assessment of a relationship (e.g. via Homework 52) often involve the balance between each party's separate independent lives, supports, interests, and activities, and the 'overlap' in their lives; for example, Relationship PMC (g) in Figure 6.8.

Problems identified can include:

- Little current overlap. Leading quite separate lives as 'housemates' or 'co-parents' or 'dual-mortgagees'.
- One partner relies heavily on the other; has little separate identity; may be housebound or disabled or dominated. Either party can resent this arrangement.
- Both partners highly enmeshed, 'co-dependent'; little or no 'me time' or privacy, or spread of supports. Again, either or both parties may suffer due to this.

Each of these imbalances can be described and assessed using Script 8. Clients can then express a global opinion.

But for a more thorough assessment, including specific areas, supports, or activities that are absent or are present in the wrong sector (overlapping versus separate), the following Homework may be offered to, ideally, both partners:

From what I've learned so far, I'm concerned that the *balance* between what you have in your life, Bill, and what is separate in your life, Mary, and what you have or do or share together, is out of wack.

For example, I'm not sure, but it looks like

(a) there isn't much in the middle that you share as a couple that brings you together, or

(b) there isn't much that you have, Mary, that's an outlet, that's just yours, and that lets you be someone apart from a wife and mother all the time, or

(c) there isn't much for both of you that gives you some 'down time' or gives you outside support or lets you 'be someone else' for a bit of the week.

But I need your feelings on this. So can I ask both of you, separately at first, to write in at least 5 things in each of the three areas I'm drawing now.

Draw two overlapping cricles [of course use appropriate first names above each circle].

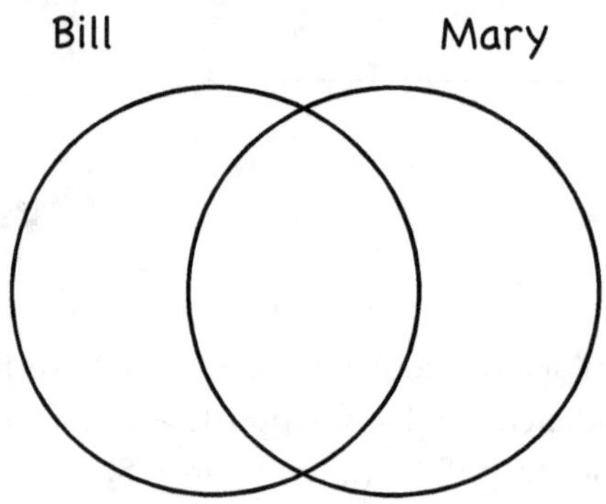

In here you write things that are part of your life, Bill, but not so much Mary's. For example we can start with your work. [Write this in?]. In this area it's *your* stuff, Mary. I understand that Beth is a friend of yours, but not so much of Bill [Write 'Beth' in?]. In here go the things you have or do in common. Could we write the girls [daughters] in here? Now we want at least 4 more in each area.

When we meet next time, I'd like to compare what you've each come up with, and then look at how balanced it all is, and ask *you* if you feel it's balanced enough.

Once again, the followup session is the critical one here. But where it goes depends entirely upon the details and stances described by the homework.

This homework allows examination and commitments to change without blame being ascribed. It focuses on *balance*, and therefore reciprocity, PMCs, and the structure of the relationship, rather than pathology or bad behaviour or fault.

HOMEWORK 58

The Reminder Codeword

When a general relationship PMC (see Table 3.1) has been identified, subsequent Homeworks are aimed at changing attitudes, circumstances, sensitivities, habits, or skills. Homework 55: How You Feel Loved or Show Love is an example of this, in which attitudes, habits, and sensitivities are addressed.

But when a *specific* relationship PMC is identified — an instance of worsening in the relationship, that could occur again tonight — then learning theory requires us to provide a link or reminder or trigger or cue between what we rationally agree in the therapy session needs to occur tonight if the PMC begins, and what actually occurs tonight. It is not enough to give general advice. What your client(s) will be fighting tonight is a causal circle or spiral that has occurred many times, is emotion-charged, and is likely to be habitual or automatic by now.

Frequently, the analysis and insights a therapist puts into words — the PMC — have been understood at some level by clients already. They may even introduce the problem in these terms. What they are missing, what they need from you, is the techniques, the technology, to break the cycle from tonight.

Such bridges from therapy session decisions to specific PMC disruption include: written Homework cards, self-monitoring tasks, placement of cues such as stickers, carrying cards with self-talk or worry questions or aphorisms on them, and so on. When working on a relationship PMC, the two people involved can be reminders/cues for each other. If this is done on therapist instruction, then reminders may be more seen as informative, rather than controlling or blaming or nagging.

Based on Figure H-58 as a specific relationship PMC example, a Reminder Codeword can be introduced.

FIGURE H-58
Example of a specific relationship PMC that can benefit from a reminder codeword.

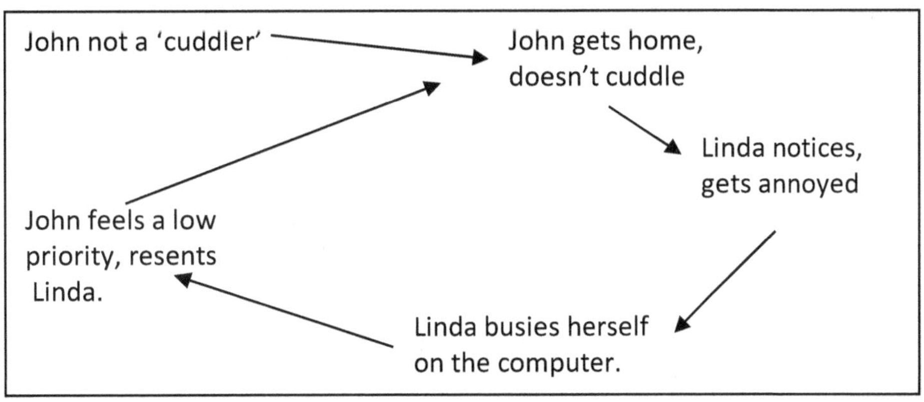

Your first Homework is to agree on a 'codeword' — any word — that from now on means 'I feel neglected and ignored right now. I need some attention and affection.' When you've decided on it, then Linda, I'd like you to say the word to John when he gets home and forgets to give you a cuddle. John, if Linda says the codeword, it's not having a go at you, it's telling you how Linda feels. Notice the codeword stands for 'I' sentences. [Explain if necessary. See Homeworks 10 and 53.] And John, you can say the codeword whenever it's true for you too.

The codeword is much better than telling someone off, or giving them a lecture, or storming off and avoiding them. It's not aggressive or passive, it's informative, and it's assertive. I'll ask you next time what your codeword is, and whether you've used it yet.

It is best to let couples choose and agree on the precise codeword. However, words used very frequently, like 'Hello', should be avoided, as confusion can ensue. And words that can be used in public are preferable too, as PMCs can occur anywhere.

The Reminder Codeword Homework can combine especially well with Homework 41: *Time-Outs*, because time-outs need to be identified so they are not seen as a rejection or 'storming off in a huff', and because either partner may need to trigger the time-out, and because lecturing or argument need to be especially avoided at heated times.

HOMEWORK 59

10 Partner Positives

PMCs that incorporate a deteriorating attitude to one's partner require a re-recognition of the positives that presumably once were recognised and appreciated. This process, and hence the 10 Partner Positives homework, parallels Homework 6: *25 Positives* when addressing self-esteem.

The introductory lines of Homework 55: *How You Feel Loved or Show Love*, emphasising the therapist's perception that both parties in the relationship are okay, loveable people, and that a 'vicious circle' has grown, are again applicable here. This especially applies because the parties once did see the positives in each other. Such an approach ties in well with a PMC formulation after initial assessment and immediately before Homeworks commence.

Then can follow:

Therefore, I'm asking both of you to write down, separately, and show me next time, 10 of the nicest things about your partner — qualities, things they do, abilities, things that you like or appreciate about them. [If the relationship is in more dire straits, they may be asked for only 7 or 5, or sometimes I have asked for 3, just to get *something* positive out of them.]

The intent here of course is to remind/reawaken some memory or awareness of the positives they have been ignoring since the relationship deteriorated. The next session is therefore critical, and half or more of it may be devoted to reading out, elaborating on, and discussing the homework produced. The therapist can ask for examples of each positive, or ask why that positive matters.

However, it is also hoped that the parties will learn or remember more about what matters to their partner. (Similar to Homework 55 goals.) The list may come in some priority order or may be ordered in discussion in session. But even what makes it to the list may be a surprise to the partner.

What is learned may be then incorporated into Homework 56: *A Behavioural Marital Contract.*

HOMEWORK 60

Couple PESs

The Pleasant Events Schedule (PES; Homework 21) is very useful as an assessment and as a therapeutic homework in many individual problems, especially in the areas of anxiety and depression. But it can also be helpful in a couple/relationship problem when, for example, few mutual enjoyable activities are reported; see Figure 6.8 (g).

In this situation, before encouraging or 'prescribing' an increase in such activities together, it may be necessary to find activities which would count as mutually enjoyable, especially if the pattern of absent or separate recreations and free time has been occurring for some time. They may have forgotten what they both enjoy. This assessment can become a positive mutual activity in itself.

After discussing the relevant PMC, such as Figure 6.8 (g):

(While presenting the PES)

If we're going to do something about the fact that there's been not much fun-together for quite a while, first we need to find some things that would count as enjoyable or fun for both of you, that are things you don't have to do by yourself, that are available and affordable, and you can do at least once a week. So I'd like you both separately to go through this questionnaire tonight. It's a huge list of lots of things that people can enjoy.

You can ignore the first column here. (Cross off 'Frequency'.) This questionnaire has been designed to measure where depressed people, for example, are with doing this sort of stuff. We don't need this. We need the second column, a 'Pleasantness' rating, from each of you.

Then we can go back over it to find those things you both can enjoy a lot, and see if we can find practical, available ones to make plans about or fit into your lives together.

This bit tells you about putting a 0, 1, or 2 in the 'Pleasantness' column next to all 320 items in the list. If one of you puts your answers down here (point to 'Pleasantness' column) then the other of you could even cover them up, and put your answers in the 'Frequency' column, even though they're about Pleasantness.

At the next session, items that received a '2' rating from both parties can be discussed regarding their affordability, availability, whether they are solo, joint, or group activities, and whether they are one-off, infrequent, or frequent activities. It is preferable then to make a plan and obtain some commitment for followup, rather than leave it undecided and at people's whim. The relevant PMC must be consciously and effortfully *broken*, else it will continue, despite insight into its existence.

HOMEWORK 61

Re-Injury Medical Advice and Other Cognitive Therapy

Psychoeducation for Chronic Pain problems should include education about the differences between acute and chronic pain. This includes the function of acute pain as a stimulus to cease use of the affected area, so it can heal. Chronic pain has the same effect, but usually should not, as further injury is unlikely. In fact, exercise, mobility, and strengthening are usually necessary in chronic conditions in order to restore function.

This is not always the case, so medical opinion should be sought, and then reinforced by the therapist, until it is firmly accepted that the pain is a 'false alarm' and needs to be worked through, rather than given into.

I often send my clients back to their most authoritative medical helper with the written specific homework instruction to get it clear as to whether, for example, sitting through a movie at the cinema with subsequent back pain will do any damage, or will just hurt.

Subsequently, this new more-true self-talk may need to be coached or reinforced through any usual Cognitive Therapy technique.

Many other unhelpful beliefs in chronic pain may be detected and addressed similarly. One difference from conventional Cognitive Therapy for depression, for example, is that the term 'unhelpful beliefs' is preferable over 'negative thinking', because some negative thoughts are adaptive and helpful in chronic pain, such as 'I have an arthritic back, so I need to lift carefully', and some positive thoughts are problematic, such as 'I'll be all better next week'.

Another difference is that low mood in chronic pain is rarely associated with low self-esteem, unlike in depression. It is more likely to be associated with low self-efficacy, so Homework 6 is likely to be less relevant than Homework 12, and it is desirable to be doing *something* for the pain rather than nothing, even if only placebo effects occur.

HOMEWORK 62

Cued Stretching or Mini-Relaxers

Although stretching and mini-relaxers are physical strategies intended to have a physical effect, the necessary *psychological* input to these techniques is in *getting them done* sufficiently and regularly, so as to have a long-term effect. Exercise therapy for depression (Homework 24) is similarly placed.

The role here of the psychological therapist in chronic pain problems, then, is to establish a system of cues that will ensure an adequate behavioural response, as described in Homework 33: Mini-Relaxers. Please read this section now.

Numerous pain management outcome studies have supported the benefits of a strategy of prevention of, rather than reaction to, the onset of pain episodes. This is especially true of stretching or muscle relaxation techniques. It is too late to attempt relaxation of an area once it is signalling acute pain. Resort to medication is likely to work better by this stage. So the goal is to prevent pain increase, or excessive associated muscle tension and circulatory effects, by developing a habit of regular, brief stretching or relaxation through the day.

Whether stretching or relaxation or tension-and-relaxation are used, and where, and in what way, and for how long, are issues often best decided by a medical practitioner, physiotherapist, or similar. I will often direct a client to one of these specifically with these questions, explaining the context of a cued, regular, through-the-day, preventive 'habit'.

The identification of cues, often with appropriate stickers (supplied, keep a stock to hand out) is a detailed, specific, vital task, guided by the cue frequency (total of 15–20 per day?), convenience (e.g. privacy of the loo), and regularity (e.g. when tooth-brushing; as the kettle boils).

HOMEWORK 63

Nonmedication Physical Techniques

It is useful for even psychological-level therapists to have some knowledge of nonmedication physical pain management techniques for several reasons. One such — that their regular use may have to be prompted using psychological/behavioural techniques — is described in Homework 62: Cued Stretching or Mini-Relaxers.

Another is mentioned under Homework 61: *Re-Injury Medical Advice and Other Cognitive Therapy.* This concerns the need for *some options* for pain management to be available so as to avoid feelings of powerlessness, hopelessness, and lowered self-efficacy. If a person has *something* they can turn to, they can likely bear the pain more in the meantime, or even choose to ignore it.

This is not a justification for crystal healing or Reiki. The method needs to have a genuine effect in order for it to maintain self-efficacy over time. A pure placebo effect suffers the risk of decreasing, or being 'found out' over time.

Hence, medical advice or some experimenting with the application of heat, or cold, massage, TENS machine, stretching, and so on, is often *psychologically* useful.

HOMEWORK 64

Pacing, Timetabling, and Disability Acceptance

The pacing of daily activities necessary in chronic pain conditions may include strategies of behavioural activation, as applied to depression problems, such as Homeworks 21, 22, 23, and 24. But it may also include behavioural moderation, limiting, and regularity strategies, as is useful in the psychological adjunctive treatment of bipolar disorder.

The overall theme, then, is timetabling, rather than activation or limitation. Hence Homework 18: Self-Organisation may be useful, as well as Homework 19: 15-Minute Time Slots, Homework 20: Achievement Recording, and even Homeworks 15, 16, and 17 on Values, Goals, and Plans.

But sometimes an analysis of pain levels through the day will pinpoint just one or two critical activities that need to be moderated or spaced, such as sitting in front of the computer, which can then be selectively addressed either ergonomically, or via diary slots, or with a phone alarm, or in some other imaginative way.

A commitment to such an intervention requires a degree of acceptance of disability. If assessment shows this to be lacking, specific CBT techniques may be called for, similar to grief work or behavioural experiments.

HOMEWORK 65

Cognitive Therapy + Exposure and Response Prevention

There are many comprehensive guides to the complete processes of cognitive therapy and exposure and response prevention for OCD (Claiborn & Pedrick, 2002; Hyman & Pedrick, 2005; March & Mulle, 1998; Purdon & Clark, 2005). This is too big a topic for the present volume. Instead I will concentrate on the preliminary critical step in OCD treatment: How to help a client 'get it'.

Schwartz (1996) described a four-step treatment process. His first step, Relabel: 'It's not me — It's my OCD', is critical. It is about insight, about 'getting it'. Insight and the model of OCD presented are mutually supportive. They can form a 'virtuous circle'. Capacity for insight can help acceptance of the model and subsequent therapy. And a good convincing model can trigger insight, acceptance, motivation, and compliance.

Others have offered similar steps, again with a recognition of the most crucial and difficult of them.

For example, Blair-West's (2009) seven phases are:

1. Unawareness
2. Awareness
3. Motivation to change
4. Knowledge and understanding of OCD
5. Acceptance of the Model
6. Exposure and response prevention
7. End point of active treatment.

Phase 5, Acceptance of the Model, 'is essential to successful treatment ... For this reason much time and energy is spent describing the model' (p.10).

Therefore, 'The 5 Steps in Managing OCD' that I write and give to the client, and refer back to, every time we are making a decision in therapy, reviewing progress, or reviewing lack of progress (See Script 11) are:

1. Accept I have OCD
2. Learn about OCD
3. Recognise which thoughts are OCD thoughts ('false alarms')
4. Stop reacting when they happen
5. Face all normal situations.

Many therapy processes can benefit from a simple plan like this. But OCD especially requires it, as sufferers will constantly doubt the process, and confuse feeling better with getting better.

FIGURE H-65
A specific example of an OCD PMC Loop, and a Linear 'Non-loop' OCD Therapy Chain.

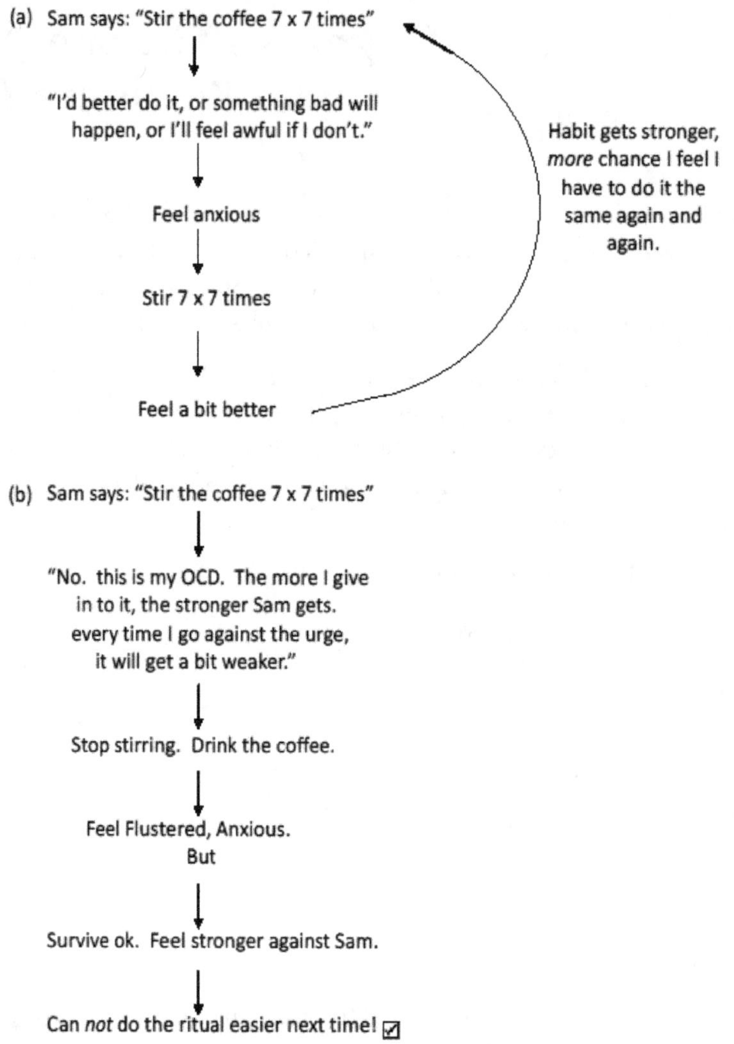

A general model of OCD in PMC terms that can be presented to clients is illustrated in Figure 6.11. The points at which therapy attempts to break the PMCs by cognitive therapy (A) or exposure therapy (B) and response prevention (C) are illustrated. As with all PMC-based case formulations, this model is especially useful in explaining and justifying the ensuing treatment plan. But it must be embedded in a thorough psychoeducational package.

Figure H-65 illustrates a (real) specific example of an individualised OCD PMC loop (a), and a linear OCD therapy chain (b). (a) is an individualised diagrammatic case formulation, and (b) is then a therapy plan. Note that 'Sam' is the name given to this OCD problem. (See Homework 69)

The psychoeducational package is necessary because it is critical that people with OCD understand that:

(a) All people have bizarre, random, repulsive, or 'egodystonic' thoughts as their brains continue incessantly to tick over.

(b) Thoughts are just thoughts. They don't equal, or inevitably lead to, actions or feelings. There is a useful literature and source of handouts on the 'thought-action fusion' (Rees, 2009; Shafran et al., 1996) that OCD usually involves.

(c) When we react strongly to a thought/fear/urge, either behaviourally or emotionally, we increase its chances of occurring again soon. (Masses of learning theory describe and explain this phenomenon.)

(d) Each time we feel relieved due to performing a superstitious/neutralising/compulsive ritual, this will entrench and broaden the ritual.

Many of the formats and techniques of CBT as applied to other problems are applicable to OCD. Most of these techniques are 'transdiagnostic'.

For example, Homework 1: *Negative Emotion Records* can be useful in OCD treatment as a self-monitoring, self-awareness, and cognitive 'self-therapy' approach. It is hoped, and can be coached, that Column 6: Useful/True/Reasonable Thoughts, when OC reactions are analysed, will not include reassuring, neutralising self-talk, but rather 'That's another of my OC thoughts' or 'That's Muriel again. I refuse to react to her. If I do, I'll make her stronger' and suchlike.

Homework 2: *NER + Coping Options* can be part of a broader 'coping skills' approach to OCD, in which will feature brief self-talk (CO3), distraction (CO2), counteraction of feelings (CO4), being brave (CO6), learning about OCD (CO8), seeing the joke (CO10), and professional support (CO12), but avoidance of the coping options of 'solving the problem' (neutralising)(CO1), getting reassurance (CO5), being rescued (CO7), being organised (CO15), praying (CO16), getting drunk (CO20), or using other drugs (CO21). (See Table H-2.)

Other frequently applicable techniques of Cognitive Therapy or Exposure and Response Prevention with OCD include Homework 4: *Challenge Diary*, Homework 14: *Decisions Book*, Homework 19: *15-Minute Time Slots*, Homework 20: *Achievement Record*, Homework 24: *Regular Exercise*, Homework 25: *Overwhelming Sensory Experiences*, Homework 30: *Worry Questions*, Homework 34: *SUDS of 7*, and Homework 36: *Thought-Stopping*.

The effective use of the last of these, thought-stopping (TS), provides an example of the complexity of some OCD treatment. It is critical that TS be used to block cognitive or behavioural rituals from occurring, not that it be used to block obsessions (Bakker, 2009). This would counterproductively aid avoidance rather than exposure.

HOMEWORK 66

OCD Questionnaires

The specific word options in the three analogies of Script 12 (danger/cleanliness/germs/safety/...) are important because OCD sufferers seem to have difficulty identifying with the specific OC problems they don't currently have. Many current checkers will laugh about the counters, and the counters will dismiss the cleaners, etc. Even when a sufferer used to count everything in 3s, they will have difficulty seeing how that had anything to do with their current problem with locking doors to leave the house. This is a problem in OCD support groups. Members often have difficulty identifying with or empathising with other members who describe obsessions, compulsions, and fears that they don't currently have themselves.

I therefore often give lists, checklists, or questionnaires like the Compulsive Activity Checklist (Steketee & Freund, 1993) or the Padua Inventory (Sanavio, 1988) or the Yale-Brown Obsessive-Compulsive Scale (Goodman et al., 1989), simply to show sufferers that they are on the list. Furthermore, I file my handouts according to specific OC symptom type, because a religiously scrupulous OC person will benefit much more from examples of treatment for this, than from examples of treatment of a germ OCD.

This use of an assessment tool is another example of the CBT clinician's treatment focus, even in assessment activities. Valid and reliable assessments are critical in research. But a clinician would much rather get an inflated score on a measure if completing it had a positive psychoeducational/therapeutic effect, as occurs with reactive self-monitoring.

The reason given for administering one of the OCD questionnaires mentioned is not to get a score. Your assessment is likely to be adequate and sufficient without such a number. Your PMC formulation is probably fairly certain.

But one PMC worth breaking is 'OCD + Lack of insight <—> Give in to compulsive urges'. OCD questionnaires may decrease 'Lack of insight'.

HOMEWORK 67

OC/OK Worries

The task recommended for many anxiety problems in 'Homework 35: Reasonable Versus Unreasonable Worries Listing' is particularly and specifically useful for OCD. Among the reasons for this is the tendency for sufferers to doubt — including to doubt which are 'OC worries' and which are normal, healthy 'OK worries'. The process of setting limits (e.g. Homework 68: Check Once Only) is one that most OCD sufferers require. How often should we wash our hands? How long should this take? What are the odds I've put poison in my child's food? Should I throw it out? Should I go home from work if I doubt the back door is locked? Is it safer to wash one shirt in the washer at a time?

Although patient education about germs, safety, and so on, has been emphasised by some (Vaccaro et al., 2008), most OCD suffers in interview will have a reasonable grasp of what is outlandish and what others do and think. OC thoughts and urges are, by diagnostic definition, 'egodystonic'. In this sense they are different from psychotic delusions. (On the other hand, there is a grey area when it comes to beliefs in Body Dysmorphic Disorder and even Anorexia Nervosa, in which clients seem to genuinely experience an hallucination at the neurological level. They don't just believe or feel ugly or fat. They can 'see' it. [Phillips, 1996].)

So when given the task of listing OC versus OK worries most OCD clients will successfully complete it, as an academic exercise. They just need to remember why they've gone to a therapist rather than a sanitation expert, or security consultant, or mathematician, or policeman, or ...

The challenge lies more in the emotion, urgency, or habit of the OC moment. To ignore a false alarm sounding in one's brain requires composure, certainty, and a plan. A pre-decided official listing of false alarms may help with this.

This makes OC/OK lists very important — something I emphasis to clients. Once the lists are agreed, they will determine one's behavior in the face of real and unreal dangers for the rest of one's life! They are a contract, not to be broken, even in the heat of the fearful moment.

The other major import of the OC/OK lists is that they dictate very different responses to perceived urges or threats. An OK worry may be processed, shared, ruminated upon, and acted upon. An OC worry must be recognised and dismissed, and the opposite to its natural consequence done. At the felt risk to people's lives, an alarm will be ignored. This is not to be done when a bus bears down on one's child. But is to be done when one feels sure there is poison in this meal.

We're up to Step 3 in our managing of your OCD (Script 11). It's really important you recognise which are OC thoughts or urges or superstitions or doubts, and which are OK normal worries you should act on. You seem to have a fair idea of this [clients with BDD may be an exception here] or else you wouldn't have come along to me. At some level you agree this is a thinking problem, not a safety problem or a germ problem or a ... But it's really important you are clear and sure about this, because we know that OC people can doubt anything, and to ignore and beat a false alarm in your head, you have to be firm and sure and consistent.

So I'm going to ask you to write down two lists of worries that jump into your head. First there are 'OK' worries. These are things I don't want you to ignore or re-label. They're real things that should be thought about, planned for, and acted on. You might write on this list 'Nearly run out of money by the end of the week', or 'Mary vomited twice tonight', and so on.

The second list we'll call 'OC' worries. They're the ones we're calling false alarms. This is when the 'Oh dear, watch out, what if, but I can't be sure, something terrible could happen' loop in your brain fires off at the wrong thing. Recently it's especially fired off when … [insert description of current OC fears and behaviours].

So we can start this list with … [Write something like, 'If I buy 3 things instead of 4, something awful will happen' or 'If I don't scrub 28 times I'll feel awful and could get sick or cause someone to die'.]

I'd like at least 3 'OK' ones and at least 8 'OC' ones.

This homework will assess the ease and clarity of the client's insight, and may reveal undisclosed content. Some prefer to write embarrassing or personal content rather than speak it to your face.

Another hoped-for therapeutic function of this exercise is that — as can occur with the NER homework — once written in words, the content of thoughts, fears, or urges can seem all the more ridiculous.

The content of the lists may guide future Cognitive Therapy or Exposure and Response Prevention.

But also, the lists serve the purpose of being serious official records of what has been positively identified as 'false alarms', and what must be acted upon, or not, in the future. This 'contractual' element can be emphasised.

HOMEWORK 68

Check Once Only

Unfortunately for most OCD sufferers it is debatable as to what is an acceptable level of cleanliness, safety, or security, and doubt is central in most OCD problems. Can you contract AIDS from a door handle? If my front door is left unlocked all day, what are the odds a stranger will find this out? Even the extreme or illogical cause-and-effect beliefs of some — such as 'If I don't tap 3 times 3 times, something bad will happen' — blend into the superstitious behaviours of some of us. Such issues or standards should be researched, discussed, and settled *once* with the therapist. If this is repeated, the process can become a neutralising ritual or reassurance in itself. An inexpert therapist may see this as cognitive therapy or reality testing, when it is just another compulsive way of coping.

However, one clear line of demarcation can be found when checkers doubt their own perception or memory to the point of *re*-checking door locks, windows, taps, power points, and so on. The eyes and memories of OCD sufferers are not defective. In fact they are so attuned to risks and habitual in their rituals, it is *less* likely they will leave dangers unchecked.

Therefore, at some point in therapy with a checker it can be useful to impose a new 'rule' for their lives:

Some things are OK to check. They're probably not a part of OCD. Like checking that the back door is locked before leaving home to go to work. But even with that, it only needs checking once, and you've told me you check the ___________ more than once. In fact lots of times, by looking and trying it.

This means you are doubting your own eyes or doubting your memory, and your eyes and memory are as good as anyone's. So this really is, for sure, a part of the 'doubting disease'.

So this is one type of OC you won't have to run past me or anyone else in deciding where to draw the line. As soon as you feel the urge to re-check anything, we know it's a part of the OCD (or it's Sam; see Homework 69). Then this is a chance to fight the OC urges (or Sam).

In fact we can make a new rule:

(Write on homework card)

From now on everything may be checked either zero or one times. Any more is definitely an OC (or Sam, or a 'false alarm'). I'd like you to write in your Challenge Diary (see Homework 4 and Homework 65: CT+E&RP) any times you follow this rule, and any times you break it.

The rule can be written on a homework card, or can be in the form of a promise or contract:

I, ____, agree that from today I will check taps, locks, power points, the stove, windows, my son's bed, that the toilet has flushed correctly, the contents of the salt shaker, ... no more than once.

Signed: ___________________ Dated: ________ Witnessed: ___________________

Further insights and other therapies/homeworks can arise from feedback as to how successful or unsuccessful the client has been with this pledge, with which behaviours they have faltered, and what strategies or self-talks have helped.

HOMEWORK 69

Name It

Although the thoughts and urges in OCD are usually 'ego-dystonic',[1] that is, the person can see the illogicality, extremeness, or dysfunctionality of their obsessions and compulsions, it still 'feels' real at the time because it occurs spontaneously within their head. It can be hard to separate out what is them, and what is the OCD.

OCD sufferers are also often embarrassed and self-blaming over their problem behaviours — see Figure 6.6 (a) and (b) — and, due to thought-action fusion (see Homework 65: CT + E&RP), over their thoughts as well.

For these reasons, I extend the strategy recommended for children with OCD (Hyman & Pedrick, 2005, p. 188) to adults, of deciding on a name for the OCD.

> The trouble here is that most of your brain — most of *you* — is working fine. The brain researchers have found that it's just one small bit of your brain that's firing off when it shouldn't, but it's doing that over and over. We've already worked out that the more you act on this firing — the more you take it seriously — the stronger that nerve pathway gets. Every time you let it fire but don't do anything about it, the weaker over time it'll get. The 'neural groove' will get shallower, not deeper.
>
> So this bit of your brain isn't you. It's a tiny bit up there that we need to step away from, work out, and then ignore.
>
> It'll help us in doing this if we see the problem as separate from the real Mary [insert name here]. So I'd like you to decide on a name we'll give it: 'Muriel' or 'Sam', or whatever you like. Preferably not the name of someone you know. And a yukky name might be good. I want you to tell me the name, and also tell (mother, father, spouse, etc.), so that from now on we can all blame Mr X, and we can see this as helping you control and ignore Mr X. It's us and you against him; not us against you, or you against you.

It is subsequently up to the therapist to consistently talk about Mr X, ask about Mr X, coach self-talk in cancelling out Mr X, and encourage family members to be negative about Mr X, not about the OCD sufferer.

---

1 There are exceptions to this. Most Body Dysmorphic Disorder sufferers fully believe in their body dysmorphia. Many chronic hoarders will argue for their lifestyle. Anorexics effectively hallucinate when they look in the mirror.

HOMEWORK 70

Loop Tape

Many OCD sufferers display few or no observable rituals or neutralising behaviours. A functional analysis may reveal, however, that internal, cognitive, or covert neutralising occurs. That is, they attempt to cope with the intrusive thought, fear, or urge by reassurance, self-talk, or a purely mental ritual such as prying, counting, internal chanting, analysing/ruminating, and suchlike. This is where OCD and GAD overlap, as both problems involve the dysfunctional belief that worrying is necessary to feel better or to avert the fear or urge. In this sense Wells' (1995; 2002) metacognitive model and therapy can apply to both problems.

The only adaptive cognitive response or reassurance allowed by our current understanding of the PMCs of OCD (see Figures 6.11 and H-65) is along the lines of 'This is my OCD again. I know it's a false alarm. So I refuse to react to it.'

The application of Exposure and Response Prevention (E&RP) to OC problems that involve an overt compulsive expression is usually clear. The situation that invokes an obsession or fear or urge must be faced rather than avoided. Even the experience of the obsession must be accepted. But it must be seen for what it is — a false alarm — and the washing or checking or repeating or counting or escaping or ... must be resisted.

If the compulsive component is entirely cognitive, however, it is harder to identify, to distinguish from the obsession, and to block or prevent. The CBT treatment of some OCDs can therefore be quite complex, and best left to a clinical psychologist experienced in the area. For example, it is common for reassurance from the therapist to become a ritual/neutraliser. Many OCD sufferers will start each session with a request that s/he be told *once again* that s/he is unlikely to be a paedophile, or to cause someone's death, or suchlike. Similar to the 'check once' rule (Homework 68), the therapist must insist that the decision as to what is an OK worry and what is an OC worry (Homework 67) must be made once, and once only, and that then 'This is my OCD again' must kick in.

A part of this complexity is the judicious use of Thought Stopping (TS) in OCD (Bakker, 2009). PMC theory and E & RP treatment require exposure to the distressing thoughts, fears, or urges. TS could interfere with this. TS is definitely a potentially effective way to block cognitive rituals or unhealthy reassurances. But whether it is useful in controlling obsessions depends on subtlties about *why* it is being used. If an OCD sufferer uses TS to block upsetting thoughts because s/he sees them as nuisance intrusive distractions, this is good. If s/he uses it because the thoughts are distressing and could lead to bad outcomes, this is not good. TS should only be used against obsessions in a 'This is my OCD again' strategy.

But if the neutralising behaviour is internal, how can we prevent it in an E & RP procedure? Salkovskis and Westbrook (1989) developed a 'loop tape' procedure, extended and modified since (especially beyond the literal use of tapes; Crino, 1993; Dunne, 2000; Freeston et al., 1997; Hyman & Pedrick, 2005; Salkovskis et al., 1998). But the critical elements appear to be: (a) selection of a recording format (loop tape, dictaphone, computer-based recording, etc.); (b) a recording in the person's own voice of distressing obsessive content; (c) exposure to this, usually via headphones, in a prolonged and uninterrupted way so as to prevent avoidance, neutralising, cognitive rituals, or maladaptive reassurance, until the person is habituated to the point of nonresponse, or even, desirably, of boredom. Where an audio recording format is not available, prolonged repeated writing of distressing obsessional content is an option. But this does not as reliably guarantee the prevention of concurrent neutralising.

Once a recording format is chosen, instructions could follow these lines.

I'd like you to write out tonight the worst thoughts you can have about ...

Write out about 2 or 3 minutes worth, if you spoke them aloud. Don't put in any 'maybes' or softeners or qualifications or reassurances. Just the worst stuff, one after another. (This needs to be checked, either on paper, or when the recording is brought in at the next session.) Then I want you to record what you've written onto ...

We need it in your own voice, so it's like listening to your own thinking. Then, I'd like you to listen to this recording, through the headphones (to aid privacy, and to imitate thoughts-in-your-head) twice a day for 10 (or 15) minutes. It *will* upset you; it's meant to. So we want no interruptions, no distractions, and especially no arguments or reassurances about what you're hearing. That's why it's a continuous/loop recording. We know now the stuff is rubbish. It's a 'false alarm', it's your OCD talking. We have to get to a point where you're sick of it, where you stop reacting to it, because we know when you take it seriously and react at all to it, this makes it worse, and you're more likely to react to it again when it comes into your mind the next time. It *will* come into your mind again. Whenever you react as if it's true you make the OCD stronger. Every time you react as if it's OCD rubbish (or 'Sam'; see Homework 69) it makes the OCD a bit weaker.

When I see you next time, bring the recording in so I can hear what you've said in it (or at least the written version). And also I'd like to check that you're paying attention to it, and that each session is long enough so you're a bit less upset toward the end of the listening session.

HOMEWORK 71

Three Imperfections

Often OCD can present on a background of general perfectionism or scrupulosity. Or a person may be referred for work on an 'obsessive-compulsive personality disorder'. Or perfectionism may be contributing to another psychological problem such as social anxiety or depression.

At such times some form of cognitive therapy may be a good starting point. This may include the provision of literature on perfectionism. Such literature can range from textooks (e.g., Flett & Hewitt, 2002), through self-help workbooks (e.g., Antony & Swinson, 1998), to an educative introductory chapter. A good example of the latter can be found in Bieling and Antony's (2003) chapter 'You don't need to be perfect: Changing perfectionism and self-criticism' in *Ending the Depression Cycle.*

But a behavioural component to therapy is perhaps even more important. Whether it is conceptualised as exposure and fear-facing, or as skills practice, or as behavioural experiments, the client will need to do some things imperfectly and learn to live with this.

(While writing on a homework card)

In the next fortnight I would like you to choose three things to do, on purpose, *imperfectly*. Firstly, I'll be interested to see what you choose — what counts or matters. Secondly, I'll be interested to see how it went — how hard it was for you. And thirdly, I'll be interested to see *how* you coped. Did you have to talk yourself through it? Did you distract yourself from it? Did you get support from someone? ... and so on.

Things that would count [derive these from the person's own presentation and history], which could include: Turn up to a meeting late; leave a mess at work or at home for a few days; submit an assignment with a deliberate typo error in it; ... [Give concrete examples!] Record these in your Challenge Diary, including the highest SUDS level you reached when doing them. (See Homeworks 4 and 34.)

Much of the psychological work then occurs upon review of this homework. Further challenges may be set, and/or self-talk and beliefs challenged, and/or coping options fine-tuned or tailored.

HOMEWORK 72

Identifying PMCs

When a client has been introduced to the basic CBT model (Script 2) and to the centrality of PMC identification (Script 3), then many can identify their own PMCs more effectively than the therapist can. We know the literature, the theories, and many of the questions to ask in seeking likely PMCs. But the client has a lifelong intimate knowledge of their own experiences, thoughts, feelings, and behaviours.

Therefore, I will frequently provide a copy of the likely PMCs in a particular problem area (e.g. any of Figures 6.1 to 6.15).

Ask the client:

I'd like you to take these home and look through them tonight. Any problem-maintaining circles that you can see have probably been happening in your life, I'd like you to put a tick next to them. I might know what to look out for, but only you know if it probably fits.

The purpose of this homework is threefold: (a) to check that the client understands PMCs; subsequent discussion will reveal this; (b) to identify relevant PMCs so that treatment can be guided; and (c) to engender a commitment to the PMC/CBT approach, especially for those clients who have been encouraged by the media or by past therapists to only seek historical precipitating causes and to expect a cure and resolution the moment one of these is identified.

More insightful clients can be asked whether PMCs not included in the sample taxonomies have applied. For example, one depressed client proposed:.

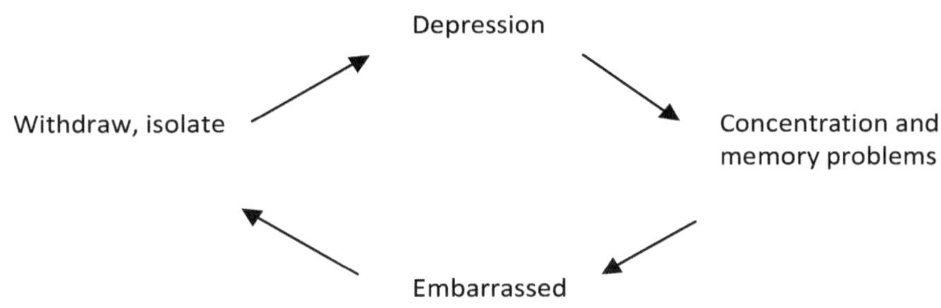

One anxious client proposed:

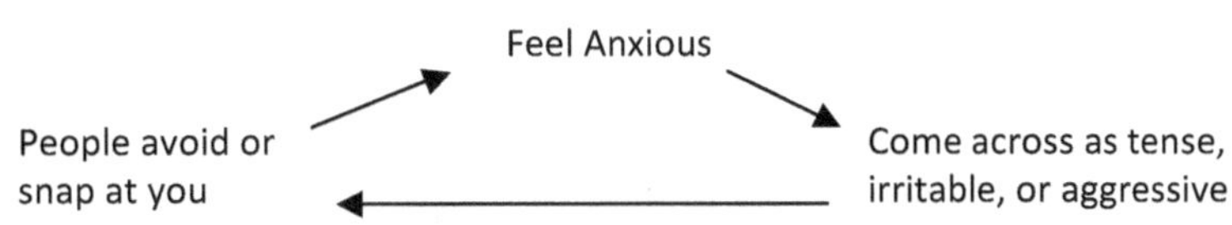

SECTION 4

Scripts

SCRIPT 1

Self-Efficacy, Self-Esteem Restoration

Psychoeducation is the ubiquitous component of all evidence-based therapy approaches, or at least of those that produce a lasting result.

There are many possible mechanisms by which psychoeducation may be efficacious. It can help clients decide which coping option to apply to which problem. For example, knowing exactly what is an OCD urge and what is a healthy worry, can guide selection of thought-stopping versus reassurance-seeking.

Some knowledge, or at least a model, of the problem can also assist in restoration of feelings of normality, better self-esteem, and thus better self-efficacy, and can thus push along any therapeutic gains.

In fact, with panic disorder such knowledge of what has occurred and is occurring, and what can cause what, and how panic attacks are not dangerous, may be the primary therapeutic ingredient.

Some version of the following script, depending upon the particular presenting problem, is often a useful first intervention. Parts of it may not apply, however, to psychotic disorders, organically based ones, and others in which PMCs are secondary rather than primary.

This is quite a common problem. People don't go around announcing it to everyone, but they do come and tell me. So some people you know are likely to have, or have had, this problem. In fact we know that about 1 in X of the population will get this problem. ***Cite approximate prevalence rate, as obtained from, for example, O'Leary & Norcross (1998)***.

This problem can happen to nearly anyone, depending on what they go through. There might be a bit of a genetic/heredity component; but that's only a susceptibility, like some people under stress will get depressed, some get tummy problems, some get skin rashes, some get panic attacks.

We need to have a reasonable, matter-of-fact, attitude to you having this problem. You've told me that you've kept the problem largely to yourself, maybe because you're a bit embarrassed or ashamed of having it. This isn't fair, and it gets in the way of beating the problem.

It isn't fair because we know that anyone can get this problem. It has **nothing** to do with intelligence; Einstein could have had this problem for all we know. So when you used words like 'stupid' or 'silly' you were wrong. People can't just brainpower their way out of these problems. It has to do with feelings and conditioning and experiences, not just being sensible or silly.

It has nothing to do with 'mental illness'. You have as much chance of getting schizophrenia as I have. ***(At this point many clients will reveal a certainty that they were going mad. Further explanation may be necessary.)***

It has nothing to do with 'willpower'. I've known people with this problem who've given up smoking just like that. You can't just **decide** to stop thinking this way/reacting this way/feeling this way. If this was possible I'd be out of business. The reason people come to see me to help beat the problem is that circles of causes get going that trap people in the problem, so they **can't** 'just stop it'. We're going to spot some of these circles, and work out where you can break them. People **can** break out of these circles/problems, when they learn how. ***(A reference to the Figure 3.1 CBT Model may help here. See Script 2.)***

So you're not responsible/at fault/to blame for having this problem, but it **will** be largely up to your effort to break out of it, when you know how.

The attitude or approach described here may be at odds with the medical model of psychological problems that the client has already been exposed to by their GP or psychiatrist. It is common for these professions to explain to a depressed patient, for example, that he/she has a 'chemical imbalance' — perhaps involving serotonin — that needs to be corrected by medication.

The motivation for such a medical model is clear. It encourages patients to take their medication. And, as with the medical model of alcoholism, it attempts to avoid issues of blame or moral weakness, in favour of acceptance of the problem and a need for help.

However, there are many problems with the 'chemical imbalance' model (Bakker, 2019a). There is no blood test to check on this 'imbalance'. The serotonin hypothesis is very simplistic. SSRIs don't work with many patients. Other drugs can work. Is grief a 'chemical imbalance'? CBT and IPT are able to correct this 'chemical imbalance'! But, above all, self-esteem, stigma and self-efficacy are not improved by being told your brain is malfunctioning. It is possible to counter self-blame by referring to PMCs, and how 'willpower' is not enough (also see Script 2).

Finally, the restoration of some self-esteem and self-efficacy can be enhanced by the provision of literature, which explains and 'normalises' the problem. And which can be shared with spouses, family, and so on, so their attitudes can be improved.

SCRIPT 2

Introducing the CBT Model

The basic CBT model (see Figure S-1, below) can be introduced to a client at several points in the latter assessment stages or early treatment stages of session one or two.

This, for me, involves holding up a sheet illustrating the model and speaking while pointing to its various elements or causal arrows.

A general introduction could be:

While you've been filling me in on what's been happening for you, I've had this model in my head, to try to understand what's been causing what. If this is you ***(point to enclosed area)***.

The purposes of introducing the model can include:

- simplifying a problem formulation:

So when you see a spider ***(point)***, your brain says 'Danger' ***(point)***, and you feel panicky ***(point)***, and you leave the room ***(point)***.

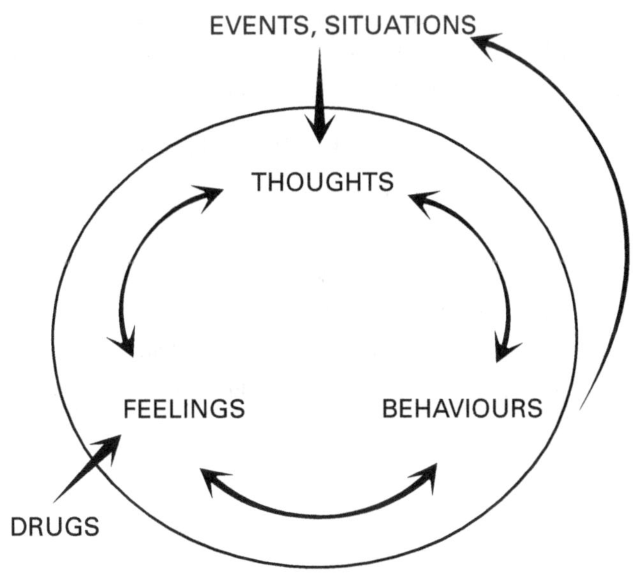

FIGURE S-1
A CBT model.

- illustrating PMCs:

When you leave the room ***(point)***, and the spider's then not near ***(point to Events, Situations)*** your brain says 'I'm safe' ***(point)***, you feel calmer ***(point)***, and you're **more** likely to run away again ***(point to Behaviours)***. This unfortunately only makes the fear stronger.

- explaining probable aetiology:

It seems that what has probably happened is that the car accident ***(point)*** has meant that you now see danger all the time on the roads ***(point)***, so you feel terrified in traffic ***(point)***, and haven't driven since ***(point)***.

Note the mixture of specific and general applications or elements of the model in the above examples, as per Table 3.1. Illustrating PMCs and explaining probable aetiology can also serve to bolster shattered self-esteem or self-efficacy (see Script 1).

- justifying therapy homework and describing treatment goals:

If you get back to going to the gym ***(point to Behaviours)*** whether you feel like it or not, because we know it'll be good for you, then you'll have a chance of some nice things happening ***(Events, Situations)***, that can change your mind a bit about whether life sucks ***(Thoughts)***, and you may feel better for a minute ***(Feelings)***, which can encourage you to go on and **do** a bit more ***(Behaviours)***.

Another example of tying the model into homework has been described in Homework 1: *Negative Emotion Records (NERs)*, where Figure 3.1 is referred to while explaining the links between 4. Situation/Event/Trigger, 5. Negative Automatic Thoughts, and 2. Feeling/Emotion.

- explaining the role of concurrent or alternative drug therapies:

The Zoloft can help by making a difference to how you feel overall ***(point)***, but we don't want to rely just on this to hopefully have a spill-over effect over time; we want to **make** changes in how you're thinking ***(point)***, what you're doing ***(point)***, the supports you've got ***(point to Events, Situations)*** and so on. So that the changes are permanent. We know that CBT has a longer-term effect than just taking the medication.

SCRIPT 3

Individualised PMCs

In Chapter 5 it was argued that one of the best ways to present a problem formulation to a client is in terms of individualised PMCs. In Script 1 reference is made to how circles of causes get going, and people with problems can't 'just stop it'. Script 2, introducing the CBT Model, gives illustrations of specific PMC examples. And many of them are outlined in Figures 6.1 to 6.15.

But it is the therapist's task to propose which PMCs apply in an individual case. The details of formulation and discussion which ensue will vary hugely from client to client. But a suitable general introduction to the process, as a whiteboard or sheet of paper is being prepared, would be:

> You've told me about several things that were probably relevant to this problem getting going in the first place. ***(Briefly mention past stressors, experiences in upbringing, family history of psychological problems, or particular traumas.)*** But with most of that, it's either long-gone, over, done, history, or it's not changeable or fixable now. We can't do much with that. But there are clear things that are keeping the problem going (or coming back) that we **can** do something about. You've gotten caught up in some 'vicious circles', like … ***(write, while explaining, factors such as those illustrated in Figures 6.1 to 6.15)***. Now, where can we break these up? It'd be good to change them at **several** points; maybe at the Thoughts points, and at the Behaviour points, and others. The homework I'm going to give you aims to do this at several points. And as an intellectual exercise if you like you can classify the things I'll ask you to do according to whether they are attacking thinking or situations or feelings or behaviours in the circles.

Depending upon the capacity for insight of clients, they can be asked to alter or add to PMC illustrations, or formulate their own, or look through copies of pages of PMCs to identify ones currently probably relevant to them.

SCRIPT 4

Common or Expected Prognosis

The following awaits full empirical support, but I have found it to be clinically useful.

The outcome studies cited in Chapters 2, 3, and 4 indicate that relapses are common after CBT for depression, anxiety problems, and so on, though less common than with pharmacotherapy alone. But such relapses tend to be less severe, less prolonged, and less frequent over time. This is consistent with the notion that people *change* when they use CBT to control a problem. They learn new skills, develop supports, increase awareness, change their circumstances, and alter attitudes and habits.

Knowledge of all this can be relevant to relapse prevention or recovery, as outcome is likely to be worse among clients who (a) expect no progress, (b) expect no hiccups and catastrophise if they occur, (c) rely solely on medication, or (d) don't know what to expect.

The following script and graph (I usually make a new drawing with each client to personalise the presentation) is meant to apply only to problems that do not have an ongoing or currently relevant precipitant, such as an organically based mental illness or an ongoing stressor (see Figure 5.2). In such circumstances, relapses can be equally as severe over time, as the illness or stressors fluctuate; but for most Type II CPPs, CBT can be the primary or singly effective intervention.

I'm going to show you how these problems usually go for most people ***(present Figure S-4a)***.

This is an upside-down graph, representing 'size of the problem' over time. So up here is bad and down here is good ***(point)***.

Now some people come along after a slow buildup of problems over time, and some after a sudden traumatic event. But this graph starts from when we first get together and get on the right track.

Notice I've drawn this graph with lots of wiggles. Everyone has good and bad days. And we can't say someone is much better or much worse after a day or two. So that's the first thing. We mustn't judge too quickly. We have to look at how things go over time.

But generally, as we work on it, and find things that help, people improve over time. Maybe on this day ***(point to a spike on the recovery slope)*** they think 'What's the use!?' but soon after they see the overall improvement. Especially if they record things, because it's easy to forget how bad you felt before.

So that's the good news — generally people get better. But the bad news is that this can happen ***(point to first relapse)***. It may be 3 weeks down the track, or 12 months, but most people have hiccups.

But notice I've drawn this hiccup as not quite so high or severe as the first episode. And notice the recovery time is quicker. That's because people have learned something or changed things from the first time. They get back to therapy exercises quicker, or they know quicker what helps, or they have their supports ready, and so on.

That's the good news. But the bad news is that this can also happen ***(point to the second relapse)***.

But notice too that the gaps between these hiccups tend to get longer. That's because, on average, the sort of stress or trigger that can cause this hiccup ***(point to the first relapse)*** is the sort that might happen to most people every few months, like an argument at home, or getting the flu. But what would be necessary to cause a hiccup way down here ***(point to third relapse)*** is bigger; it is the sort of thing that happens to most people only every few years, like a death in the family, or a car accident.

Now the reason it's important to know this, is that hiccups can happen, but they're not necessarily a bad sign. And what you say to yourself here ***(point to X in Figure S-4b)*** can make a big difference. If you say to yourself, 'Well, this is awful, I'm back to square one, this must mean there's something permanently wrong with me, I've got a brain disorder!' then you'll still get better over time, but it'll be harder. You'll follow **this** line ***(see Figure S-4b)***. If you say to yourself 'I knew this could happen. It's probably the stress at work, and not sleeping well for a week. I'd better get stuck into some of my old homework,' then you'll keep on the better line on the graph ***(see Figure S-4b)***.

Take this graph with you, and put it in a drawer somewhere with your homework, because it might be useful to remind yourself of all this when hiccups happen — even the day-to-day ones.

Where possible it is good to mark, or ask the client to mark, where they are on the graph at the moment, especially if seeing them during a relapse.

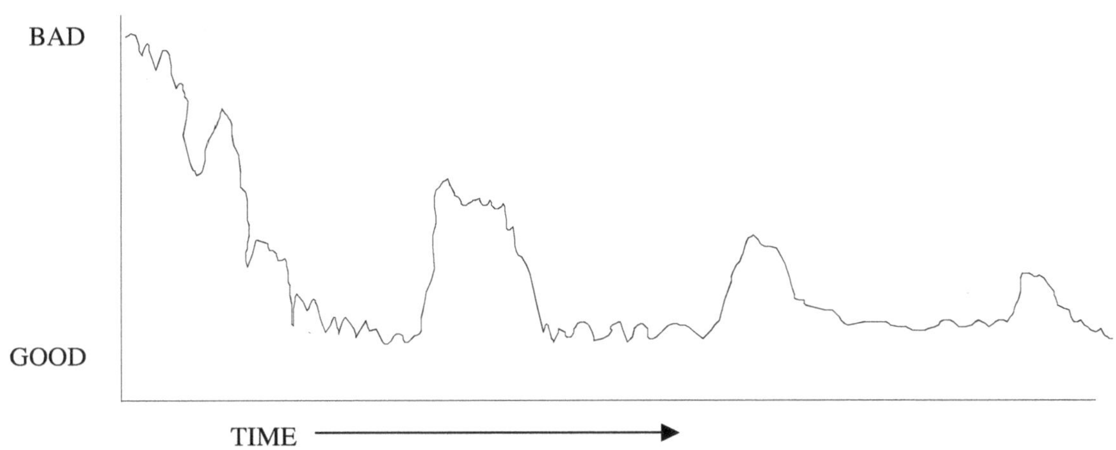

FIGURE S-4A
Usual progress after CBT.

(Available as a free download from www.australianacademicpress.com.au)

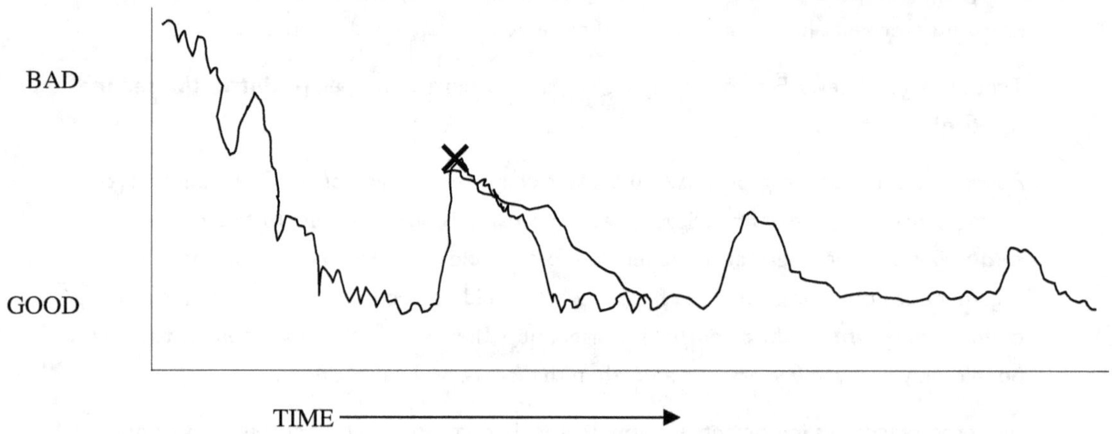

FIGURE S-4B
Variations in progress after CBT.

(Available as a free download from www.australianacademicpress.com.au)

SCRIPT 5

Not Just 'Talk Therapy'

Most clients reveal that they have no clear expectations of what therapy will involve. Many who do, explicitly say they want or expect someone to talk to. They may carry such an expectation from previous counselling or therapy, or from media portrayals of psychoanalysis or counselling.

Some report they feel better for having talked things out. There may be a temptation to merely satisfy this expectation. But we know there is a distinction between pleasing clients in a session and producing progress. In fact, it is arguable that an undisrupted client is one who is able to maintain their current dysfunctional or inadequate homeostasis.

So if any indication of such a talk therapy expectation emerges, I will, even in Session 1, explain that I will be giving homework in every session, and that I expect most of the benefits of our work to occur ***between*** rather than ***within*** our sessions.

If the response is blank or even argumentative, I may elaborate with:

There are two and a half things that determine everything in your life and in my life. They are:

1. your genes
   This makes a difference to your appearance, your talents, your sensitivity even. But there's not much we can do about what you start with in your genes.
2. your environment
   By this I mean everything that goes on from Day One that affects you: your role models, your luck, your traumas, what you learn, what you're rewarded for, your experiences.

But, I said there are two-and-a-half things. Because, since we are conscious humans, and not just cows, we see all this happening, and can make a difference to it. Cows are 100% a product of (1) and (2).

But **we've** got a third bit — (3) our 'reason' or 'consciousness' or 'awareness'. And if we want to change how we're turning out, we can do it, a bit. But we do it **by changing or controlling no. 2 — our environment**. After a while this then changes us. Let's take an example. If I don't like how nervous I get around people, I can't just see that and be different from today. Pure 'reason' doesn't do much. But I can decide to change what I go through over the next few weeks or months that I know will change me. So I can decide to be with people more, even if I'm uncomfortable. I can decide to deliberately talk to myself better before or during or after social occasions — maybe even write down my successes. I can decide to take three slow deep breaths before I go into the staff room at work. I can join a public speaking club, and so on.

So it's useful for you and I to talk, and analyse, and understand. But it's mainly useful if this then starts a process of real changes in your experiences, your influences, over time.

That's what your homework will aim to do.

SCRIPT 6

Education About Normal Anxiety, Grief, and Trauma Reactions

This process is too variable to offer a generic script.

Education can be useful where the judgment is made that an appropriate, understandable, proportionate, or useful emotional response to a very real circumstance is occurring — as in short-term stress symptoms, uncomplicated grief reactions, or acute stress disorder following trauma. These can be assumed to be self-limiting, but some relief and some security against PMC formation may result from education.

Or education can be useful where PMCs have formed, and misunderstanding or 'catastrophising' is maintaining some of them; for example, Figures 6.1 (d), (g), (h), (i), 6.2 (a), 6.4 (g), (i), (q), 6.5 (d), and 6.8 (e). This especially occurs in panic disorder, illness phobias, social phobia, and generalised anxiety disorder.

Materials for the process of education are very available. For general anxiety symptoms The Burns Anxiety Inventory (Montgomery & Morris, 1992, pp. 19–22) is useful. For panic attacks, I use the DSM-IV criteria list. The same source has a good listing for acute stress disorder, and coming from a big impressive book may give it more weight?

A hyperventilation symptom list is included in Homework 38.

A nonacademic introduction to the experience of grief is provided by Mal McKissock's *Coping With Grief* (1995).

And educative scripts are included in Homework 24 (Regular Exercise) and 33 (Mini-Relaxers), including the Cues for Tensions and Anxiety Survey Schedule (Table H-33).

SCRIPT 7

Negative Emotion Records (NERs)

Imagine a boy called Phil who comes home every day after school and is sat in front of the computer or the TV with a glass of milk. He goes to bed, gets up, goes to school, and lives through another day.

Then imagine Bob, who gets home and is sat down by mum who asks 'How was your day? … What happened? … How did you feel about that? … What was the best bit? … What was the worst bit? … How come you got worried and nervous? … What will you do different next time?', and so on. This boy 'lives' his day twice. This means he learns more from it, and maybe even remembers his childhood more when he grows up?

To Phil, life is a blur. Things happen one after another. But he isn't coached in recognising the links between events and thoughts and feelings. And doesn't learn as much about life, his feelings, and how to recognise or control them.

SCRIPT 8

Relationship Types

This activity comprises a very short, nifty means of assessment of a relationship that is so brief it is rarely necessary to give it as homework.

I'd like your opinion about how the relationship has felt to you, overall, along these lines:

(While drawing on a whiteboard/system card)

This [draw (a)] represents 2 people (each line is one person) who are both very reliant, maybe dependent, on each other. We call this a 'tepee' relationship. This can work okay, but it's risky because if either partner isn't there, or gets sick, or leaves the relationship, then the other one can fall over.

This [draw (b)] we call a 'lean-to' relationship. Here the dependence is pretty much one way. If this person goes away, this one may fall over.

This [draw(c)] is a 'parallel lives' relationship. The two people don't have much of a connection, but they can put up with each other. They're both pretty independent. Maybe they just have the house or kids or the mortgage in common. Sometimes this is how it feels when the kids have grown and moved out, and it's just the two left.

This [draw (d)] is the ideal in our culture. You've got two people. They're both potentially okay if on their own, but there's a solid bridge or support or connector between them that makes each one even more solid when they're together.

Which does your relationship feel like these days?

Which did it used to feel like?

And which would you like to have now?

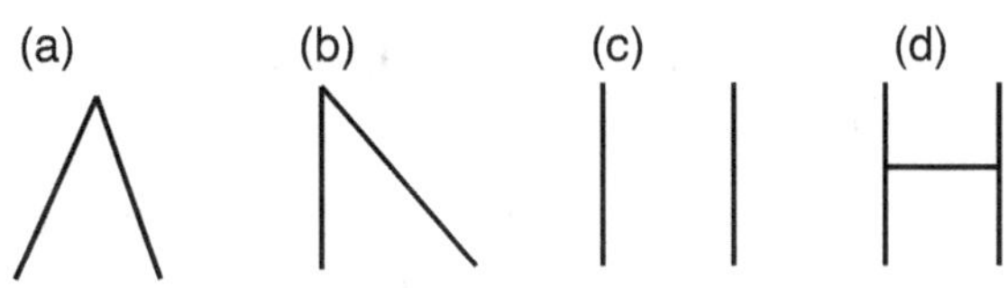

SCRIPT 9

A Visual (Venn Diagram) Model of OCD

Many OCD sufferers are visually inclined and respond best to imagery. In fact such a tendency may contribute to the disorder (Hirsch & Holmes, 2007). A descriptive model of OCD and the aims of treatment can be presented visually using Venn diagrams.

For such people, a 'normal' person's mental world is illustrated below. The relative sizes of the labelled areas represent the numbers or proportions of positive, negative, worry, and reflexive/automatic thoughts we have per day. In the 'normal' person, the universe of thoughts (the large circle) comprises positive or neutral ones (+) ('The sun feels warm'), and negative (-) ones ('The sun can cause cancer'). Hopefully, people have more positive/neutral ones per day than negative ones.

A 'normal' mental world is illustrated in the following diagram — Diagram (1).

In Diagram (1) a 'normal' mental world is represented where:

Diagram (1)

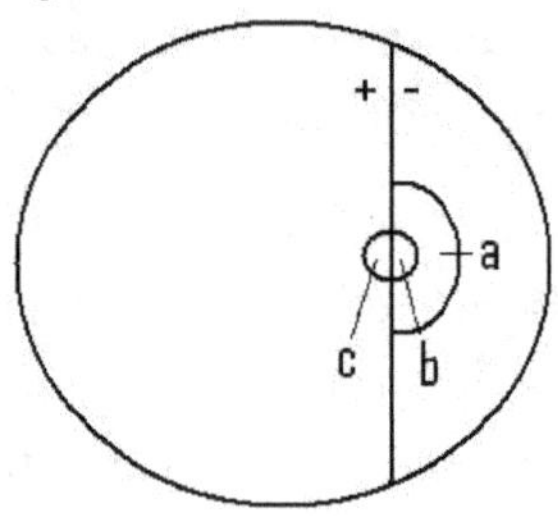

+ = Positive or neutral thoughts

- = Negative thoughts

a = Worries: Negative thoughts that produce an anxiety reaction (versus depression, jealousy, anger, etc.)

b+c = Reflexive, automatic thoughts and associations.

b = 'False alarms'

c = Neutral or positive reflexive thoughts and associations e.g. tunes that get 'stuck in your head'. These are trivial, except in OCD treatment.

Among the negative thoughts are 'What if … 's. We can label these 'worries' (the semi-circle 'a'). So worries are negative, as opposed to positive, 'What if… 's that produce anxiety. Other negative thoughts may produce depression.

In OCD, the negative 'What if … 's become reflexive, automatic, and frequent. They occur spontaneously or due to strong associations with triggers, and often become preoccupations. It is possible to also have positive or neutral reflexive automatic associative thoughts. For example, I think of a certain conversation with my father-in-law whenever I peel potatoes. Many people get a certain tune 'stuck in their heads'. Such examples are like OCD thoughts, but don't have the negative/worry flavour and so don't become problems, and also tend to reduce over time. OCD thoughts/urges/obsessions, on the other hand, produce large emotional and sometimes behavioural reactions (compulsions), and so tend to grow over time. That is, they occur more frequently, more consistently, and more dramatically over time, due to the large reactions to them. (See 'The Long Drive' in Script 12.)

OCD is illustrated in Diagram (2), below. The negative, worry, false alarms are bigger than those in Diagram (1) that represented a 'normal' mental world.

Therefore, the aim in CBT treatment of OCD is to move initially from OCD — Diagram (2) to Diagram (3), not to Diagram (4). In Diagram (3), the person is still having their reflexive/automatic/obsessive thoughts — their false alarms — but is not reacting as much to them. They are more positive/neutral now. For example, 'Oh, that's Muriel (or my OCD, or another false alarm). I refuse to do anything about it!'. Then, over time, the frequency, consistency, and impact of the thoughts can decline, and Diagram (4) applies.

Aim in OCD, to move from:

(i.e., Don't try to squash or escape from the false alarms. Turn them into nuisance automatic thoughts by seeing them as false alarms.)

Diagram (2) Diagram (3) Diagram (4)

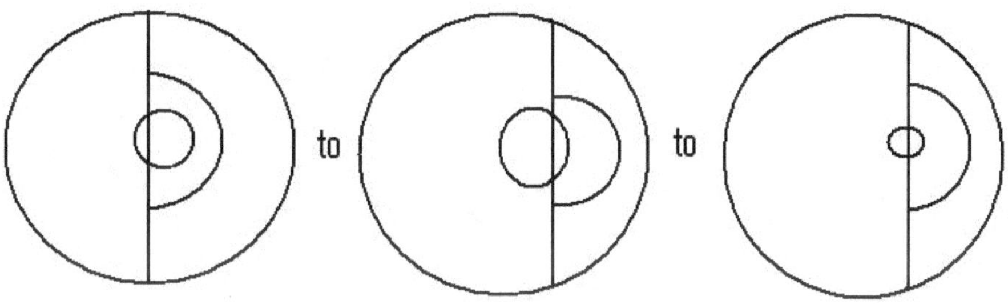

Then they'll die.

This visual descriptive model can help to understand many other disorders. Proposed depictions are presented, in Diagram (5) (see over page), of OCD, OCD with (subsequent?) depression, depresson, agitated depression, generalised anxiety, and psychopathic insensitivity.

Diagram (5)

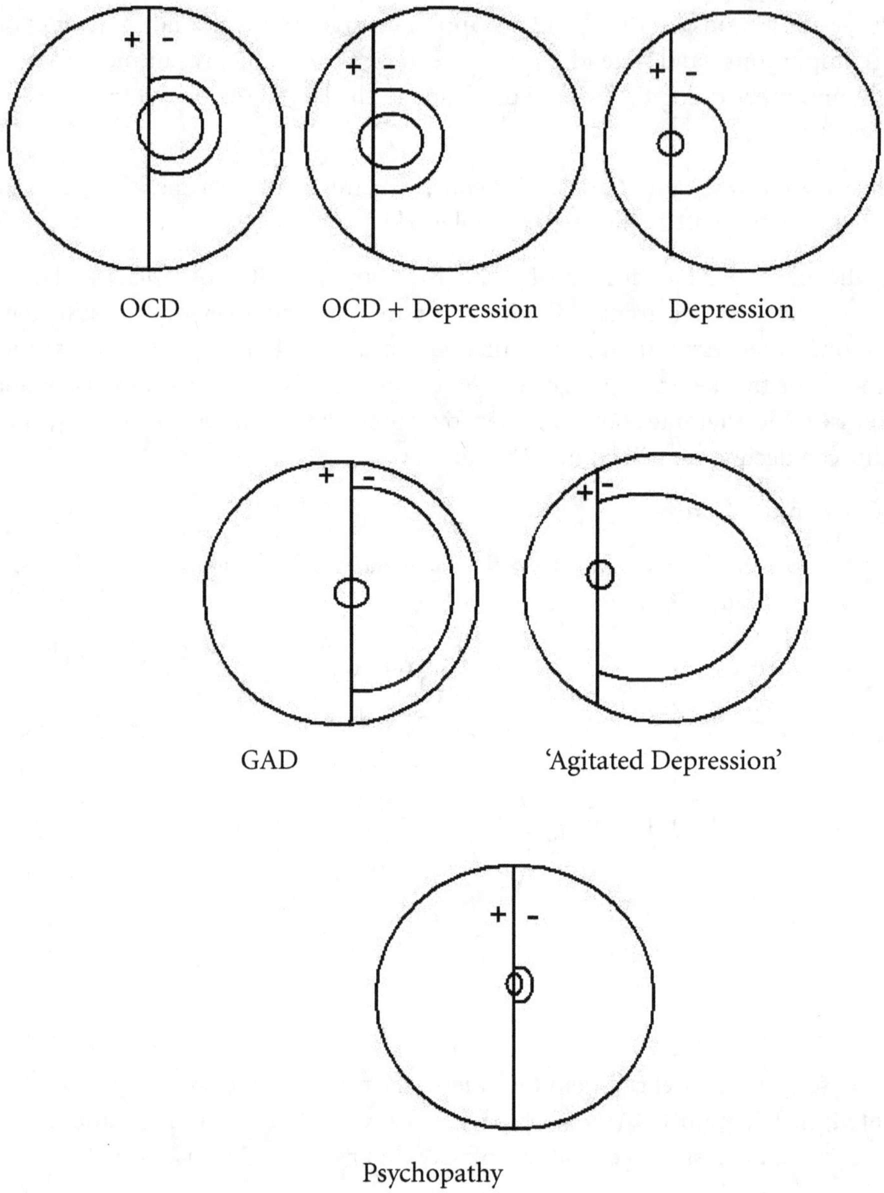
+
-
OCD
OCD + Depression
Depression
GAD
'Agitated Depression'
Psychopathy

SCRIPT 10

Calories and Vomiting

Many binge eaters deliberately vomit afterward. This can produce negative medical consequences, such as dental decay. But it can also, within a PMC, result in more frequent binges, as the person gives in to binges in the expectation that they can compensate by purging afterward.

A medical fact that can disrupt this PMC is as follows:

Did you know that as soon as you swallow the food, you start to absorb it? Maybe not the big complex proteins, but definitely the little glucose molecules. So, next time you're in a binge, remember it's being digested already. Vomiting only 'reduces the damage'. Ask your doctor about this. (Ensure the client's doctor is of the same understanding.)

SCRIPT 11

The Five Steps in Managing OCD

There is a great range of insight among people presenting with OCD. Some see the problem, understand the PMCs, and hence comply with treatment very well. Some 'just don't get it' (Bakker, 2011), and then have great difficulty either in motivation for treatment or in complying properly with treatment. Problems with insight, motivation, and hence compliance, are especially common with Body Dysmorphic Disorder, and with Anorexia Nervosa. Compliance is important because most Exposure and Response Prevention occurs independently between sessions, and if a client does not truly grasp what is a ritual or a reassurance or a safety behaviour they will perpetuate rather than extinguish an OC response.

It is therefore useful to introduce a simple model of OCD treatment that the client can take with them, and that can be referred to whenever blocks to progress occur.

Following is the one that I provide. It is self-explanatory when one understands CBT treatment of OCD, but needs to be explicitly taught to clients. Homeworks can be classified according to which Step they address. Therapeutic blocks and failures can be classified according to which Step has not been taken.

The 5 Steps in Managing OCD:

1. Accept I have OCD.

2. Learn about OCD.

3. Recognise which thoughts are OCD thoughts. ("false alarms")

4. Stop reacting when they happen.

5. Face all normal situations.

(Available as a free download from www.australianacademicpress.com.au)

SCRIPT 12

Three Analogies To Help OCD Sufferers 'Get It'

Often professional/clinical authority (e.g. a diagnosis, or even better, a PMC-based case formulation) and rational explanation may be enough to convince an OCD sufferer of what problem they have. That is, they have a *thinking* problem, rather than a cleanliness problem, or a dangerous urge problem, or a safety problem. But they may still not grasp the implications of this. They persist in fretting about safety and so on, rather than about having these persistent nuisance distressing intrusive thoughts/fears/urges/false alarms.

When appropriate, I offer the following three analogies:

1. The Smell Problem

I'd like you to imagine that you wake up one morning and you can smell something burning. So you get up and go looking. You can't find any cause. There's no smoke. You see no flames. But the smell persists. You try some experiments. You walk around to see whether the smell gets stronger or weaker in different rooms or outside the house. Let's say there's no pattern with this. You may wait to see if it gets stronger or weaker over time. It may come and go a bit, but with no clear pattern. You even ask someone 'Can you smell burning?', but everyone says no. But the smell feels real and it's alarming, so it really interferes with your life. It's still there when you go to work, so eventually you go to the doctor. They do tests and end up telling you *it's in your brain*. The smell centre is firing off, a bit like epilepsy, all the time by itself. Some pills might quieten it down, but they have side effects, so you're better off trying to ignore it, and this will help over time. It can go away if you stop paying attention and reacting to it. Meantime, you've worked out that if you jump up and down, the smell dies down a bit. So you start doing this several times a day. But the doctor tells you, and you can see, that this makes the smell even worse later in the day.

Now, the only difference between the smell problem and your OCD problem is that instead of a sensory part of your brain firing off whenever it feels like it, it's a thinking part of your brain that's doing the same thing. It's the 'Oh dear, what if, but maybe, it's dangerous, this could happen...' false alarm part of your brain that keeps going off. The more you react to it as though it's real, the more it will fire off. If you can identify it, relabel it, and ignore it, or even go *against* it, and do the *opposite* of the OC thought, the quicker it will shut up.

2. The Car Alarm

Let's imagine we're sitting here and a car alarm goes off outside the window. [I hope you have one.] So we get up and have a look. We can see a car out there. Its lights are flashing, and there's no one about, and the wind is blowing strongly. So we identify it as a false alarm. What should we do? Will we go out and stand by the car? Will we phone the police? No. We shut the window, sit down, and continue our sessions, and try really hard to ignore the noise, until it stops. To do anything else with a false alarm is just time wasting, or upsetting, or interferes with our session, with our lives.

We need to do the same with the false alarm OC thoughts going off in your head.

3. The Long Drive

If I'm driving to [insert distant city], my mind wanders all over the place. One thought I had once was: 'If I move my hands just 6 inches for just a second, the consequences would be *massive*. I could die. Others could die'. So what I did when I had that thought was I decided not to move my hands that way, and that was the end of it.

Now, if I had reacted to the thought with: 'How could I think that?! Why did I think that? I could do that!', then I would have had to pull over and calm down somehow, and struggle to drive on. Because of my big reaction, the same thought is likely to hit me again 5 minutes later, or on the trip back from [insert].

I didn't overreact to my random awful thought because I don't have OCD. (I don't suffer from thought-action fusion.) So it came and went. If I had OCD I'd overreact, and off goes a self-perpetuating OC thought/fear problem. All this has nothing to do with my safety.

You don't have a dangerous/cleanliness/safety/… problem. You have a thinking problem. So from now on I don't want us to talk about germs/urges/risks/… I want us to talk about your nuisance thoughts.

SCRIPT 13

I'm OK, The World's OK

A variation and deviation from the terminology of Transactional Analysis (Harris, 1967; Jongeward & James, 1973) can explain to clients in a simple model each of the major negative emotions (anxiety, anger, depression) and why they are being given Cognitive Therapy Homeworks such as Numbers 3, 6, 36, or 40 to address them.

For example, sometimes anger, though negative, is a more adaptive and desirable response to a problem or stress than depression. This can explain why a therapist will work on someone's self-esteem and hence self-efficacy before anything else.

The model relates attitudes to self and the world to subsequent likely emotional states, and by implication to subsequent problem-response behaviour.

The Model

Attitude to Self and World	→	Subsequent Likely Frequent Emotion
A. I'm OK, the World's OK.	→	Content, confident, optimistic.
B. I'm OK, the World's not OK.	→	Angry, arrogant, suspicious.
C. I'm not OK, the World's OK.	→	Anxious, guilty, dependent.
D. I'm not OK, the World's not OK.	→	Depressed, hopeless.

(Available as a free download from www.australianacademicpress.com.au)

A useful explanatory script is:

If a problem crops up and I'm in frame-of-mind A, then who will fix it? I can, or I can get some help. Either way, it'll be OK.

If a problem crops up and I'm in frame-of-mind B, then who will fix it? Well, I will have to, and look out any useless sod who tries to get in my way.

If a problem crops up and I'm in frame-of-mind C, then who will fix it? Someone else will have to, because I can't. I'm 'not OK'. But I daren't tell too many people about it because I'm too embarrassed, so I'll keep quiet and just suffer. It's what I deserve anyway. I just hope someone will rescue me.

If a problem crops up and I'm in frame-of-mind D, then who will fix it? Well, no one. I can't. I'm useless. And no one else will. They don't care. So we'll get nowhere.

References

Al-Kubaisy, T., Marks, I.M., Lagsdail, S., Marks, M.P., Lovell, K., Sungur, M., & Araya, R. (1992). Role of exposure homework in phobia reduction: A controlled study. *Behavior Therapy, 23*, 599–621.

Allerti, R.E., & Emmons, M.L. (1974). *Your perfect right: A guide to assertive behavior*. San Luis Obispo, CA: Impact Press.

Almas, E., & Landmark, B. (2010). Non-pharmacological treatment of sexual problems — A review of research literature 1970–2008. *Sexologies: European Journal of Sexology and Sexual Health, 19* (4), 202–211.

American Psychiatric Association. (1980). *Diagnostic and statistical manual of mental disorders* (3rd ed.) Washington, DC: Author.

American Psychiatric Association. (1987). *Diagnostic and statistical manual of mental disorders* (3rd ed. revised ed.) Washington DC: American Psychiatric Association.

American Psychiatric Association. (1994). Diagnostic and statistical manual of mental disorders. Washington, DC: Author.

American Psychiatric Association. (2000). *Diagnostic and statistical manual of mental disorders* (4th ed., revised) Washington, DC: Author.

Anand, S., & Malhi, G.S. (2011). From manual to Bible: The questionable hegemony of DSM IV. *Australian and New Zealand Journal of Psychiatry, 45* (5), 348–350.

Anderson R., Saulsman, L., & Nathan, P. (2011). *Helping health anxiety.* Perth, WA: Centre for Clinical Interventions.

Andrasik, F., Coleman, D., & Epstein, L.H. (1982). Biofeedback: Clinical and research considerations. In D.M. Doleys, R.L. Meredith, & A.R. Ciminero (Eds.), *Behavioral medicine: Assessment and treatment strategies*. New York, NY: Plenum Press.

Angermeyer, M.C., Holzinger, A., Carta, M.G. & Schomerus, G. (2011). Biogenetic explanations and public acceptance of mental illness: Systematic review of population studies. *British Journal of Psychiatry, 199*, 367–372.

Antonuccio, D.O., Thomas, M., & Danton, W.G. (1997). A cost-effectiveness analysis of cognitive behavior therapy and fluoxetine (Prozac) in the treatment of depression. *Behavior Therapy, 28*, 187–210.

Antony, M.M., & Swinson, R.P. (1998). *When perfect isn't good enough: Strategies for coping with perfectionism*. Oakland, CA: New Harbinger.

Argyle, M. (1987). *The psychology of happiness*. New York, NY: Routledge.

Arntz, A. (2003). Cognitive therapy versus applied relaxation as treatment of generalized anxiety disorder. *Behaviour Research and Therapy, 41*, 633–646.

Atlantis, E., & Sullivan, T. (2012). Bidirectional association between depression and sexual dysfunction: A systematic review and meta-analysis. *Journal of Sexual Medicine, 9*(6), 1497–1507.

Australian Pain Society. (2002). Position statement: The role of the psychologist in the management of persistent pain. Retrieved from www.physiotherapy.asn.au

Australian Psychological Society. (2010). *Evidence-based psychological interventions in the treatment of mental disorders: A literature review* (3rd ed.). Melbourne, VIC: Author.

Azrin, N.H., Sneed, T.J., & Foxx, R.M., (1973). Dry bed: A rapid method of eliminating bedwetting (enuresis) of the retarded. *Behaviour Research and Therapy, 11*, 427–434.

Bachrach, H., Galatzer-Levy, R., Skolnikoff, A., & Waldron, S. (1991). On the efficacy of psychoanalysis. *Journal of the American Psychoanalytic Association, 39,* 871–916.

Baglioni, C., Battagliese, G., Feige, B., Spiegelhalder, K., Nissen, C., Voderholzer, U., Lombardo, C., & Riemann, D. (2011). Insomnia as a predictor of depression: A meta-analytic evaluation of longitudinal epidemiological studies. *Journal of Affective Disorders, 135,* 10–19.

Bakker, G.M. (2008a). *Practical CBT: Using functional analysis, problem-maintaining circles, and standardised homework in everyday therapy.* Bowen Hills, Qld: Australian Academic Press.

Bakker, G.M. (2008b). Problem-maintaining circles: Case illustrations of formulations that truly guide therapy. *Clinical Psychologist, 12*(1), 30–39.

Bakker, G.M. (2009). In defence of thought stopping. *Clinical Psychologist, 13*(2), 59–68.

Bakker, G.M. (2011). Paranormal beliefs and insight. *Skeptical Inquirer, 35*(1), 54–55.

Bakker, G.M. (2019a). A new conception and subsequent taxonomy of clinical psychological problems. *BMC Psychology*, *7*, 46.

Bakker, G.M. (2019b). Nine evidence-based guidelines for a 'good life'. *Skeptical Inquirer*, *43*(6), 34-37.

Bakker, G.M. (in submission). Psychotherapy outcome research: Implications of a new clinical taxonomy. *Clinical Psychology and Psychotherapy*.

Baller, W.R. (1975). *Bed-wetting: Origins and treatment*. New York, NY: Pergamon Press.

Bandura, A. (1969). *Principles of behavior modification*. New York, NY: Holt.

Bandura, A. (1977). Self-efficacy: Toward a unifying theory of behavioral change. *Psychological Review, 84*, 191–215.

Bandura, A. (1982). Self-efficacy mechanism in human agency. *American Psychologist, 37*, 122–147.

Bandura, A. (1997). *Self-efficacy: The exercise of control*. New York, NY: Freeman.

Barlow, D.H., Allen, L.B., & Choate, M.L. (2004). Toward a unified treatment for emotional disorders. *Behavior Therapy, 35,* 205–230.

Barlow, D.H., Ellard, K.K., Fairholme, C.P, Farchione, T.J., Boisseau, C.L., Allen, L.B., and Ehrenreich-May, J.T. (2011a). *Unified Protocol for transdiagnostic treatments of emotional disorders*. Oxford, England: Oxford University Press.

Barlow, D.H., Ellard, K.K., Fairholme, C.P, Farchione, T.J., Boisseau, C.L., Allen, L.B., and Ehrenreich-May, J.T. (2011b). *Unified Protocol for transdiagnostic treatments of emotional disorders: Therapist guide*. New York, NY: Oxford University Press.

Barsky, A.J., & Ahern, D.K. (2004). Cognitive behavior therapy for hypochondriasis: A randomized controlled trial. *Journal of the American Medical Association, 291*, 1464–1470.

Baumeister, R.F., Smart, L., & Boden, J.M. (1996). Relation of threatened egotism to violence and aggression: The dark side of high self-esteem. *Psychological Review, 103*, 5–33.

Baxter, L.R. (1992). Caudate glucose metabolic rate changes with both drug and behaviour therapy for obsessive-compulsive disorder. *Archives of General Psychiatry, 49*, 681–689.

Beck, A.T. (1976). *Cognitive therapy and the emotional disorders*. New York, NY: International Universities Press.

Beck, A.T., Kovacs, M., & Weissman, A. (1975). Hopelessness and suicidal behavior: An overview. *Journal of the American Medical Association, 234*, 1146–1149.

Beck, A.T., Rush, A.J., Shaw, B.F., & Emery, G. (1979). *Cognitive therapy of depression*. New York, NY: Guilford Press.

Beck, J.S. (1995). *Cognitive therapy: Basics and beyond*. New York, NY: Guilford Press.

Becker, J.V., & Skinner, L.J. (1983). Assessment and treatment of rape-related sexual dysfunctions. *Clinical Psychologist, 36* (4), 102–105.

Becker, R.E., & Heimberg, R.G. (1988). *Assessment of social skills. In A.S. Bellack & M. Hersen (Eds.), Behavioral assessment: A practical handbook*. New York, NY: Pergamon Press.

Beevers, C.G., Wenzlaff, R.M., Hayes, A.M., & Scott, W.D. (1999). Depression and the ironic effects of thought suppression: Therapeutic strategies for improving mental control. *Clinical Psychology: Science and Practice, 6*, 133–148.

Bem, D.J. (1972). Self-perception theory. In L. Berkowitz (Ed.), *Advances in experimental social psychology*, Vol. 6, (pp. 1–62). New York, NY: Academic Press.

Benson, H. (1975). *The relaxation response*. New York, NY: Morrow.

Beutler, L.E., Bongar, B., & Shurkin, J.N. (1998). *Am I crazy, or is it my shrink? How to get the help you need*. New York, NY: Oxford University Press.

Beutler, L.E., Harwood, T.M., & Caldwell, R. (2001). Cognitive-behavioral therapy and psychotherapy integration. In K.S. Dobson (Ed.), *Handbook of cognitive-behavioral therapies*. New York, NY: Guilford Press.

Bieling, P.J., & Antony, M.M. (2003). *Ending the depression cycle*. Oakland, CA: New Harbinger.

Bieling, P.J., & Kuyken, W. (2003). Is cognitive case formulation science or science fiction? *Clinical Psychology: Science and Practice, 10* (1), 52–69.

Bilodeau, L. (1992). *The anger workbook*. Minnesota, MN: Hazelden.

Bissett, R.T., & Hayes, S.C. (1999). The likely success of functional analysis tied to the DSM. *Behaviour Research and Therapy, 37* (4), 379–383.

Blair-West, S. (2009). Obsessive-compulsive disorder (OCD) — Awareness, understanding and treatment. *Anxiety Matters: Anxiety Recovery Centre Victoria, 13*, 9–12.

Blanchard, E.B., Arena, J.G., & Pallmeyer, T.P. (1981). Psychosomatic properties of a scale to measure alexithymia. *Psychotherapy and Psychosomatics, 35*, 64–71.

Bloom, L.Z., Coburn, K., & Pearlman, J. (1975). *The new assertive woman*. New York, NY: Dell.

Bloom, P.B. (1994). Is insight necessary for successful treatment? *American Journal of Clinical Hypnosis, 36*, 172–174.

Blumenthal, J.A., Fredrikson, M., Kuhn, C.M., Ulmer, R.L., Walsh-Riddle, M., Appelbaum, M. (1990). Aerobic exercise reduces levels of cardiovascular and sympathoadrenal responses to mental stress in subjects without prior evidence of myocardial ischemia. *American Journal of Cardiology, 65*, 93–98.

Borkovec, T.D., & Mathews, A.M. (1988). Treatment of nonphobic anxiety disorders: A comparison of nondirective, cognitive, and coping desensitization therapy. *Journal of Consulting and Clinical Psychology, 56*, 877–884.

Borkovec, T.D., & Sides, J.K. (1979). Critical procedural variables related to the physiological effects of progressive relaxation: A review. *Behaviour Research and Therapy, 17*, 119–126.

Borsboom, D., Epskamp, S., Kievit, R. ., Cramer, A.O., & Schmittmann, V.D. (2011). Transdiagnostic networks: Commentary on Nolen-Hoeksema and Watkins (2011). *Perspectives on Psychological Science, 6*(6), 610–614.

Boulanger, J.L., Hayes, S.C., & Pistorello, J. (2010). Experiential avoidance as a functional contextual concept. In J.L. Boulanger, S.C. Hayes, & J. Pistorello (Eds.), *Emotion regulation and psychopathology: A transdiagnostic approach to etiology and treatment*. (pp. 107–136). New York, NY: Guilford Press.

Bourne, E.J. (1995). *The anxiety and phobia workbook*. Oakland, CA: New Harbinger.

Bradford, D., Stroup, S., & Lieberman, J. (2002). Pharmacological treatments for schizophrenia. In P.E. Nathan & J.M. Gorman (Eds.), *A guide to treatments that work* (2nd ed., pp.169–200). New York, NY: Oxford University Press.

Braswell, L., & Kendall, P.C. (2001). Cognitive-behavioral therapy with youth. In K.S. Dobson (Ed.), *Handbook of cognitive-behavioral therapies*. New York, NY: Guilford Press.

Britt, E., Blampied, N.M., & Hudson, S.M. (2003). Motivational interviewing: A review. *Australian Psychologist, 38*, 193–201.

Brody, A.L., Saxena, S., et.al. (1998). FDG-PET predictors of response to behavioral therapy and pharmacotherapy in obsessive compulsive disorder. *Psychiatry Research, 84*, 1–6.

Brooke, S. (2004). Formulation in clinical psychology: Past, present and future. *Clinical Psychology, 41*, 36–39.

Brown, G.W., & Harris, T.O. (1989). *Life events and illness*. New York, NY: Guilford Press.

Brown, T.A., & Barlow, D.H. (2009). A proposal for a dimensional classification system based on the shared features of the DSM-IV anxiety and mood disorders: Implications for assessment and treatment. *Psychological Assessment, 21* (3), 256–271.

Bryant, R.A. (2003). Acute Stress Disorder: Is it a useful diagnosis? *Clinical Psychologist, 7*, 67–79.

Bryant, R.A., Sackville, T., Dang, S.T., Moulds, M., & Guthrie, R. (1999). Treating acute stress disorder: An evaluation of cognitive behavior therapy and counseling techniques. *American Journal of Psychiatry, 156*, 1780–1786.

Burk, E.M., Randolph, D.L., & Probst, C. (1985). Effects of several thought stopping treatments on worry cognitions. *Psychology: A Journal of Human Behaviour, 22*, 31–41.

Burks, N., & Martin, B. (1985). Everyday problems and life change events: Ongoing versus acute sources of stress. *Journal of Human Stress, 11*, 27–35.

Burns, D.D. (1980). *Feeling good: The new mood therapy*. New York, NY: Harper Collins.

Bushman, B.J., & Baumeister, R.F. (1998). Threatened egotism, narcissism, self-esteem, and direct and displaced aggression: Does self-love or self-hate lead to violence? *Journal of Personality and Social Psychology, 75*, 219–229.

Butler, A.C., & Beck, J. (2001). Cognitive therapy outcomes: A review of meta-analyses. *Tidsskrift for Norsk Psykolog forening, 38*, 698–706.

Butler, A.C., Chapman, J.E., Forman, E.M., Beck, A.T. (2006). The Callahan empirical status of cognitive-behavioral therapy: A review of meta-analyses. *Clinical Psychology Review, 26*, 17–31.

Butler, L.D., & Nolen-Hoeksema, S. (1994). Gender differences in responses to depressed mood in a college sample. *Sex Roles, 30*(5–6), 331–346.

Butler, P.E. (1991). *Talking to yourself*. New York, NY: Harper Collins.

Butler, P.V. (1999). Diagnostic line-drawing, professional boundaries, and the rhetoric of scientific justification: A critical appraisal of the American Psychiatric Association's DSM project, *Australian Psychologist, 34*(1), 20–29.

Callahan, S.A., Panichelli-Mindel, S.M., & Kendall, P.C. (1996). DSM-IV and internalizing disorders: Modifications, limitations, and utility. *School Psychology Review, 25*(3), 297–307.

Cammin-Nowak, S., Helbig-Lang, S., Lang, T., et al. (2013). Specificity of homework compliance effects on treatment outcome in CBT. *Journal of Clinical Psychology, 69*(6), 616–629.

Campo, J.V., & Fritsch, S.L. (1994). Somatization in children and adolescents. *Journal of the American Academy of Child and Adolescent Psychiatry, 33*, 1223–1235.

Carey, M.P., Spector, T.P., Lantinga, L.J., & Krauss, D.J. (1993). Reliability of the Dyadic Adjustment Scale. *Psychological Assessment, 5, 238*–240.

Carey, T.A., & Pilgrim, D. (2010). Diagnosis and formulation: What should we tell the students? *Clinical Psychology and Psychotherapy, 17*, 447–454.

Carlat, D.J. (2010). *Unhinged: The trouble with psychiatry – A doctor's revelations about a profession in crisis*. New York, NY: Free Press.

Carter, W. (1997). *Macquarie medical matters*. Sydney, Australia: Macquarie.

Cautela, J.R. (1979). The use of covert conditioning in modifying pain behaviour. In D. Upper & J.R. Cautela (Eds.), *Covert conditioning*. New York, NY: Pergamon Press.

Cautela, J.R., & Kastenbaum, R. (1967). A reinforcement survey schedule for use in therapy, training and research. *Psychological Reports, 20*, 1115–1130.

Cautela, J.R., & Kearney, A.J. (1986). *The covert conditioning handbook*. New York, NY: Springer.

Cautela, J.R., & Rosenstiel, A.K. (1979). The use of covert conditioning in the treatment of drug abuse. In D. Upper & J.R. Cautela (Eds.), *Covert conditioning*. New York, NY: Pergamon Press.

Cautela, J.R., & Upper, D. (1975). The process of individual behavior therapy. In M.H. Eisen & R.M. Eilser (Eds.), *Progress in behavior modification*. New York, NY: Academic Press.

Chapman, L.J., & Chapman, J.P. (1969). Illusory correlation as an obstacle to the use of valid psychodiagnostic signs. *Journal of Abnormal Psychology, 74,* 271–280.

Chu, B.C., Colognori, D., Weissman, A.S., & Bannon, K. (2009). An initial description and pilot of group behavioral activation therapy for anxious and depressed youth. *Cognitive and Behavioral Practice, 16*(4), 408–419.

Claiborn, J., & Pedrick, C. (2002). *The BDD workbook: Overcome body dysmorphic disorder and end body image obsessions*. Oakland, CA: New Harbinger.

Clark, D.A., & Beck, A.T. (2010). *Cognitive therapy of anxiety disorders: Science and practice*. New York, NY: Guilford Press.

Clark, D.M. (1986). A cognitive approach to panic. *Behavior Research and Therapy, 24*, 461–470.

Clark, D.M. (1999). Anxiety disorders: Why they persist and how to treat them. *Behaviour Research and Therapy, 37*(1), S5–S27.

Clark, D.M., & Wells, P.A. (1995). A cognitive model of social phobia. In R.G. Heimberg, M.R. Liebowitz, D.A. Hope, & S.A. Schneier (Eds.), *Social phobia: Diagnosis, assessment and treatment* (pp. 69–93). New York, NY: Guilford Press.

Clark, L.A., Watson, D., & Reynolds, S. (1995). Diagnosis and classification of psychopathology: Challenges to the current system and future directions. *Annual Review of Psychology, 46,* 121–153.

Cleophas, T.J.M. (2000). Depression and myocardial infarction. In K.J. Palmer (Ed.), *Depression associated with medical illness*. Hong Kong: Adis International.

Cloitre, M., Heimberg, R.G., Liebowitz, M.R., & Gitow, A. (1992). Perceptions of control in panic disorder and social phobia. *Cognitive Therapy and Research, 16,* 569–577.

Cohen, P., & Cohen, J. (1984). The clinician's illusion. *Archives of General Psychiatry, 41,* 1178–1182.

Cosci, F., Knuts, I.J.E., Abrams, K., Griez E.J.L., & Schruers, K.R. (2010). Cigarette smoking and panic: A critical review of the literature. *Journal of Clinical Psychiatry, 71*(5), 606–615.

Cottraux, J., Mollard, E., Bouvard, M., Marks, I,. Sluys, M., Nury, A.M., … Cialdella P. (1990). A controlled study of fluvoxamine and exposure in obsessive-compulsive disorder. *International Clinical Psychopharmacology*, *5*, 17–30.

Cramer, A.O.J., Waldorp, L.J., van der Maas, H.L.J., & Borsboom, D. (2010). Comorbidity: A network perspective. *Behavioral and Brain Sciences, 33,* 137–193.

Cramer, H., Haller, H., Lauche, R., & Dobos, G. (2012). Mindfulness-based stress reduction for low back pain. A systematic review. *BMC Complementary and Alternative Medicine, 12,* 162.

Crino, R.D. (1993). The cognitive behavioural treatment of obsessional thoughts. *First Australian Conference on Obsessive-Compulsive Disorder* (pp. 87–93).

Cuijpers, P., Geraedts, A.S., van Oppen, P., Andersson, G., Markowitz, J.C., & van Straten, A. (2011). Interpersonal psychotherapy for depression: A meta-analysis. *American Journal of Psychiatry, 168*(6), 581–592.

Cuipers, P., van Straten, A., Andersson, G., & van Oppen, P. (2008). Psychotherapy for depression in adults: A meta-analysis of comparative outcome studies. *Journal of Consulting and Clinical Psychology, 76*(6), 909–922.

D'Zurilla, T.J., & Nezu, A.M. (2001). Problem-solving therapies. In K.S. Dobson (Ed.), *Handbook of cognitive–behavioral therapies*. New York, NY: Guilford Press.

Dattilio, F.M. (1989). A guide to cognitive marital therapy. In P.A. Keller & S.R. Heyman (Eds.), *Innovations in clinical practice: A source book*. (pp. 27–42). Sarasota, FL: Professional Resource Exchange.

Davidson, J.R.T., Strickland, R., Turnbull, C.D., & Belyea, M. (1984). Comparative diagnostic criteria for melancholia and endogenous depression. *Archives of General Psychiatry, 41*, 506–511.

Davis, M., Eshelman, E.R., & McKay, M. (2008). *The relaxation and stress reduction workbook*. Oakland, CA: New Harbinger.

DCP. (2013). *Position statement on the classification of behaviour and experience in relation to functional psychiatric diagnoses: Time for a paradigm shift*. Leicester: British Psychological Society.

de Craen, A.J., Moerman, D.E., Heisterkamp, S.H., Tytgat, G.N., Tijssen, J.G., & Kleijnen, J. (1999). Placebo effect in the treatment of duodenal ulcer. *British Journal of Clinical Pharmacology, 48*(6), 853–860.

de Jong-Meyer, R., Beck, B., & Riede, K. (2009). Relationships between rumination, worry, intolerance of uncertainty and metacognitive beliefs. *Personality and Individual Differences, 46*(4), 547–551.

de Jong, P.J., van Lankveld, J., & Elgersma, H.J. (2010). Sexual problems. In D. McKay, J.S. Abramowitz & S. Taylor (Eds.), *Cognitive-behavioral therapy for refractory cases: Turning failure into success*. (pp. 255–275). Washington, DC: American Psychological Association.

Deacon, B., & Maack, D.J. (2008). The effects of safety behaviors on the fear of contamination: An experimental investigation. *Behaviour Research and Therapy, 46*(4), 537–547.

Deacon, B.J. (2013). The biomedical model of mental disorder: A critical analysis of its validity, utility, and effects on psychotherapy research. *Clinical Psychology Review, 33,* 846–861.

Dengrove, E. (1985). Obsessional thinking. In M. Hersen & C.G. Last (Eds.), *Behavior therapy casebook*. New York, NY: Springer.

Denman, F. (1995). What is the point of formulation. In C. Mace (Ed.), *The art and science of assessment in psychotherapy* (pp. 167–181). New York, NY: Routledge

Dennett, D.C. (1995). *Darwin's dangerous idea: Evolution and the meanings of life*. New York, NY: Touchstone.

Department of Health. (2001). *Treatment choice in psychological therapies and counselling*. London, England: HMSO.

DeRubeis RJ, Hollon SD, Amsterdam JD, Shelton RC, Young PR, Salomon RM, et al. (2005). Cognitive therapy vs. medications in the treatment of moderate to severe depression. *Archives of General Psychiatry, 62*(4), 409–416.

DeRubeis, R.J., & Feeley, M. (1990). Determinants of change in cognitive therapy for depression. *Cognitive Therapy and Research, 14*(5), 469–482.

DeRubeis, R.J., Gelfand, L.A., Tang, T.Z., & Simons, A.D. (1999). Medications versus cognitive behaviour therapy for severely depressed outpatients: Mega-analysis of four randomized comparisons. *American Journal of Psychiatry, 156*, 1007–1013.

DeRubeis, R.J., Tang, T.Z., & Beck, A.T, (2001). Cognitive therapy. In K.S. Dobson (Ed.), *Handbook of cognitive–behavioral therapies*. New York, NY: Guilford Press.

Devilly, G.J. (2005). Power therapies and possible threats to the science of psychology and psychiatry. *Australian and New Zealand Journal of Psychiatry, 39*, 437–445.

Devilly, G.J., & Cotton, P. (2003). Psychological debriefing and the workplace: Defining a concept, controversies and guidelines for intervention. *Australian Psychologist, 38*(2), 144–150.

Devilly, G.J., Gist, R., & Cotton, P. (2006). Ready! Fire! Aim! The status of psychological debriefing and therapeutic interventions: In the workplace and after disasters. *Review of General Psychology, 10*(4), 318–345.

Dobson, D., & Dobson, K.S. (2009). *Evidence-based practice of cognitive-behavioral therapy*. New York, NY: Guildford Press.

Dobson, K.S. (2001). *Handbook of cognitive-behavioral therapies*. New York, NY: Guilford Press.

Dobson, K.S., & Joffe, R. (1986). The role of activity level and cognition in depressed mood in a university sample. *Journal of Clinical Psychology, 42*, 264–271.

Dobson, K.S., Hollon, S.D., Dimidjian, S., Schmaling, K.B., Kohlenberg, R.J., Gallop, R., … Jacobson, N.S. (2008). Randomized trial of behavioral activation, cognitive therapy, and antidepressant medication in the prevention of relapse and recurrence in major depression. *Journal of Consulting and Clinical Psychology, 76* (3), 468–477.

Dobson, K.S., Quigley, L., & Dozois, D.J.A. (2014). Toward an integration of interpersonal risk models of depression and cognitive-behaviour therapy. *Australian Psychologist, 49*, 328-336.

Dryden, W. (1985). Challenging but not overwhelming: A compromise in negotiating homework assignments. *British Journal of Cognitive Psychotherapy, 3*, 77–80.

Dryden, W., & Ellis, A. (2001). Rational emotive behavior therapy. In K.S. Dobson (Ed.), *Handbook of cognitive-behavioral therapies*. New York, NY: Guilford Press.

Dryden, W., & Walker, J. (1996). *REBT self-help form*. New York, NY: Albert Ellis Institute for REBT.

Dunn, A.L., Trivedi, M.H., Kampert, J.B., Clark, C.G., & Chambliss, H.O. (2005). Exercise treatment for depression: Efficacy and dose response. *American Journal of Preventive Medicine, 28*, 1–8.

Dunne, P. (2000). Overvalued ideas and obsessions: Some clinical considerations. *Behaviour Change, 17*, 265–274.

Ehlers, A., & Clark, D.M. (2000). A cognitive model of posttraumatic stress disorder. *Behavior Research and therapy, 38,* 319–345.

Eisen, A.R., & Silverman, W.K. (1993). Should I relax or change my thoughts? *Journal of Cognitive Psychotherapy, 7,* 265–279.

Eisen, A.R., & Silverman, W.K. (1998). Prescriptive treatment for generalized anxiety disorder in children. *Behavior Therapy, 29*, 105–121.

Eisner, D.A. (2000). *The death of psychotherapy: From Freud to alien abductions*. Westport, CT: Praeger.

Eitzen, D.S. (1976). The self-concept of delinquents in a behavior modification treatment program. *Journal of Social Psychology, 99*, 203–206.

Elkin, I., Gibbons, R.D., Shea, M.T., Sotsky, S.M., Watkins, J.T., Pilkonis, P.A., Hedeker D. (1995) Initial severity and differential treatment outcome in the National Institute of Mental Health Treatment of Depression Collaborative Research Program. *Journal of Consulting and Clinical Psychology, 63*, 841–847.

Ellis, A. (1962). *Reason and emotion in psychotherapy*. New York, NY: Lyle Stuart.

Ellis, A. (1994). *Reason and emotion in psychotherapy*. Secaucus, NJ: Birch Lane Press.

Ellis, A. (1995). Rational emotive behavior therapy. In R. Corsini & D. Wedding (Eds.), *Current psychotherapies*. Itasca, IL: Peacock.

Ellis, A., & Harper, R.A. (1997). *A guide to rational living*. North Hollywood, CA: Melvin Powers.

Ellis, P.M., & Smith, D.A.R. (2002). Treating depression: The beyondblue guidelines for treating depression in primary care. *Medical Journal of Australia, 176*, S77–S83.

Empson, J. (1989). *Sleep and dreaming*. London, England: Faber & Faber.

Endler, N.S., & Parker, J.D.A. (1994). Assessment of multidimensional coping: Task, emotion, and avoidance strategies. *Psychological Assessment, 6*, 50 60.

Epstein, N. & Baucom, D.H. (1989). Cognitive-behavioral marital therapy. In A. Freeman, K.M. Simon, L.E. Beutler, & H. Arkowitz (Eds.), *Comprehensive handbook of cognitive therapy*. (pp. 491–513). New York, NY: Plenum Press.

Evans, L., Eadie, M.J., Hollister, L., & Tyrer, J.H. (1983). *Drug use in psychiatry*. Sydney, Australia: ADIS Health Science Press.

Evans, M.D., Hollon, S.D., DeRubeis, R.J. et.al. (1992). Differential relapse following cognitive therapy and pharmacotherapy for depression. *Archives of General Psychiatry, 49*, 802–808.

Fairburn, C.G. (2008). *Cognitive behavior therapy and eating disorders*. New York, NY: Guilford Press.

Fairburn, C.G., Cooper, Z., & Shafran, R. (2003). Cognitive behaviour therapy for eating disorders: A 'transdiagnostic' theory and treatment. *Behaviour Research and Therapy, 41*, 509–528.

Fairburn, C.G., Cooper, Z., Shafran, R., & Wilson, G.T. (2008). Eating disorders: A transdiagnostic protocol. In D.H. Barlow (Ed.), *Clinical handbook of psychological disorders: A step-by-step treatment manual* (4th ed.) (pp. 578–614). New York, NY: Guilford Press.

Fairholme, C.P., Boisseau, C.L., Ellard, K.K., Ehrenreich, J.T., & Barlow, D.H. (2010). Emotions, emotion regulation, and psychological treatment: A unified perspective. In A.M. Kring & D.M. Sloan (Eds.), *Emotion regulation and psychopathology: A transdiagnostic approach to etiology and treatment*. (pp. 283-309). New York, NY: Guilford Press.

Fava, G.A. (1999). Sequential treatment: A new way of integrating pharmacotherapy and psychotherapy. *Psychotherapy and Psychosomatics, 68*, 227–229.

Fava, G.A., Rafanelli, C., Grandi, S., Conti, S., & Belluardo, P. (1998). Prevention of recurrent depression with cognitive behavioural therapy: Preliminary findings. *Archives of General Psychiatry, 55*, 816–820.

Fazio, R.H., Zanna, M.P., & Cooper, J. (1977). Dissonance and self-perception: An integrative view of each theory's proper domain of application. *Journal of Experimental Social Psychology, 13* (5), 464–479.

Feeley, M., DeRubeis, R.J., & Gelfand, L.A. (1999). The temporal relation of adherence and alliance to symptom change in cognitive therapy for depression. *Journal of Consulting and Clinical Psychology, 67*, 578–582.

Fensterheim, H., & Baer, J. (1975). *Don't say yes when you want to say no*. London, England: Futura.

Fensterheim, H., & Baer, J. (1977). *Stop running scared!* New York, NY: Dell.

Festinger, L. (1957). *A theory of cognitive dissonance*. Stanford University Press.

First, M.B., Pincus, H.A., Levine, J.B., et al. (2004). Clinical utility as a criterion for revising psychiatric diagnoses. *American Journal of Psychiatry, 161*(6), 946–954.

Fisher, J.E., & O'Donohue, W.T. (2006). *Practitioner's guide to evidence based psychotherapy*. New York, NY: Springer.

Flanagan, E.H., & Blashfield, R.K., (2006). Do clinicians see Axis I and Axis II as different kinds of disorders? *Comprehensive Psychiatry, 47*, 496–502.

Flanagan, E.H, & Blashfield, R.K. (2007a). Clinicians' folk taxonomies of mental disorders. *Philosophy, Psychiatry, & Psychology, 14* (3), 249–269.

Flanagan, E.H., & Blashfield, R.K. (2007b). Should clinicians' views of mental illness influence the DSM? *Philosophy, Psychiatry, & Psychology, 14* (3), 285–287.

Flanagan, E.H., & Blashfield, R.K. (2010). Increasing clinical utility by aligning the DSM and ICD with clinicians' conceptualizations. *Professional Psychology: Research and Practice, 41* (6), 474–481.

Flanagan, E.H., Keeley, J., & Blashfield, R.K. (2008). An alternative hierarchical organization of the mental disorders of the DSM-IV. *Journal of Abnormal Psychology, 117* (3), 693–698.

Flett, G.L., & Hewitt, P.L. (2002). *Perfectionism: Theory, research, and treatment*. Washington, DC: American Psychological Association.

Foa, E.B., Liebowitz, M.R., Kozak, M.J., Davies S., Campeas R., Franklin M.E ... Tu, X. (2005). Randomized, placebo-controlled trial of exposure and ritual prevention, clomipramine, and their combination in the treatment of obsessive compulsive disorder. *American Journal of Psychiatry, 162,* 151–161.

Follette, W.C. (1996). Introduction to the Special Section on the development of theoretically coherent alternatives to the DSM system. *Journal of Consulting and Clinical Psychology, 64* (6), 1117–1119.

Follette, W.C., & Houts, A.C. (1996). Models of scientific progress and the role of theory in taxonomy development: A case study of the DSM. *Journal of Consulting and Clinical Psychology, 64* (6), 1120–1132.

Follette, W.C., Houts, A.C., & Hayes, S.C. (1992). Behavior therapy and the new medical model. *Behavioral Assessment, 14* (3-4), 323–343.

France, R., & Robson, M. (1997). *Cognitive behavioural therapy in primary care: A practical guide*. London, England: Jessica Kingsley.

Frank, E. (2007). Interpersonal and social rhythm therapy: A means of improving depression and preventing relapse in bipolar disorder. *Journal of Clinical Psychology, 63*(5), 463–473.

Franklin, J.A. (1999). *Self-mastery training. A complete 28 day home treatment program for agoraphobia*. Queanbeyan, Australia: Highland Press.

Freeston M.H., Ladouceur R., Gagnon F., Thibodeau N., Rhéaume J., Letarte H., & Bujold A. (1997). Cognitive-behavioral treatment of obsessive thoughts. *Journal of Clinical and Consulting Psychology, 65,* 405–413.

Furer, P., Walker, J.R., & Stein, M.B. (2007). *Treating health anxiety and fear of death*. New York, NY: Springer Publishing.

Galassi, M.D., & Galassi, J.P. (1977). *Assert yourself: How to be your own person*. Oxford, England: Human Sciences.

Ghaderi, A. (2010). Eating disorders. In D. McKay, J.S. Abramowitz & S. Taylor (Eds.), *Cognitive-behavioural therapy for refractory cases: Turning failure into success*. (pp. 155–182). Washington, DC: American Psychological Association.

Gillian, P., & Rachman, S. (1974). An experimental investigation of desensitization in phobic patients. *British Journal of Psychiatry, 124,* 392–401.

Glancy, G., & Saini, M.A. (2005). An evidence-based review of psychological treatments of anger and aggression. *Brief Treatment and Crisis Intervention, 5,* 229–248.

Glass, C.R., & Arnkoff, D.B. (1997). Questionnaire methods of cognitive self-statement assessment. *Journal of Consulting and Clinical Psychology, 65,* 911–927.

Gold, I. (2009). Reduction in psychiatry. *Canadian Journal of Psychiatry, 54,* 506-512.

Goldfried, M., & Trier, C.S. (1974). Effectiveness of relaxation as an active coping skill. *Journal of Abnormal Psychology, 83,* 348–355.

Goldfried, M.R. (1979). Anxiety reduction through cognitive-behavioral intervention. In P. Kendall & S.D. Hollon (Eds.), *Cognitive–behavioral interventions: Theory, research and procedures*. New York, NY: Academic Press.

Goodman, W.K., Price, L.H., Rasmussen, S.A., & Mazure, C. (1989). The Yale-Brown Obsessive Compulsive Scale: I. Development, use, and reliability. *Archives of General Psychiatry. 46* (11), 1006–1011.

Green, R.A., & Murray, E.J. (1973). Instigation to aggression as a function of self-disclosure and threat to self-esteem. *Journal of Consulting and Clinical Psychology, 40*, 440–443.

Greenberg, J.S. (1996). *Comprehensive stress management*. Madison, WI: Brown & Benchmark.

Gresham, F.M., & Gansle, K.A. (1992). Misguided assumptions of DSM-III-R: Implications for school psychological practice. *School Psychology Quarterly, 7*(2), 79–95.

Griffin, M., & Hudson, A. (1979). *Children's problems: A guide for parents*. Melbourne, Australia: Circus.

Grimm, L.G. (1980). The evidence for cue-controlled relaxation. *Behavior Therapy, 11*, 283–293.

Gross, J.J. (1998). The emerging field of emotion regulation: an integrative review. *Review of General Psychology, 2* (3), 271–299.

Gross, J.J. (2002). Emotion regulation: Affective, cognitive, and social consequences. *Psychophysiology, 39* (3), 281–291.

Gross, J.J., & Thompson, R.A. (2007). *Handbook of emotion regulation*. New York, NY: Guilford Press.

Gruber, K., & Heimberg, R.G. (1997). A cognitive-behavioral treatment package for social anxiety. In W.T. Roth & I.D. Yalom (Eds.), *Treating anxiety disorders*. San Francisco, CA: Jossey-Bass.

Hackmann, A. (1998). Cognitive therapy with panic and agoraphobia: Working with complex cases. In N. Tarrier & A. Wells (Eds.), T*reating complex cases: The cognitive behavioural therapy approach*. New York, NY: Wiley.

Hall, A.M., Kamper, S.J., Maher, C.G., Latimer, J., Ferreira, M.L., & Nicholas, M.K. (2011). Symptoms of depression and stress mediate the effect of pain on disability. *Pain, 152*(5), 1044-1051.

Hannan, S.E., & Tolin, D.F. (2005). Acceptance and mindfulness-based behavior therapy for obsessive-compulsive disorder. In S.M. Orsillo, & L.Roemer (Eds.), *Acceptance and mindfulness-based approaches to anxiety: Conceptualization and treatment* (pp. 271–299). New York, NY: Springer.

Hansen, E.S., Hasselbalch, S., Law, I., & Bolwig, T.G. (2002). The caudate nucleus in obsessive-compulsive disorder. *International Journal of Neuropsychopharmacology, 5*, 1–10.

Harris, T.A. (1967). *I'm OK - You're OK*. New York, NY: Harper & Row.

Harvey, A.G. (2008). Sleep and circadian rhythms in bipolar disorder: Seeking synchrony, harmony, and regulation. *American Journal of Psychiatry, 165*(7), 820-829.

Harvey, A.G. (2010). Insomnia. In D. McKay, J.S. Abramowitz & S. Taylor (Eds.), *Cognitive-behavioral therapy for refractory cases: Turning failure into success*. (pp. 277–295). Washington, DC: American Psychological Association.

Harvey, A.G., Belanger, l., Talbot, L., et al. (2014). Comparative efficacy of behavior therapy, and cognitive behavior therapy for chronic insomnia: A randomized controlled trial. *Journal of Consulting and Clinical Psychology, 82*(4), 670–683

Harvey, A.G., Watkins, E.R., Mansell, W., & Shafran, R. (2004). *Cognitive behavioural processes across psychological disorders: A transdiagnostic approach to research and treatment*. Oxford, England: Oxford University Press.

Haslam, N. (2002). Kinds of kinds: A conceptual taxonomy of psychiatric categories. *Philosophy, Psychiatry, & Psychology, 9* (3), 203–217.

Haslam, N., & Kvaale, E.P. (2015). Biogenetic explanations of mental disorder: The mixed blessings model. *Current Directions in Psychological Science, 24*(5), 399-404.

Hawton, K., Catalan, J., Martin, P., & Fagg, J. (1986). Long-term outcome of sex therapy. *Behaviour Research and Therapy, 24*, 665–675.

Hayes, S.C., & Follette, W.C. (1992). Can functional analysis provide a substitute for Syndromal classification? *Behavioral Assessment, 14* (3-4), 345–365.

Hayes, S.C., & Smith, S. (2005). *Get out of your mind and into your life: The new acceptance and commitment therapy*. Oakland, CA: New Harbinger Publications, Inc.

Hayes, S.C., Strosahl, K.D., & Wilson, K.G. (1999). *Acceptance and commitment therapy*. New York, NY: The Guilford Press.

Haynes, S.N. (1992). *Models of causality in psychopathology*. New York, NY: Macmillan.

Haynes, S.N., & O'Brien, W.H. (1990). Functional analysis in behavior therapy. *Clinical Psychology Review, 10* (6), 649–668.

Heiby, E.M. (1982). A self-reinforcement questionnaire. *Behaviour Research and Therapy, 20*, 397–401.

Heiby, E.M. (1983). Toward the prediction of mood change. *Behavior Therapy, 14*, 110–115.

Heiman, J.R., Lo Piccolo, L., & Lo Piccolo, J. (1976). *Becoming orgasmic: A sexual growth program for women*. Englewood Cliffs, NJ: Prentice-Hall.

Helbig, S., & Fehm, L. (2004). Problems with homework in CBT: Rare exception or rather frequent? *Behavioural and Cognitive Psychotherapy, 32*(3), 291–301.

Herman, J. (2005). The need for a transitional model: A challenge for biopsychosocial medicine? *Families, Systems, & Health, 23* (4), 372–376.

Hersen, M., & Bellack, A.S. (1976). *Behavioral assessment: A practical handbook*. Oxford, England: Pergamon Press.

Hetherington, E.M., Cox, M., & Cox, R. (1985). Long-term effects of divorce and remarriage on the adjustment of children. *Journal of the American Academy of Child Psychiatry, 24*, 518–530.

Hetherington, E.M., & Kelly, J. (2002). *For better or for worse: Divorce reconsidered*. New York, NY: W.W. Norton.

Hilderink, P.H., Burger, H., Deeg, D.J., Beekman, A.T., & Voshaar, R.C.O. (2012). The temporal relation between pain and depression: Results from the Longitudinal Aging Study Amsterdam. *Psychosomatic Medicine, 74*(9), 945-951.

Hirsch, C., & Holmes, E.A. (2007). Mental imagery in anxiety disorders. *Psychiatry, 6* (4), 161–165.

Hoelscher, T.J., Lichstein, K.L., Fischer, S., & Hegarty, T.B. (1987). Relaxation treatment of hypertension: Do home relaxation tapes enhance treatment outcome? *Behavior Therapy, 18*, 33–37.

Hofmann, S.G. (2014). Toward a cognitive-behavioral classification system for mental disorders. *Behavior Therapy, 45*, 576-587.

Hofmann, S.G., Asnaani, A., Vonk, I.J.J., Sawyer, A.T., & Fang, A. (2012). The efficacy of cognitive behavioral therapy: A review of meta-analyses. *Cognitive Therapy and Research, 36* (5), 427–440.

Hollander, E., Braun, A., & Simeon, D. (2008). Should OCD leave the anxiety disorders in DSM-V? The case for Obsessive Compulsive-Related Disorders. *Depression and Anxiety, 25*, 317–329.

Hollon, S.D., & Beck, A.T. (1994). Cognitive and cognitive-behavioral therapies. In A.E. Bergin & S.L.Garfield (Eds.), *Handbook of psychotherapy and behavior change* (p. 428–466). John Wiley & Sons.

Hollon, S.D., Shelton, R.C., & Loosen, P.T. (1991). Cognitive therapy and pharmacotherapy for depression. *Journal of Consulting and Clinical Psychology, 59*, 88–99.

Holmes, T.H., & Rahe, R.H. (1967). The Social Readjustment Rating Scale. *Journal of Psychosomatic Research, 11*(2), 213–218.

Howard, K.I., Moras, K., Brill, P.L., Martinovich, Z., & Lutz, W. (1996). Evaluation of psychotherapy: Efficacy, effectiveness, and patient progress. *American Psychologist, 51*, 1059-1064.

Hsu, L.K.G., & Holder, D. (1986). Bulimia nervosa: Treatment and short-term outcome. *Psychological Medicine, 16*, 65–70.

Hyman, B.M., & Pedrick, C. (2005). *The OCD workbook: Your guide to breaking free from obsessive-compulsive disorder.* (2nd ed.). Oakland, CA: New Harbinger.

Hyman, S.E. (2007). Can neuroscience be integrated into DSM-V? *Nature Reviews: Neuroscience, 8*, 725-732.

Hyman, S.E. (2010). The diagnosis of mental disorders: The problem of reification. *Annual Review of Clinical Psychology, 6*, 155–179.

Jacobson N.S., Dobson K.S., Truax P.A., Addis M.E., Koerner K., Gollan J.K., ..., Prince S.E. (1996). A component analysis of cognitive-behavioral treatment for depression. *Journal of Consulting and Clinical Psychology, 64*(2), 295-304.

Jacobson, E. (1974). *Progressive relaxation*. Chicago, IL: The University of Chicago Press.

Jarrett, R.B., Kraft, D., Doyle, J. et.al. (2001). Preventing recurrent depression using cognitive therapy with and without a continuation phase: A randomized clinical trial. *Archives of General Psychiatry, 58*, 381–388.

Jeffreys, D. (1993). *OCD in the decade of the brain*. First Australian Conference on Obsessive-Compulsive Disorder, 'A hidden disability', April 30 to May 2, 1993. Scientific programme proceedings, PCD Foundation.

Johnstone, L. (2006). *Formulation in psychology and psychotherapy: Making sense of people's problems*. New York, NY: Routledge.

Johnstone, L. (2014). *A straight talking introduction to psychiatric diagnosis*. Ross-on-Wye: PCCS Books.

Jongeward, D., & James, M. (1973). *Winning with people*. Addison-Wesley.

Kahneman, D. (2011). *Thinking fast and slow*. Farrar, Straus and Giroux.

Kanfer, F.H. (1975). Self-management methods. In F.H. Kanfer & A.P. Goldstein (Eds.), *Helping people change*. New York, NY: Pergamon Press.

Kanfer, F.H. (1990). Research and theory as guides for therapeutic strategies. In H. Zapotoczky & T. Wenzel (Eds.), *The scientific dialogue: From basic research to clinical intervention* (pp. 21-26. Swets & Zeitlinger.

Kanner, A.D., Coyne, J.C., Schaefer, C., & Lazarus, R.S. (1981). Comparison of two modes of stress measurement: Daily hassles and uplifts versus major life events. *Journal of Behavioral Medicine, 4*(1), 1-39.

Kausman, R. (2004). *If not dieting, then what?* Crows Nest, NSW: Allen & Unwin.

Kazantsis, N., Deane, F.P., Ronan, K.R., & L'Abate, L. (Eds.) (2005). *Using homework assignments in cognitive behavior therapy*. Routledge/Taylor & Francis Group.

Kazantzis, N., Deane, F.P., & Ronan, K.R. (2004). Assessing compliance with homework assignments: Review and recommendations for clinical practice. *Journal of Clinical Psychology, 60*(6), 627-641.

Kazdin, A.E. (1977). *The token economy: A review and evaluation*. New York, NY: Plenum Press.

Kazdin, A.E. (1982). Symptom substitution, generalization, and response covariance: Implications for psychotherapy outcome. *Psychological Bulletin, 91*, 349–365.

Kendall, P.C., Panichelli-Mindel, S.M., Sugarman, A., & Callahan, S.A. (1997). Exposure to child anxiety: Theory, research, and practice. *Clinical Psychology: Science and Practice, 4* (1), 29–39.

Kendell, R., & Jablensky, A. (2003). Distinguishing between the validity and utility of psychiatric diagnoses. *The American Journal of Psychiatry, 160* (1), 4–12.

Kennedy, M., & Franklin, J. (2002). Skills-based treatment for alexithymia: An exploratory case series. *Behaviour Change, 19*, 158–171.

Kent, G., & Gibbons, R. (1987). Self-efficacy and the control of anxious cognitions. *Journal of Behaviour Therapy & Experimental Psychiatry, 18*, 33–40.

Kessler, R.C., Chiu, W.T., Demler, O., & Walters, E.E. (2005). Prevalence, severity, and comorbidity of 12-month DSM-IV disorders in the National Comorbidity Survey Replication. *Archives of Genereal Psychiatry, 62* (6). 617–627.

Kidman, A. (1986). *Tactics for change: A self-help manual*. St Leonards, New South Wales: Biochemical & General Services.

Kidman, A. (1999). *Feeling better: A guide to mood management*. St Leonards, New South Wales: Biochemical & General Services.

Kilmann, P.R., Boland, J.P., Norton, S.P., Davidson, E., & Caid, C. (1986). Perspectives of sex therapy outcome: A survey of AASECT providers. *Journal of Sex & Marital Therapy, 12* (2), 116–138.

Kilpatrick, D.G., & Amick, A.E. (1985). Rape trauma. In M. Hersen & C.G. Last (Eds.), *Behavior therapy case book*. New York, NY: Springer.

Kim, N.S., & Ahn, W. (2002). Clinical psychologists' theory-based representations of mental disorders predict their diagnostic reasoning and memory. *Journal of Experimental Psychology: General, 131* (4), 451–476.

King, N.J., Gullone, E., & Ollendick, T.H. (1998). Etiology of childhood phobias. *Behaviour Research and Therapy, 36*, 297–309.

Kingdon, D., & Young, A.H. (2007). Research into putative biological mechanisms of mental disorders has been of no value to clinical psychiatry. *British Journal of Psychiatry, 191,* 285-290.

Kirsch, I. (2009). Antidepressants and the placebo response. *Epidemiology and Psychiatric Sciences, 18*(4), 318-322.

Knopf, J., & Seiler, M. (1990). *ISD: Inhibited sexual desire*. New York, NY: William Morrow and Company.

Kohlenberg, R.J., & Tsai, M. (1991). *Functional analytic psychotherapy: Creating intense and curative therapeutic relationships*. New York, NY: Plenum Press.

Kovacs, M., Rush, A.J., Beck, A.T., & Hollon, S. (1981). Depressed outpatients treated with cognitive therapy or pharmacotherapy. *Archives of General Psychiatry, 38*, 33–39.

Kratochwill, T.R., & McGivern, J.E. (1996). Clinical diagnosis, behavioral assessment, and functional analysis: Examining the connection between assessment and intervention. *School Psychology Review, 25* (3), 342–355.

Kring, A.M., & Sloan, D.M. (2010). *Emotion regulation and psychopathology: A transdiagnostic approach to etiology and treatment*. New York, NY: Guilford Press.

Krohne, H.W., & Laux, L. (1982). Achievement, stress, and anxiety. Washington, DC: Hemisphere.

Krupnick, J.L., Elkin, I. Collins, J. et.al. (1994). Therapeutic alliance and clinical outcome in the NIMH Treatment of Depression Collaborative Research Program: Preliminary findings. *Psychotherapy: Theory, Research, Practice, Training, 31*, 28–35.

Kupfer, D.J., First, M.B., & Regier, D.A. (Eds.) (2002). *A research agenda for DSV-5*. Arlington, VA: American Psychiatric Association.

Kuyken, W., Padesky, C.A., & Dudley, R. (2009). *Collaborative case conceptualization: Working effectively with clients in cognitive-behavioral therapy*. New York, NY: The Guilford Press.

Kvaale, E.P., Gottdiener, W.H., & Haslam, N. (2013). Biogenetic explanations and stigma: A meta-analytic review of associations among laypeople. *Social Science and Medicine, 96,* 95-103.

Kwon, S., & Oei, T.P.S. (1992), Differential causal roles of dysfunctional attitudes and automatic thoughts in depression. *Cognitive Therapy and Research, 16*, 309–328.

Lam, R.W., & Kennedy, S.H. (2004). Evidence-based strategies for achieving and sustaining full remission in depression: Focus on meta-analyses. *Canadian Journal of Psychiatry, 49*(Suppl. 1), 17S–26S.

Lange, A.J., & Jakubowski, P. (1976). *Responsible assertive behavior: Cognitive/behavioral procedures for trainers*. Champaign, IL: Research Press.

Lawrence, A.E., Rosellini, A.J., & Brown, T.A. (2009). *Current perspectives on the anxiety disorders: Implications for DSM-V and beyond*. New York, NY: Springer Publishing Co.

Laws, D.R., & Marshall, W.L. (1991). Masturbatory reconditioning with sexual deviates: An evaluative review. *Advances in Behavior Research and Therapy, 13*, 13–25.

Lazarus, A.A. (1981). *The practice of multimodal therapy*. New York, NY: McGraw Hill.

Lazarus, A.A. (1992). Multimodal therapy: Technical eclecticism with minimal integration. In J.C. Norcross & M.R. Goldfried (Eds.), *Handbook of psychotherapy integration* (pp. 231–263). New York, NY: Basic Books.

Leahy, R.L., & Tirch, D.D. (2008). Cognitive behavioral therapy for jealousy. *International Journal of Cognitive Therapy, 1* (1), 18–32.

Lekes, N., Hope, N.H., Gouveia, L., et al. (2012). Influencing value priorities and increasing wellbeing: The effects of reflecting on intrinsic values. *The Journal of Positive Psychology*, *7*, 249-–261.

Lepine, J.P., & Pelissolo, A. (1998). Social phobia and alcoholism: A complex relationship. *Journal of Affective Disorders, 50,* 23–28.

Levant, R.F. (1998). Assessing and treating normative male alexithymia. In G.P. Koocher, J.C. Norcross, & S.S. Hill (Eds.), *Psychologists' desk reference*. New York, NY: Oxford University Press.

Levenson, H., & Strupp, H.H. (1997). Cyclical maladaptive patterns: Case formulation in time-limited dynamic psychotherapy. In T.D. Eells (Ed.), *Handbook of psychotherapy case formulation*. New York, NY: Guilford Press.

Lewinsohn, P.M., Munoz, R.F., Youngren, M.A., & Zeiss, A.M. (1986). *Control your depression*. New York, NY: Prentice Hall Press.

Liedl, A., O'Donnell, M., Creamer, M., Silove, D., McFarlane, A., Knaevelsrud, C., Bryant, R.A. (2010). Support for the mutual maintenance of pain and post-traumatic stress disorder symptoms. *Psychological Medicine, 40* (7), 1215–1223.

Linde, S.M., & Savary, L.M. (1974). *The joy of sleep*. New York, NY: Harper & Row.

Lindwall, M., Larsman, P., & Hagger, M.S. (2011). The reciprocal relationship between physical activity and depression in older adults. *Journal of Sport & Exercise Psychology, 33* (5), 748–749.

Linehan, M.M. (1993). *Cognitive–behavioral treatment of borderline personality disorder.* New York, NY: Guilford Press.

Linton, S.J., Nicholas, M.K., MacDonald, S., Boersma, K., Bergborn, S., Maher, C., & Refshauge, K. (2011). The role of depression and catastrophizing in musculoskeletal pain. *European Journal of Pain, 15* (4), 416–422.

Llorca, P.-M., Courtet, P., Martin, P., Abbar, M., Gay, C., Meynard, J.-A., … Samalin, L. (2013). Formalized Consensus Guidelines (FCG) screening and management of bipolar disorder. In N. Boutros (Ed.), *The international psychiatry*

and behavioral neurosciences yearbook – 2012 (Vol. 2, pp. 87–114). Nova Biomedical Books.
MacPhillamy, D.J., & Lewinsohn, P.M. (1982). The Pleasant Events Schedule: Studies on reliability, validity, and scale intercorrelation. *Journal of Consulting and Clinical Psychology, 50*, 363–380.
Mahoney, M.J. (1971). *The self-management of covert behavior: A case study.* Behavior Therapy, 2, 575–578.
Mahoney, M.J. (1974). *Cognition and behavior modification*. Cambridge, MA: Ballinger.
Mahoney, M.J., & Arnkoff, D.B. (1978). Cognitive and self-control therapies. In S.L. Garfield & A.E. Bergin (Eds.), *Handbook of psychotherapy and behaviour change: An empirical analysis*. New York, NY: Wiley.
Mansell, W., Harvey, A., Watkins, E., & Shafran, R. (2009). Conceptual foundations of the transdiagnostic approach to CBT. *Journal of Cognitive Psychotherapy, 23* (1), 6–19.
March, J., & Mulle, K. (1998). *OCD in children and adolescents: A cognitive-behavioral treatment manual*. New York, NY: The Guilford Press.
Marks, I. (1973). New approaches to the treatment of obsessive-compulsive disorders. *Journal of Nervous and Mental Disease, 156*, 420–426.
Marks, I.M. (1978a). *Living with fear*. New York, NY: McGraw-Hill.
Marks, I.M. (1978b). Rehearsal relief of a nightmare. *British Journal of Psychiatry, 133*, 461–465.
Marks, I.M. (1985). Behavioral psychotherapy for anxiety disorders. *Psychiatric Clinics of North America, 8*, 25–35.
Masters, W., & Johnson, V. (1970). *Human sexual inadequacy*. Boston: Little Brown.
Mather, A., Rodriguez, C., Guthrie, M., McHarg, A., Reid, I., & McMurdo, M. (2002). Effects of exercise on depressive symptoms in older adults with poorly responsive depressive disorder: Randomised controlled trial. *British Journal of Psychiatry, 180*, 411–415.
Mathew, A.R., Pettit, J.W., Lewinsohn, P.M., Seeley, J.R., & Roberts, R.E. (2011). Co-morbidity between major depressive disorder and anxiety disorders: Shared etiology or direct causation? *Psychological Medicine, 41*, 2023–2034.
McCarthy, B.W. (2001). Integrating sex therapy strategies and techniques into marital therapy. *Journal of Family Psychotherapy, 12* (3), 45–53.
McEvoy, P.M., Nathan, P., & Norton, P.J. (2009). Efficacy of transdiagnostic treatments: A review of published outcome studies and future research directions. *Journal of Cognitive Psychotherapy, 23* (1), 20–33.
McGuire, J., & Priestley, P. (1985). *Offending behaviour: Skills and strategies for going straight*. London, England: Batsford.
McHugh, R.K., Murray, H.W., & Barlow, D.H. (2009). Balancing fidelity and adaptation in the dissemination of empirically-supported treatments: The promise of transdiagnostic interventions. *Behaviour Research and Therapy, 47*, 946–953.
McKay, M., Davis, M., & Fanning, P. (2007). *Thoughts & Feelings*. (3rd ed.). Oakland, CA: New Harbinger.
McKissock, M. (1995). *Coping with grief.* Sydney, Australia: ABC Books.

McNally, R.J. (1998). Information-processing abnormalities in anxiety disorders: Implications for cognitive neuroscience. *Cognition and Emotion, 12*, 479–495.

Meichenbaum, D.H. (1977). *Cognitive–behavior modification*. New York, NY: Plenum Press.

Meichenbaum, D.H. (1985). *Stress inoculation training: A clinical guidebook*. New York, NY: Pergamon Press.

Melzak, R., & Wall, P. (1983). *The challenge of pain*. New York, NY: Basic Books.

Mendelsohn, G. (1982). Alexithymia and chronic pain: Prevalence, correlates and treatment results. *Psychotherapy and Psychosomatics, 37*, 154–164.

Menzies, R.G., & Clarke, J.C. (1993). The etiology of fear of heights and its relationship to severity and individual response patterns. *Behavior Research and Therapy, 31*(4), 355–365.

Menzies, R.G., & Clarke, J.C. (1994). Retrospective studies of the origins of phobias: A review. *Anxiety, Stress, and Coping, 7, 305–318.*

Menzies, R.G., & Clarke, J.C. (1995). The etiology of phobias: A nonassociative account. *Clinical Psychology Review, 15*, 23–48.

Messer, S., Slife, B.D., Williams, R.N., & Barlow, D. (Eds.) (2001). *Critical issues in psychotherapy: Translating new ideas into practice*. Thousand Oaks, CA: SAGE.

Miller, G.A. (2010). Mistreating psychology in the decade of the brain. *Perspectives on Psychological Science, 5*, 716-743.

Miller, M.A., & Rahe, R.H. (1997). Life changes scaling for the 1990s. *Journal of Psychosomatic Research, 43*, 279–292.

Miller, P.M., Surtees, P.G., Kreitman, N.B., Ingham, J.G., & Sashidharan, S.P. (1985). Maladaptive coping reactions to stress. *Journal of Nervous and Mental Disease, 173*, 707–716.

Miller, W.R. (1983). Controlled drinking: A history and critical review. *Journal of Studies and Alcohol, 44*, 68–83.

Mischel, W. (1973). Toward a cognitive social learning reconceptualization of personality. *Psychological Review, 80*, 252–283.

Montgomery, B., & Morris, L. (1992). Living with anxiety. Victoria, Australia: Lothian.

Montgomery, G.T., & Crowder, J.E. (1972). The symptom substitution hypothesis and the evidence. *Psychotherapy: Theory, Research, and Practice, 9*, 98–102.

Montgomery, R., & Morris, L. (1987). *You & Sex: How to make sex more enjoyable and solve common sexual problems*. Melbourne: Nelson Publishers.

Moorey, S. (2010). The six cycles maintenance model: Growing a 'vicious flower' for depression. *Behavioral and Cognitive Psychotherapy, 38*, 173–184.

Morawetz, D. (2001). Depression and insomnia: Which comes first? *Australian Journal of Counselling Psychology, 3*, 19–24.

Murray, G., & Harvey, A. (2010). Circadian rhythms and sleep in bipolar disorder. *Bipolar Disorders, 12*(5), 459-472.

Muse, K., McManus, F., Hackmann, A., Williams, M., & Williams, M. (2010). Intrusive imagery in severe health anxiety: Prevalence, nature and links with memories and maintenance cycles. *Behaviour Research and Therapy, 48* (8), 792–798.

Nathan, P.E., & Gorman, J.M. (2015). *A guide to treatments that work*. Oxford, England: Oxford University Press.
Nelson-Gray, R.O. (2003). Treatment utility of psychological assessment. *Psychological Assessment, 15* (4), 521–531.
Nelson, J.C., & Quinlan, D.M. (1981). Evaluation of the DSM-111 criteria for melancholia. *Archives of General Psychiatry, 38*, 555–561.
Nelson, R.D., Hayes, S.C., Felton, J.L., & Jarrett, R.B. (1985). A comparison of data produced by different behavioural assessment techniques with implications for models of social-skills adequacy. *Behaviour Research and Therapy, 23*, 1–11.
Newport, D.J., & Nemeroff, C.B. (2000). Neurobiology of posttraumatic stress disorder. *Current Opinion in Neurobiology, 10*, 211–218.
Nezu, A.M., Nezu, C.M., & Perri, M.G. (1989). *Problem-solving therapy for depression: Theory, research, and clinical guidelines*. New York, NY: Wiley.
Nezu, A.M., Nezu, C.M., Friedman, S.H., & Haynes, S.N. (1997). Case formulation in behavior therapy: Problem-solving and functional analytic strategies. In T.D. Eells (Ed.), *Handbook of psychotherapy case formulation*. New York, NY: Guilford Press.
Nolen-Hoeksema, S. (1987). Sex differences in unipolar depression: Evidence and theory. *Psychological Bulletin, 101*(2), 259-282.
Nolen-Hoeksema, S. (1991). Responses to depression and their effects on the duration of depressive episodes. *Journal of Abnormal Psychology, 100*(4), 569-582.
Nolen-Hoeksema, S., & Watkins, E.R. (2011). A heuristic for developing transdiagnostic models of psychopathology: Explaining multifinality and divergent trajectories. *Perspectives on Psychological Science, 6* (6), 589–609.
Norfolk, D. (1986). Executive stress. London, England: Arrow.
Novaco, R.A. (1975). *Anger control*. Lexington, MA: Lexington Books.
O'Keeffe, M., Purtill, H., Kennedy, N., Conneely, M., Hurley, J., O'Sullivan, P., … O'Sullivan, K. (2016). Comparative effectiveness of conservative interventions for nonspecific chronic spinal pain: Physical, behavioral/psychologically informed, or combined? A systematic review and meta-analysis. *The Journal of Pain, 17*(7), 755-774.
O'Leary, B.J., & Norcross, J.C. (1998). Lifetime prevalence of mental disorders in the general population. In G.P. Koocher, J.C. Norcross & S.S. Hill (Eds.), *Psychologists' desk reference*. New York, NY: Oxford University Press.
Oei, T.P.S., & Yeoh, A.E.O. (1999). Pre-existing antidepressant medication and the outcome of group cognitive-behavioural therapy. *Australian and New Zealand Journal of Psychiatry, 33*, 70–76.
Olatunji, B.O., Etzel, E.N., Tomarken, A.J., Ceisielski, B.G., & Deacon, B. (2011). The effects of safety behaviors on health anxiety: An experimental investigation. *Behaviour Research and Therapy, 49* (11), 719–728.
Ost, L. (1988). Applied relaxation versus progressive relaxation in the treatment of panic disorder. *Behaviour Research and Therapy, 26*, 13–22.
Ost, L.G. (1987). Applied relaxation: Description of a coping technique and review of controlled studies. *Behaviour Research and Therapy, 25*, 88–91.

Oswald, I. (1987). Dreaming. In R.L. Gregory (Ed.), *The Oxford companion to the mind*. Oxford, England: Oxford University Press.

Ougrin, D. (2011). Efficacy of exposure versus cognitive therapy in anxiety disorders: Systematic review and meta-analysis. *BMC Psychiatry, 11*, 200. doi:10.1186/1471-244X-11-200.

Padesky, C.A., & Greenberger, D. (1995). *Clinician's guide to Mind over Mood*. New York, NY: Guilford Press.

Padus, E. (1992). *The complete guide to your emotions and your health*. PA: Rodale Press.

Page, A. (2000). *A millennial checkup for cognitive behavioural therapists*. Paper presented at the AACBT conference, Melbourne, Australia.

Paris, J. (2000). *Myths of childhood*. New York, NY: Brunner/Mazel.

Parkes, C.M. (1993). Grief as a psychosocial transition process of adaptation to change. In M. Stroebe, W. Stroebe, & R.O. Hanson (Eds.), *Handbook of bereavement: Theory, Research and Intervention*. New York, NY: Cambridge University Press.

Parkes, K.R. (1984). Locus of control, cognitive appraisal, and coping in stressful episodes. *Journal of Personality and Social Psychology, 46*, 655–668.

Patterson, G.R. (1982). *Coercive family process*. Eugene, OR: Castalia.

Patterson, G.R., Dishion, T.J., & Chamberlain, P. (1993). Outcomes and methodological issues relating to treatment of antisocial children. In T.R. Giles (Ed.), *Handbook of effective psychotherapy*. New York, NY: Plenum Press.

Pauli, P., Marquardt, C., Hartl, L., Nutzinger, D., Hölzl, R., Strian, F. (1991). Anxiety induced by cardiac perceptions in patients with panic attacks: A field study. *Behaviour Research and Therapy, 29*, 137–145.

Pavlov, I.P. (1927). *Conditional reflexes: An investigation of the physiological activity of the cerebral cortex*. New York, NY: Oxford University Press.

Paykel, E.S., Scott, J., Teasdale, J.D., Johnson, A.L., Garland, A., Moore, R., …Pope, M. (1999). Prevention of relapse in residual depression by cognitive therapy. *Archives of General Psychiatry, 56*, 829–835.

Peden, A.R., Rayens, M.K., & Hall, L.A. (2005). A community-based depression prevention intervention with low-income single mothers. *Journal of the American Psychiatric Nurses Association, 11*, 18–25.

Persons, J.B. (1986). The advantages of studying psychological phenomena rather than psychiatric diagnoses. *American Psychologist, 41* (11), 1252–1260.

Persons, J.B. (1989). *Cognitive therapy in practice: A case formulation approach*. New York, NY: W.W. Norton & Co.

Persons, J.B. (2008). *The case formulation approach to cognitive-behavior therapy*. New York, NY: Guilford Press.

Persons, J.B., & Davidson, J. (2001). Cognitive–behavioral case formulation. In K.S. Dobson (Ed.), *Handbook of cognitive-behavioral therapies*. New York, NY: Guilford Press.

Persons, J.B., & Tompkins, M.A. (1997). *Handbook of psychotherapy case formulation*. New York, NY: Guilford Press.

Peterson, C., & Bossio, L.M. (1991). *Health and optimism*. New York, NY: The Free Press.

Phan, K.L., Fitzgerald, D.A., Nathan, P.J., & Tancer, M.E. (2006). Association between amygdala hyperactivity to harsh faces and severity of social anxiety in generalized social phobia. *Biological Psychiatry, 59, 424–429.*

Phillips, K.A. (1996). *The broken mirror: Understanding and treating body dysmorphic disorder.* New York, NY: Oxford University Press.

Phillips, K.A., Stein, D.J., Rauch, S.L., Hollander, E., Fallon B.A., Barsky, A., … Leckman J. (2010). Should an obsessive-compulsive spectrum grouping of disorders be included in DSM-V? *Depression and Anxiety, 27,* 528–555.

Pitt, L., Kilbride, M., Welford, M., Nothard, S., & Morrison, A.P. (2009). Impact of a diagnosis of psychosis: User-led qualitative study. *Psychiatric Bulletin, 33* (11), 419–423.

Powers, M.B., Sigmarsson, S.R., & Emmelkamp, P.M.G. (2008). A meta-analytic review of psychological treatments for social anxiety disorder. *International Journal of Cognitive Therapy, 1* (2), 94–113.

Purdon, C., & Clark, D.A. (2005). *Overcoming obsessive thoughts: How to gain control over your OCD*. Oakland, CA, US: New Harbinger Publications.

Rachman, S., & Hodgson, R. (1974). Synchrony and desynchrony in fear and avoidance. *Behaviour Research and Therapy, 12*, 311–318.

Rachman, S., & Hodgson, R. (1980). *Obsessions and compulsions*. Englewood Cliffs, NJ: Prentice-Hall.

Radford, J.C. (2001). Cognitive behavioural therapy influenced medical care model: A comprehensive model of personal health and personal health care. [Masters thesis], University of New South Wales.

Radua, J., van den Heuvel, O.A., Surguladze, S., & Mataix-Cols, D. (2010). Meta-analytical comparison of voxel-based morphometry studies in obsessive-compulsive disorder vs. other anxiety disorders. *Archives of General Psychiatry, 67* (7), 701–711.

Ramond-Roquin, A., Bouton, C., Gobin-Tempereau, A.S., Airagnes, G., Richard I., Roquelaure, Y., & Huez, J. (2014). Interventions focusing on psychosocial risk factors for patients with non-chronic low back pain in primary care — A systematic review. *Family Practice, 31*(4), 379-388.

Rapee, R.M., Gaston, J.E., & Abbott, M.J. (2009). Testing the efficacy of theoretically derived improvements in the treatment of social phobia. *Journal of Consulting and Clinical Psychology, 77,* 317-327.

Rees, C.S. (2009). *Obsessive-compulsive disorders: A practical guide to treatment*. Melbourne: IP Communications.

Regestein, Q.R., & Rechs, J.R. (1980). *Sound sleep*. New York, NY: Simon and Schuster.

Rehm, L.P. (1984). Self-management therapy for depression. *Advances in Behaviour Research and Therapy, 6,* 83–98.

Rehm, L.P., Kaslow, N.J., & Rabin, A.S. (1987). Cognitive and behavioural targets in a self-control therapy program for depression. *Journal of Consulting and Clinical Psychology, 55*, 60–67.

Repp, A.C., Felce, D., & Barton, L.E. (1988). Basing the treatment of stereotypic and self-injurious behaviors on hypotheses of their causes. *Journal of Applied Behavior Analysis, 21* (3), 281–289.

Rimm, D.C., & Masters, J.C. (1979). *Behavior therapy: Techniques and empirical findings*. New York, NY: Academic Press.

Rind, B., & Tromovitch, P. (1997). A meta-analytic review of findings from national samples on psychological correlates of child sexual abuse. *Journal of Sex Research, 34,* 237–255.

Robinson, J., Sareen, J., Cox, B.J., & Bolton, J.M. (2011). Role of self-medication in the development of comorbid anxiety and substance use disorders: A longitudinal investigation. *Archives of General Psychiatry, 68* (8), 800–807.

Rokke, P.D., & al'Absi, M. (1992). Matching pain coping strategies to the individual: A prospective validation of the Cognitive Coping Strategy Inventory. *Journal of Behavioral Medicine, 15*, 611–625.

Rokke, P.D., & Lall, R. (1992). The role of choice in enhancing tolerance to acute pain. *Cognitive Therapy and Research, 16*, 53–65.

Rokke, P.D., & Rehm, L.P. (2001). Self-management therapies. In K.S. Dobson (Ed.), *Handbook of cognitive-behavioral therapies*. New York, NY: Guilford Press.

Roth, A., & Fonagy, P. (2005). *What works for whom?* New York, NY: Guilford Press.

Rotter, J. (1966). Generalized expectancies for internal versus external control of reinforcement. *Psychological Monographs, 80*, Whole No. 609.

Russell, R.K., & Sipich, J.F. (1973). Cue-controlled relaxation in the treatment of test anxiety. *Journal of Behavior Therapy and Experimental Psychiatry, 4*, 47–49.

Sabourin, S., Valois, P., & Lussier, Y. (2005). Development and validation of a brief version of the Dyadic Adjustment Scale with a nonparametric item analysis model. *Psychological Assessment, 17,* 15–27.

Salkovskis, P.M. (1985). Obsessive-compulsive problems: A cognitive-behavioral analysis. *Behavioral Research and Therapy, 23* (5), 571–583.

Salkovskis, P.M. (1996). The cognitive approach to anxiety: Threat beliefs, safety-seeking behavior, and the special case of health anxiety and obsessions. In P.M. Salkovskis (ed.), *Frontiers of cognitive therapy*, pp.48-74. Guilford Press.

Salkovskis, P.M., & Westbrook, P.M. (1989). Behaviour therapy and obsessional ruminations: Can failure be turned into success? *Behaviour Research and Therapy, 27,* 149–160.

Salkovskis, P.M., Forrester, E., & Richards, C. (1998). Cognitive-behavioural approach to understanding obsessional thinking. *British Journal of Psychiatry, 173,* 53–63.

Salmivalli, C. (2001). Feeling good about oneself, being bad to others? Remarks on self-esteem, hostility, and aggressive behavior. *Aggression & Violent Behavior, 6*, 375–393.

Salter, D., McMillan, D., Richards, M., Talbot, T., Hodges, J., Bentovim, A., … Skuse, D. (2003). Development of sexually abusive behaviour in sexually victimized males: A longitudinal study. *Lancet, 361,* 471–476.

Sanavio, E. (1988). Pre-sleep cognitive intrusions and treatment of onset-insomnia. *Behaviour Research and Therapy, 26,* 451–459.

Sarkes, T. (2014). *Situational PMCs perpetuating unemployment status*. Personal communication.

Sarwer, D.B., & Durlak, J.A. (1997). A field trial of the effectiveness of behavioral treatment for sexual dysfunctions. *Journal of Sex & Marital Therapy, 23* (2), 87–97.

Satel, S., & Lilienfeld, S.O. (2013). *Brainwashed: The seductive appeal of mindless neuroscience*. New York, NY: Basic Books.

Schachter, S., & Singer, J.E. (1962). Cognitive, social, and physiological determinants of emotional state. *Psychological Review, 69*, 379–399.

Schindel-Allon, I., Aderka, I.M., Shahar, G., Stein, M., & Gilboa-Schechtman, E. (2010). Longitudinal associations between post-traumatic distress and depressive symptoms following a traumatic event: A test of three models. *Psychological Medicine, 40* (10), 1669–1678.

Schmidt, G., & Arentewicz, G. (1983). Etiology. In G. Arentewicz & G. Schmidt (Eds.), *The treatment of sexual disorders: Concepts and techniques of couple therapy*. (pp. 34–58) New York, NY: Basic Books.

Schonpflug, W. (1983). Coping efficiency and situational demands. In G.R.J. Hockey (Ed.), *Stress and fatigue in human performance*. New York, NY: Wiley.

Schulte, D., Kunzel, R., Pepping, G., & Schulte-Bahrenberg, T. (1992). Tailor-made versus standardized therapy of phobic patients. *Advances in Behaviour Research and Therapy, 14*, 67–92.

Schwartz, J.M. (1996). *Brain lock: Free yourself from obsessive-compulsive behavior.* New York, NY: Harper Collins.

Schwartz, J.M. (1998). Neuroanatomical aspects of cognitive-behavioral therapy response in obsessive-compulsive disorder: An evolving perspective on brain and behavior. *British Journal of Psychiatry, 35*, 38–44.

Schwartz, J.M., Stoessel, P.W., Baxter, L.R., Martin, K.M., & Phelps, M.E. (1996). Systematic changes in cerebral glucose metabolic rate after successful behavior modification treatment of obsessive-compulsive disorder. *Archives of General Psychiatry, 53,* 109–113.

Scott, M.J., & Stradling, S.G. (1992). *Counselling for post-traumatic stress disorder*. London, England: SAGE.

Segal, Z., Williams, M., & Teasdale, J. (2002). *Mindfulness-based cognitive therapy for depression: A new approach to preventing relapse*. New York, NY: Guilford Press.

Seiffge-Krenke, I. (2000). Casual links between stressful events, coping style, and adolescent symptomatology. *Journal of Adolescence, 23,* 675–691.

Seligman, M.E. (1972). Learned helplessness. *Annual Review of Medicine (1972),* 207-412.

Seligman, M.E.P. (1990). *Learned optimism*. New York, NY: Knopf.

Seligman, M.E.P. (1995). *The optimistic child*. Sydney, Australia: Random House.

Seligman, M.E.P. (2007). *What you can change and what you can't*. Sydney: Random House.

Shafran, R., Thordarson, D.S., & Rachman, S. (1996). Thought-action fusion in obsessive compulsive disorder. *Journal of Anxiety Disorders, 10* (5), 379–391.

Shaw, B.F., Elkin, I., Yamaguchi, J., et al. (1999). Therapist competence ratings in relation to clinical outcome in cognitive therapy for depression. *Journal of Consulting and Clinical Psychology, 67,* 837–846.

Shortt, A.L., & Spence, S.H. (2006). Risk and protective factors for depression in youth. *Behaviour Change, 23*(1), 1-30.

Silverman, W.K., La Greca, A.M., & Wasserstein, S. (1995). What do children worry about? Worries and their relation to anxiety. *Child Development, 66,* 671–686.

Simon, G.E. (2002). Management of somatoform and factitious disorders. In P.E. Nathan & J.M. Gorman (Eds.), *A guide to treatments that work.* (2nd ed.) (pp. 447–461) Oxford, England: Oxford University Press.

Simons, A.D., & Thase, M.E. (1992). Biological markers, treatment outcome, and 1-year follow-up in endogenous depression Electroencephalo graphic sleep studies and response to cognitive therapy. *Journal of Consulting and Clinical Psychology, 60,* 392–401.

Simons, A.D., Murphy, G.E., Levine, J.L., & Wetzel, R.D. (1986). Cognitive therapy and pharmacotherapy for depression. *Archives of General Psychiatry, 43*, 43–48.

Simpson, H.B., Maher, M.J., Wang, Y., Bao, Y., Foa, E.B., & Franklin, M. (2011). Patient adherence predicts outcome from cognitive behavioral therapy in obsessive-compulsive disorder. *Journal of Consulting and Clinical Psychology, 79* (2), 247–252.

Skinner, B.F. (1953). *Science and human behaviour*. New York, NY: Macmillan.

Smith, D., & Over, R. (1987). Does fantasy-induced sexual arousal habituate? *Behaviour Research and Therapy, 25*(6), 477-485.

Sonkin, D.J., & Durphy, M. (1985). *Learning to live without violence: A handbook for men*. Volcano, CA: Volcano Press.

South, S.C., Krueger, R.F., & Iancono, W.G. (2009). Factorial invariance of the Dyadic Adjustment Scale across gender. *Psychological Assessment, 21*, 622–628.

Spanier, G.B. (1976). Measuring dyadic adjustment: New scales for assessing the quality of marriage and similar dyads. *Journal of Marriage & the Family, 38,* 15–28.

Spielberger, C.D. (1972). Anxiety: Current trends in theory and research. New York, NY: Academic Press.

Stein, D.J., Seedat, S., vander Linden, G.J.H., & Zungu-Dirwayi, N. (2000). Selective serotonin reuptake inhibiters in the treatment of posttraumatic stress disorder: A meta-analysis of randomized controlled trials. *International Clinical Psychopharmacology, 15*, 531–539.

Stein, M.B., Roy-Byrne, P.P., Craske, M.G., et al. (2011). Quality of and patient satisfaction with primary health care for anxiety disorders. *Journal of Clinical Psychiatry, 72*(7), 970-976.

Steketee, G., & Freund, B. (1993). Compulsive Activity Checklist (CAC): Further psychometric analyses and revision. *Behavioural Psychotherapy, 21* (1), 13–25.

Steketee, G.S. (1993). *Treatment of obsessive-compulsive disorder*. New York, NY: Guilford Press.

Storch, E.A., Abramowitz, J., & Goodman, W.K. (2008). Where does Obsessive-Compulsive Disorder belong in DSM-V? *Depression and Anxiety, 25,* 336–347.

Strauss, J., Muday, T., McNall, K., & Wong, M. (1997). Response Style Theory revisited: Gender differences and stereotypes in rumination and distraction. *Sex Roles, 36*(11-12), 771-792.

Strunk, D.R., Brotman, M.A., & DeRubeis, R.J. (2010). The process of change in cognitive therapy for depression: Predictors of early inter-session symptom gains. *Behaviour Research and Therapy, 48* (7), 599–606.

Suinn, R. (1977). Manual: Anxiety management training (AMT). Boulder, CO: Rocky Mountain Behavioral Sciences Institute.

Suinn, R. (1995). Anxiety management training. In K. Craig & K. Dobson (Eds.), *Anxiety and depression in adults and children*. Thousand Oaks, CA: SAGE.

Sussman, N. (2009). Why replication matters. *Primary Psychiatry, 16,* 14–15.

Swartz, H.A., & Swanson, J. (2014). Psychotherapy for bipolar disorder in adults: A review of the evidence. *Focus (Am Psychiatr Publ), 12*(3), 251–266.

Tang, T.Z., & DeRubeis, R.J. (1999). Sudden gains and critical sessions in cognitive-behavioural therapy for depression. *Journal of Consulting and Clinical Psychology, 67*, 894–904.

Taylor, C.T., & Amir, N. (2010). Attention and emotion regulation. In A.M. Kring & D.M. Sloan (Eds.), *Emotion regulation and psychopathology: A transdiagnostic approach to etiology and treatment* (pp. 380–404). New York, NY: Guilford Press.

Taylor, G. (1984). Alexithymia: Concept, measurement and implications for treatment. *American Journal of Psychiatry, 141*, 725–732.

Taylor, S., & Asmundson, G.J.G. (2004). *Treating health anxiety: A cognitive-behavioral approach*. New York, NY: Guilford Press.

Taylor, S., & Clark, D.A. (2009). Transdiagnostic cognitive-behavioral treatments for mood and anxiety disorders: Introduction to the special issue. *Journal of Cognitive Psychotherapy, 23* (1), 3–5.

Taylor, S., Thordarson, D.S., Maxfield, L.Fedoroff, I.C. Lovell, K., & Ogrodniczuk, J. (2003). Comparative efficacy, speed, and adverse effects of three PTSD treatments: Exposure therapy, EMDR, and relaxation training. *Journal of Consulting and Clinical Psychology, 71*, 330–338.

Teasdale, J.D. (1985). Psychological treatments for depression: How do they work? *Behaviour Research and Therapy, 23*, 157–165.

Teasdale, J.D. (1988). Cognitive vulnerability to persistent depression. *Cognition and Emotion, 2*(3), 247-274.

Tennant, C., Bebbington, P., & Hurry, J. (1981). The short-term outcome of neurotic disorders in the community: The relation of remission to clinical factors and to 'neutralizing' life events. *British Journal of Psychiatry, 139,* 213–220.

Terr, L.C. (1983). Chowchilla revisited: The effects of psychic trauma four years after a school-bus kidnapping. *American Journal of Psychiatry, 140,* 1543–1550.

Tiller, J.W.G. (2001). Cognitive behaviour therapy in medical practice. *Australian Prescriber, 24*, 33–37.

Titov, N., Gibson, M., Andrews, G., & McEvoy, P. (2009). Internet treatment for social phobia reduces comorbidity. *Australian and New Zealand Journal of Psychiatry, 43* (8), 754–759.

Tracy, S.W. (2007). Medicalizing alcoholism one hundred years ago. *Harvard Review of Psychiatry, 15* (2), 86–91.

Trask, P.C., & Sigmon, S.T. (1999). Ruminating and distracting: The effects of sequential tasks on depressed mood. *Cognitive Therapy and Research, 23*(3), 231-246.

Treatment Protocol Project: World Health Organization Collaborating Centre. (2004) *Management of mental disorders* (4th ed.), Volume 1. Sydney: WHO.

Trower, P., Bryant, B., & Argyle, M. (1978). *Social skills and mental health*. Pittsburgh, PA: University of Pittsburgh Press.

Truax, C.B., & Carkhuff, R.R. (1967). *Toward effective counseling and psychotherapy*. Chicago, IL: Aldine.

Tryon, G.S., & Palladino, J.J. (1979). Thought stopping: A case study and observations. *Journal of Behaviour Therapy and Experimental Psychiatry, 10,* 151–154.

Tucker, G.J. (1998). Putting DSM-IV in perspective. *The American Journal of Psychiatry, 155* (2), 159–161.

Tyrer, P., Cooper, S., Crawford, M., et al. (2011). Prevalence of health anxiety problems in medical clinics. *Journal of Psychosomatic Research, 71* (6), 392–394.

Ulrich, H., Randolph, M., & Acheson, S. (2006). Child sexual abuse: Replication of the meta-analytic examination of child abuse by Rind, Tromovitch, and Bauserman (1998). *Scientific Review of Mental Health Practice, 4* (2), 37–51.

Upper, D., & Cautela, J.R. (1979). *Covert conditioning*. New York, NY: Pergamon Press.

Vaccaro, L.D., Jones, M.K., Menzies, R.G., & St Clare, T. (2008). *DIRT [Danger Ideation Reduction Therapy] for obsessive compulsive checkers: A comprehensive guide to treatment*. Bowen Hills, Queensland: Australian Academic Press.

Van der Ploeg, H.M., Schwartzer, R., & Spielberger, C.D. (1984). *Advances in test anxiety research*. Hillside, NJ: Erlbaum.

Velten, E. (1988). Withdrawal from heroin and methadone with RET: Theory and practice. In W. Dryden & P. Trower (Eds.), *Developments in rational-emotive therapy*. Philadelphia: Open University Press.

Visser, S., & Bouman, T.K. (2001). The treatment of hypochondriasis: Exposure plus response prevention vs. cognitive therapy. *Behaviour Research and Therapy, 39,* 423–442.

Vlaeyen, J.W.S., & Linton, S.J. (2000). Fear-avoidance and its consequences in chronic musculoskeletal pain: A state of the art. *Pain, 85*(3), 317-332.

Wachtel, P.L. (1991). From eclecticism to synthesis: Toward a more seamless psychotherapeutic integration. *Journal of Psychotherapy Integration, 1*, 43–54.

Walker, J.R., & Furer, P. (2008). Interoceptive exposure in the treatment of health anxiety and hypochondriasis. *Journal of Cognitive Therapy, 22* (4), 366–378.

Warwick, H.M.C., & Salkovskis, P.M. (1989). Hypochondriasis. In J. Scott, J.M.G. Williams, & A.T. Beck (Eds.), *Cognitive therapy in clinical practice* (pp. 45–58). London, England: Croom Helm.

Waterman, G.S. (2007). Clinicians' 'folk' taxonomies and the DSM: Pick your poison. *Philosophy, Psychiatry, & Psychology, 14*(3), 271–275.

Watson, J.B. (1924). Behaviorism. Chicago: University of Chicago Press.

Watson, J.B., & Rayner, R. (1920). Conditioned emotional reactions. *Journal of Experimental Psychology, 3*, 10–14.

Weeks, G.R., & L'Abate, L. (1982). *Paradoxical psychotherapy*. New York, NY: Brunner/Mazel.

Wei, Y., Szumilas, M., & Kutcher, S. (2010). Effectiveness on mental health of psychological debriefing for crisis intervention in schools. *Educational Psychology Review, 22* (3), 339–347.

Weinberger, M., Hiner, S.L., & Tierney, W.M. (1987). In support of hassles as a measure of stress in predicting health outcomes. *Journal of Behavioral Medicine, 10*(1), 19-31.

Wells, A. (1995). Meta-cognition and worry: A cognitive model of generalized anxiety disorder. *Behavioural and Cognitive Psychotherapy, 23*, 301–320.

Wells, A. (1997). *Cognitive therapy of anxiety disorders: A practical manual and conceptual guide*. Chichester: Wiley.

Wells, A. (2002). Worry, metacognition, and GAD: Nature, consequences, and treatment. *Journal of Cognitive Psychotherapy: An International Quarterly, 16*, 179–192.

Wells, A. (2011). Metacognitive therapy. In J.D. Herbert & E.M. Forman (Eds.), *Acceptance and mindfulness in cognitive behavior therapy: Understanding and applying the new therapies*. (pp.83-108). John Wiley & Sons Inc.

Westen, D., Novotny, C., & Thompson-Brenner, H. (2004). The empirical status of empirically supported therapies: Assumptions, methods, and findings. *Psychological Bulletin, 130*, 631-663.

Wheatley, D. (1997). Stress, anxiety and depression. *Stress Medicine, 13*, 173–177.

Wheatley, D. (1998). Sex, stress and sleep. *Stress Medicine, 14*, 245–248.

Wheatley, D. (2000). The role of stress in psychiatric disorders. *Primary Care Psychiatry, 6*, 93–100.

Whitaker, R. (2010). *Anatomy of an epidemic: Magic bullets, psychiatric drugs, and the astonishing rise of mental illness in America*. New York, NY: Crown Publishers/Random House.

White, J. (1999). *Overcoming generalized anxiety disorder: A relaxation, cognitive restructuring and exposure-based protocol for the treatment of GAD*. Oakland, CA: New Harbinger.

Whitehead, A., & Mathews, A. (1986). Factors related to successful outcome in the treatment of sexually unresponsive women. *Psychological Medicine, 16*, 373–378.

Wilding, C., & Milne, A. (2010). *Cognitive behavioural therapy*. London, England: Hodder Education.

Wilson, G.T. (1998). Manual-based treatment and clinical practice. *Clinical Psychology: Science and Practice, 5*, 363–375.

Windholz, M.J., Marmar, C.R., & Horowitz, M.J. (1985). A review of the research on conjugal bereavement: Impact on health and efficacy of intervention. *Comprehensive Psychiatry, 26*, 433–447.

Wisocki, P. (1985). Thought stopping. In A.S. Bellack & M. Herson (Eds.), *Dictionary of behavior therapay techniques*. New York, NY: Pergamon Press.

Wolfe, S.W. (1974). Avoid sickness: How life changes affect your health. In J.H. Brennecke & R.G. Amick (Eds.), *Readings in psychology and human experience*. London, England: Glencoe.

Wolpe, J. (1954). Reciprocal inhibition as the main basis of psychotherapeutic effects. *Archives of Neurology and Psychiatry, 72*, 205.

Wolpe, J. (1973). *The practice of behaviour therapy*. New York, NY: Pergamon Press.

Wolpe, J. (1986). Misconceptions about behavior therapy: Their sources and consequences. *Behaviour Change, 3*, 9–15.

Wolpe, J., & Lazarus, A.A. (1966). *Behavior therapy techniques*. New York, NY: Pergamon Press.

Woolf, C.J. (2011). Central sensitization: Implications for the diagnosis and treatment of pain. *Pain, 152*(3), S2-15.

Worchel, P. (1960). Status restoration and the reduction of hostility. *Journal of Abnormal and Social Psychology, 63*, 443–445.

Wykes, T. (2002). Effects on the brain of a psychological treatment: Cognitive remediation therapy: Functional magnetic resonance imaging in schizophrenia. *British Journal of Psychiatry, 188*, 144–152.

Yoman, J. (2008). A primer on functional analysis. *Cognitive and Behavioral Practice, 15* (3), 325–340.

Young, J.E. (1990). *Cognitive therapy for personality disorders: A schema-focused approach*. Sarasota, FL: Professional Resource Exchange.

Young, M.A., Scheftner, W.A., Klerman, G.L., Andreason, N.C., & Hirschfield, R.M. (1986). The endogenous subtype of depression: A study of its internal construct validity. *British Journal of Psychiatry, 148*, 257–267.

Zachar, P. (2008). Real kinds but no true taxonomy. In R. Kendler & J. Pamas (Eds.), *Philosophical issues in psychiatry*. John Hopkins University Press.

Zayfert, C., & Becker, C.B. (2007). *Cognitive–behavioral therapy for PTSD*. New York, NY: The Guilford Press.

Zimmerman, M., Corryell, W., Pfohl, B., & Stangl, D.A. (1986). The validity of four definitions of endogenous depression. *Archives of General Psychiatry, 43*, 234–244.

Index

C

D

P

R

S

T

www.ingramcontent.com/pod-product-compliance
Lightning Source LLC
LaVergne TN
LVHW080026210926
848481LV00011B/3110
9781925644449